INSURRECTION

INSURRECTION

SCOTLAND'S
FAMINE WINTER

JAMES HUNTER

BIRLINN

First published in 2019 by
Birlinn Limited
West Newington House
10 Newington Road
Edinburgh
EH9 1QS
www.birlinn.co.uk

ISBN 978 1 78027 622 9

British Library Cataloguing in Publication Data

A catalogue record for this book is available from the British Library.

Typeset by Hewer Text UK Ltd, Edinburgh
Printed and bound by Gutenberg Press, Malta

Food riots have been spreading in the North of Scotland to so great an extent that several parties of military have been despatched from Edinburgh. In some parts the country is described to be nearly in a state of insurrection.

Spectator, 6 February 1847

Contents

List of illustrations

Map 1: West Highlands and Islands

Map 2: Moray Firth Area

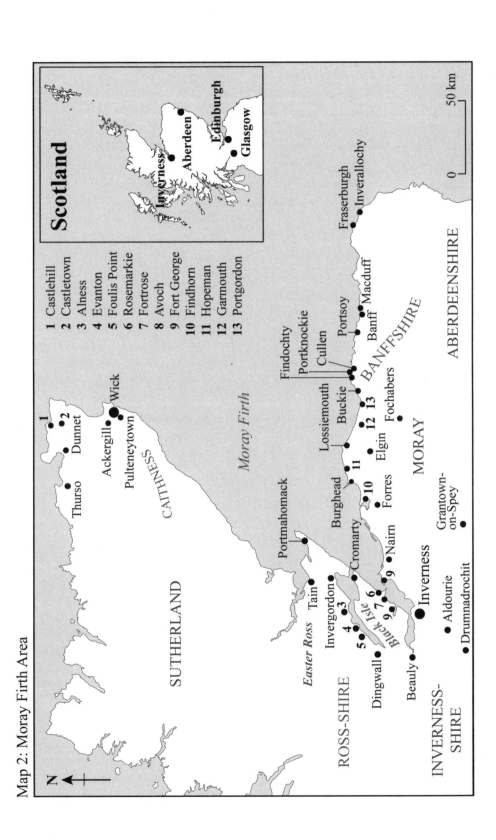

Scotland

Inverness
Aberdeen
Edinburgh
Glasgow

50 km

0

1 Castlehill
2 Castletown
3 Alness
4 Evanton
5 Foulis Point
6 Rosemarkie
7 Fortrose
8 Avoch
9 Fort George
10 Findhorn
11 Hopeman
12 Garmouth
13 Portgordon

Fraserburgh
Inverallochy

Macduff
Banff
Portsoy
Cullen
Portknockie
Findochty

BANFFSHIRE

ABERDEENSHIRE

Lossiemouth
Buckie
12 13
Elgin
Fochabers

MORAY

Moray Firth

Wick
Ackergill
Pulteneytown

Thurso

1
2
Dunnet

CAITHNESS

SUTHERLAND

Portmahomack

Burghead
11
10
Forres
Grantown-
on-Spey

Nairn
9

Tain
Invergordon
3
4
5
Dingwall
Black Isle
6
7
9
7

Easter Ross

Cromarty

Inverness

Aldourie
Drumnadrochit

Beauly

ROSS-SHIRE

INVERNESS-
SHIRE

N

Some key characters

Several hundred individuals are named in this book. Most feature in only one episode. A number, however, turn up more frequently. They are listed here.

Aldcorn, Andrew Medical doctor, Oban, active in Free Church famine relief efforts.

Allan, John Grain-dealer, Elgin.

Balmer, Thomas Richmond Estate commissioner, Fochabers.

Cameron, Patrick Elginshire (Moray) Sheriff-Substitute, based Elgin.

Coffin, Commissary-General Sir Edward Pine Senior officer, Commissariat.

Colquhoun, William Inverness-shire Sheriff-Substitute, based Inverness.

Currie, Alexander Sheriff of Banffshire.

Davidson, Angus Cooper, Burghead.

Evans-Gordon, Captain Charles Army officer, 76th Regiment.

Falconer, James Shoemaker, Burghead.

Fraser, Andrew Inverness-shire Sheriff-Substitute, based Fort William.

Fraser-Tytler, William Sheriff of Inverness-shire.

Gordon, Colonel John Owner of Barra, South Uist and Benbecula.

Gregg, James Caithness Sheriff-Substitute, based Wick.

Grey, Sir George Home Secretary.

Harney, Julian Chartist activist and editor.

Hope, Lord John High Court judge.

Innes, Cosmo Sheriff of Elginshire (Moray).

Jardine, John Sheriff of Ross-shire.

Lindsay, John Crown Agent, Edinburgh.

Loch, James Sutherland Estate commissioner and Wick MP.

MacDonald, Donald   Parish priest, Barra.

MacKay, John   Procurator Fiscal, Inverness.

MacLeod, Alexander   Barra, South Uist and Benbecula factor.

MacLeod, John   Church of Scotland minister, Morvern.

Main, John   Fisherman, Hopeman.

Miller, Hugh   Cromarty-born writer and newspaper editor.

Nicolson, Alexander   Church of Scotland minister, Barra.

Nicolson, James   Shoemaker, Pulteneytown.

Pole, George   Investigating officer, Commissariat.

Pringle, John   Banffshire Sheriff-Substitute, based Banff.

Rhind, Josiah   Banker and provost, Wick.

Rutherfurd, Andrew   Lord Advocate.

Shaw, Charles   Inverness-shire Sheriff-Substitute, based Lochmaddy.

Simpson, William   Provost of Inverness.

Sutherland, Daniel   Fisherman, Hopeman.

Thomson, Robert   Sheriff of Caithness.

Trevelyan, Charles   Treasury civil servant.

Waters, David   Free Church minister, Burghead.

Young, John   Fisherman, Hopeman.

Young, William   Principal proprietor, Burghead.

Introduction

Kinlochlaggan • Ardverikie • Hopeman

The three women walking down the road from Newtonmore to Kinlochlaggan on an August day in 1847 were strangers to this part of the Scottish Highlands. That might have been guessed from their clothes, which, though standard where they came from, are likely to have jarred a little with the more sober styles then favoured hereabouts. Still more suggestive of the three being far from home would have been the way they talked. The women's conversation, and there must have been quite a bit of that as they neared their destination, was not in Gaelic, the everyday language of most of this inland area's mid nineteenth-century residents. Instead, they spoke in the Scots dialect of a distant and coastal community.

At the close of a document compiled for them in the days following their long tramp to Kinlochlaggan, each of the three walkers, none of whom could write, put 'her mark', in the shape of a shakily inscribed X, beside her name. All were married. In the old Scots style, however, the surnames entered on this document, preserved today in Britain's National Archives in Kew, were not the surnames of the women's husbands. Mary Jack, Isabella Main and Margaret Main, when marrying, had seen no reason to give up names that had been theirs since childhood.[1]

In normal times, to be an outsider in Badenoch, the district Margaret, Isabella and Mary were passing through, was automatically to attract attention. But this August things were different. Especially in and around Kinlochlaggan, it had suddenly become an everyday occurrence to see, and meet with, lots of people from elsewhere. Many of those people – some of them landed gentry, others professional men – were the sort who travelled by private carriage. But the road to Kinlochlaggan, whether from Newtonmore to the east or from Spean Bridge and Fort William in the other direction, was also busy with foot traffic. Much of this, grumbled one of the newspapermen thronging Kinlochlaggan's only inn, resulted from a 'perfect plague' of peddlers and trinket-sellers. It is perfectly possible, then, that anyone encountering Mary, Isabella and Margaret might have thought them itinerant traders of some kind. This would have been a misjudgement. But there was, for all that, something the three women shared with the hawkers – and indeed the press reporters – crowding into this usually quiet corner of Badenoch. All of them were here because of the presence, just three or four miles from Kinlochlaggan, of Queen Victoria and Prince Albert.[2]

The royal couple had arrived at Kinlochlaggan on Saturday 21 August. The day was wet. But 'in spite of the pouring rain', the queen commented in her journal, Ewen MacPherson of Cluny, who owned a lot of the surrounding land, had assembled a guard of honour to receive her. This consisted of around 50 men kitted out in kilts and carrying swords and targes of the sort their forebears had taken into battle when, a century before, MacPherson's grandfather had mobilised his clan in support of Prince Charles Edward Stuart's attempt to remove George II from Britain's throne. Had that attempt succeeded, Victoria, George II's great-granddaughter, never would have worn a crown. But the queen, a devotee of the romantic cult that had taken Charles Edward and his rebel Highlanders out of history and into myth, gave no thought to such might-have-beens. In their new guise of loyal retainers, men swathed in tartan were, from Victoria's perspective, intrinsic to Highland Scotland's appeal. Equally key to this appeal was the region's scenery. 'It is quite close to the lake,' the queen noted that evening of the building that was to be her home for the next four weeks, 'and the view from the windows, as I now write, though somewhat obscured by rain, is very beautiful and extremely wild.'[3]

This building was Ardverikie Lodge.* It stood on MacPherson of Cluny's estate. But the lodge, together with thousands of acres around it, had been let to the Marquess of Abercorn, one of Prince Albert's close friends and now his and Victoria's host. Apart from 'a few cottages inhabited by gamekeepers', remarked another of the journalists who had come north in the royal party's wake, Ardverikie's hinterland was deserted. 'Yet the ruins of old corn-kilns and other traces of social life and industry, which meet the eye in several quarters, point back to a time when population was a great deal more numerous.' Some 50 or 60 years previously, that population had been removed to make way for sheep. But by 1847 the sheep too had gone – replaced by red deer,

---

* The lodge, a relatively modest residence, was destroyed by fire in 1871. It was replaced by a larger and more ornate edifice that, in recent times, has featured in television series and films like *Monarch of the Glen* and *Mrs Brown*.

which Abercorn had imported from another part of the Highlands with a view to creating a hunting preserve.[4]

'I have never seen so uncomeatable a place,' a man from the *Illustrated London News* reported of Ardverikie. 'Coaches passing near it, there are none; villages in its vicinity, there are none; farmhouses within sight of it, there are none . . . The queen, it is said, wants retirement; and certainly, in her present quarters, she has got it.' Seclusion was guaranteed by the lodge's position on the southern shore of Loch Laggan – the 'lake' Victoria mentioned in her journal's first Ardverikie entry. On the opposite shore was the public road, constructed 30 years before, which had enabled the queen and Prince Albert to get speedily to Kinlochlaggan from Fort William where they had landed from the royal yacht. The narrower track linking Kinlochlaggan with Ardverikie, however, was strictly private. Unobserved by anyone other than the closest of close retainers, then, Albert was free to stalk deer while Victoria walked, rode into the hills and fished for trout in the nearby loch or its tributary burns. Nothing, it seems, blighted the queen's enjoyment of those activities; not the frequent rain and chill of what was an exceptionally inclement summer; not even the midge bites which left her, she wrote, 'a perfect object'. Victoria and Albert's Highland jaunt, it followed, was to be no one-off occurrence. Months after their trip to Ardverikie, they would acquire their own very similar retreat at Balmoral.[5]

As would be the case at Balmoral, privacy at Ardverikie gave way sometimes to spectacle. This was most evident on 26 August when a Highland Games was staged to celebrate Albert's 28th birthday. On that occasion, all and sundry were free to approach Ardverikie and to glimpse the queen and her husband – Victoria in 'a shawl of Royal Stewart tartan', Albert 'arrayed in . . . Highland garb and wearing the eagle feather of a chieftain in his bonnet'. Next day, however, the public were again excluded, with the exception, as it turned out, of Margaret Main, Isabella Main and Mary Jack. That they had arrived too late for the games would not have concerned them. They had not come to Kinlochlaggan to catch sight of the queen from a distance. Their plan was to meet with her, speak with her and ask her to exercise the royal prerogative of mercy in the case of three men then in London's Millbank Prison where they were being held prior to being shipped to a penal colony in Australia.[6]

The Millbank prisoners were Daniel Sutherland, John Young and John Main. Sutherland was 24, Young 21 and Main 18. They were fishermen from Hopeman, a village on the Moray coast. At the end of March, all three had appeared in Scotland's High Court on charges of mobbing, rioting and assault. Their trial had been brief because they pled guilty. In part, it seems, they did so in the expectation that this would reduce the severity of their punishment. It did not. Each was sentenced to seven years transportation. Those sentences, or so it was hoped by Mary, Isabella and Margaret, might be overturned by Queen Victoria if only she could be persuaded to listen to their explanations of why this should be done.[7]

Margaret and Isabella were probably in their late forties or fifties. Isabella was Daniel Sutherland's mother; Margaret was John Young's mother; and one of the two (which is unclear) was also an aunt of John Main whose own mother was dead. Mary Jack, in her mid twenties and thus much younger than her companions, was Daniel Sutherland's wife. When, in April, her husband was taken to Millbank, she was said to be 'just about to be confined with her first child' – a boy who had been christened James and who, when his mother and grandmother set out with Margaret Main from Hopeman to Ardverikie, must have been left in the care of someone (perhaps one of Mary's friends) prepared to act as his wet-nurse.[8]

On nearing Kinlochlaggan, Mary, Isabella and Margaret would have quit the main road and turned left on to the track leading to Ardverikie. A minute or two's walk along this track would have taken them to a 'floating bridge' – a barge-like contrivance hauled to and fro across the River Pattack at the spot where that deep (and here slow-flowing) watercourse enters the eastern end of Loch Laggan.* When this flat-decked vessel was moored on the Pattack's southern bank, as it was most of the time, Ardverikie was rendered inaccessible. One or two aspiring intruders, to be sure, made it across the Pattack at points further upstream. But they were soon apprehended, it was reported, by 'the police officers whose care it [was] to keep [all such people] at a distance'. It was as well for the Hopeman women, then, that a well-wisher had made strenuous – and, as it proved, successful – efforts to win them safe passage to Ardverikie.[9]

The well-wisher was Elizabeth Waters. Her husband, David Waters, was one of 450 clerics who, four years before, had walked out of the Church of Scotland and set up a new denomination, the Free Church. David Waters was also Margaret, Isabella and Mary's minister. This meant that they were well known to Elizabeth who, a week or so prior to the trio's departure from Hopeman, had penned a letter – 'in the cause of humanity', as she put it – to Sarah MacPherson, Ewen MacPherson of Cluny's wife. Mentioning that she herself had been a MacPherson before her marriage† and that the laird of

---

* The floating bridge was located nearer to the loch than the fixed bridge that has since taken its place.

† Middle-class married women like Elizabeth had long since adopted the habit, soon to become universal, of taking their husband's surnames.

Cluny was thus her 'chief', Elizabeth urged Sarah to do what she could to ensure that the Hopeman women were not barred from Ardverikie. 'Your husband,' Elizabeth wrote, 'is likely to come into much contact with the queen [and] I thought perhaps he might be able to admit them [Mary, Isabella and Margaret] to some part of the [Ardverikie] grounds where they might possibly see Her Majesty.' Thus it came about that three close relatives of men confined to what Charles Dickens called 'the great blank prison' at Millbank were conveyed across the Pattack and taken to the lodge that had become the British royal court's temporary headquarters.[10]

Possibly because they had chosen to focus on the comings and goings of the great and good, the journalists clustered around Kinlochlaggan missed out on the chance to interview, and write about, Ardverikie's visitors from Hopeman. But a week or so after they got home, someone, and Elizabeth Waters must be a likely candidate, supplied details of the women's mission to the *Witness*, an Edinburgh newspaper strongly supportive of the Free Church. In the resulting coverage, replicated by dailies and weeklies in many parts of Britain, the journey made by the three 'fisherwomen' (who, by a press less intrusive than today's, were not named) was compared to that undertaken by one of the most renowned female characters in nineteenth-century Scottish fiction. This was Jeannie Deans, heroine of Walter Scott's novel *The Heart of Midlothian*, and a woman whose religious faith (a faith shared, it was implied, by the Hopeman women) was combined with courage, perseverance and, above all, unwavering loyalty to family.[11]

When, in 1730s Scotland, Jeannie's sister Effie is unjustly condemned to death for the supposed murder of her illegitimate child, Jeannie quits her father's farm near Edinburgh and walks to London where she aims to have Effie pardoned by King George II. On reaching the capital, Jeannie is put in touch with the then Duke of Argyll (in real life a politician and military man of considerable standing) who is sufficiently touched by the young Scotswoman's story to take her to meet the king's consort, Queen Caroline. 'Oh madam,' Jeannie says to the queen, 'if ever ye ken'd what it was to sorrow for . . . a sinning and a suffering creature, whose mind is sae tossed that she can be neither ca'd fit to live or die, have some compassion on our misery! Save an honest house from dishonour, and an unhappy girl, not eighteen years of age, from an early and dreadful death!' This entreaty, and more in the same vein, have the hoped-for effect. The queen (and the historical Caroline certainly wielded just such influence) makes clear that Effie will at once be pardoned and set free.[12]

How far could she walk in a day, Jeannie is asked by a curious Caroline. 'Five and twenty miles and a bittock', Jeannie replies – that bittock, Argyll tells the queen, taking Jeannie's daily mileage to 30. Margaret Main, Isabella Main and Mary Jack (women well used to criss-crossing the Moray country-side in search of buyers for fish carried in heavy creels strapped to their backs) are likely to have matched Jeannie's record. They would thus have covered in under three days the 75 or 80 miles between Hopeman and Ardverikie. Once there, and this could only have happened as a result of intervention by Ewen MacPherson of Cluny, the three women (whose experiences now came clos-est to paralleling those of Jeannie Deans) found themselves in the company of a senior member of the British government.

This was the Colonial Secretary, Earl Grey, the cabinet minister who – it then being thought necessary for a politician to accompany the head of state when she was out of London – had travelled to Scotland with Victoria and Albert. Grey, much of whose time was spent wrestling with governance issues in British possessions as diverse as Canada, New Zealand and South Africa, is most unlikely to have been familiar with the background to the sentencing of John Main, John Young and Daniel Sutherland. It is probable, however, that he had been told something of that background by Ewen or Sarah MacPherson, and it is virtually certain that he had read the letter (afterwards sent to Whitehall from Ardverikie) Sarah had received from Elizabeth Waters. Elizabeth's letter does not dispute that Sutherland, Young and Main had taken part in a riot. But it stresses that those 'three unfortunate lads' had done what they did in response to a food supply crisis so severe as to make them fear that 'they and their families would die of starvation'.[13]

Had he responded to his Hopeman visitors in the gallant manner of the Duke of Argyll in Scott's tale, Earl Grey would have conducted those visitors into the presence of royalty. This did not happen. But according at least to the *Witness*, the earl gave the Hopeman women an assurance that, if a petition for clemency were drawn up in their names, 'it would be laid before the sovereign'. Grey then listened, again according to the *Witness*, while Mary Jack, Isabella Main and Margaret Main, 'told their story . . . in their own homely way'. That story doubtless touched, as Elizabeth Waters's letter to Sarah MacPherson had done, on the wider, and often grim, circumstances that had caused John Main, John Young, Daniel Sutherland and thousands of other people to break the law. What those circumstances were is what this book is about.[14]

I

'A winter of starvation'

*Isle of Barra • Banagher • Skibbereen • Windsor
Castle • Westminster • Wick • Pulteneytown*

When George Pole made his way into the Barra township of Bruernish on the morning of Wednesday 13 January 1847, he was at once confronted by indications of the sort of crisis a later age would call a humanitarian catastrophe. The immediate cause of the misery affecting this crofting settlement's 27 families was a runaway plant disease that had deprived them of potatoes. That would not have mattered had alternative foodstuffs been available in quantity. But this was not the case. Barra, said by a sixteenth-century cleric, Dean Donald Munro, to be 'fertill and fruitful . . . in cornes', might once have been a grain-producing locality where oatmeal and barley-meal were common foodstuffs. Now little of either was to be got on an island where nearly every scrap of arable land had been given over to potatoes. In Bruernish, George Pole reported, 'I found few families with any meal at all.' What he did find, on 'entering the dwellings' constituting this 'little village', were 'diarrhoea and typhus fever' – standard accompaniments of famine. Outside, crunching under Pole's boots, was 'evidence', as he put it, of Bruernish people's desperate search for food: 'The approach to the cottages was paved with . . . shells'. Those shells came from Barra's beaches. Mostly they had contained cockles.[1]

'The famous blue cockles of Barra,' a visiting scientist observed some five years prior to George Pole's arrival on the island, 'are probably the finest, largest and most abundant in the kingdom.' Writing in 1840, Barra's Church of Scotland minister, Alexander Nicolson, was equally emphatic. Cockles could be taken from his parish's shores in 'immense quantities', the minister remarked. Barra's 2,500 or so people, Nicolson went on, turned to 'this article' in 'scarce seasons'. Those occurred when a potato crop, perhaps because of prolonged rains or early frosts, did not come up to expectations, and when, as a result, one year's 'old' potatoes gave out in advance of the next year's 'new' potatoes being ready. 'Sometimes they eat them, when boiled, out of the shell,' Nicolson commented of the cockles on which Barra people relied during those emergencies; 'at other times, such as have milk boil it and the cockles together, making them into soup . . . They commence the use of [cockles] in times of scarcity in April and continue . . . till the beginning of August.' Islanders, Nicolson added, thought 'that the quantity of this [shell]fish on the shores is much greater in scarce seasons than at any other time'.[2]

This comforting notion, that cockles were most prolific when most needed, did not survive the 1840s. Its demise may have been delayed had food shortages been kept confined, in the way Alexander Nicolson described, to the months between April and high summer. But what George Pole encountered in Bruernish was a crisis of a different order from any that had gone before. As had also happened elsewhere in Barra and, for that matter, in much of the rest of north and north-west Scotland, the bulk of people's staple – often only – source of nutrition had been destroyed during July and August 1846 when potato blight reduced field after field, plot after plot, to a sickeningly reeking mass of blackened, rotting vegetation. 'We frequently had bad [meaning hungry] springs,' one of Alexander Nicolson's fellow churchmen remarked of what came next, 'but this is a winter of starvation.' Many Barra people would not have survived that winter had food not reached them from outside. The person tasked with its delivery was George Pole.[3]

From Bruernish, when Pole came knocking at its doors, the ship that had brought him to Barra could be seen at anchor in a sheltered inlet immediately to the north. This was HMS *Firefly*, one of the Royal Navy's newer vessels. A steam-powered, paddlewheel-driven gunboat that, since its 1832 launch, had seen service in several of the British Empire's far-flung outposts, *Firefly* that morning was discharging, on Pole's orders, 50 large sackfuls – or 6¼ tons – of barley-meal. Landed by sailors crewing the ship's boat that had earlier ferried George Pole ashore, this aid was meant, at the minimum, to stop Barra's plight worsening further. It had been delivered, Pole reckoned, not a moment too soon.[4]

George Pole was an 'inspecting officer' on the staff of the Commissariat, the government agency made responsible the previous autumn for famine relief in Scotland's Highlands and Islands. The Commissariat's principal role was to ensure the efficient provisioning of fighting troops in times of conflict, and its consequent expertise in transport and logistics made it the obvious organisation to take on the job of getting food to malnourished communities.

There was to be no question, however, of such aid being anything other than strictly limited. Government ministers, therefore, entrusted the Commissariat with neither a blank cheque nor a free hand. Instead its personnel were subjected to the strictest of supervision and direction by the Treasury and, in particular, by Charles Trevelyan, the senior civil servant who, since 1840, had been a controlling influence on the workings of that key department.

Pole, who would frequently be in correspondence with Trevelyan, was, like many of his Commissariat colleagues, an ex-serviceman. In 1825, when still a youth, he had joined the army with the rank of cornet – comparable to a present-day second-lieutenancy. After long stints overseas, first in the West Indies and then in Canada, where his regiment helped put down an armed rebellion, Pole, now a captain, quit the forces in September 1844 and came home to England. Despite qualifying for the half-pay that was the mid nineteenth-century equivalent of a military pension, Pole, newly married, needed a job. Hence his application for the Commissariat post he obtained in March 1846. Since that post carried a salary of a guinea a day, almost three times a captain's half-pay, Pole's money troubles were now at an end.* So, however, was his freedom to be with his wife. Because Commissariat deployments followed quickly on recruitment, George Pole, within a week of his being hired, was *en route* for Ireland. There blight had struck a year prior to its appearance in the Scottish north; and there, because millions of Irish people were every bit as reliant on potatoes as were folk in Barra, there was a pressing risk of many deaths.[5]

In the event, there was no mass mortality in Ireland in the immediate aftermath of the 1845 potato failure. This was due in no small part to a British politician. Most such politicians were thought by many Irish people to show little concern for Ireland, all of it then part of the United Kingdom. Occasionally, however, there were exceptions. One was Tory prime minister Sir Robert Peel who responded to Ireland's loss of well over half its 1845 potato crop by ordering the establishment of an extensive network of food stores. From those depots, as such stores were called, big quantities of maize or Indian corn, purchased at public expense on international markets, were distributed at cost, or near-cost, price. This life-saving operation, which moved into high gear as hunger gripped more and more of the Irish population in the spring and early summer of 1846, was handled by the Commissariat.

---

* Pole's total income now stood at some £520 annually – between £50,000 and £60,000 at present-day values.

Thus it came about that George Pole, on his arrival in Ireland, was made superintendent of a corn-filled warehouse in Banagher, a County Offaly market town on the banks of the River Shannon.

Both in Banagher's immediate vicinity and in what he called 'the wretched fastnesses' of the Tipperary hill country, a little to the south, Pole encountered 'great distress'. But this, he felt, he was helping to alleviate. 'I cannot too often affirm,' Pole wrote of the foodstuffs dispensed from his Banagher depot, 'that . . . but for the introduction of these supplies the poor . . . would now be starving.' This was in June 1846 when, with a new potato crop doing well, George Pole and lots of others thought that Ireland had been rescued from calamity. 'The interest I feel in my duties,' Pole went on, 'increases with their importance; and in 19 years military service I never enjoyed what I now experience, an active duty with the happy effects of my exertions constantly presenting themselves around me.'[6]

That positivity would not last. By the beginning of August, Pole was reporting the appearance of 'blackened stalks and spotted stems' in potato fields all too obviously manifesting 'fatal signs' of blight's return. And not only was blight back; its virulence was greater than in 1845. Then a reasonable proportion of Ireland's potato harvest had been brought home unscathed. But in the late summer and early autumn of 1846, whether in Ireland or in the more newly affected Highlands and Islands, few – very few – potato fields would yield a worthwhile crop. By September, when he got orders to leave Banagher for Oban, the North Argyll harbour town where the Commissariat was putting in place a Scottish base, George Pole was in pessimistic mood. Ireland, he wrote, was 'in a fearful state as regards the future prospects of the poor'. Those prospects had not been improved by a change of government in London.[7]

The Commissariat's Banagher depot was shut down just prior to Pole's departure. So was every other such store in Ireland. This was in compliance with instructions from the ministers to whom Charles Trevelyan and his Treasury team had been reporting since June when Whigs or Liberals (as some of this party's members now called themselves) took the place of Peel and his Tory colleagues. Liberals of that era were more in thrall than Tories or Conservatives (another then novel designation) to economists of the sort who preached the sanctity of free markets. This made the incoming government susceptible to the complaint that Commissariat depots of the Banagher kind served mainly to disrupt trade while also making the Irish population overly reliant on the UK state. Peel's Irish policy was accordingly abandoned.

Charles Trevelyan, personally in sympathy with free market theorising of the most extreme type, was happy to give effect to a change of plan in Ireland. A handful of food depots might be reopened in hard-to-access areas on Ireland's west coast, he announced. Elsewhere, the new government's response to blight's re-emergence would consist primarily of a programme of public works — for example, road construction. This, it was claimed, would deliver multiple benefits. Ireland's infra-structure would be improved. Irish people, thought hopelessly feckless by Britain's political class, would be subjected to a salutary dose of labour discipline. And public work earnings, payable in either cash or kind, would ensure that no one went hungry.

This might have made sense in Whitehall. Across the Irish Sea, it made none. British-run Ireland, as events showed all too clearly, lacked the admin-istrative machinery that would have been needed to get large-scale public works underway in the time available. Amid the ensuing chaos, to say nothing of the bad feeling that accompanied it, Ireland, as an exceptionally cold and snowy winter set in, began to starve. This was made plain by a letter published in the *Times* on Christmas Eve.

That letter was written by Nicholas Cummins, a businessman and Justice of the Peace in Cork city. 'Having for many years been intimately connected with the western portion of the County of Cork and possessing some small property there,' Cummins began, 'I thought it right personally to investigate the truth of the several lamentable accounts which had reached me of the appalling state of misery to which that part of the county was reduced.' On 15 December, therefore, Cummins embarked on a 50-mile journey to Skibbereen. To make that trip today is to thread one's way through busy tour-ist towns like Kinsale and Clonakilty. Then, judging by Nicholas Cummins's experiences, to go where he went was akin to descending into hell.[8]

Being aware that he 'should have to witness scenes of frightful hunger', Cummins, before leaving home, had filled his carriage 'with as much bread as five men could carry'. Some of that bread was intended for South Reen. This was a West Cork townland* of which, it seems, Nicholas Cummins had previ-ous knowledge. 'On reaching the spot,' the Cork JP wrote, 'I was surprised to find the wretched hamlet apparently deserted. I entered some of the hovels to ascertain the cause, and the scenes that presented themselves were such as no tongue nor pen can convey the slightest idea of. In the first, six famished and ghastly skeletons, to all appearance dead, were huddled in a corner on some

---

* The term applied in Ireland to a smallholding community of the sort called a crofting township in Scotland.

filthy straw, their sole covering what seemed a ragged horsecloth ... I approached with horror and found, by a low moaning, that they were alive. They were in fever, four children, a woman and what had once been a man. It is impossible to go through the detail. Suffice to say that, in a few minutes, I was surrounded by at least 200 of such phantoms.'

In other townlands and in the more substantial settlement of Skibbereen itself, things were no better. In one place, Cummins found himself 'grasped by a woman with an infant just born' – the 'remains of a filthy sack across her loins' constituting this mother's 'sole covering of herself and babe'. In another locality, when people opened the door of a house where no sign of life was to be seen, the 'two frozen corpses' discovered there were found, Cummins reported, to have been 'half-devoured' by rats. In a Skibbereen home entered by a local doctor were seven individuals whose only source of warmth was the single cloak or coat that covered them: 'One had been dead many hours, but the others were unable to move either themselves or the corpse.'

During December 1846, the month that saw Nicholas Cummins undertake his fact-finding mission to West Cork, William Fraser-Tytler, Sheriff of Inverness-shire, began to warn that conditions in some parts of his Highlands and Islands sheriffdom were getting as bad as those in Ireland. Fraser-Tytler worried most about the Outer Hebrides, the island chain extending north-to-south from Lewis, by way of Harris, North Uist, Benbecula and South Uist, to Barra. Apart from Lewis, those islands were in Inverness-shire. This made them Fraser-Tytler's responsibility. On-the-ground justice there, however, was administered by one of the Inverness-shire sheriff's deputes or 'substitutes', Charles Shaw, whose home was in the North Uist village of Lochmaddy and whose regular reports to Fraser-Tytler were the chief source of the latter's growing alarm as to what was unfolding in the Long Island, as the Outer Hebrides were then known.

Stressing that Sheriff-Substitute Shaw was 'one whose information [was] worthy of all confidence', Fraser-Tytler took to forwarding his depute's dispatches to the authorities in Edinburgh. 'I regret to say,' ran one such dispatch of 22 December, 'that ... a large proportion of the people of this district [meaning the Long Island from Harris southwards] are on the eve of starvation ... I refer especially to the parishes of South Uist and Barra. A third of the population of these parishes, amounting to upwards of 3,000*

---

* At the 1841 census, the total population of South Uist and Barra was 9,690.

[people] . . . subsist on, perhaps, a little fish or shellfish, without either vegetables, gruel or anything else, and of this half a meal a day is all that in many cases can be procured.' He understood, Shaw added, that deaths from hunger had already occurred in Barra. Days later, in a further dispatch, Shaw was informing Fraser-Tytler 'of another [Barra] death from the same cause'.[9]

Communications of this kind, their impact increased by their being leaked in part to the *Inverness Courier*, Highland Scotland's leading newspaper, were quickly to result, as William Fraser-Tytler wanted, in steps being taken to establish exactly how bad conditions were on Barra. That was why, on New Year's Day 1847, George Pole was instructed 'to proceed' to an island that, according to the *Inverness Courier*, was 'perhaps the most wretched' locality in all of Scotland. Nor was this new. If potato blight's consequences were grimmer in Barra than anywhere else in the Highlands and Islands, then that owed a good deal to circumstances long antedating blight's onset.[10]

Something of those circumstances was captured in Alexander Nicolson's 1840 account of the island. This told of homes where walls of 'undressed stones without mortar of any kind' supported 'roofs of divot* or straw bound together by heather ropes'. Floors in such houses, typically consisting of just one room, were of beaten-down earth. There were 'neither windows nor chimneys'. Smoke from peat-fuelled fires fogged and darkened interiors before exiting through gaps left in wind-battered thatch. 'The . . . dwellings of the [Barra] peasantry,' Nicolson wrote by way of summary, 'are of the most miserable description.' Much the same could have been said, to be sure, about housing conditions in most crofting areas.† But there were not many other places in Scotland where homes were so bereft of the most basic amenities. 'They have seldom much furniture,' Alexander Nicolson commented of Barra families; 'sometimes not a chair to sit upon, a bed to sleep on, or bed-clothes to cover them.'[11]

This was confirmed in June 1843 when Barra homes were inspected by members of a government-appointed commission of inquiry then looking into the workings of Scotland's Poor Law – a sixteenth-century measure believed widely, and correctly, to be badly in need of updating. The 'very poor hut' occupied by Donald MacLean, his wife and five children was found

---

* Roofing divots were thin strips of grassy turf cut from nearby fields and laid across roof timbers. The divots were then covered with thatch.

† Why this was so is explored in Chapter 3.

to contain 'one bedstead'. But the MacLeans owned 'no bedclothes', and parents and children alike were 'in rags'. Lots more islanders were similarly placed. The four children being raised by Daniel MacDougall and his wife were 'nearly naked', and, apart from a 'very wretched bed', the family's possessions amounted to just 'one broken jug, one pot [and] one small tub'. Widow Cumming, as a 50-year-old single mother was described, had no bed of any description – just 'some straw or other bedding laid upon the floor'. 'Has no means of subsistence but what she and her children can gather', the 1843 investigators noted of Mrs Cumming. 'They [the Cummings] live chiefly on shellfish, but get a little potato ground here and there from their kind neighbours.'[12]

Absolute poverty of the sort uncovered by the 1843 commission was by no means universal on Barra. But even families who were marginally better off were so reliant on potatoes that, when blight took potatoes away, they soon went hungry. That was evident to George Pole from what he discovered in Bruernish. Pole, however, was keen to 'see and hear [of] the state of . . . people' in the rest of Barra. Mounting a horse he had managed to borrow, he duly set off on a tour of the island.[13]

From Bruernish, in Barra's north-eastern corner, Pole headed west by way of a little glen – today one of Barra's few wooded corners – that took him, after three or four miles, to the 'very commodious' manse that had been home to Alexander Nicolson. Although the minister had died the previous April, his widow, Susan, and one or more of her three daughters were still in residence. The Nicolson 'ladies', Pole wrote, 'represent the state of the poor as surpassing description; their servants are in the habit of saving a portion of . . . [the household's] meals to give to . . . starving applicants at the door. Mrs Nicolson feels quite certain that many have died from . . . [having] insufficient food.'[14]

On an island where folk spoke mostly or only Gaelic, Pole, no Gaelic-speaker, was in search that January day of people able to tell him, in English, how Barra was faring. But for all that he could communicate easily with Susan Nicolson, Pole may have suspected that a Presbyterian minister's widow might not be best placed to provide him with insights of the sort he wanted. Barra, after all, was a place where the Scottish Reformation of 300 years before had never taken hold and where, in consequence, the late Alexander Nicolson's congregation had always been a small one. And so George Pole rode on to Craigston, one of a number of townships in a broad and westward-facing valley opening out on to the sea.

At Bruernish, its homes scattered across a series of rocky knolls above a tangle of little bays and tidal creeks, Pole had been in the part of Barra that borders the Minch – the name given to the wide waters separating the Outer Hebrides from the Inner Isles of Skye, Rum, Eigg and Canna. Now he was on Barra's Atlantic coast where calcium-rich shell-sand, washed in from the ocean, neutralises the acidity of what would otherwise be sour and peaty soils – which is why land in the west of Barra is much grassier and more productive agriculturally than land further east. It was in localities like Craigston, then, that Barra people would have sown much of the grain or 'cornes' mentioned in Dean Munro's account of the island. But by the 1840s, though one or two people here and in neighbouring settlements still managed to grow some oats or barley, potatoes had mostly taken over as completely as they had done in Bruernish. The consequences were spelled out for Pole by Donald MacDonald, Barra's Catholic priest.

MacDonald's church, St Brendan's, then Barra's only Catholic place of worship, stood at the lower end of Craigston.* A few hundred yards to the east, at a spot called Gearradhmor, was the priest's home – today a roofless and windowless shell – where Pole, that day in January 1847, was to hear that Donald MacDonald's congregation was in as bad a state as it was possible to be. 'Priest MacDonald,' the Commissariat man reported, 'describes the poor of Barra as on the point of starvation . . . [H]e says, with melancholy, that [the few folk who still grew grain] have eaten, or are eating, their seed corn [usually husbanded carefully until spring]. He confesses that . . . all the various degrees of want and disease present themselves to his notice . . . People come to him who, after reaching his door, cannot speak to him from weakness.'[15]

George Pole was much affected by what he saw and was told on Barra. Partly, perhaps, his response was bound up with pressures he was under personally. Some of those stemmed from his extraordinarily demanding role; others may have originated in news that reached him not long after he got to Oban. There, at the beginning of October 1846, Pole learned from his wife that their child (a first child it seems) had died. Understandably, Pole thought about resigning and heading for home. However, he did not do so, something that drew praise from Charles Trevelyan. 'I sincerely sympathise with you and Mrs Pole in the affliction which it has pleased God to send you,' the deeply pious Trevelyan told his subordinate, 'but I approve of, and admire, the resolution you have come to not to be deterred by this domestic calamity from completing the critical and important public duty on which you are engaged.'[16]

---

* Today's St Brendan's is the product of much rebuilding in the later nineteenth century.

For the next three months, that 'public duty' would be all-consuming. Aboard the *Firefly*, and in weather that was often cold as well as stormy, Pole visited islands and island groups as far apart as Islay (within sight of Ireland) and Shetland (parts of which are nearer Norway than to much of mainland Scotland). Pole's traverses of bigger islands like Skye were mostly made on horseback. But when investigating conditions on the hilly and often roadless West Highland mainland, he was sometimes obliged to make long treks on foot. One such trek, completed just before Christmas, took Pole through Ardnamurchan, Moidart, Morar and Arisaig. He had found this a 'very severe' undertaking, Pole admitted, his 'progress' having been repeatedly 'retarded' by 'mountain streams and snow-clogged paths'.[17]

Those efforts left Pole not just exhausted but ill. Within a week of his being in Barra, where the *Firefly*'s departure was delayed for two or three days by renewed gales, he informed his superiors that his 'state of health [was] becoming such that a further continuation in this service and climate would only lead to its total derangement'. By February, George Pole, whose departure was a cause of 'very great concern' to Charles Trevelyan, would be with his wife in England. But the several pages he penned on quitting Barra had meanwhile done their work. No one reading Pole's account of what he had found there could have been anything other than convinced that Barra's predicament was every bit as serious as Sheriff Fraser-Tytler feared.[18]

In both Scotland and Ireland, Whig ministers believed, rural populations at risk of starvation needed to look for assistance, in the first instance, to landlords who, given their insistence that governments should have nothing to do with how they managed their estates, could hardly object (in public at least) to being handed this responsibility. But what if no such assistance was forthcoming? This was the position in Barra. That island, along with neighbouring South Uist and Benbecula, belonged to someone who, in the months following blight's annihilation of potato crops, showed next to no concern for the 10,000 or so famine-threatened people living on his Outer Hebridean properties. This someone was Colonel John Gordon. An absentee owner who seems to have only once set foot on his Long Island domains, Gordon – an individual of the sort Jane Austen might have described as 'a gentleman of large fortune' – divided his time between two well-appointed residences, Cluny* Castle in Aberdeenshire and a substantial house in Edinburgh's New Town.

---

* This Aberdeenshire Cluny is not to be confused with the Badenoch Cluny that was home to Ewen and Sarah MacPherson.

As famine loomed, Gordon,* like other Highlands and Islands landlords, was advised repeatedly by government to embark on estate improvement schemes. These, ministers pointed out, could be financed by means of Treasury-provided loans made available on the basis that to generate employment was also to enable hungry families to get by. Gordon, however, declined to fall in line. 'The proprietor,' Sheriff Charles Shaw† commented in one of his reports on Benbecula, South Uist and Barra, 'has not done anything either by providing work or food.' Perhaps because John Gordon's stance so spectacularly gave the lie to the Scottish establishment's tendency to portray the country's lairds as unfailingly benevolent, his conduct provoked outrage on the part of politicians, not least Andrew Rutherfurd MP, Scotland's lord advocate and thus the Whig administration's main man north of the border.‡ 'It grieves me to the heart,' Rutherfurd remarked at the beginning of January 1847, 'that destitution should have made a progress so stern and alarming on a property belonging to one of the most wealthy proprietors in this country.' Those feelings were reinforced by what Rutherfurd and his colleagues learned from George Pole.[19]

In Ireland, Pole had incurred official displeasure because he expressed himself too freely. When communicating with higher authority, he was told, he needed to be 'cautious'. This instruction Pole now disregarded. 'I cannot conclude,' he wrote, 'without saying that I have found upon Colonel Gordon's property, especially in the Isle of Barra, greater wretchedness and privation from want of food than it has been my painful duty to investigate on other properties in the Highlands and Islands.' Nor did Pole draw back from attributing blame for the sufferings endured by what he called a 'neglected people': 'What an awful reflection it is that at this moment the wealthy heritor§ of these islands is not employing the poor population . . . But this I affirm, that if the poor on [Gordon's estate] are not employed . . . and that forthwith, scenes will occur in South Uist, Barra and Benbecula which would be disgraceful to his [Gordon's] name and injurious to the reputation of Great Britain.'[20]

★　　★　　★

---

* There is more on Gordon's background in Chapter 3. He was a colonel by virtue of an Aberdeenshire Militia rank he had held years before.
† A sheriff-substitute like Shaw was commonly given the same shorthand title as a sheriff principal like Fraser-Tytler.
‡ Then and for another 40 years Lords Advocate exercised administrative functions that would later become the responsibility of Secretaries of State for Scotland.
§ A Scots law term for a proprietor.

George Pole's findings were corroborated by Charles Shaw who, just four or five days after Pole's departure, arrived on Barra to take sworn statements about the circumstances surrounding the growing number of deaths caused, islanders said, by hunger. Like Pole, Sheriff Shaw spent time in Bruernish where one of the township's residents, Archibald MacMillan, was in no doubt that his daughter Catherine, 'then about 14 years of age', had died in mid December as a result of 'her being [for] so long a period on a small allowance of food'.[21]

Because of blight, MacMillan said, 'his crop of potatoes ... afforded himself and [his] family subsistence for [only] about a week'. Since August, it followed, the MacMillan household – Catherine, her two sisters and three brothers, Archibald and his wife Jean – had 'frequently ... been without food'. So far, so unequivocal. At once, however, there began to be back-tracking on Archibald MacMillan's part. Every evening, he said, the family made 'half a lippie,* or about a pound, of meal' into gruel. In the mornings, a further half lippie of meal, this time in the form of oatcakes, was eaten with, on occasion, 'a little fish' – by which Archibald (whose Gaelic was translated into English in Shaw's interview transcript) very possibly meant cockles.[22]

All through the autumn and into the winter, Archibald MacMillan next insisted, Catherine 'had fallen [away] greatly in strength and appearance ... in consequence of the scarcity of food' available to her. That was why she had become 'so weak as to be unable to withstand' the illness (perhaps typhus or dysentery of the sort Pole observed in Bruernish) that had been 'the immediate cause' of her eventual death.

Nothing of this, Shaw realised, made sense; for if the MacMillans' food intake was as Archibald described, then Catherine, despite her diet's evident inadequacy, should not have become quite so emaciated as her father claimed. In search of clarification, the sheriff turned to Catherine MacMillan's eldest brother, John, a young man of 18. Clearly reluctant to break too radically with his father's account, John nevertheless qualified that account in key respects. The family had 'not consume[d] a lippie of meal a day' or indeed anything like that amount. Often, they had been forced to make do with just one 'scanty' serving of gruel – made from 'a little' oatmeal mixed with warm water. As a result, John said, he himself had been 'getting quite weak' and had 'fallen off very much'. Catherine, John added, 'had fallen off much more'.[23]

---

* A Scots measurement of meal by volume.

Additional information was provided by Alexander MacPhie, another Bruernish resident and a man who had been present in the MacMillan home on the day Catherine died. 'It was his opinion,' MacPhie told Charles Shaw, 'that [Catherine] died of want of food.' This 'want of food', Alexander MacPhie went on, had arisen from 'her father's family' having been 'for some time previously . . . very destitute'. The MacMillans, Shaw heard, 'seldom had meal' in their possession. Yes, they might have picked up some shellfish. But for lengthy periods, it appeared, the family had 'lived principally upon the remains of diseased potatoes' that had earlier been left to rot where they lay.[24]

Shaw next re-examined Archibald MacMillan. For week after week, MacMillan now admitted, neither he nor his family had been able to access food of the kind he had previously described. That was why he had 'sent his children . . . to collect . . . all the potatoes which they thought they could with safety eat'. In fact, as MacMillan would have been aware, to eat any such potatoes was to risk sickness. But having no alternative, his children, himself and his wife, MacMillan said, had made 'two meals a day' of scavengings from Bruernish's blighted potato patches. Despite this, they had 'never [had] anything like a sufficient quantity to satisfy the cravings of hunger'. That was why – and here Archibald MacMillan returned to his original starting point – 14-year-old Catherine had died.[25]

Charles Shaw might have told the man in front of him that to lie under oath was a serious offence. The sheriff, however, confined himself to asking for an explanation of the divergences between MacMillan's two statements. Shaw, it seems likely from the mildness of his manner, had already deduced the man's likely response. That response, when it came, was certainly one that George Pole, had he been involved in questioning Archibald MacMillan, could have predicted exactly. This was because Pole, when in Ireland, had been party to lots of similar encounters.

One such encounter began on a July morning in 1846 when a man described as a 'small farmer' was shown into Pole's Banagher office. This farmer, it transpired, had made a 12-mile walk in the hope of acquiring from the Commissariat the supplies needed to rescue his family from 'the verge of famine'. Pole, aware that there was a locally organised relief committee operating in the vicinity of the farmer's home, asked his visitor why he had not applied to its members for help. 'By going to the committee,' the man replied, 'I proclaim myself a pauper.' During his time in Banagher, Pole wrote, he had come across 'many instances . . . of this description' – instances of people going to great lengths to conceal from others (maybe even from themselves) how dire their situation had become.[26]

As in Banagher, so in Bruernish. 'He did not state all this in his former declaration,' Archibald MacMillan said of his eventual revelations, 'because he felt ashamed to make the admission.' What had happened to Catherine MacMillan was not her father's fault. But a parent unable to rescue their child from starvation is unlikely ever to be free of a sense of failure, culpability, self-reproach.[27]

The emotions discernible in Archibald MacMillan's account of the reasons for his daughter's passing, emerge over and over again from the scores of neatly inscribed foolscap pages on which Charles Shaw (or an accompanying clerk) recorded the results of his meticulous inquiries into other Barra deaths – deaths affecting, in every instance, the children or old people who are always a famine's first victims.

In Borve, a mile or so south of Fr Donald MacDonald's church at Craigston, Neil MacNeil spoke about his four-year-old son who had died less than a week before Shaw met with the boy's father. He and his family, MacNeil said, were so lacking in resources that, for months, they had 'depended upon the charity of . . . friends'. Those friends, however, were 'themselves so scarce' that they had little food to spare. Sometimes, it followed, there were days when 'the only thing . . . tasted' by MacNeil, his wife and their five children 'was warm water'. Like the MacMillans, the MacNeils had been seen 'digging in the fields' for 'diseased potatoes'; while such oatmeal as they had managed to beg from neighbours was eked out so sparingly that, 'during the last fort-night of his life', the boy who died (and whose name has not been preserved) could be given no more than 'about a gill* of thin gruel sometimes once and sometimes twice in [each] 24 hours'. 'He never complained of pain,' Neil MacNeil said of his dead son, 'but . . . he wasted away day by day till he became so weak that he could not sit [up], and he at last expired [in the early morning of Friday 15 January] without . . . ever having had a moment's illness'. His little boy 'had not tasted a morsel the previous day', MacNeil added, because there had been 'nothing to give him'.[28]

In Tangasdale, not far from Borve, Anne MacDonald told how her elderly aunt, Jessie MacDonald, who had died on Thursday 7 January, 'often wept bitterly for want of food' before her death. In the autumn, Anne's father, Jessie's brother, now also dead, had sold the family's cow and calf. But such

---

* A quarter of a pint.

provisions as were bought with the cash thus raised had long since been consumed – something Jessie, it seems, found hard to accept. He had often heard the old lady 'imploring the family to give her food when they had none to give', Sheriff Shaw was informed by one of the MacDonalds' neighbours.[29]

A further narrative of trauma and bereavement awaited Shaw at another MacDonald household, this one in Cliad, a coastal settlement occupying a little valley two or three miles north of Tangasdale and Borve. Shaw's principal informant here was Mary MacDonald, a woman of 'about 30 years'. Mary was unmarried but had two small sons – described formally at the time as 'natural' or 'illegitimate'. This, in what was a censorious age, would have made for difficulties enough for Mary. But added to these were responsibilities arising from her being, in today's terminology, sole carer of her ageing mother, Margaret.[30]

Margaret and Mary MacDonald grew potatoes on a diminutive croft rented, like all such Barra smallholdings, from Colonel John Gordon. When their croft's 1846 potato crop was wiped out by blight, Mary said, she had first slaughtered the little flock of 'ducks and hens' that, in better times, had provided the family with eggs. Her poultry eaten, Mary had next turned to her savings – consisting of '50 shillings' earned at some point from the sale of a horse. Back in the summer, 30 of those shillings had been spent on oatmeal. But by winter, when this oatmeal was exhausted, 'her two boys,' Mary said, 'frequently for five or six days together tasted nothing but dulse and tangle' – these being varieties of seaweed that could be gathered from coastal outcrops within an easy walk of the MacDonald croft. But what, Charles Shaw queried, had Mary done with the cash, amounting in total to a pound, she had not so far accounted for? Although neighbours had been 'very kind', Mary explained, they had never been able to spare more than a little of their own scanty stocks of food, and it had thus become obvious that her mother, already ailing, could not long survive. She accordingly 'gave the remaining pound' of the family's savings to a trusted friend for safekeeping. This meant that when Margaret died in December, there were 20 shillings with which 'to bury her'. 'She would look upon it as an indelible disgrace,' Mary MacDonald told Charles Shaw, 'if she had not [had] money to expend upon her mother's funeral.'[31]

A stitched-together set of Charles Shaw's Barra transcripts, together with a 'confidential note' summarising Shaw's assessment of the state of matters on the island, reached Sheriff William Fraser-Tytler in early February 1847. 'The evidence there given presents a picture second in nothing to what we read of in Ireland,' Fraser-Tytler wrote of those documents. This, in the light of what Nicholas Cummins had discovered in West Cork, was arguably to go too far. But if Barra's people were not yet facing horrors of the sort afflicting places like Skibbereen, there was certainly no lack of signs that they might be about do so. 'No words [could] express the feelings with which [he had] read' Shaw's material, Inverness-shire's sheriff informed Lord Advocate Rutherfurd. What especially offended Fraser-Tytler was John Gordon's disregard for his Hebridean tenants. But such conduct, though reprehensible morally, infringed no statute. Barra's proprietor would thus remain, as Fraser-Tytler put it, 'beyond the reach of human law'. This was to imply that Gordon might face punishment in the next world if not in this – something from which the Sheriff of Inverness-shire appears to have derived some comfort. In the meantime, however, Fraser-Tytler wanted to discover if Barra residents were at least getting such aid as they were entitled to under the provisions of the recently reformed Poor Law. Andrew Rutherfurd shared that wish. A somewhat harassed Charles Shaw – one of whose letters stressed that 'the island [was] far' from his North Uist home and 'often inaccessible' for long periods in winter – was accordingly sent back to Barra. This time he was accompanied by William Peterkin, a senior employee of the Board of Supervision for the Relief of the Poor.[32]

That Edinburgh-based organisation was a product of legislation resulting from the 1843 commission of inquiry whose members had found, not just in Barra but throughout Scotland, good reasons to put care of the poor on a new basis. Previously, poor relief had been handled by the Church of Scotland. Now each of the country's 880 parishes was required to set up a parochial board, usually consisting in the first instance of a mix of clerics and property owners. Those boards, along with the inspectors they were duty-bound to appoint, had to conduct themselves in accordance with rules and regulations enshrined in a Poor Law Act of 1845. The Board of Supervision, established by the same Act, had the job, as its name suggests, of ensuring that every locality complied with these requirements. In the case of Barra, as William Peterkin soon realised, the level of compliance was so low as to place the island, in effect, outside the scope of what were meant to be Scotland-wide arrangements.

In November 1845, it appeared, a number of men had met in order to set up a Barra Parochial Board. Attendees had included the then parish minister, Alexander Nicolson, his Catholic counterpart, Donald MacDonald, and, most crucially, John Gordon's factor or estate manager, Alexander MacLeod, who had at once taken charge of proceedings. On MacLeod's recommendation, a Barra crofter, Archibald MacDonald, was made the island's inspector of the poor. Sheriff Shaw – who believed the November 1845 meeting to have been so slipshod that, strictly speaking, the Barra Parochial Board had 'not been legally constituted' – was dismissive of MacDonald. Although 'a most respectable man', the inspector, in the sheriff's estimation, was 'unfit for his office from want of education', being at best, it seems, only semi-literate. Why, then, had such a person been selected to fill so vital a post? Because, Shaw commented, he was 'entirely under the control of the factor'.[33]

That Charles Shaw, in 1847 anyway, thought little of this factor is apparent from the many critical comments he made about him in documentation arising from his visits to Barra. This makes it odd that, years later, Shaw would describe the self-same Alexander MacLeod as 'a most benevolent, kind-hearted man'. Maybe Shaw, by that stage, simply did not wish to speak ill of someone who had died a long time previously. Or maybe he was simply falling into line with a then growing tendency, in some parts of the Highlands and Islands, to insist that memories of Alexander MacLeod were so positive as to prove him an 'outstanding exception' to the general rule that no such land manager, whether alive or dead, was thought by crofters to merit anything other than loathing.[34]

Favourable opinions of MacLeod, who was born in North Uist in 1788 and who went on to study medicine at Edinburgh University, appear to have been held mostly in localities – North Uist was one and Skye another – where MacLeod practised for a time as a doctor. On John Gordon's estate, however, he was remembered primarily as a ruthless enforcer of his employer's wishes – with the result that, when MacLeod died in 1854 from a fall, people on Gordon's island properties (where another factor had by then been installed) greeted news of their former oppressor's fatal accident by saying that divine retribution had at last overtaken him.[35]

Charles Shaw's negative take on Alexander MacLeod, then, was firmly in line with Barra sentiment. That, however, does not rule out the possibility of bias on Shaw's part. Ten years before the famine, and just prior to John Gordon's acquisition of the island, Shaw had himself factored Barra for some months. The position had come to him on the basis that he had worked closely for a period with his father who had managed more than one Hebridean estate. But for all that the post had been strictly temporary, the island having then been up for sale, might it have rankled with Shaw that Gordon, on buying Barra, had hired Alexander MacLeod rather than him? Perhaps. But by 1847, surely, Shaw is most unlikely to have thought it would be better to be managing famine-ravaged Barra than to be an Inverness-shire sheriff-substitute – a role that had come to him in 1841 and which he was to retain for 40 years.

Certainly, there is no discrepancy between Charles Shaw's reports from Barra and those of the Board of Supervision's William Peterkin. On the latter interviewing Archibald MacDonald, for example, the MacLeod-appointed poor inspector was open about inadequacies of the sort that Shaw believed had caused the factor to give MacDonald the job. He had 'never got a copy of the Act of Parliament' that set out his duties, MacDonald admitted. He had seen the 'printed notes' supplied by the Board of Supervision, but he no longer had them. He 'did not know anything' of the requirement that he organise a minimum of two parochial board meetings each year – with the result that those meetings had 'never been held'. The 'register of poor' compiled at the November 1845 meeting had not been updated and there was no 'list of those who [despite application] were refused relief'. The inspector, in fact, possessed 'no [minute or account] books of any kind' and had not been informed by Alexander MacLeod that 'it was his duty to keep them'. Nor was he aware that he was expected to 'visit the poor at their dwelling houses'. In short, as Sheriff Shaw had already observed, Archibald MacDonald 'did not know how to act and . . . entirely leant upon the factor by whom alone he was guided'.[36]

Might others have challenged Alexander MacLeod's dominance? One who could perhaps have done so was Fr Donald MacDonald. But the priest, as he told Shaw, was 'dependent upon the factor and proprietor for many things and did not like to give umbrage by [an] . . . active interference'. It was for this reason, Shaw observed cynically, that the absence of parochial board meetings had made no difference to the course of events in Barra – because the board's members lacked the will, the capacity or both, to 'carry the factor along with them'.[37]

Had poor relief on Barra been managed on standard lines, much of the resulting cost, recouped by way of the rates parochial boards were empowered to levy on land and other assets, would have fallen on John Gordon in his role as the island's sole laird. As it was, this potential burden was eliminated by Alexander MacLeod's success in keeping relief expenditure to the barest minimum. At what was ostensibly the founding meeting of the Barra Parochial

Board, MacLeod had agreed to have 53 names placed on the poor roll then compiled. None of the individuals in question, several of whom died during 1846 and early 1847, had received cash payments of the kind common in other parts of Scotland. Instead they got sporadic hand-outs of meal from an estate store. And when Archibald MacDonald spoke 'over and over again' with MacLeod about the need, as he saw it, to add to the poor roll people like the two elderly women, Margaret MacDonald in Cliad and Jessie MacDonald in Borve, whose deaths Charles Shaw had earlier investigated, 'the factor,' the poor inspector said, 'always put him off'.[38]

Alexander MacLeod, for his part, contended that hunger had played no part in the deaths of either Margaret or Jessie. 'I [knew] the individuals,' the factor told John Gordon. 'They had been sickly for years.' Barra, MacLeod insisted in a letter to the *Inverness Courier*, was doing well. On his regular visits there from his home at Kilbride on the adjacent island of South Uist, he had seen nothing of the 'scenes of misery . . . so industriously and groundlessly set forth in the public prints'. Both Jessie MacDonald and Margaret MacDonald might have been kept off the poor roll at the factor's instigation. So might the 'many [other] applicants' for poor relief of whom Shaw and Peterkin heard in the course of their enquiries. But several older folk, it seemed, had neverthe-less received 'occasional aid' – an assertion put in context by Board of Supervision calculations showing that, during the second half of 1846, the 'aid' thus extended to the elderly averaged just four ounces of oatmeal per person per day.*[39]

William Peterkin, whose Barra reports read like the work of a man so wedded to orderliness as to have been truly shocked by his discoveries, wondered how (given the niggardly nature of a daily hand-out equivalent to not much more than a single bowl of porridge) Margaret MacDonald's daughter Mary, together with Mary's two boys, had not died at much the same time as Margaret: 'The parochial allowance [meaning Margaret's oatmeal allocation] being evidently insufficient to support life in four individuals [Margaret, her daughter and her daughter's sons], the question comes to be, how did this family subsist? It appears to have been almost entirely owing to the charity of their neighbours and their having recourse, when *in extremis*, to the last resort of destitution, eating seaweed.'[40]

---

* The charitable agency which became (as will be seen) a key source of Highlands and Islands famine relief fixed the daily meal ration at 12 ounces per adult female and 24 ounces per adult male. Children under 12 got 8 ounces.

What made such episodes all the more inexcusable, in the opinion of both Peterkin and Charles Shaw, was the fact that Margaret and Mary MacDonald should have been able to draw on a fund put in place to help people like them. This fund's creators were two Barra men who had long before gone overseas and, on doing well financially, had made a joint bequest of £400 (equivalent to several tens of thousands of pounds today) to Barra's poor. This sum was banked and, as mentioned in the Revd Alexander Nicolson's 1840 account of his parish, interest from it was 'distributed . . . annually' to needy islanders. Why, Peterkin and Shaw now asked, had no such distribution been forthcoming 'while the poor were on the eve of starvation'? The answer – an extraordinary one – was provided by Donald Nicolson, adult son of Barra's late minister.[41]

Some three years earlier, Nicolson said, his father had been persuaded to relinquish control of the £400 legacy of which he had been trustee and which, up to that point, had been deposited with the Bank of Scotland in Edinburgh. 'This sum,' Donald Nicolson continued, 'is now in the hands of Colonel Gordon of Cluny.' Quite how that had happened was unclear. Only two things were certain. First, in a promissory note, dated 27 May 1844 and available for inspection at Barra's manse, Gordon undertook to invest the £400 bequest in such a way as to deliver an annual return of 3.5 per cent. Second, he had since remitted to Barra not one penny of that supposed return. This meant that, by early 1847, their rich landlord had, in effect, stolen accumulated interest payments of around £40 from Barra's poor. Even at the famine-inflated prices then prevailing, this amount could have provided the island's hungriest families with a modicum of food. In those circumstances, it was as well that the Commissariat, in the person of George Pole, had come to Barra's assistance. It was as well too that, in Scotland's cities and in other centres further south, lots of contributions were beginning to be made to famine relief funds.[42]

When Nicholas Cummins wrote to the *Times* about the gruesome scenes he saw in South Reen and Skibbereen, he copied his letter to the Duke of Wellington. By so doing, Cummins hoped to persuade the duke – military hero, elder statesman and, most crucially in this context, a man whose origins were in Ireland – to raise Irish people's torments at the highest level. 'You have access to our young and gracious queen,' the Cork JP urged the duke. 'Lay these things before her. She is a woman. She will not allow decency to be outraged. She has at her command the means of at least mitigating the sufferings of the wretched survivors of this tragedy.'[43]

When Cummins's letter appeared in the press, Queen Victoria, then 27, was spending the Christmas and New Year season at Windsor Castle with Prince Albert and the first four of their eventually nine children. The queen was again pregnant and presumably taking no pleasure in a condition that reduced her, she wrote later, to the status of a breeding animal 'like a cow or a dog'. Nor was the weather a source of cheer, Victoria's journal filling with references to bitter frosts, which, though enabling Albert to skate on a nearby lake, got in the way of morning strolls and other outings. Evenings, on the other hand, were enlivened by an array of dinner guests. The Duke of Wellington was not among them. But Ireland, Nicholas Cummins would have been pleased to know, intruded more than once, as did the worsening crisis in the Hebrides.[44]

'We walked out for a short while and found it extremely cold,' Victoria noted on 31 December. 'Received some heartrending accounts of the state of Ireland – really too terrible to think of. In one district alone, 197 people have died from fever, produced by want, and half as many have died in their cabins, and in the lanes and streets, of starvation. To save expense, they are buried without . . . the services of any clergy. The scenes of horror, the starving people, shivering with cold and devouring raw turnips . . . Too dreadful . . . I saw a private letter from a lady saying that the poor people in the . . . Western Isles [of Scotland] are equally in a state of starvation, existing only on seaweed.'[45]

Partly because the queen's journal entries are more in the nature of hasty jottings than considered musings, sentiments like these can appear trite and superficial. But that would be to overlook the extent to which much of this intensely emotional woman's long life was lived as a protracted melodrama – her prime ministers, for instance, being either loved (Disraeli most famously) or (as with Gladstone) hated. In Ireland, already experiencing the early stirrings of an eventually triumphant republicanism, it would be thought widely that Victoria cared not a jot for hunger's victims. But on the last day of 1846 at least, her sympathies for them were surely real, as was the anger that caused her to write: 'In the midst of all this, the landlords appropriate the people's corn!' There the queen touched on something that has coloured Irish attitudes to the 1840s' famine ever since, the export from a starving country of huge quantities of grain. Had that grain not been sold to shippers by the often malnourished farmers who produced it, then those same farmers would have been unable to pay their rents to landowners of the sort castigated by the queen – landowners who mostly reacted to non-payment, as Victoria knew, by having non-payers driven from their homes.[46]

What, then, was to be done? In an era much given to humanitarian and charitable campaigns with objectives ranging from ending slavery to building hospitals, one answer seemed obvious. Famine relief fund-raising had begun in Scotland towards the end of 1846. Now England followed suit with the early-January launch in London of the British Association for the Relief of Extreme Distress in Ireland and in the Highlands and Islands of Scotland. Headed by bankers and financiers like Baron Lionel de Rothschild, the association looked to Victoria for support. First, she gave £1,000 – upped to £2,000 when it was discovered that the Sultan of Turkey, then looking to curry favour with Britain, was about to match her initial donation. Next, in her capacity as head of the Church of England, she told the Archbishops of Canterbury and York to ensure, as Victoria's letter of instruction put it, that Anglican clergy 'in each parish do effectively excite their parishioners to [make] a liberal contribution' to the British Association. This letter, signed on the day that took George Pole to Bruernish, would help to put a final total of around £470,000 (equivalent to some £50 million today) at the association's disposal. That was impressive. But ultimately, as the queen and everyone else knew, only government could deal effectively with the multifaceted devastation unleashed by potato blight. And her latest set of ministers impressed Victoria not at all.[47]

On the then teenage Victoria becoming queen in 1837, she had developed so close a bond with her first prime minister, Lord Melbourne, as to have been appalled when Melbourne, a Whig, was obliged to give way to Tory leader Robert Peel, as stolidly and unexcitingly middle-class as Melbourne was raffishly aristocratic. But Prince Albert, Victoria's German-born cousin whom she married in 1840, saw in Peel a man who shared his interest in the technological advance and economic expansion that were to be the defining characteristics of the Victorian age. With Albert's encouragement, therefore, Victoria began to discern in Peel qualities that had initially eluded her – with the result that, months after the event, she continued to lament Peel's 1846 fall from power. 'Good, excellent Sir Robert Peel sat next to me [at dinner]', the queen wrote on 5 January 1847, 'I never cease regretting his loss as a minister.' Like many more of Britain's political upheavals throughout the nineteenth century and beyond, that loss was bound up with Ireland – specifically, on this occasion, with the 1845

failure of the Irish potato crop having become the rationale for Peel's decision to repeal the UK's Corn Law.[48]

This law, which imposed hefty import duties on inexpensively produced
grain from countries like the United States and Russia, was a means of under-
writing and propping up the position and power of Britain's 'landed interest'
– meaning the owners of the country's great estates. To move against the
Corn Law, then, was to signal that landlords, whose rental incomes rose with
agricultural prices, were to lose out at the expense of the manufacturers, business people and others who wanted Britain to have cheaper food. Given the
complexities of a party structure that did not divide neatly along landed and
non-landed lines, the politics of Corn Law repeal were far from simple. Many
supporters of Peel's own Tory Party, for example, were much more committed to keeping domestic grain prices high than to helping the prime minister
buy American maize for Ireland. Peel, however, was unyielding – seeing off
opponents of Corn Law repeal with the same resolve as he countered critics
of Irish food depots like the one managed by George Pole. When MPs questioned expenditure on forestalling a famine that, they argued, might prove less
severe than forecast, Peel was savage. 'Are you to hesitate in averting famine
which may come, because it possibly may not come?' he asked. 'Are you to
look to and depend upon chance in such an extremity? Or, good God! are
you to sit in Cabinet and consider and calculate how much diarrhoea, and
bloody flux, and dysentery a people can bear before it becomes necessary for
you to provide them with food?'[49]

Amid much acrimony, the Corn Law was consigned to history. But so,
with the Tory or Conservative Party now hopelessly split, was Sir Robert
Peel's government. In Ireland, even in anti-British circles, this was seen as a
misfortune. 'No man died of famine during his administration,' it would be
said of Robert Peel by *Freeman's Journal*, one of Dublin's nationalist newspapers. No such commendations were to come the way of Peel's successor,
Lord John Russell, whose Whig or Liberal cabinet, in the course of a year
remembered in Ireland as 'Black Forty-Seven', presided over a famine death
toll numbered, insofar as it could be numbered at all, in hundreds of
thousands.[50]

The awful scale of Ireland's *Gorta Mór* or Great Hunger was not yet
evident when, a few days into 1847, Russell visited Windsor to discuss the
content of the Queen's Speech to be delivered, as was customary, at the
start of a new parliamentary session on 19 January. But 'the fearful state of
Ireland', Victoria recorded, nevertheless loomed large when she and

Russell 'talked of the Speech and how it could be framed'. There would need to be some acknowledgement, it was agreed, of Ireland's trauma and of the risk of something similar occurring in the Highlands and Islands. But perhaps because neither Lord John Russell nor his colleagues quite grasped the sheer immensity of the challenges they faced, the Queen's Speech, as finalised in cabinet, dealt less in policy initiatives than in what *Freeman's Journal* called 'vague and formal' expressions of pity for the hungry, for the dying, for the dead.[51]

'Gentlemen,' Victoria told the MPs and peers who gathered in the House of Lords to hear her, 'It is with the deepest concern that upon your assembling I have to call your attention to the dearth of provisions which prevails in Ireland and parts of Scotland.' Outside, as the queen went on to talk of 'disease' and 'mortality', the day had been made dreary by one of the smoke-thickened fogs so emblematic of winter in nineteenth-century London. The 'atmosphere', according to Victoria, 'was . . . cold, thick and yellow'; and so 'extreme' was the 'darkness occasioned by the fogginess and gloominess of the weather', the press reported, that, prior to 2 p.m., all parliament's numerous candles had to be called into service. 'In consequence of the place being lit up,' the *Times* commented, 'the ceremony was more brilliant even than usual.' The queen's dress 'blazed with diamonds', while 'the magnificent jewels' favoured by the Duchess of Sutherland, accompanying Victoria in her role as the royal court's Mistress of the Robes, 'also shone with conspicuous splendour.'[52]

There was scope for satire in that scene: in the queen being so expensively arrayed while talking, 'in [a] rather subdued tone', of her people's 'severe sufferings'; in the duchess, whose territorial designation derived from her husband's ownership of most of an extensive Highland county, choosing to put so much wealth on display at a point when many of her family's Scottish tenants were experiencing the hardest of hard times. In the event, however, those incongruities – the mid nineteenth century, like the early twenty-first, being inured to extreme inequality – occasioned little comment. Of more interest to politicians and to journalists, it seems, were the differing ways that people in Ireland on the one hand, and in the Highlands and Islands on the other, had responded to the disasters confronting them.[53]

While still at Windsor, the queen heard how Hebridean communities were 'bearing their terrible plight with exemplary patience'. Not so the Irish. In their often troubled country, the Queen's Speech asserted, there had been 'outrages . . . directed against property', while 'the transit of provisions [had] been rendered unsafe' as a result of attacks on, or thefts from, supply convoys. While *Freeman's Journal* 'acknowledge[d] this state of things with profound sorrow', the violence occurring in Ireland provoked more complex reactions in Scotland. What an Isle of Skye clergyman called 'the great forbearance and the submissive deportment of our Highlanders' should surely attract, the same minister argued, the 'favourable . . . attention' of the politicians to whom those same Highlanders were looking for help. But was this necessarily so? Hugh Miller, the Highlander in charge of the pro-Free-Church *Witness*, then one of Scotland's biggest circulation newspapers, worried that, with events in Ireland tending to monopolise parliamentary attention, the opposite might be the case. 'The peaceful and loyal demeanour of a humble population,' Miller declared in an editorial on what was happening in the Highlands and Islands, 'may have caused their afflictions to be overlooked and their calamities to be unknown'.[54]

In a private letter, Hugh Miller went further, responding to rumours of rebellion in Ireland by lamenting Highland and Hebridean quiescence: 'They [the Irish] are buying guns, and will be by-and-by shooting magistrates . . . by the score, and parliament will in consequence do a great deal for them. But the poor Highlanders will shoot no-one, not even . . . a brutal factor, and so they will be left to perish unregarded in their hovels . . . Government will yield nothing to justice, but a great deal to fear.'[55]

In thus writing off the possibility of insurgency in the Scottish north, however, Miller was premature. His point was certainly true of Barra. There the only demonstration mounted during the famine winter of 1846–47 took place on the day George Pole sailed for Oban – island families marking his departure by gathering on the shore to signal, as Pole put it, 'their gratitude for the temporary plenty' he had brought them. Elsewhere, however, the opening weeks of 1847 were to bring no end of dispute. Soon villages and towns across the eastern half of the mainland Highlands, among them Grantown-on-Spey, Inverness, Beauly, Avoch, Cromarty, Dingwall and Invergordon, would be convulsed by riot and disorder as, in blight's aftermath, food ran short and prices soared. Here and further east, in Moray, Banffshire and Aberdeenshire where similar protests were organised in places like Fraserburgh, Macduff, Portgordon, Burghead and Elgin, thousands of men, women and children mobilised with a single aim in view. What they wanted to bring about was the cessation of a trade identical to the one that had so offended Queen Victoria when she learned of its continuation in famine-stricken Ireland. This trade consisted of grain shipments destined for the Scottish Lowlands and for England.[56]

The scale of the efforts now made to stop these shipments is reflected in the alarmed nature of the national press's response to there being suddenly so much unrest in a part of the United Kingdom not usually associated with widespread turmoil. 'Food riots have been spreading in the north of Scotland to so great an extent,' reported the London-based *Spectator* at the start of February, 'that several parties of military have been despatched from Edinburgh. In some parts the country is described to be nearly in a state of insurrection.' Among the most turbulent localities were two closely linked communities in Caithness, mainland Scotland's most northerly county. Those communities, separated only by a river and the harbour at its mouth, were Wick and Pulteneytown.[57]

In 1847 no part of the substantial and fast-growing settlement of Pulteneytown was much more than 30 years old. The town, a place of numerous business premises and hundreds of stone-built homes, had been laid out to the west and south of the harbour that had given rise to it. From this harbour, there were various ways of getting to the bridge connecting Pulteneytown with the much longer-established burgh of Wick. Of these, one of the most direct consisted, as it still does, of Bank Row which, after a few hundred yards, becomes Union Street. Along Bank Row and into Union Street at about nine o'clock in the evening of Wednesday 24 February 1847, there marched some 30 men of the British army's 76th Regiment. For the previous three or four hours those men, together with 70 or so of their comrades, had battled at Pulteneytown's harbourside with 1,500 or more people intent on preventing what the army was there to facilitate: Caithness-produced grain being taken aboard a waiting cargo vessel.

While trying in vain to clear Pulteneytown of protesters, bayonet-wielding troops had drawn blood from at least 50 individuals. Increasingly enraged crowds, for their part, had begun by 'shouting, yelling [and] spitting' at the soldiers before going on to assault them with 'sticks', 'staves', 'stones and filth'. Understandably, then, the troops making their way into Union Street were not in the best of tempers. Their mission was to convey to jail in Wick two Pulteneytown men, John Shearer and James Nicolson, whom they had earlier helped arrest; and when, from doorways facing on to Bank Row, a handful of residents had tried to impede the soldiers' progress, those folk – men, women, youngsters – were instantly and roughly brushed aside.[58]

Bank Row was and is flanked on both sides by houses. But on reaching Union Street, the military found that, though still protected by homes and other buildings to their right, they were open to attack from the left. On that side, Union Street was bordered only by the steep embankment separating it from Sinclair Terrace, a parallel but higher roadway which, that Wednesday night, was occupied by hundreds of people – some from elsewhere in Pulteneytown, others from Wick – whose purpose was to inflict as much damage as possible on the troops below.

Today the slope between Sinclair Terrace and Union Street is fenced and wooded. In 1847, however, there were neither trees nor fences to obstruct the missiles that now descended on the soldiers of the 76th. On getting into Union Street, their commander reported, he and his men were at once exposed to 'tremendous volleys of large stones'. So heavy were some of those stones that one of them shattered the wooden stock of a soldier's musket; others, 'thrown with great violence' and curving down from high above, inflicted injury after injury on men whose progress was thus brought to a halt. 'I was struck with stones several times,' said Corporal Cormick Dowd who 'had his head cut through his cap'. 'My arm was black [from a] severe blow,' said Private John Carr. A stone 'knocked the firelock' from his grasp, said Private Richard Broome. 'The stones were rattling on our bayonets,' said Private Daniel Connery. 'I was hit between the shoulders with a large stone which knocked me flat to the ground . . . When I got the blow I said I would stand this no longer, and it was as good to kill another as for oneself to be killed.'[59]

Daniel Connery's wish to retaliate was doubtless shared by lots of men around him. But in circumstances such as those facing the 76th Regiment in Pulteneytown, the army was not empowered to do as Connery wanted. The military was in Pulteneytown 'to aid,' in the legal jargon of that time, 'the civil power'; and it was for a senior representative of this civil power, not Captain Charles Evans-Gordon, the officer heading the now stalled advance up Union Street, to decide on the best means of extricating Connery, Broome, Carr, Dowd and other soldiers from their hopelessly unprotected position.

How the chain of command operated in situations of this sort had been explained by a veteran soldier, Sergeant Thomas Morris, in a best-selling account of his time with one of the regiments the Duke of Wellington led to victory over Napoleon at Waterloo. When, a year or so after that war-winning battle, Morris's unit was sent to quell disorders in Birmingham – where workers had gathered to denounce wage cuts that followed the peace – the sergeant, whose sympathies were with the protesters, was much impressed by a local law officer who made it his business to countermand the orders of a military man hell-bent, Morris felt, on 'killing a few people'.[60]

'On some brickbats and stones being thrown at us,' Thomas Morris wrote, 'our brave captain gave orders [to us] to load [our muskets], and he then gave directions that we should fire among the mob.' At this point, however, a Birmingham magistrate standing beside the captain 'interposed', as Morris put it, and said 'there was no necessity for that': ' "Then," said our officer, "if I am not allowed to fire, I shall take my men back." "Sir," said [the magistrate], "you are called on to aid and assist the civil power, and if you fire on the people without my permission, and death ensues, you will be guilty of murder; and if you go away, without my leave, it will be at your peril." '[61]

That Birmingham exchange was not replicated in Pulteneytown's Union Street. There the impetus for drastic action on the military's part did not come from Captain Evans-Gordon of the 76th but from Robert Thomson, Sheriff of Caithness, a man whose conduct could scarcely have been more at odds with the pacifying role adopted by the Midlands magistrate Thomas Morris so admired. For this, in the days that followed, Thomson would be condemned widely.

Among the sheriff's numerous critics was the *Times*, which, in an excoriating analysis of what the paper's leader-writer called 'a most deplorable incident', found nothing to suggest that Thomson 'was justified in the course he adopted'. 'Military power should at all times be most sparingly used in dealing with an excited populace,' the *Times* contended. But in Pulteneytown Sheriff Thomson, instead of treating the army's guns as a resource to be deployed only in 'the very last extremity', had reached for this resource so speedily that he could not have given proper thought to what might follow.[62]

Thomson, who had earlier presided over a series of mostly unsuccessful attempts to clear streets and alleys in the lower part of Pulteneytown, had felt it his duty to ensure that his prisoners, Nicolson and Shearer, were got safely into jail. That was why the sheriff was accompanying Evans-Gordon and his men. Walking alongside Thomson, and acting as the sheriff's personal bodyguard, was Constable Donald Sinclair, the Wick area's single policeman. Sinclair was a big man and, on stones starting to fly 'like hail', he said, 'I told [the sheriff] to keep in my shelter as much as he could'. But those protective efforts notwithstanding, Thomson was soon hit by a stone that drew blood. 'The sheriff,' according to Sinclair, 'then called to Captain [Evans-Gordon] and said we cannot stand this longer, you must fire on them.'[63]

That, the *Times* reckoned, was the moment when Robert Thomson's emotions got the better of the considered judgement he should have exercised: 'Becoming alarmed apparently for his personal safety or irritated at the blow he had received, [the sheriff] immediately and, as we think, most hastily and improperly, ordered the soldiers to fire.'[64]

The inquiry the *Times* demanded into the circumstances surrounding this order was not conceded by Lord John Russell's Whig administration. Had it been and had it had access to Constable Donald Sinclair's sworn testimony as to the events of the night of 24 February, its verdict on Sheriff Thomson's conduct may not have been too far removed from that of the *Times* – all the more so in view of the fact that Charles Evans-Gordon, writing just a couple of hours after the Union Street debacle, was every bit as clear as Sinclair as to the origins of Thomson's instructions to him. 'The sheriff who was with me was struck in the head,' Evans-Gordon informed his superiors, 'and he then loudly gave [me] the command to fire.'[65]

It was not for Captain Evans-Gordon, whose military career would culminate in his reaching the rank of major-general, to dispute that command. But he appears to have done everything possible to minimise the risk of its giving rise to fatalities. 'I loudly shouted to the people above that I was about to fire,' Evans-Gordon said. This, the captain feared, would be treated as a bluff by folk unlikely to give up just when they were gaining the upper hand. By way of reinforcing his warning, therefore, Evans-Gordon next ensured that his men made as much noise as possible with the ramrods used to drive powder and ball down the barrels of the muzzle-loading muskets that were then British infantrymen's standard-issue firearms. The resulting clatter, the captain hoped, would make it clear to those with ears to hear that previously unloaded weapons were being loaded and that gunfire would shortly follow. 'The crowd must have heard him [shout] and [heard] the ramrods working,' he said. 'Some of them did go away.' Most, however, did not.[66]

'The night,' the captain said, 'was dark.' There was no moon and such illumination as was available from the gas-fuelled street lamps installed in Pulteneytown some years before was faint and fitful at best. Muskets were notoriously inaccurate even in optimum conditions. When fired uphill in next-to-zero visibility, they became all the more so. It may be, too, that soldiers like the vengeance-seeking Daniel Connery were in no mood to heed Evans-Gordon's directive to aim, not at the thickly occupied upper slopes of the embankment down which stones were still being heaved, but at its empty lower reaches. That is speculation. What is certain is that, despite

Evans-Gordon's best efforts, the smoke and crash of a military musket volley – a thing never before experienced in Caithness – proved a prelude to bloodshed.[67]

As always in calamity's aftermath, there were stories of narrow escapes. 'One man had the sole of his shoe torn off by a bullet,' Wick's weekly newspaper, the *John O'Groat Journal*, reported. 'Another had his boot split.' Deaths had somehow been avoided. However, 'a girl named MacGregor was wounded in the left arm, the ball passing through the fleshy part . . . The girl's wound is a large one.' Still more serious was the injury sustained by William Hogston, a foreman cooper with one of Pulteneytown's several manufacturers of barrels destined for the Caithness fish trade. 'A ball went through [Hogston's] right hand which was so shockingly mutilated that the fingers had to be cut off,' *Journal* readers were informed in the immediate aftermath of the Union Street shootings. Nor was this the end of Hogston's torments. Because amputation was then the standard medical response when wounded limbs began to become infected, William Hogston, days after the loss of his fingers, lost his hand in its entirety.[68]

Since a cooper with only one hand was unemployable, Hogston, his wife and five children were left destitute. Irrespective of what the now former tradesman had or had not been doing on the night of 24 February, his disability would have attracted sympathy. But there was a further reason for the near universal feeling in Pulteneytown and Wick that William Hogston and his family had suffered a huge injustice. Hogston, by his own account and the account of others, had taken no part in the events preceding the musket volley that left him both mutilated and jobless. 'It seems [Hogston] was climbing the brae for the very purpose of avoiding the mob and being safe from the military,' the *John O'Groat Journal* asserted. 'He was standing a minute before at the [Union Street] door of an acquaintance, and on being ordered off by one of the [soldiers] he went the way he was directed.' Because many of the complaints made about Sheriff Thomson were rooted in this conviction that David Hogston had been guiltless of any offence, the authorities were bound to have produced any contrary evidence available to them. That did not happen.[69]

Editorial staff at the *Times* were unsurprised by the apparent innocence of the man most affected by what had happened in Pulteneytown. When, in other places and at other times, the army had fired on rioters, uninvolved bystanders had frequently been killed, and only the merest chance, the paper's leader-writer felt, had prevented this new recourse to military firepower 'from resulting in a [similar and] most lamentable sacrifice of life'. Even so, the *Times* concluded, 'the too common consequence on these melancholy occasions ensued; for the individuals most severely wounded were a man who had taken no part whatever in the fray . . . and a girl who must have been one of the last persons to deserve the cruel fate she experienced.'[70]

That verdict chimed strongly with majority opinion in Caithness. But if, in Pulteneytown and Wick, Sheriff Thomson was seen as primarily responsible for what occurred on the night of 24 February, the 76th Regiment too attracted censure. That was maybe unavoidable. Troops who fire on civilians are never likely to be popular in the area where such firing takes place. But adding to the 76th Regiment's reputational difficulties was the fact that, elsewhere in the Scottish north, a number of its soldiers had themselves been charged with serious crimes. One of those crimes was committed in the West Highland town of Fort William.

2

'Disorderly, tumultuous and turbulent assemblages'

Fort William • Inverness • Wick • Pulteneytown

In 1846, as for many years previously, the second of Fort William's two annual fairs (the first was held in June) took place in mid November. A highlight in the life of this Lochaber town, the fair, which began on a Wednesday and went on over the next couple of days, attracted folk from every part of the surrounding countryside. And not just people were on the move. Because much of the business done that week turned on the selling and buying of cattle and horses from all over western Inverness-shire, Fort William's streets became thronged, for as long as the fair lasted, with often noisy livestock. Adding to the stir and bustle was the presence of merchants and tradespeople – some of them local, others from further afield – dealing in boots, shoes, clothes, pots, pans, candles, sweets and anything else that might find purchasers. Also in the habit of turning up on such occasions were itinerant musicians and entertainers, some of whom, it is reasonable to suppose, must have found their way to the dances or parties held in private homes on the Friday evening that brought the November 1846 fair to a conclusion.[1]

Among the guests at one such party was a young woman called Mary Cameron. What happened to Mary in the hour or two following this get-together would lead, the next morning, to her being examined by Charles Crichton, a Fort William surgeon. Crichton found Mary 'to be greatly agitated' and to be 'generally bruised and pained in various parts of her body'. This information he passed on to Andrew Fraser whose home was in Fort William and who, like Charles Shaw in the Long Island, was one of Inverness-shire's sheriff-substitutes. To Fraser there fell the task of establishing who should be held responsible for Mary's injuries.[2]

'I was at a dance last night in the house of John MacPhee, spirit dealer, Fort William,' runs the sworn statement taken by Andrew Fraser from Mary

Cameron. She had gone to the MacPhee home, Mary went on, 'with two of my sisters and other friends, having got permission [to be there] from my mistress, Mrs Cochrane, wife of Colonel Cochrane.'[3]

George Cochrane was in charge, as he had been for 25 years or more, of the military installation which had given its name to the town that had developed within half a mile of its walls. Cochrane, a veteran of Britain's wars with Napoleonic France, had grown up in Edinburgh. But his wife, Susan MacColl before her marriage, was a Highlander who came most probably from Duror, one of several small communities straddling the road between Fort William and Oban, some 45 miles to the south. Druimarbin, where Mary Cameron had been raised, was closer than Duror to Fort William. But it was the same sort of place – a small, Gaelic-speaking settlement where everyone was known to everybody else. There was a social gulf between Mrs Cochrane and her maid: the one a clergyman's daughter as well as a senior military man's wife; the other from a crofting family. But might their backgrounds have been sufficiently similar to make for at least some sense of solidarity between them? It is to be hoped this was the case; for Mary Cameron, in the closing weeks of 1846 and in the months that followed, is sure to have been greatly in need of her employer's help and understanding.[4]

The Cochrane family – the colonel, Susan and their seven or more children – lived with Mary and perhaps two other servants at the fort known locally as 'the barracks' or, in Gaelic, *an gearasdan*, the garrison. It was to the Cochrane home, then, that Mary headed on leaving the MacPhee household's still-continuing festivities. 'I remained till it was pretty late,' she told Sheriff Fraser, 'and I was accompanied to the barrack gates by an acquaintance of the name of John Lamont . . . We found the gates shut and could not obtain admittance. Lamont suggested that soldiers whom he had seen at the dance might perhaps get the gates opened for us, and [so] we returned to the [town].'[5]

The soldiers in question were James Miller and Dennis Driscoll. Both belonged to the 76th Regiment – the regiment that, three months later, would be deployed in Pulteneytown. A part of this regiment had been in the Highlands since the summer of 1846 when around 55 of its soldiers were stationed at Fort George. A far more formidable installation than the one George Cochrane was responsible for, Fort George is located on the Moray Firth coast some 12 miles east of Inverness. At Fort George in early November it had been decided to send Driscoll, Miller and a number of their comrades to Fort William. Why this was done is unclear – though it is by no means unlikely that the town's November fair was seen as the sort of occasion that might merit the presence of an army recruiting party. What is certain is that the arrival at Fort William of a 76th Regiment detachment had the effect of disrupting Colonel George Cochrane's arrangements.[6]

Cochrane's household, along with a few retired soldiers serving as care-takers and handymen, were usually the sole residents of garrison buildings dating from a time when faraway governments were struggling to impose their will on rebellious Highland clans. But now that the colonel and the rest of the fort's skeleton staff had been joined by serving troops, the casual way that things were normally done there was greatly tightened up. This explains why the heavy doors that Mary described as barrack gates were closed on the night of Friday 13 November – not to keep intruders out but to keep the newly arrived men of the 76th in their quarters.

Under cover of darkness, Driscoll and Miller got round that restriction by climbing over the fort's increasingly dilapidated ramparts. Had Mary Cameron's friend John Lamont known this, he might have hesitated before entrusting Mary's safekeeping to the two soldiers – both of whom were instantly agreeable to his request that they escort Mary home. But Lamont, seeing no reason to be anything other than welcoming of Miller and Driscoll's willingness to do as he asked, told Mary he 'thought it unnecessary' for him to accompany her any longer. That proved a serious misjudgement.[7]

Today's Fort William extends well beyond the site of the long-demol-ished fortifications that were Mary Cameron's destination. In 1846, however, those fortifications, accessed by way of what has since become Belford Road, were separated from the town by a wide expanse of mostly open ground. At night, this area was not a place where people were inclined to linger. But as she and her supposed protectors made their way across it, Mary told Andrew Fraser, 'one of the soldiers' walking alongside her 'desired me to sit down with him . . . I refused and, seizing me, he threw me on [to] the road and was above me. He attempted to lift up my clothes, but I resisted and I screamed.' A hand was pressed across her mouth to stifle her cries, Mary said. But despite this she managed somehow to yell 'Murder!' or '*Muirt!*', the English word's Gaelic equivalent. At this, Mary went on, the man attacking her, James Miller, was thrust aside by Dennis Driscoll who, Mary said, 'told me that if I would be quiet I would be allowed to get up'. Having little alternative, Mary complied. At this, Miller quit the scene while Driscoll, gripping Mary's arm, announced that he would see her safely back to town.[8]

This did not happen. Instead Mary was dragged off the road and on to a path skirting a church that, years before, had been put there to cater for English – and thus non-Presbyterian – troops attached to the Fort William garrison. Between the path and the church's grounds was a wall surmounted by iron railings to which Mary tried desperately to cling. 'He then proceeded to drag me [free of the railings],' she said of Driscoll. Pushed, kicked and again thrown down, Mary nevertheless went on trying to fight off her assailant who, as she put it in her account to Andrew Fraser, 'succeeded in lifting my clothes above my knees'.[9]

Although Driscoll's efforts to silence her would leave Mary's mouth and lips swollen and bleeding, her 'half-choking' shouts, as they described them, were heard at last by a group of homeward-bound local men who rushed to her aid. When Driscoll became aware of 'the sound of [those men's] footsteps,' Mary said, '[he] attempted to make his escape but I kept hold of him until they came.' One of her rescuers, John Cameron, a Fort William weaver, at once 'caught [Driscoll] in the middle,' he explained afterwards, 'and, in so doing, felt that his trousers were unbuttoned at the front. The girl's clothes,' John Cameron added, 'were raised up about her body . . . [She] was in a state of great agitation and gasping for breath'. As she was helped to her feet, Cameron added, the still sobbing Mary turned to one of his companions, a man she could scarcely see because it was so dark but whose voice she had immediately recognised. 'Donald,' she said in Gaelic to this man, 'it was the Lord that sent you here.'[10]

This and more third-party testimony to the same effect was what enabled Andrew Fraser to charge Dennis Driscoll with the crime of 'assault with intent to ravish' – in other words, attempted rape. Because nobody other than Mary Cameron could testify that James Miller had also attacked her, and because Miller, on being questioned by Fraser, insisted he 'did not behave with any rudeness to the girl', the sheriff's attempt to have him charged along with Driscoll had to be abandoned. This, Fraser commented regretfully, was because Mary's account of what Miller had done to her was unsubstantiated by independent 'corroboration' of the sort Scots law required.[11]

For Dennis Driscoll, however, there was no escape. Dragged back into town by John Cameron and others, he was arrested by Fort William's resident police inspector whom Driscoll's captors roused from his bed in what were now the early hours of the morning of 14 November. Interrogated later that day by Sheriff Fraser, Driscoll said that, while he had been 'the worse of drink' the night before, 'he did not strike or kick [Mary Cameron] in any way'. Nothing of this being thought credible, Private Dennis Driscoll was soon on his way to jail in Inverness – military records showing that, on 16 November, his pay was stopped as a result of his having that day been taken 'into custody of the civil power'.[12]

In Inverness prison, a set of cells in the then recently constructed and still prominent 'castle' that also served as the Highland capital's courthouse, Dennis Driscoll was joined by more of the 76th Regiment's soldiers. One, John Triston, would receive a six-month sentence for theft and forgery. Another, Private James Ball, was accused, like Driscoll, of attempted rape – his victim being a woman living not far from Fort George. Of the 55 men of the 76th shipped to Fort George at the end of June 1846, then, no fewer than three were to be incarcerated – two on extremely serious charges – within six months of their arrival in the Highlands. This could have done nothing for the regiment's standing. But even if Ball, Triston and Driscoll had not committed the crimes of which they were soon to be found guilty, the 76th is unlikely to have inspired much affection among the civilians with whom its soldiers came in contact. By the greater part of the British public of that time, Queen Victoria's army was seldom viewed with anything other than suspicion. This stemmed in large part from the nature of army recruitment.

In the later eighteenth century, and for some time after, communities across the northern half of Scotland had developed close ties with the military because of there having been, for much of that period, a close association between particular regiments and particular districts. When, for instance, the army's 93rd Regiment was raised in the late 1790s by the then Countess of Sutherland,* almost all the regiment's officers and men came either from the countess's estate or from nearby localities. In the decades following Waterloo, however, links of this sort were broken.† George Pole of the Commissariat, a man whose 19 years as an army officer were mostly spent with the 93rd,

---

* The countess afterwards became the first Duchess of Sutherland. She was the mother-in-law of the later duchess who, as noted in the preceding chapter, accompanied Victoria to Westminster on the occasion of the 1847 Queen's Speech.

† Partly with a view to strengthening bonds between the military and the society it existed to serve, strenuous efforts would subsequently be made to restore a degree of what the army called 'territoriality' to its formations. That was why regimental numbering eventually gave way to titles like Argyll and Sutherland Highlanders. In the 1840s, however, this process had not started.

appears to have had no family connection with the Scottish north. The same was true of lots of the soldiers serving with him – Pole's regiment, like every other such formation, enlisting men wherever they could be found.[13]

Making recruitment difficult was the fact that rank-and-file soldiering, even in peacetime, was a grimly unattractive occupation. Fort George, the principal military base in the north, might have looked impressive. But the extensive barracks complex inside its perimeter bastions offered little in the way of comfort. 'The sanitary condition of the fort is a disgrace,' commented an 1830s visitor. 'To the men it is little better than a prison.' At Fort George, as in every other garrison, discipline was harsh, floggings frequent, food poor, pay minimal. Dozens of single men were crammed into ill-lit and scarcely heated quarters where flimsy canvas screens provided such scanty privacy as was granted to the one-in-twelve soldiers permitted to have wives and children with them.[14]

While Daniel Defoe might have exaggerated when he remarked, more than a century earlier, that the only options available to the poorest of the poor were to 'starve, thieve or turn soldier', it was very much the case that the army of the 1840s drew many of its troops from groups that political theorists Karl Marx and Friedrich Engels were to label, in that same decade, the *lumpenproletariat*. By Marx and Engels this term was applied to the most precariously positioned social strata to be found in growing urban centres like Glasgow, Liverpool and Manchester – people to whom a soldier's two indifferent (but regular) meals a day might have seemed at least a little more appealing than wagelessness, vagrancy, beggary or worse. From the perspective of settled and more cohesive communities, it followed, there was little that was surprising in the 76th Regiment being found to contain criminals like Dennis Driscoll, James Ball and John Triston. Not every soldier was believed to be in that category of course. But the generality of troops were nevertheless so different in background and upbringing from most folk living in northern Scotland that they could easily be categorised, by those folk, as altogether alien.[15]

In the Scottish north as elsewhere, moreover, army units tended to put in an appearance (other than in barrack towns) only when called upon to crush the sort of disorder that, though thought threatening by the authorities, might have a great deal of popular backing. This was an unavoidable consequence of police forces being non-existent or (in places where they were developing) having so little manpower that they could not possibly engage in crowd-control. The 76th Regiment, as it happened, was well used to having a front-line role in such situations. Three years prior to some of its soldiers being stationed at Fort George, those same soldiers or their immediate predecessors had been commended officially for the 'zeal and alacrity' they showed when putting down widespread disturbances in Wales. That commendation is unlikely to have been endorsed by more than a small minority of Welsh people. Nor was there any greater enthusiasm in Caithness when, around midday on Tuesday 23 February 1847, it became known that a steamship carrying just over 100 men of the 76th was approaching Pulteneytown.[16]

This ship, the *Pharos*, belonged to the organisation responsible for the care and maintenance of lighthouses. It was commandeered by Lord John Russell's government when ministers found that the Royal Navy, because of its having only a small presence in Scottish waters, could not get soldiers to the many places in northern Scotland where, it had become apparent, military intervention was urgently required. Though skilfully skippered and totally seaworthy, the *Pharos* lacked cabins capable of accommodating anything like the number of troops who boarded the vessel at Fort George on the evening prior to its being sighted off Caithness.* This meant that most of those troops were forced to spend a night and morning on the *Pharos's* open deck. That was no way to make a winter crossing of the Moray Firth, which separates Caithness, Sutherland and Easter Ross on its northern shore from the 100-mile length of eastward-tending coastline between Inverness and Fraserburgh. Making conditions all the more unpleasant was a rising wind out of the southeast. As well as kicking up a swell that left a lot of soldiers seasick, this made it impossible for the *Pharos* to land anyone in Pulteneytown – a place badly exposed to south-easterlies – without the assistance of a locally based pilot. No such pilot, according to Sheriff Robert Thomson, could be got. People in Pulteneytown and Wick, Thomson commented, were almost unanimously committed to stopping outgoing grain shipments of the sort the 76th had been sent to expedite. Such was 'the force of the [resulting] combination', the sheriff added, that Pulteneytown's pilots 'refused to assist in landing the troops'. The *Pharos*, in consequence, steamed on north, entered Sinclair Bay – sheltered from the south-east by the cliffs of Noss Head – and anchored off Ackergill where, it was hoped, the military could at last be ferried ashore.[17]

Again there were problems. Fishermen living around Ackergill, about 3 miles overland from Wick, turned out to be of the same mind as Pulteneytown

---

* The 76th Regiment's presence at Fort George had been greatly expanded by this point. How and why that happened is explored in Chapter 5.

pilots – with the result that the army, as the *John O'Groat Journal* reported, was 'sternly refused . . . the use of their boats'. Eventually, however, 'one or two' craft were 'procured' and local coastguard staff drafted in to man them. Equally helpful from Robert Thomson's standpoint was the fact that a Pulteneytown pilot called William Williamson (a man the sheriff felt should be rewarded for his having broken ranks with colleagues) now volunteered his services. With Williamson's aid, all the troops from the *Pharos* were soon 'ranged in military order on Ackergill beach' preparatory to setting off along the road to Wick. 'About four o'clock,' the *John O'Groat Journal* commented, 'the [whole] party . . . under the command of Captain [Charles] Evans-Gordon . . . entered the town with fixed bayonets.' 'The soldiers, being newly off the sea, had a worn-out and jaded appearance,' the paper noted. But if their evident exhaustion resulted in Evans-Gordon and his men looking less well turned-out than they might have done, the sight of so many bayonets – all gleaming and readied for use – clearly had, as intended, an intimidatory effect on the 'anxious spectators' filling Wick's streets and staring from 'every window'. That evening, by which point Evans-Gordon and his men had withdrawn to requisitioned quarters, 'all was quiet'.[18]

Today's Wick, which includes the once distinct community of Pulteneytown, is not as it was at the start of Queen Victoria's reign. Much that is now 200 years old was then new. That was true of Pulteneytown in its entirety. It was true of a great deal of Wick as well. In Bridge Street, the older town's civic and commercial heart, building after building had gone up. Shops, banks, an imposing town hall, an equally imposing courthouse: all those took shape in the 1820s and 1830s; together they showed, as did the many deals done behind Bridge Street's then unweathered frontages, that this corner of Caithness had begun to do well financially.

The source of Wick's prosperity, and the reason for Pulteneytown's existence, was the harbour created, during the nineteenth century's first 20 years, at the spot where the Wick River enters the sea. This harbour belonged to the British Fisheries Society. Formed in 1786, the society was an early public–private partnership. Its geographical focus, despite the wider remit suggested by its name, was the Highlands and Islands; its objective was to get government to work with north of Scotland interests in ways that would aid commercial exploitation of the region's potentially enormous fisheries resource.[19]

To begin with, the British Fisheries Society concentrated on Atlantic waters. Hence its construction of harbours and associated villages at

Tobermory on the Isle of Mull and at Ullapool in Wester Ross. Pulteneytown, named for one of the society's directors, Sir William Pulteney, was a slightly later undertaking. It was also the only British Fisheries Society venture on Scotland's east coast where, society bosses felt, there would be money to be made from boosting catching efforts in the Moray Firth and, beyond the firth, in the North Sea.

This proved correct. From the first, Pulteneytown grew far more rapidly than either Ullapool or Tobermory. That was due largely to the immense quantities of herring brought ashore here each summer. Starting in July and going on into September, those landings were the work of a huge fleet. Much of this fleet was manned by Caithness crews. The rest consisted of boats from elsewhere: from the West Highlands; from ports on the Moray Firth's southern coast; from still more distant fishing communities in Fife and Berwickshire. 'This is truly a wonderful place,' wrote one 1840s visitor to what had become much the biggest population centre in Scotland's far north. 'What . . . Manchester is in cotton manufacture, what Sheffield is in steel, what Birmingham is in iron goods . . . so is Wick the emporium of the Scottish herring fishery.' By Wick, that visitor meant both the original burgh and the more recent settlement on its doorstep. 'Here . . . on a fine summer's evening,' he commented of Pulteneytown, 'the eye might be regaled with as lovely a sea-view as any in [Britain]. The signs of fishing life commence usually towards four or five o'clock in the afternoon. About this time may be seen hundreds of stalwart fishermen clad characteristically in . . . fear-nothing jackets* and high fishing boots . . . and with [a knapsack] across the back containing refreshment for the night. In an hour or two, the . . . ocean is studded with a thousand tiny barques, each under canvas . . . [and each] bounding along in the direction of the fishing ground . . . A more interesting sight cannot be imagined.'[20]

Today it may seem improbable that there were ever as many as 1,000 fishing boats operating out of Pulteneytown. But this, by the 1840s, was definitely the case. By modern standards, admittedly, those boats were as small as they were frail. Undecked and powered by oars as well as sail, the typical boat was wooden-hulled, clinker-built and around 30 feet long. All such craft were crewed by five or six men whose job it was to set and then haul in the drift nets that were the herring industry's key pieces of equipment. Woven by hand

---

* In that pre-oilskin era, a fear-nothing jacket – a bulky and hooded garment – gave such protection as there was to be got from rain and spray.

from cotton by fishermen's wives and daughters, for whom this was a routine occupation in winter, those nets – each of their meshes measuring, as the law demanded, at least one inch from knot to knot* – hung curtain-like in the sea. Below, they were weighted with lead. Above, they were suspended from inflatable buoys or floats made, at a time when synthetic materials remained far in the future, from cattle bladders or from sewn-up and waterproofed dogskins.

Herring spend daylight hours at depths. At night, they rise towards the surface with the plankton they feed on. That is why Pulteneytown's herring fleet left harbour when it did, why it returned not long after dawn, and why open-boat herring fishing was often described, though mostly by land-based observers, in language that made it seem unfailingly romantic. 'There is something very pleasing and exciting [about fishing for herring],' runs one such account, 'when the night is very dark and the moon . . . not shining. The water sends phosphorescent particles† round the boat at every stroke of the oar . . . At the bows are piled the nets ready for casting into the sea. Now and then we come near the herrings which . . . quickly dart off . . . leaving a line of fiery light.'[21]

A more hard-headed portrayal of the herring-catching business was provided by a man met with in the preceding chapter – a man raised in the port town of Cromarty. 'The profession of the herring fisherman,' Hugh Miller commented at the start of a writing career that would take him to a newspaper editor's chair, 'is one of the most laborious and most exposed both to hardship and danger. From the commencement to the close of the fishing, the men who prosecute it only pass two nights of each week in bed.‡ In all the others they sleep in open boats with no other covering than the sail . . . The watchfulness necessary in these circumstances becomes so habitual that, during the fishing, their slumbers rather resemble those of watchdogs than of men. They start up at the slightest motion or noise, cast a hurried glance over

---

* This was an early stock conservation measure. It ensured that immature fish could pass through a net.

† The author, when a boy, often went with his father to net sea trout and salmon at night in the tidal waters of Loch Linnhe. Phosphorescence (caused by plankton and other organisms emitting flashes of light when seawater is disturbed) was an endless source of fascination. Fish did indeed leave flame-like trails and our net, when being lifted, often looked to be on fire.

‡ Because Sunday was then a day of rest in Scotland, no boat could sail from port on a Saturday or Sunday night.

the buoys of their drift, ascertain their position with regard to . . . the other boats around, and then fling themselves down again.'[22]

Discomfort could be endured. The death of friends, relatives and colleagues was less easy to bear. As Hugh Miller indicated, however, the pursuit of the fish that fishermen called 'silver darlings' was never without risk. In August 1848 in just one morning – a morning when an especially ferocious south-easterly gale rose with next to no warning – boat after boat was sunk and almost 40 men lost within sight of families gathered on Pulteneytown's quays. That was a worse than usual tragedy. But sinkings and drownings, even if not often on that scale, took place, year in year out, all through the nineteenth century.

Women worried about what could happen to fathers, husbands, sons. They were also every bit as hard-worked as their men. But for women's input, in fact, there would have been no herring industry. This was at once apparent to Robert Wilson, a naturalist who, when voyaging around Britain, put into Pulteneytown one summer morning in the early 1840s. 'After breakfast we went ashore,' Wilson reported, 'and there witnessed one of the most extraordinary sights . . . All along the inner harbour, and in every street and quay, as well as within many large enclosed yards and covered buildings, there are numerous square wooden boxes as big as ordinary-sized rooms, [their] . . . sides, however, being only two or three feet high. Into these huge troughs the herring are carried in panniers from the boats the instant they arrive. There [the catch is] . . . all tumbled in helter-skelter, pannier after pannier, in a long-continued stream of fish, until the boats are emptied and the troughs are filled. Then come troops of sturdy females, each armed with knife in hand, [who] range themselves round the trough. The process of gutting [next] commences and is carried on with such ceaseless and untiring rapidity that, unless we had . . . request[ed] one of the . . . prettiest of these eviscatrixes so to moderate the rancour of her knife as to let us see what she was doing, we could scarcely have followed her manipulations with the naked eye.'[23]

When left to work at speed, Robert Wilson noted, that same woman gutted 24 herrings a minute – or one every two and a half seconds. Others of her three-person team were meanwhile placing layer after layer of newly cleaned fish, together with layer after layer of salt, into new-made barrels – 'thousands and tens of thousands' of which stood everywhere along the harbourside. And so it went; hour by hour, day by day, week by week, as herring by the million were unloaded, gutted, packed, inspected and otherwise made ready for the cargo ships that carried them to distant markets.[24]

★　　★　　★

When, in 1803, the British Fisheries Society acquired the 400 or so acres on which Pulteneytown was built, those acres contained no more than half-a-dozen cottages. Forty years later, the same area was home to scores of commercial concerns. Alongside the curing sheds described by Robert Wilson were at least a dozen cooperages, just as many boatyards, a shipyard, chandleries, four ropeworks, foundries, sawmills, grain mills, a distillery, a brewery and all sorts of warehousing facilities. Most of those businesses were located beside, or close to, the harbour, which had itself required extension within 20 years of its original completion. Nor, in marked contrast to the way urban development was then occurring in most other parts of the UK, was any of this at all haphazard. From the start, Pulteneytown's expansion, though breakneck, took place in accordance with plans commissioned by the Fisheries Society from one of early nineteenth-century Britain's leading civil engineers, Thomas Telford, whose other north of Scotland projects would include roads, bridges and the Caledonian Canal.[25]

Telford gave as much thought to housing the Pulteneytown workforce as he did to providing space for industry. This meant that Pulteneytown – 'a gently astonishing place', a Telford biographer calls it – did better by its residents than southern cities such as Manchester where, in the 1840s, Friedrich Engels was working on his investigatory classic, *The Condition of the Working Class in England*. In 'Manchester and its environs', Engels reported, working people lived, 'almost all of them', in 'damp, filthy cottages' surrounded by equally dirty streets. 'In a word,' he went on, 'we must confess that in the working-men's dwellings of Manchester, no cleanliness, no convenience and consequently no comfortable family life is possible . . . All alike are degraded by want, apathy and wretchedness.' In comparison with Manchester or, for that matter, many parts of Glasgow and Edinburgh, where (as Engels acknowledged) thousands lived in housing even worse than Manchester's, Pulteneytown was positively futuristic. Behind the harbour and its adjacent industrial district, in what was known as Lower Pulteneytown, were street after street of solidly built homes. Further inland and on higher ground was Upper Pulteneytown, its grid of wider roadways centring on the open spaces of Argyle Square. The cumulative effect owed a good deal to the layout adopted earlier in Bath, a city that Telford knew well. And though Caithness weather ensures that Telford failed in his 'great objective' of 'exclud[ing] the north wind' from streets that mostly have (for this reason) an east–west alignment, to visit Pulteneytown is at once to get a sense of the care that went into its design.[26]

Pulteneytown, for all that, was no earthly paradise. During the herring season, when its permanent population was trebled by the arrival of as many as 10,000 fishermen, gutters and others from the rest of Scotland, overcrowding – 'sometimes to the number of ten or twelve in one small room' – was every bit as rife as in Engels's Manchester. In these circumstances, a Wick clergyman complained, 'unchastity, both in man and woman, is lamentably frequent'. Almost equally prevalent, the same minister noted, was infectious disease. Twice in the 1830s Pulteneytown was ravaged by cholera; and in summer, when the harbourside and adjacent streets were 'everywhere' awash with 'fish offals', the general lack of cleanliness in a place with little in the way of piped water could readily result in outbreaks of 'fever of a typhoid type'.[27]

The summer of 1846, as it happened, brought little in the way of illness. Nor, on the face of things, were there other causes for concern. '[From] the middle of July,' the *John O'Groat Journal* observed at the herring season's close, 'our population was augmented by not a few thousands and . . . our bay was crowded with boats . . . all eagerly proceeding to the fishing grounds. On Saturday evenings our streets were impassable, being thronged with multitudes of nearly all descriptions of the human species.' Everywhere in Pulteneytown and across the river in Wick there was 'the hum of strange voices', but, despite the availability of endless pubs and drinking places, visitors and locals alike, the *Journal* reported, were well behaved. 'Scarcely a drunken man was to be seen on the streets and, with one or two exceptions, not a single "row" was observed.' This absence of ill-temper stemmed, perhaps, from what had proved a most successful fishery. 'The season has been one of unbroken and uninterrupted good weather.' Landings, in consequence, were heavy.[28]

Difficulties loomed, however. Pulteneytown curers, the businessmen who bought the herring catch and organised its processing, might have had more than 110,000 barrels* of cured herring on hand by the season's end. What they lacked was demand for their product. This was not an entirely new problem. One formerly important market, the West Indies, had been lost in the 1830s when slavery was abolished throughout the British Empire – freed slaves having no interest in purchasing the salt herring on which their former owners had often fed them.† Now Ireland, an even more vital market, had

---

* Those barrels would have altogether contained something like 125 million herrings.
† Cured herring were a cheap source of nutrition. It was also believed that a diet rich in cured herring helped replenish the salt lost by slaves as they sweated in plantation cane-fields.

become equally problematic. Partly this was because the impoverishing effects of Ireland's famine meant that fewer and fewer Irish people could afford to buy herring. So soaked in brine were cured herring, moreover, that – in the absence of the boiled potatoes used to mask their ferociously salty taste – they were thought inedible. 'The fatal potato disease which deprived the . . . Irish of that root which long habit had made so essential an accompaniment to the consumption of herrings,' explained the fishing industry's government-appointed monitors, 'produced . . . a great stoppage in the sale of the fish, and the price continued so very low . . . that the curers were by no means remunerated.'[29]

Curers feared ruin. Fisherfolk and others, on it becoming clear that the 1846 potato crop had failed every bit as comprehensively in the Scottish north as it had done in Ireland, began to worry that they might run out of food. An early indicator of those anxieties was a marked shift in the spending patterns of West Highland fishermen who had spent the summer fishing out of Pulteneytown. Because curers had bought catches at prices agreed before the autumn and winter collapse of the cured herring market, those fishermen had cash in their pockets. In previous Septembers, the *John O'Groat Journal* commented, this cash would have found its way to 'clothiers and hardware merchants' where it would have been exchanged for goods of a sort that were hard to come by in west coast communities. Instead it had been 'expended on the purchase of [oat]meal'. 'Every boat that left for the [West] Highlands,' the paper continued, 'had as much as . . . 10 to 20 bolls* of meal on board . . . In former years the vast majority had not as much as an ounce.'[30]

The purchasers of those supplies belonged mostly to crofting localities like Wester Ross. They may have been urged in letters from home to bring back from Pulteneytown as much oatmeal as their boats could carry; or they may simply have reckoned that their own districts were unlikely to have escaped devastation of the sort that, as summer turned into autumn, was causing alarm in Caithness. At least four-fifths of the county's potato crop had been destroyed by blight, Wick Town Council calculated. This loss, the council stated, would have the most serious consequences. 'During ten months of the year the labouring classes, cottagers and mechanics [or tradesmen] with their families, depend for two-thirds of their subsistence on potatoes.' What, the council queried, was to take potatoes' place?[31]

---

* A boll, long a standard Scottish measure, was equivalent to 140 pounds (63.5 kilos) – as compared to an English hundredweight of 112 pounds.

An ostensibly reassuring answer to that question was supplied by Caithness's Commissioners of Supply. Bodies of this type then ran all of Scotland's counties and would do so until superseded in 1890 by elected councils.* As laid down in legislation dating from the seventeenth century, each county's commissioners of supply consisted of its principal landowners. The Caithness commissioners, it followed, had first-hand knowledge of the state of the area's crops. Potatoes, they acknowledged, had been lost 'to an extent to be deplored'. But theirs, the commissioners of supply stressed, was a 'corn-growing county' and the 1846 cereal harvest, they pointed out, 'amount[ed] to more than an average'. That was why the commissioners felt able to express, at a September meeting, 'the most confident hope that the distress which threatens certain other districts in so aggravated a form may be comparatively unfelt in Caithness'.[32]

The *John O'Groat Journal* was sceptical. Founded in 1836 by Peter Reid, son of a Pulteneytown fish-curer, the *Groat*, as Reid's paper came to be known, had no very high opinion of what it called 'our country gentlemen'. The *Groat*'s politics were self-consciously progressive. It very much favoured, for example, Corn Law repeal – which most 'country gentlemen' in Caithness, as elsewhere, opposed vociferously. On this and other matters, the *Groat*, if only for the reason that to have done otherwise would have made no commercial sense, was doing no more than aligning itself with prevailing opinion among the Wick and Pulteneytown business community which provided the paper with most of its readers and advertisers. The leading men of this community – fish-curers, boat-builders, cooperage owners and the like – were no revolutionaries. But on a whole variety of issues, local as well as national, they tended to take up stances that put them at odds with landed proprietors of the sort serving as the county's commissioners of supply.[33]

A typical such issue loomed large throughout the summer and autumn of 1846 at meetings of the Wick Parochial Board whose members took their duties a lot more seriously than did their counterparts in Barra. At stake was a suggestion that, as well as distributing cash allowances to 'pauper families', the board might meet the cost of providing the children of such families with some 'elementary' schooling. On the grounds that 'few things tend more to repress the growth of pauperism than education', this proposal, pushed strongly by Pulteneytown and Wick property owners, was carried narrowly

---

* Burghs like Wick already possessed elected councils – though the right to vote in burgh elections was restricted.

at one meeting only to be overturned at the next – when the Wick and Pulteneytown faction was outvoted by previously missing representatives of the rural part of Wick parish. There was no way, it was made clear by Sir George Dunbar of Ackergill, then spending heavily on his fine home, that he was prepared to contribute even the tiniest share of the £60 a year the parochial board reckoned it would cost to teach the children of the local poor to read and write. Clashes of this sort – Pulteneytown and Wick business people on one side, Caithness lairds and their more substantial farming tenants on the other – were to be a constant feature of the crisis arising from what the *John O'Groat Journal* called 'the entire destruction' of a key component of 'the people's food'.[34]

That there would be such a crisis the paper was sure by late summer. 'In the neighbourhood of Wick,' it reported at the end of August, 'the [potato] disease has been making fearful ravages, and whole fields of withered stems, emitting an odd, musty effluvium, are to be seen.' 'Under such circumstances,' the *Groat* went on, 'we cannot but look forward with fear and trembling to the coming winter . . . Pity the poor!'[35]

In places like Wick and Pulteneytown, most working families grew their own potatoes in garden-like plots they rented from farmers. With this source of cheaply produced nutrition gone, they were forced to turn to more expensive cereal substitutes, primarily oatmeal, the price of which went up further as demand for it increased. Household budgets, in consequence, were soon under strain. This would have made for testing times in any event. But making matters worse – far worse – was the way in which the herring slump quickly pushed the wider Pulteneytown and Wick economy into deep recession.

Fishermen had long depended in winter on upfront payments made by curers who, in order to bind particular crews to them, were prepared to advance a proportion of the cash those crews were expected to earn the following summer. So uncertain were curing trade prospects by the end of 1846, however, that all such advances were suspended. Nor, for the same reason, was anyone willing to make investments of the sort that usually kept a whole range of fishery-related businesses afloat. Cooperages, it followed, were obliged to lay off coopers. Other sectors, most notably boatbuilding, were still more severely affected. Something like 100 fishing boats had been built and launched in Pulteneytown during the later months of 1845 and the early months of 1846. The figure for the corresponding period in 1846 and 1847 was virtually zero.[36]

With incomes shrinking or disappearing on all sides, and with food becoming dearer by the week, there inevitably began to be what the Wick and Pulteneytown Chamber of Commerce called 'a great amount of destitution'. 'The state of the labouring population,' chamber members felt, 'was lamentable'. Government fishery officers agreed. 'I am sorry to report,' one Caithness-based officer wrote at the start of January, 'that . . . there is considerable suffering in [this] district. Some families are already subsisting, in a great degree, on turnips and cabbage.'[37]

At the September 1846 meeting of the Caithness Commissioners of Supply there had been well-publicised statements to the effect that winter work would be provided on local estates. These were not empty promises. By the year's end, extensive land improvement projects were underway on a number of properties as the county's lairds took advantage of cheap government loans made available under the terms of a recently passed Drainage Act – a measure which enabled UK landowners, many of them still grumbling about Corn Law repeal, to draw down a grand total of £3 million from the Exchequer. So depressed was the Caithness labour market, however, that the county's landlords, despite the public funding at their disposal, were able to get away with offering minimal wages.

One Caithness worker channelled resulting discontents into verses he and his comrades sang (at some risk of instant dismissal) to the tune of a then popular song:

> With body weary and worn,
> With visage seedy and sad,
> A ditcher wrought from early morn,
> With shovel and pick and spade –
> And still as he delved among water and clay,
> He sang to himself from day to day,
> The sorrowful Song of the Drain.
> Ditch! Ditch! Ditch!
> For twopence an hour I'm here.
> Ditch! Ditch! Ditch!
> For twopence an hour this year.
> I'm doomed to toil midst frost and snow,
> When the torrents fall, and the breezes blow,
> I delve and ditch, and lay down the drains,
> And I'm paid with twopence an hour for my pains.[38]

To obtain that twopence an hour, a man might have to set off in the deep dark of a January morning to get to his place of work by dawn. There, during the eight hours (at most) of daylight to be had in Caithness at that time of year, he would earn (as long as one of the 1846–47 winter's frequent snowstorms did not bring operations to a halt) 16 pence or 1s 4d. If such a man had a wife and three children to support, Wick and Pulteneytown Chamber of Commerce pointed out, his family's daily expenditure on oatmeal 'almost swallowed up the whole [of his wages] . . . and left nothing for fire, milk and other necessaries'. Little wonder, then, that a January meeting of Wick Town Council heard 'strong opinions' about the 'utter insufficiency' of the earnings to be got from Caithness landowners – some of whom, the council was informed, were making strenuous efforts to reduce the twopence-an-hour rate by a further farthing.* Such meagre earnings as could be got, then, were in decline at a point when, the council noted, already high food prices were again spiralling upwards.[39]

Caithness's Commissioners of Supply did nothing to ease Wick Town Council's anxieties. Although once more stressing that 'the [cereal] crop of 1846 in the county' had been 'amply sufficient' to meet local needs, the commissioners made clear their determination, as representatives of landowning and farming interests, to obtain the highest possible prices for grain still in storage. This could most effectively be accomplished, the commissioners of supply stated, by selling Caithness grain into the wider British market where, by the start of 1847, prices were well ahead of those that Caithness merchants (most of whom traded only in their own localities) were prepared to pay. 'Owing to the comparatively low prices . . . given by dealers in this county,' the commissioners of supply stated bluntly on 11 January, 'a considerable quantity of [Caithness] grain will probably be exported.'[40]

Outward shipments, in fact, had already begun. It was for this reason that Josiah Rhind, the Wick banker who was Wick and Pulteneytown Chamber of Commerce's chairman, was instructed by chamber members on 16 January to write on their behalf to 33 of Caithness's 'landed proprietors' and 'principal farmers'. The Pulteneytown and Wick 'public mind', Rhind informed his letter's recipients, had 'been rendered somewhat uneasy by . . . sales of grain for shipment' at a point when it was 'obvious that the consumption of the county will be very much larger than usual'. Hence the Chamber of Commerce's decision 'respectfully to express a hope' that landowners and farmers would 'not hurriedly dispose' of further grain in this way.[41]

---

* A farthing was a quarter of a penny.

This appeal elicited just three replies. Two, from farmers, were supportive of the chamber's initiative. The third, from an estate owner, expressed outrage that anyone should try to stop agriculturalists 'selling in the dearest, and buying in the cheapest, market'. It seemed, one Caithness clergyman responded wryly, that men who had previously been staunch advocates of protectionism in the shape of the Corn Law were now equally staunch in defence of free trade: 'Nothing is so blinding as selfishness; and I presume it arises from the lairdocracy being too deeply imbued with this principle, that, while hitherto they have sternly prohibited corn from coming into the country when it was cheap, they now feel indignant that the poor should demur upon seeing it shipped off beyond their reach.'[42]

On Friday 5 February 1847, an Orkney-registered cargo ship, the *William Bowers*, sailed into Pulteneytown and moored at the harbour's north quay. His ship was there, said *William Bowers*'s skipper James Robertson, to load grain for Leith. But this, Robertson soon discovered, was to be no easy task. On the morning following his arrival, the skipper said, 'a good many people of the town came about my vessel and told me that I would not be allowed to ship any grain'. At that point, Robertson went on, he had not 'put out any of [the] ballast' that would have to be unshipped from the *William Bowers*'s holds prior to a cargo taking its place. He could thus have left Pulteneytown that same Saturday, the skipper said, and – foreseeing trouble – would gladly have done so but for the fact that, by so doing, he would have incurred heavy financial penalties for breaking his agreement with men set on getting Caithness grain to south of Scotland markets.[43]

Among those men was William Davidson who farmed on a substantial scale at Oldhall, about 10 miles west of Wick. Oldhall grain destined for Leith was known to be already stored in a Wick warehouse where, it became apparent on the evening of Monday 8 February, a lot of people thought it should stay. 'That night,' the *John O'Groat Journal* reported, 'a large crowd assembled in Wick and, accompanied by a piper, marched . . . to the north quay of Pulteneytown harbour.' This crowd, from Skipper James Robertson's perspective, was more in the nature of 'a mob' whose members, Robertson said, 'came down to my vessel and . . . wished me to promise that I would not take any grain on board'. The terms of his 'charter' or contract, Robertson again explained, meant that he could make no such promise. This, the *William Bowers*'s skipper went on, was not well received. 'I am alarmed for the safety of my vessel and myself,' he said. His crew, he added, had been so panicked by what they had seen and heard that they were 'threatening to leave me if grain is taken in'.[44]

Also on Monday night, said Peter Taylor, harbour-master at Pulteneytown, 'the roadway to the north quay' had been 'obstructed by boats pulled across it'. 'There are two fishing boats of the largest size, and a broken one, placed there,' Taylor continued. 'It would require 30 men . . . to remove these boats,' the harbour-master reckoned, 'they are so heavy . . . On Tuesday morning I tried to get assistance to remove [them] but nobody would help me.' When it had been put to the harbour workforce that they should clear the roadway, Taylor said, the suggestion had been 'met . . . with shouts of derision'. This did not bode well for the carters employed by William Davidson who, this same Tuesday morning, gave orders that, roadblock or no roadblock, a part of his Leith-bound grain consignment should be taken out of storage in Wick and moved to Pulteneytown.[45]

Just before midday, in accordance with the Oldhall farmer's instructions, several sackfuls of grain were carried from a warehouse on Wick's outskirts and loaded on to a horse-drawn cart, which was then driven through the burgh into Bridge Street and onto the Wick River crossing from which the street got its name. The day, as it happened, was one of heavy snow. This both slowed the grain cart's progress and ensured – because all outdoor work had been suspended – that there were more people around than might otherwise have been the case. To 'loud and long [if somewhat derisive] cheers', William Davidson's carters were permitted to cross into Pulteneytown. At 'the south end' of the Wick River bridge, however, there was 'such a complete block-ade,' as the *Groat* put it, 'that the parties in charge of the cart had to turn [their] horse's head and retrace their steps amid the most deafening chorus.'[46]

An angry William Davidson now turned for aid to James Gregg, Wick's resident sheriff-substitute who, Davidson insisted, should at once restore order. This Gregg was willing to do. What he lacked, 1840s Caithness having vanishingly few uniformed policemen, was the necessary manpower. Hence his decision to mobilise a force of special constables drawn from what was considered to be the 'respectable' end of the local social spectrum. More than 100 tradesmen, shopkeepers, businessmen, solicitors and others were accord-ingly instructed to make their way to Gregg's Bridge Street courthouse where, they were told, the sheriff would swear them in and get them ready for imme-diate deployment.[47]

What happened next is suggestive of even 'respectable' opinion in Pulteneytown and Wick having been more supportive of attempts to prevent grain shipments than it was of efforts to speed such shipments on their way. No less than two-thirds of the men summoned formally by Gregg refused to put in an appearance – opting instead to run the risk of heavy fines for non-compliance. Nor were the 36 who turned up and who swore to do the sheriff's bidding at all keen to help Gregg clear Wick's roadways. When, some three hours after William Davidson's initial failure to get his cartload of grain into Pulteneytown, the farmer resolved to try again, Sheriff Gregg thought it his duty to confront, and speak with, the hundreds of people who had assembled by this point in Bridge Street. Those people, it seems likely, wished Gregg no great harm. But the circumstances, for all that, were nervy, tense, potentially hazardous. That may be why all but two of the sheriff's newly recruited constables declined to follow him down the courthouse steps.[48]

Alongside Gregg was Caithness's procurator fiscal, John Henderson, and one of the county's Justices of the Peace, James MacKenzie, a Wick lawyer. 'The sheriff,' MacKenzie said in the course of a statement taken down next day, 'addressed the people and enquired into the cause of their assembling . . . The substance of their answer was that they were there to prevent the shipment of grain.' On Gregg then 'remonstrating with the crowd and saying that they must allow the grain to be shipped', remarked another observer of the afternoon's events, 'the people would not hear the sheriff' whose words were drowned in a welter of 'hooting and hissing'. At this, said James MacKenzie, 'Gregg stated that . . . as the law must be enforced . . . he would proceed to read the Riot Act commanding [the crowd] to disperse, and this was accordingly done.'[49]

Because the Riot Act, in force since 1714, required that any sheriff, Justice of the Peace or other magistrate invoking it should do so 'with a loud voice', and because James MacKenzie's voice was judged louder than Gregg's, MacKenzie, at the sheriff's request, made the formal proclamation the Act insisted on: 'Our sovereign Lady the Queen chargeth and commandeth all persons, being assembled, immediately to disperse themselves, and peaceably to depart to their habitations, or to their lawful business, upon the pains contained in the Act made in the first year of King George the First for preventing tumults and riotous assemblies. God save the Queen!'[50]

The several hundred people thronging a snowy Bridge Street listened to MacKenzie in comparative silence. But they made no move; and though Sheriff Gregg, by virtue of the powers the Riot Act conferred on him, could have ordered their forcible dispersal, the non-appearance or melting away of his hoped-for battalion of special constables had left him bereft of any ability to make this happen. Instead the sheriff, accompanied by James MacKenzie and John Henderson, walked over to where William Davidson and some of his employees were standing beside their cart, which, when driven for a second time into Bridge Street, had there been brought to a halt. Perhaps hoping that the reading of the Riot Act might have dissuaded the crowd from renewed obstructionism, Gregg told the Oldhall farmer to be on his way to the harbour.

On seeing Davidson's cart set off, said James MacKenzie, 'the mob made a rush towards the [Wick River] bridge' where they 'received an accession of numbers from Pulteneytown and blockaded the road so completely that there was danger [to] life in proceeding, the horse . . . [being at risk] of running away from the noise and [from the] shaking of caps and hats in his [the horse's] face'. The sheriff, his colleagues, Davidson and his men, MacKenzie said, duly headed back to Wick. He 'considered [it] hopeless', MacKenzie added, to think about a further attempt to provide the *William Bowers* with its promised cargo.[51]

James MacKenzie's expectation that such an attempt would be met by renewed opposition was underlined by the widespread circulation on 10 February of a handbill 'announcing that a great victory had been obtained [the day before] and calling upon the people to prepare for another'. Taken in conjunction with the fact that Pulteneytown and Wick had for some days been 'placarded' with posters urging residents to rise up and stop grain shipments, this handbill's speedy appearance pointed to the 9 February protest having been no spontaneous outbreak. The preparation and distribution of handbills, posters and other material; the rapidity with which the Bridge Street crowd had gathered; the same crowd's almost military-like manoeuvres: all this was proof, or so Sheriff Gregg and everyone else in authority believed, that there was an organising mind, or minds, behind a lot of what was taking place.[52]

In the immediate aftermath of the 9 February occurrences, suspicion centred on a Wick cooper called William Davidson, a namesake, though definitely not a relation, of the farmer whose proposed grain shipment had caused so much uproar. 'He seemed to take a lead in the crowd,' one of Gregg's colleagues commented of Davidson, 'and was their principal spokesman.' Davidson had spoken 'harshly' to the sheriff, someone else said, and 'had asked him if the people were to be starved for want of wages and meal'.[53]

Perhaps, it began to be suggested in the light of these reports, the Wick and Pulteneytown campaigners were motivated by more than a wish to secure affordable food. Perhaps, in fact, they had a wider agenda. This was very much the opinion of James Loch, the Whig MP who represented Wick and several other Highlands and Islands burghs in the House of Commons. There was much 'radical and levelling feeling' among 'the lower classes' in Caithness, Loch asserted in March 1847. 'I have for years been convinced,' the MP wrote on another occasion, 'that there is no . . . attachment to [Britain's] constitution or [to] the present order of society among the working classes of the towns and villages in the north of Scotland . . . They are great readers and their local press is of the worst description, tending . . . to preach socialism and its accompanying doctrines.'[54]

Loch, to be sure, was by no means the most objective of commentators. His parliamentary seat was owed mainly to the string-pulling capabilities of the Duke of Sutherland by whom Loch was employed, as he had been by the duke's father, to run the ducal estates and to manage the ducal family's extensive business interests. In this dual capacity, Loch had been lead organiser of the mass evictions or clearances that had depopulated the Sutherland interior during the nineteenth century's second decade. The sometimes violent opposition those evictions had engendered, together with the many attacks launched on Loch and his employers by anti-clearance journalists, had left the MP prone to discern revolutionary conspiracies on all sides. But if the *John O'Groat Journal* was not usually as radically inclined as Loch alleged, the paper's take on what it described as the 'excitement and commotion' of Tuesday 9 February would have done nothing to alter the Wick MP's low opinion of all such news sheets.

The *Groat's* stirring account of the final retreat of the forces of law and order from the Wick River bridge – during which a 'cheering, yelling, hissing and hooting . . . mob took to pelting several of the officials with snowballs' – made clear where the paper's sympathies lay. So did an accompanying editorial. Wick and Pulteneytown people 'might have assembled in their thousands, [and] in an illegal manner, to prevent the further exportation of grain', the *Groat* observed. But as long as families were 'in a state of alarming want and driven by dozens to the turnip field', it was inevitable that there should be hostility to 'carrying [grain] away to overfill the already filled . . . stores of unscrupulous speculators in the south'. These provocations notwithstanding, the Pulteneytown and Wick population had behaved, the *Groat* felt, with commendable restraint: 'They attacked no provisions store, they plundered no meal house, they stole no food, they injured no property; they merely proclaimed their sufferings (who would not?) and asked aid. We trust their prayer will be heard.'[55]

Caithness's sheriff principal, Robert Thomson, unlike his Inverness-shire counterpart, William Fraser-Tytler, did not live in his sheriffdom. As was then common, Thomson combined his public office with a more lucrative legal practice in Edinburgh, contenting himself with occasional forays to the north, and otherwise relying on his sheriff-substitute, James Gregg, to handle the bulk of routine business. The difficulties confronting Gregg in early February 1847, however, were anything but routine. With mail from Caithness bringing ever more alarming news, and with the government's Edinburgh-based civil servants insisting that he must take personal charge of law enforcement in Wick and Pulteneytown, Robert Thomson left the Scottish capital for his sheriffdom on Saturday 13 February.

His journey was far from straightforward. Scotland's rail network, though expanding rapidly in the 1840s, had not reached much beyond Fife, and the coach taking Thomson into the Highlands, the sheriff reported, could get no further than the Easter Ross town of Tain 'on account of the snow'. There being no alternative, the sheriff, a man in his late fifties, pressed on, whether by boat or on horseback is unclear, finally reaching Wick – some 70 miles from Tain – four full days after he left Edinburgh.[56]

The briefings Thomson now got from his sheriff-substitute and from Procurator Fiscal Henderson were not reassuring. On 11 February, Thomson learned, Hugh MacKay, a British Fisheries Society manager in Pulteneytown, had ordered men in society employment to accompany him to the harbour's north quay with a view to their removing the boats that had been dragged across it. While still 'a few hundred yards short' of the quay, MacKay said, 'we were met by a crowd of about 200 people . . . and the men turned back'. Both the quay and the *William Bowers* thus remained inaccessible, and two further vessels that had arrived in the harbour to load grain had accordingly been obliged to leave without cargoes.[57]

Because of the proven impossibility of mustering a worthwhile number of special constables, Thomson informed the authorities in Edinburgh, there was nothing he could do to counter the 'tumultuous obstruction' now becoming commonplace. Gregg, John Henderson and the several other 'gentlemen' he had consulted, Thomson wrote, were 'unanimously of the opinion that no [further] shipment can be attempted without the aid of a military force'. He had accordingly 'sent . . . a requisition to . . . Fort George' with a view to having soldiers dispatched to Caithness. This, the sheriff stressed, 'admits of no delay as we have not for nearly ten days had any force to assist the authority of the law'.[58]

That was written on Wednesday 17 February, the day after Robert Thomson's arrival in Wick. On Friday, the sheriff's powerlessness was under-lined when, according to Procurator Fiscal Henderson, 'a mob' headed by a piper 'marched in noisy . . . procession through the streets' prior to making for Pulteneytown's north quay where several men from among the crowd took possession of the *William Bowers*. They 'threatened to put the vessel to sea,' Thomson said of these men, 'and I believe nothing but an adverse wind prevented them from doing so'. With Henderson and Gregg, Thomson continued, he had gone to the harbour to try to reason with the people gath-ered there. 'We walked down [from the Wick River bridge],' the sheriff said, 'but speedily found ourselves in the midst of a watch established by the riot-ers, a signal from whom brought [around] us from 20 to 30 men. To their credit . . . I must say, they did not attempt to injure [us] . . . [although we were] entirely in their power.'[59]

From Robert Thomson's perspective, this Friday night incident – because it showed that Pulteneytown and Wick were now controlled entirely by 'the mob' – was a further confirmation of his urgent need for troops. It was with real relief, therefore, that the sheriff went to Ackergill on the following Tuesday afternoon to watch the disembarkation, as he noted carefully, of 109 officers and men of the 76th Regiment.[60]

With those troops safely installed in Wick's Temperance Hall, a new and roomy building just four or five minutes' walk from the Bridge Street court-house that Thomson had made his headquarters, the sheriff at last felt able to assert himself. He began by organising the delivery of a pre-prepared flyer to 'every house in Wick and Pulteneytown'. While expressing some 'sympathy with the apprehensions of those who [had] been reduced to straits' by the 'great national calamity' of potato blight, this 'statement and warning', as the sheriff's leaflet was described, insisted on an immediate end to 'excesses and outrages'. It was his 'determined purpose' to restore calm, Thomson warned: 'The means of doing so being now placed in our power by the blessing of God, who is the author of order and not of confusion, we . . . will not permit . . . designing men . . . [to engage in] disturbing the public peace or interfering . . . by violence or by threats with the rights of private property or the free exportation of commodities . . . We therefore prohibit, under the pains of law, all disorderly, tumultuous and turbulent assemblages . . . all parading the streets or roads . . . all attempts to erect or maintain barricades or obstructions . . . all attempts to enter any of the vessels in or near the port . . . [and] all attempts to impede or interrupt the free passage of grain, meal or other provisions.'[61]

Next, Sheriff Thomson set about assembling a force of special constables. Now that he had soldiers at his back, the earlier failure to mobilise worthwhile numbers of constables was not repeated – not least because the men summoned to the courthouse on the morning of Wednesday 24 February were well aware that, had they not turned out, Thomson would simply have deployed the military in their place. What the sheriff described as 'a most respectable number' of constables was duly sworn in, issued with batons and marched to the harbour. There the north quay barricade was removed and the business of loading the *William Bowers* got underway.[62]

On this occasion, in order to avoid the need to expose William Davidson's carters to renewed trouble of the sort they had encountered a fortnight previously in Bridge Street, grain was obtained not from Davidson's comparatively distant warehouse but from a much handier storage facility (stocked some time before, it seems, by other farmers) in Pulteneytown. But for all that a carter was on hand to take this grain to the north quay, little progress was made. 'Although every means was tried to get men to assist in handing down the corn from the store to the cart and triple the ordinary wages offered,' said Robert Thomson, 'not one finger was raised to assist. Every attempt to get help was unsuccessful, and only met with derisive cheers from [a] surrounding crowd. The carter was the only man who would load [the cart] . . . and at last he also refused to proceed.' His special constables, the sheriff went on, showed increasing 'symptoms of impatience at [this] delay'. They had their own work and businesses to attend to, the constables told Thomson who, admitting defeat, agreed at last to send them on their way – telling them, however, 'to hold themselves in readiness to answer a summons by the town bell'.[63]

For much of the rest of Wednesday, reported Captain Charles Evans-Gordon of the 76th Regiment, Wick was 'quiet' with few people about – 'which,' Evans-Gordon added, 'I was told by Mr Gregg, sheriff-depute, was a bad sign'. And so it proved, word reaching Robert Thomson in the late afternoon 'that it had been resolved [by whom exactly nobody seemed certain] that night to scuttle the vessel [still lying at the north quay] . . . and to throw any person who might oppose [those] proceedings into the harbour'.

This intelligence was brought to Thomson by Donald Sinclair, a former soldier who had not long before been enrolled as one of only two policemen in the eastern half of Caithness. Because Sinclair lived in Pulteneytown and knew the place well, his 'information,' the sheriff decided, 'was not to be treated lightly'. Accordingly, Thomson sent word to Evans-Gordon to place a military guard on the *William Bowers*. This was done, Evans-Gordon himself leading 20 men, a sergeant and one of his lieutenants, Wilford Brett, from the Temperance Hall to the harbour just as daylight was fading.[64]

Word of this development spread swiftly and, with folk streaming towards the harbour from every part of Pulteneytown, Evans-Gordon soon found himself confronting a 'large and determined mob'. Ordering his men to fix bayonets, the captain quickly set about pushing the crowd up the quay and away from the *William Bowers*. But what he had not realised (night having fallen) was that, further down the quay, were more people who had been assisting with repairs to a Prussian ship, the *Elise* of Swinemünde,* damaged as a result of grounding on rocks near the harbour entrance. This group now came up behind Evans-Gordon and his soldiers. Strung out among them was a length of heavy rope or hawser which, the captain suspected, those new arrivals meant to run around his soldiers in such a way as to force them to the quay's edge and into the water. This threat, if threat it was, his men foiled – the entire quay, as a result, being brought under the military's control.[65]

But if Evans-Gordon was master of the quay, the still growing crowd was in charge of the rest of the harbour area. Gradually it became apparent to the captain – all the more so when, through the darkness, came the sound of heavy boats again being hauled across the top of the quay – that he and the soldiers with him were cut off from, and unable to communicate with, the much larger body of troops still in the Temperance Hall. This dilemma was solved with the aid of some of the *Elise*'s Prussian sailors who agreed to ferry Evans-Gordon across the harbour in their ship's boat. Once landed on the harbour's Wick shore, the captain made his way to Robert Thomson's lodgings where he found the sheriff at dinner. His meal abandoned, Thomson, taking Evans-Gordon with him, hurried off in search of one or two of the Wick notables he had been taking pains to keep on side – prominent among them the town's provost.

---

* Now Świnoujście in Poland. The *Elise* had come to Pulteneytown to take back to Prussia a consignment of cut-price, because otherwise unsaleable, cured herring.

This was Josiah Rhind who, by virtue of his overlapping roles as banker,* civic head and chamber of commerce chairman, had a far surer feel than Thomson for what might or might not be thought acceptable by the Wick and Pulteneytown population. If the harbourside crowd was to be faced down, Rhind now suggested to the sheriff, the task might most appropriately be given to the special constables whom Thomson himself, after all, had told to be ready to report again for duty should they hear the town bell rung. He could speedily have the bell sounded the provost informed Thomson, 'but the sheriff,' or so Rhind said later, 'thought that the emergency was too pressing and that too much time might be taken up if this course was adopted'. Instead Thomson, with the provost's reluctant agreement, ordered Captain Evans-Gordon to turn out those troops still at the Temperance Hall and march them into Pulteneytown where 'the mob' would then be confronted not by 20 soldiers but by 100.[66]

With Thomson and Rhind following close behind, Evans-Gordon, as instructed, led his remaining troops across the Wick River bridge and down to the harbour where, within minutes of their arrival, the captain and his men were drawn into a new confrontation. What ensued was altogether uglier than the fracas of two weeks earlier. Then nothing more lethal than snowballs had been thrown. This time blood would flow.

'The mob,' Evans-Gordon commented, 'were . . . very much excited.' Stones began to be hurled and women in particular started to arm themselves by entering nearby cooperages and picking up wooden 'staves' of the sort used to make barrels. 'They were brandishing [those staves], using very bad language and otherwise provoking the troops,' Evans-Gordon said of the women in question. 'The mob,' Sheriff Thomson said, 'were highly excited, noisy, tumultuous and threatening.' That was why he had had no alternative but to read the Riot Act and 'implor[e] the people, for God's sake, to go home'. This,' the sheriff added, 'they refused to do.' It thus became 'indispensable to clear the streets'.[67]

To begin with, Evans-Gordon's troops were deployed in a manner the captain described as 'walking at the charge'. This meant that, though bayonets were fixed and muskets held in the 'charge' position, soldiers moved only

---

* Rhind managed the Commercial Bank branch at 1 Bridge Street. The same building afterwards housed the Wick branch of the Royal Bank of Scotland, the Royal Bank having taken over the Commercial Bank network in the 1960s. The branch was closed by the Royal Bank in 2018, bringing some 200 years of banking at 1 Bridge Street to an end.

slowly along the Pulteneytown quaysides and into the neighbouring streets. 'This had no effect,' Evans-Gordon reported, 'as the people came back again and again.' No sooner had a street been cleared, it seemed, than it was reoccupied by men, women and youngsters who 'continued to molest the soldiers with stones'. 'We then charged briskly and touched some of the worst of [the crowd] with the bayonet,' Evans-Gordon said. This, according to the *John O'Groat Journal*, led to 'a great many' people being wounded, albeit slightly, and to one woman 'receiv[ing] a pretty severe sword cut' from one of Evans-Gordon's junior officers. Far from calming things down, however, actions of this type served mainly to aggravate the situation – as did Sheriff Thomson's decision to 'apprehend some ringleaders'.[68]

Responsibility for making arrests was given by the sheriff to Donald Sinclair who, being known personally to members of the crowd and being thought by them to be betraying the community of which he was part, became a favoured target. 'I . . . was struck several times with stones,' Sinclair said. 'The mob called out, "knock the bugger down," and began to close in on me.' With the help of some soldiers, Constable Sinclair went on, he managed both to fend off his attackers and to seize two young men, John Shearer and James Nicolson. Though both were to deny this, Nicolson and Shearer were alleged by Sinclair, Sheriff Thomson and others to have helped direct the night's events. That was why Thomson wanted them conveyed speedily to jail; and that, in turn, was what resulted in the sheriff and his army escort becoming caught up in the Union Street melee that ended in the military opening fire.[69]

'It is impossible,' the *John O'Groat Journal* reported of the Union Street volley's immediate aftermath, 'to depict the state of excitement which was visible in every direction. Men [and] women . . . fled on hearing the report of musketry and on learning that damage had been done. Parents were anxiously running in search of their children, while the crowd were giving expression to the most vociferous shouts and yells. Soon after, with the exception of the guard at the [*William Bowers*], all the military were ordered to their quarters, but throughout the greater part of the night groups of the inhabitants were assembled at every corner.'[70]

At those impromptu gatherings, the *Groat* observed, 'the unpleasant events of the evening' were much 'canvassed' – with the result that, at first light, Provost Josiah Rhind took receipt of a hand-delivered letter from a number of Wick and Pulteneytown businessmen. 'We request you will immediately call a public meeting of the electoral inhabitants,' this letter stated, 'to take into consideration what steps should be adopted for the protection of their lives and property from the reckless proceedings at present pursued by the sheriff of the county backed by the military.'[71]

By 'electoral inhabitants' was meant people entitled to vote in local and national elections. Because the franchise, despite its having been extended during the 1830s, was limited to the wealthier eighth (or thereby) of adult males, only a small proportion of Wick's population was eligible to attend the meeting Rhind now set about organising. But when that meeting – with the provost himself in the chair – was convened just 15 hours after the previous evening's shootings, practically everyone entitled to be there put in an appearance. 'The Town Hall,' the *John O'Groat Journal* reported, 'was crowded to suffocation . . . Few speeches were made, but such of the gentlemen as spoke . . . expressed an earnest desire for the immediate removal of the military.' Unsurprisingly, then, there was unanimous backing for a strongly worded resolution to the effect 'that the bringing of the military into this place . . . was a step highly unnecessary, injudicious and unwarrantable'. On Wednesday morning, it was pointed out, as many as 200 men had made themselves available for service as special constables. Had they been given the opportunity by Sheriff Thomson, it was asserted, those men would have turned out again on Wednesday evening. Yes, it was conceded, there had been 'considerable excitement' in Pulteneytown. But the sheriff could and should have dealt with the situation in ways that kept soldiers off the streets.[72]

To reinforce these points and by way of showing themselves better able than Sheriff Thomson and the military to get things back to normal, men who were at the town hall meeting went that afternoon to Pulteneytown's north quay, cleared it of all obstacles and organised the long delayed loading of grain on to the *William Bowers*. This, of course, was exactly what the sheriff had been trying to bring about. But its having at last been accomplished was overshadowed by continuing disquiet about the events of the night before.

Very much to the fore in giving voice to this disquiet was a Wick town councillor, John Cleghorn, who owned an ironmongery business in Bridge Street and who was also an amateur scientist with a national reputation.* Among others involved were James Bremner, a civil engineer who had assisted

---

* In a paper presented to a meeting of the British Association for the Advancement of Science, Cleghorn originated the term 'overfishing', today a key concept in marine conservation.

with harbour construction throughout Britain, and William Miller, a Wick lawyer. These were men of standing; men who expected their concerns to be taken seriously by Robert Thomson; men who, on Thomson refusing to engage with them, reacted furiously. With so many people experiencing a 'scarcity of food', Cleghorn and his colleagues declared, there needed to be 'forbearance' when those people took exception to the 'selfish heartlessness' of 'proprietors and farmers' who were 'selling so much grain for exportation'. 'But . . . there [had been] no such forbearance . . . no means taken [of dealing with protest] but the bullet and the bayonet.'[73]

Sheriff Thomson was dismissive. 'I deeply regret that two persons were injured,' he said of his ordering the military to open fire, 'but I would have regretted still more if, by indecision, I had failed to check criminal proceedings.' In a series of self-justificatory letters to the authorities in Edinburgh, the sheriff took a similar line – while also castigating Josiah Rhind for what Thomson regarded as the provost's double-dealing. Because Rhind had assented to the calling out of Evans-Gordon and his men, the sheriff contended, the provost shared his, Thomson's, responsibility for what followed. That Rhind would have preferred to mobilise special constables rather than troops; that Rhind had not been in Union Street when firing was ordered: nothing of this was of consequence, the sheriff argued. The provost 'had concurred with him as to the necessity of calling out the military', Thomson insisted. Rhind, therefore, should have taken no part in the town hall meeting of Thursday 25 February. He most certainly should not have chaired that gathering. Nor, by his failure to dissent from the meeting's outcome, should he have made himself party to its condemnations of what had transpired in Union Street.[74]

In Wick and Pulteneytown, however, the people who mattered, whether politically or economically, stuck by their provost. On Tuesday 2 March, a number of them attended a meeting of Wick's Parochial Board. There, as noted in the board's minute book, they considered an aid request from the cooper whose hand had had to be amputated as result of the bullet wound he had received six days before: 'Application of William Hogston for himself, having got his right hand shattered and completely disabled by a shot from the military on Wednesday last . . . The Board allow him twenty shillings per month.' It would have been hard for Hogston, his wife and their three children to get by on an income well below the cooper's previous earnings. That is why, in due course, more was done for them. But the rapidity with which the parochial board extended help to a man whose injuries arose from Robert

Thomson's conduct was one more indication that Pulteneytown and Wick's sympathies did not lie with the sheriff.[75]

Nor was Thomson assured of support in Edinburgh where the editor of one of the city's longest-established newspapers, the *Caledonian Mercury*, was astonished to learn that the army had been instructed to open fire in Caithness. 'This stern exercise of civil authority,' the *Mercury* commented, 'is so rare . . . especially in Scotland . . . that [word of this development] has caused no little sensation here.' That sense of shock extended into the Edinburgh office of Andrew Rutherfurd, the lord advocate. 'I look with great anxiety for each post,' Rutherfurd, then in London, was informed by the most senior of his Edinburgh officials. 'It is a time when coolness and discretion are particularly required of those to whom the preservation of the peace is committed, and I hope it will turn out that these qualities have not been wanting . . . in Caithness.'[76]

Rutherfurd's own instinct was to say nothing in public about what had occurred in Pulteneytown. But this became impossible when, on 4 March, the *Times* published its caustic critique of what the paper's leader-writer called Sheriff Robert Thomson's 'cruel and needless' actions. The sheriff, Rutherfurd had been told by one of his political allies, was a man of 'nervous tempera-ment'. But that was not how the lord advocate chose to portray Thomson when, in the House of Commons, he responded to the *Times*. The sheriff, Rutherfurd said, 'was a man not only of humanity but of great firmness of character'.[77]

In Caithness too, Robert Thomson had backers. One, predictably, was *William Bowers*'s skipper James Robertson who contacted the sheriff to 'express . . . [his] best thanks' for the efforts Thomson had made to restart grain shipments. Other commendations came from the farmers and landown-ers who were those shipments' source. At the Caithness Agricultural Association's annual dinner, held days after the Pulteneytown shootings, the sheriff's health was drunk with much acclaim. Just as supportive were Caithness's Commissioners of Supply. Their 'most cordial thanks', the commissioners resolved at their meeting of 12 March, were 'due to Mr Sheriff Thomson' who had done nothing other than what was 'indisputably necessary'.[78]

At that same meeting, however, a dissenting note was struck. Sir George Sinclair, who owned a substantial slice of Caithness and who had served more than once as the county's MP, was of the view that people opposing grain shipments were deserving of at least some sympathy. 'Great allowance must be made,' Sir George observed, 'for the feelings of individuals who read the distressing accounts of the calamities in which Ireland is involved and dread the possibility of similar evils befalling themselves and their families.'[79]

With coverage of Ireland's tragedy filling column after column in Britain's national and regional press, people in Wick and Pulteneytown – where public reading rooms took delivery of several daily papers – would certainly have been familiar, as George Sinclair suggested, with the speed at which scarcity could become catastrophe. And not just in Ireland. From Barra and several other parts of the West Highlands and Islands came more and more reports of hunger and starvation. These, or so the *Caledonian Mercury*'s editor maintained, were what had caused so much uproar in Caithness. 'They see grain shipped from their shores,' he wrote of Pulteneytown and Wick's protesters, 'and, knowing the destitution that prevails . . . [in other] districts of the Highlands, they imagine that this exportation is the forerunner of famine among themselves.'[80]

3

'The year potatoes went away'

*Morvern • Sutherland • Barra • Inverness • Mull • Oban •
Skye • Lismore • Lewis • Islay • Drumnadrochit
Lochaber • Moidart • Arisaig • Knoydart • Kintail • South
Uist • North Uist • Harris • Bernera • Aldourie*

When putting together an 1843 appraisal of his North Argyll locality, John MacLeod, Church of Scotland minister in Morvern,[*] drove home a key point with an anecdote. This featured 'a little boy of the parish' and, in particular, the boy's 'unvarying answer' on being asked 'of what his three daily meals consisted'. What was he given for breakfast? 'Mashed potatoes.' At midday? 'Mashed potatoes.' And in the evening? 'Mashed potatoes.' A sensitive questioner, MacLeod implied, would have stopped there. As it was, the 'too inquisitive inquirer' went on to ask, 'What else?' For a moment, this puzzled the boy. But then, 'with great artlessness', he came up with the answer: 'A spoon!'[1]

This story was set down in Morvern's manse at Fiunary, a south-facing spot that overlooks the Sound of Mull. John MacLeod was born there in 1801 and, in 1824, became Morvern's minister in succession to his father, Norman, who had held the position since 1775.[†] Fiunary's setting would be celebrated by John's nephew, also Norman and also a Church of Scotland minister, in an 1867 book, *Reminiscences of a Highland Parish*, that became a Victorian

---

[*] When Scotland's local government map was redrawn in the 1970s, Morvern was removed from Argyll and added to the Highland Council area. This book sticks with older boundaries.

[†] John MacLeod remained at Fiunary until his death in 1882. Between them, then, father and son, provided Morvern with its Church of Scotland ministers for an extraordinary 107 years.

best-seller. Norman's style is a bit flowery for today's tastes. But to read his *Reminiscences* is at once to sense why Fiunary, where he spent part of his boyhood, would remain always in his mind. 'The glebe was the glory of the manse,' Norman wrote of the 60-acre tract of farmland where Morvern's ministers raised crops and kept livestock. 'It was bounded on one side by a burn whose torrent rushed . . . between lofty, steep banks clothed with . . . ash, birch, hazel, oak and rowan . . . On the other side . . . was the sea, with here a sandy beach, and there steep rocks and deep water.'[2]

The Fiunary manse's immediate surroundings had not altered greatly in the four or five decades prior to John MacLeod completing his 1843 assessment of how matters then stood in Morvern. But that was not true of the rest of the parish. Both in his 1843 account and in evidence he gave at much the same time to two government-appointed inquiry teams, John MacLeod, whose principled stance on these matters won him a great deal of local backing, was clear as to the extent, and clearer still as to the causes, of the many disruptive changes that had taken place in Morvern during his lifetime. At the start of the nineteenth century, he wrote, 'almost every spot [in the parish] was occupied'. That, however, had ceased to be the case. Virtually all of Morvern's 'inland glens' had been 'converted into sheep-walks' and, by way of prelude to this drastic change in land use, family after family had been evicted or, in MacLeod's phrase, 'turned out'.[3]

Thanks to Norman MacLeod's *Reminiscences*, one victim of just such a turning-out or clearance – a victim tracked down and interviewed in Gaelic by Norman's father – was provided with an opportunity to tell the sort of story that usually went unrecorded. Her name was Mary and, with her husband James and all their neighbours, she was ejected from the township of Unnimore or Aonaidh Mòr – a group of 20 or so homes in a little glen to the west of the present-day road into Morvern from the north. 'The officers of the law came,' Mary* recalled of the day Unnimore ceased to exist, 'and the shelter of a house, even for one night more, was not to be got.' Her last memory of her home, Mary went on, was one that for her, as for thousands of other Highlanders and Hebrideans, was emblematic of the enforced extinction of communities where peat-fuelled fires had been kept burning, day and night, for many years. 'The hissing of the fire on the flag of the hearth as they [the evicting party] were drowning it,' Mary said, 'touched my heart.' 'It was

---

* Most Aonaidh Mòr families were Camerons. It is probable that Mary too was Cameron by name.

there that the friendly neighbourhood was,' she added. But now the people she remembered were all gone and 'the one smoke . . . to be seen' in Unnimore's vicinity came, as Mary put it, from the home of 'the Lowland shepherd'* who had taken her folk's place.[4]

Mary and James, with their baby and with James's elderly mother, left Morvern. But numerous displaced families continued to live locally. His parish, John MacLeod contended, had thus experienced both 'depopulating' and 'overpeopling' – 'the dispossessed tenantry hav[ing] . . . become the occupants of small allotments [meaning crofts]' in congested coastal settlements where, having little land and next to no chance of employment, people necessarily lived 'in a very abject state of poverty'. On crofts like that – crofts often comprising not much more than two, three or four acres of barely cultivable land – potatoes were the only crop that could be grown in sufficient quantity to keep families in food. Hence John MacLeod's tale of a small boy who is baffled by the notion that he should be given anything else to eat. In much of the Highlands and Islands of the 1840s, MacLeod commented, that boy's unchanging diet was standard, potatoes having everywhere become the region's 'staff of life'.[5]

This inherently precarious situation had its origins in the period when John MacLeod's father, who came originally from Skye, was first settling in at Fiunary. That was when ways of life deriving from earlier times began to come apart as landed proprietors whose forebears had been warrior chiefs set about reorganising their estates in ways that prioritised financial returns over the bonds and traditions of clanship. According to Samuel Johnson, then one of England's leading literary figures and a man whom the first of Morvern's MacLeod ministers met when Johnson made his 1773 tour of the Highlands and Islands, this land management revolution showed that where there had once been 'patriarchal rulers' there were now 'rapacious landlords'. As first hundreds and then thousands of communities suffered the same fate as Unnimore, plenty of people were to echo Johnson's verdict.[6]

Many such people were attracted by the thought of quitting Scotland for North America. There, as stressed in Gaelic songs and poems composed in places like the Carolinas, Nova Scotia, Prince Edward Island and Ontario,†

---

* When MacLeod's *Reminiscences* were published, the 'Lowland shepherd' responsible for the flocks then grazing around Unnimore's ruins was James or Jimmy Dempster. He was the author's great-grandfather.

† Today's Ontario was then known as Upper Canada.

newly arrived families could get farms of their own and, it followed, shape their lives in ways that were impossible back home. What Samuel Johnson called 'an epidemical fury of emigration' thus gripped much of the late eighteenth-century Highlands and Islands. But all such outward movement alarmed north of Scotland lairds who lobbied hard, and successfully, for legislation intended to put the cost of Atlantic passages beyond most folk's reach. This is what John MacLeod had in mind when he commented that people who had been keen to emigrate 'were prevented from doing so by influential proprietors'. What such proprietors feared was the loss of the workforce they needed to provide them with a commodity which, in the opening decades of the nineteenth century, became an even bigger cash-generator than the wool produced on the sheep farms then taking the place of communities like Unnimore.[7]

This commodity was kelp. Made as its name indicates from seaweed, kelp was an alkaline material required in quantity by southern industrialists. But how were the owners of West Highland and Hebridean estates with seaweed-rich coastlines to equip themselves with the huge numbers of people it took to turn this resource into a marketable product? One answer was to put obstacles in the way of emigration. Another was to move displaced families on to newly established coastal crofts laid out in such a way as to deny their occupiers anything like the acreages needed for the sort of farming – a mix of cattle-rearing and cereal-growing – they had previously relied on. To pay their rents and to cover other outgoings, freshly installed crofting families had to have some source of non-agricultural employment. In effect, then, they were forced into making kelp – men, women and children turning out each spring and summer to cut and harvest seaweed, bring it ashore, dry it and, ultimately, incinerate it in purpose-built kilns from which there was collected an ashy substance that could be sold at immense profit. This profit, perhaps needless to say, accrued to landlords whose control over the kelp trade was as absolute as their control over everything else that took place on their properties.

Despite its having gone a long way to reshaping settlement patterns in much of the Highlands and Islands, the kelp boom was transient. By the 1820s, when scientific breakthroughs made it possible to create industrial alkalis cheaply from salt, prices for the seaweed-based product were in free fall. Estate owners experienced a consequent, and often very sizeable, reduction in their incomes. For the crofting population, however, the collapse of the kelp trade had more calamitous implications. Entirely dependent now on the limited produce of their landholdings, crofters and their families became ever more impoverished and ever more reliant on the single crop that, for the small boy in John MacLeod's story, had become synonymous with food. 'Many of them do not taste animal food [meaning meat, cheese, butter and other dairy products] in a twelvemonth,' MacLeod said in 1843 when asked about his Morvern parishioners' living standards. 'He remember[ed] the time when the poorest person in the parish had a sheep [to slaughter for home consumption] at Christmas; but that is not so now.'[8]

Nor was Morvern in any way unique. 'Poorly fed, scantily clothed and miserably lodged,' one Wester Ross minister noted of crofters in his neighbourhood, 'theirs is a life of penury and toil . . . The ordinary food of this class consists of potatoes . . . Oatcakes and flesh meat are luxuries which they can seldom afford; and butter and cheese, though favourite articles, they can but rarely indulge in . . . The universal beverage is cold water.' 'No people on earth live on a more simple or scanty diet,' it was said of Skye's crofting households. 'The greater number of them subsist on potatoes.'[9]

Comments of this sort could be multiplied endlessly, as could shocked reactions to housing of the kind the Poor Law Commission of 1843 encountered in Barra and lots of other places. The crofting population, one visiting journalist commented, had to make do with 'hovels which a working man in England would consider unfit for the use of his pig'. That this was so, the same reporter stressed, was due to landlords' insistence on tenurial arrangements of a sort that would not have been tolerated in any other agricultural context. Victorian Britain's tenant farmers – and the overwhelming bulk of the country's farmland was then tenanted – were usually provided, at their landlords' expense, with homes, barns and other 'fixed equipment'. Farms were also leased for comparatively lengthy periods – often for 19 or 21 years. Crofts, in contrast, were made available on a 'bare land' basis – meaning that crofters, not their lairds, were responsible for putting up houses and other buildings. Unlike farmers, crofters were also denied leases – their land being rented to them for periods of just 12 months at a time. Even had crofting households possessed spare cash, then, their lack of security of tenure would have discouraged investment in improved housing. As it was, such money as might come to hand was swallowed up by rent demands that were, by tenant farming standards, wildly excessive. The reporter who compared croft houses adversely to pigsties reckoned that crofters, many of them confined to the poorest of poor soils, were paying substantially more per acre than were farmers occupying some of southern England's finest arable land. Still more startling is the fact

– evident only in retrospect – that those crofters were having to find rents which, in real terms, were as much as 50 times greater than would be charged for the same crofts today.*[10]

If observers of the crofting scene were at one in decrying the prevalence of high rents and the universal absence of croft leases, they were equally united in deploring the way that clearance had combined with the introduction of crofting to do away with the intricately graded social structure once characteristic of the Highlands and Islands. The older order had not lacked people who were poor. But glens that were afterwards depopulated to make way for sheep had also contained families whose agricultural and other activities were such as to make them reasonably prosperous. Hugh Miller, editor of the *Witness*, went regularly from his boyhood home in Cromarty to spend time with his mother's kinsfolk in an afterwards emptied part of Sutherland. 'If asked to sum up in one word the main difference between the circumstances of the Highlander in these and in later times,' the adult Miller wrote, 'our one word would be . . . capital.' This capital, in the form of cattle herds, cash reserves and other resources, had been lost to the Highlands and Islands, Miller argued, because of 'the destruction of [the] middle and comfortable class of tenantry' and 'the lining of barren tracts of sea-coast with . . . potato patches and wigwam huts sheltering a population struggling for animal existence'.[11]

When meeting with clergymen whose parishes included post-clearance crofting settlements on Sutherland's north coast, the Poor Law Commission heard a good deal of testimony to the effect that, as Hugh Miller contended, the population movements insisted on by the county's owners had everywhere made people poorer. 'I am inclined to think that in a majority of cases the comforts of the labouring classes have been diminished by their removal to the coast,' said William Findlater, minister in Durness. Farr's minister, David MacKenzie, agreed. 'I remember very well the change which took place in removing the small tenants from the interior to the seashore,' he commented. 'In my opinion the people have been decidedly losers by [that] change. They cannot command the same amount of the comforts of life as they did formerly. Their condition has . . . deteriorated both in food and

---

* Because croft rents have been subject to judicial control since crofters eventually gained security of tenure and other rights in 1886, present-day rents, which take account both of soil conditions and of the fact that landlords never supplied fixtures like homes and buildings, are tiny fractions, in real terms, of those formerly imposed by estate owners and their factors.

clothing. They used to keep many cattle, and they had an excellent supply of milk and of butcher-meat. They likewise . . . were far better supplied with bedding and with clothing than they are now.'[12]

By no means all the people expelled from the Sutherland interior were prepared to accept the crofts earmarked for them by estate managements. Some families managed to get away to Manitoba and to Nova Scotia. Others moved into Caithness. There members of those families, operating from diminutive harbours strung out along the Moray Firth coast south of Wick, became involved in fishing of the sort commemorated by one of twentieth-century Scotland's leading writers, Neil Gunn. In *The Silver Darlings,* arguably his finest novel, Gunn – himself descended from folk 'driven', as he put it, from 'valleys . . . where . . . their people had lived from time immemorial' – was clear as to how poverty and hunger could be kept at bay with the help of wealth extracted from the sea. 'There was hardly a household,' he wrote of the nineteenth-century locality at the centre of his story, 'that did not directly or indirectly make a few pounds out of the summer [herring] fishing; and these few pounds, in a simple economy, put the household beyond fear of want.'[13]

Why, then, did many more Highlanders and Hebrideans not do what was done by those Sutherland-descended fishermen who, when at sea, followed up the shooting of their drift nets by giving voice to what one shore-based listener described in 1840 as 'heart-stirring' Gaelic psalms? Mainly, it seems, because there was everywhere else an absence of the sort of finance injected into Caithness's fishing industry by the curers and other moneymen who loom large in *The Silver Darlings.* Here and there on the west coast of the Highland mainland and in the islands, a few people managed to secure or retain a toehold in the fishing industry. But there were plenty of other areas where, in the absence of that 'comfortable class of tenantry' whose disappearance was regretted by Hugh Miller, investment in boats, nets and other gear had become, by the 1820s and 1830s, well-nigh impossible.[14]

One such place – a place that would suffer more than most in the course of Scotland's famine winter – was Barra. 'The Barra men,' it was reported in 1816, 'are among the most active and industrious fishermen in Scotland. They carry on an extensive . . . fishery solely by their own exertions and on their own accounts, disposing . . . of the produce at the Greenock market to which they go in their fishing boats.' These Barra-built craft, crewed by up to a dozen men and 'extremely sharp both fore and aft', were lineal descendants of the birlinns* or galleys that, in the middle ages, gave island clans much of their military heft. But because Barra (like the rest of the Outer Hebrides) was treeless, the timber that went into such boats had to be imported. This involved heavy cash outlays; and when Barra began to be hard hit by plummeting returns on kelp-making, which islanders had been compelled to take up, those outlays could no longer be afforded. 'The people at present are too poor to carry on fishing on an extensive scale,' Barra minister Alexander Nicolson stated in 1840. This, Nicolson went on, was owing to 'their inability to purchase or build boats capable of encountering the boisterous seas they have to contend with'. Boats that had once carried cargoes of Barra-dried fish to Greenock (by way of the Crinan Canal at the top of the Kintyre peninsula) had long since been left to rot and fall apart. This, the *Inverness Courier* explained, was because Barra people lacked the means 'to keep their boats in proper repair or [to] purchase fishing materials'. Thus it came about that, during the winter of 1846–47, family after family in Barra, as in the West Highlands and Islands more generally, went hungry despite many of them having in plain view some of the richest fishing grounds in all the world.[15]

'Nothing can be finer than the appearance of the potato crop in the neighbourhood of Inverness and in the northern counties generally,' the *Inverness Courier* noted on Wednesday 29 July 1846. That same Wednesday, however, a resident of the Isle of Mull was penning an account of the instantly devastating impact of blight's appearance in his corner of the Highlands and Islands: 'Fields that [a day or two before] appeared beautiful and in full bloom, and promised an abundant harvest to the consumer, are this day as if overrun by fire. I tremble at what may be the consequence [of] the complete failure of this staple article of consumption.' Those fears were well-founded. There could be no good ending to what would be remembered in Mull and other places as '*a'bhliadhna a dh'falbh am buntàta*', the year the potato went away.[16]

Across Scotland the summer of 1846 had initially been dry and hot. But a week or so into July the *Courier* was reporting on a dramatic break in the weather: 'The late remarkable drought which shrank up our streams and lakes, leaving the River Ness like a scanty burn easily forded by children, has been followed by tremendous rain and consequent floods.' Next came a succession of still warm but now damp and misty days and nights. These provided ideal

---

* Birlinns were, in turn, modelled on longships of the type that brought Norwegian Vikings in large numbers to the Hebrides in the ninth and tenth centuries.

conditions for the proliferation of potato blight. The causes of blight, a spore-borne fungal disease, were not then understood. But the rapidity of its spread, together with the immediately obvious indications of its arrival, had been all too apparent since it reached Europe from North America in 1845.[17]

Just two varieties of potato were grown in the early Victorian Highlands and Islands. These were *cups* and *calicos*. The latter, 'universally used' in the north and 'considered hardy and prolific', was much the most popular. But like the *lumper*, the variety favoured in Ireland, the calico* possessed no resistance to blight which, within weeks, was everywhere. The 'disease,' the *Courier* commented in August, 'manifests itself at first by black and yellow spots on the leaves of the shaws [or stems], which rapidly wither and rot, emitting a most offensive and intolerable smell.' Soon that stench was inescapable. 'A friend had a few days ago gone to Knoydart, Skye, Lochalsh and Kintail,' a *Courier* correspondent reported that same month. 'In all that extensive district he had scarcely seen one field which was not affected.' Crofts that should have yielded tons of potatoes were 'enveloped in one mass of decay' and over and over again there were to be heard 'fearful forebodings' of the hunger winter that now seemed inescapable.[18]

Nor was blight confined to the north. At the start of September, Lord Advocate Andrew Rutherfurd, who had been collating reports from across Scotland, was clear that 'the failure' was as general as it was 'absolute': 'Little or nothing would be saved.' What varied hugely, however, was the severity of the resulting impact. High Court judge Henry Cockburn, while lamenting 'the extinction' of what he called his 'beloved potatoes', was all too aware that the alternatives that could be purchased by his class were unavailable to most people: 'We are getting on the best we can with rice, Indian corn,† macaroni and other substitutes; and we who can purchase these think ourselves vastly resigned and easily pleased when we joke over these novelties amidst our wines, old mutton, carpets, fires and every comfort. But Ireland and the Hebrides!'[19]

One organisation that needed no prompting as to blight's likely effects on the Hebrides and on adjacent mainland districts was the Free Church. Although rooted in evangelically minded sections of the urban middle class, this new denomination had won a huge following in the Highlands and Islands where

---

* The calico, now considered a 'heritage' potato, can still be found. Mostly, however, it was given up in the second half of the nineteenth century when, in reaction to the devastation caused by blight, new and more disease-resistant varieties began to be developed by plant breeders.

† *Indian corn* was the common name for maize.

the Free Church was greeted as a welcome alternative to the Church of Scotland. Because the latter was the country's established church, its ministers were appointed, as parliament had ruled, by each parish's landed proprietors from whom those ministers also received their stipends or salaries. Despite the obviously constraining influence of this arrangement, some Church of Scotland clergymen (John MacLeod in Morvern was one) did not hesitate to voice criticism of clearance and eviction. Lots of others, however, were believed to have gone along quietly with even the harshest of such measures – something that could never be said of the Free Church whose title proclaimed its rejection of all state or proprietorial interference in its governance. The fact that 'thousands [of people] . . . [had] been swept away to make room for colossal sheep farms' was, according to a Free Church publication, just one of the 'serious evils' arising from Scotland's landholding structure: 'We have seen, too, as the fruit of the *clearing* system, the mass of our Highland population gradually sinking deeper and deeper into a condition of abject poverty.'[20]

This already deplorable state of affairs, Free Church representatives announced as early as mid September 1846, was about to get worse. The potato crop having, 'totally and universally failed' across the Highlands and Islands, much of the area's population was certain to experience the 'severest destitution and suffering'. To combat this, the Free Church initiated an immediate relief effort.[21]

Perhaps the most prominent organiser of that effort was a leading Free Church layman, Andrew Aldcorn, a doctor who practised in Oban. As autumn turned to winter, Aldcorn and a number of colleagues commandeered a Free Church schooner (normally used to transport ministers around the Hebrides) and set about shipping emergency supplies of meal (bought with the proceeds of their own fund-raising) to numerous localities in Argyll, Inverness-shire and beyond. Remarkably, in an era when sectarianism was often rampant, they made no distinction between Free Church, Church of Scotland or Roman Catholic recipients – delivering, for example, a first invaluable consignment of external aid to mainly Catholic Barra and doing the same for other, equally Catholic, localities like Moidart, Arisaig and the Isle of Eigg.* In all these places, and many more besides, Aldcorn and his associates were exposed, as they recorded, to scene after scene of suffering.[22]

---

* The Free Church record in this regard contrasts with that of Protestant denominations in Ireland – alleged widely to have made aid to Catholic families conditional on their giving up their faith.

It had become common, Aldcorn reported, for children to go 'crying to bed from hunger' and for parents to keep them 'longer [than usual] there in the mornings' in the mostly vain hope that sleep might dull demands for food. In one small harbour, a member of Aldcorn's team wrote, 'a woman with a suckling infant at her breast came aboard . . . the schooner to beg for a handful of oatmeal. I looked at her and the sight went to my heart: the natural nourishment of her infant [meaning the woman's breastmilk] was clean gone.' On Ulva, an island off the much larger Isle of Mull's west coast, a widow with six young children was found to have been 'days without food': 'The charity of her humble neighbours, or rather indeed their means, had become exhausted, and she was helpless. Her . . . children wept till weakness stopped their moanings of hunger. She rose frequently during the night, as she herself told . . . a neighbour in almost equal distress, to lay her ear to the bed . . . where her children lay, to listen whether they still breathed.'[23]

Christmas Day 1846 found Andrew Aldcorn distributing oatmeal in the Skye parish of Strath where, around and to the west of Broadford, conditions were especially bad 'and every day . . . getting worse'. 'A low typhus fever prevails here in several families,' the Oban medical man went on, and the occupants of homes, 'or rather . . . hovels', where this had taken hold were often 'left to their fate by their neighbours' who feared, Aldcorn explained, that they too would become infected. 'In one most deplorable case, the whole of the family of seven persons had been laid down, not quite at the same time, in this fever. The eldest of the children, a son about nineteen years of age, had died just when his mother was beginning to get on foot. No one would enter the house with the coffin for the son's remains. It was left at the outside of the door, and the enfeebled parent and a little girl, the only other member of the family on foot, were obliged to drag the body to the door and put it into the coffin there, whence it was carried by the neighbours with fear and alarm to its last resting place.'[24]

Aldcorn* was the one member of his relief party prepared to enter this stricken home. Inside, he reported, 'I found the father lying on the floor on a wisp of dirty straw, his bedclothes, or rather rags of blanket, as black nearly as soot, his face and hands of the same colour, never having been washed since

---

* During the 1850s, Andrew Aldcorn settled in the Otago district of New Zealand where he died in 1877. If there were ever to be a memorial put up to honour people who did their best to bring aid to famine victims in the Highlands and Islands, his name would surely have a prominent place.

he was laid down . . . The whole aspect of the man, with his hollow features and sunken eyes . . . was such as I had never beheld before. In a miserable closet, beyond the kitchen where the father lay, I found the rest of the family, four daughters, from about eleven years of age to seventeen, all crammed into one small bed, two at one end and two at the other. The rags of blanket covering them were worse, if possible, than those on the father . . . [and] the two youngest [had] no night clothes of any kind. The effluvia and stench in this . . . miserable dwelling were such that I felt I could not remain long . . . The poor woman said she had got a stone or two of meal, she said she did not know from whom, which had barely served to make gruel for the unfortunate patients. The family had no means whatever of their own.'

As news of those and other horrors spread across Scotland, the Free Church appealed to its members in every part of the country to help finance its relief operations. Over a single weekend, and principally by way of church door collections, the present-day equivalent of more than £1 million was raised. 'There has been nothing like [this] before,' commented Lord Advocate Rutherfurd, adding that what had been accomplished was testimony to 'the extraordinary power' of a church that, according to one London newspaper, was 'making itself remarkable for taking the lead in all humane and benevolent enterprises in Scotland'. This was gratifying. As Andrew Rutherfurd well knew, however, getting aid to the Highlands and Islands could not be left entirely to the Free Church. Government, even if unwillingly, was going to have to get involved.[25]

Reporting to cabinet colleagues on the situation in the Highlands and Islands at the start of September 1846, the lord advocate was of the view that 'these districts are in a state very similar to the worst parts of Ireland'. It had suited landowners to have 'a surplus population' to assist with 'the manufacture of kelp', Rutherfurd continued. Kelp had since 'failed'. But 'the population remained . . . living in wretched huts, with small patches of land, and brought up to exist on the lowest quantity and quality of food'. North of Scotland lairds, Rutherfurd believed, had 'neglected both their duty and their interests' in allowing this state of affairs to arise and, during kelp's heyday, had 'even in many cases encouraged' the proliferation of the sort of croft that left its occupants reliant, as one observer put it, 'on a single root for [their] existence'.[26]

All this was true. But irrespective of who was ultimately to blame for people in much of the Highlands and Islands having become so impoverished as to be wholly dependent on potatoes, there was no escaping the consequences of the blight-induced crisis arising from this dependence. These were summed up by Charles Trevelyan, the Treasury civil servant who was soon to be coping with famine in Scotland as well as in Ireland: 'A population whose ordinary food is wheat and beef . . . can retrench in a period of scarcity and resort to cheaper kinds of food . . . But those who are habitually and entirely fed on potatoes, live upon the extreme verge of human subsistence and, when they are deprived of their accustomed food, there is nothing cheaper to which they can resort. They have already reached the lowest point on the descending scale, and there is nothing beyond but starvation or beggary.'[27]

As calls for government intervention proliferated across the Highlands and Islands, the home secretary, Sir George Grey, made known that 'an experienced Commissariat officer [would] proceed immediately to Scotland with instructions personally to inspect the districts within which the greatest distress is to be apprehended'. This officer was Commissary-General Edward Pine Coffin whom Trevelyan and the Commissariat had earlier put in charge of famine relief operations in the south-western part of Ireland. There Coffin, a veteran of Britain's war with Napoleon and a man who had more recently seen service in Mexico and China, operated out of Limerick where he was reckoned on all sides to have played a big part in ensuring that, for the first nine months of 1846, no Irish people died of hunger. Coffin's Irish efforts earned him a knighthood. Like others, however, the commissary-general, who came originally from Devon, worried that policy changes introduced by the UK's newly installed Whig administration would make it hard to sustain this success. 'The gratification that I have felt at the successful conduct of this . . . difficult duty,' he noted towards the end of his time in Limerick, 'is more than counterbalanced by . . . gloomy anticipation of the coming season.'[28]

Days after his departure from Ireland, Coffin was in Oban, which, for several months, was to be his headquarters. 'This is the gem of sea villages,' Henry Cockburn had written when, in 1840, he passed through that same Argyll community in the course of his High Court duties: 'A small bay locked in by hills; five little vessels sleeping in the quiet water; a crescent of white houses almost touching the sea, backed by a corresponding curve of cliff . . . All this completes one's idea . . . of a peaceful summer retreat.' Even in Edward Pine Coffin's time, then, Oban was beginning to be what it has ever since remained, a holiday resort. But the little town (and, by Highland standards, that is what Oban was) had also become something of a communications hub.

'Owing to its . . . safe and commodious harbour and good quays,' it was noted of 1840s Oban, 'it is visited almost daily . . . by steamers.' Some of these connected Oban with Glasgow, Fort William and Inverness – reached by way of the then 25-year-old Caledonian Canal. Others arrived from, or departed for, Lewis, the Uists, Skye, Mull, Islay and other islands. What brought Coffin to Oban, then, owed nothing to its tourism potential and everything to its being the obvious stepping-off point for anyone looking to access sea routes both to the Hebrides and to the Highland mainland's west coast – these being the localities, it was already evident, where food shortages were likely to be most pressing.[29]

Coffin was joined in Oban by George Pole. This was at Coffin's request. Pole, when in charge of the Commissariat depot at Banagher, had proven one of the commissary-general's most effective subordinates. Now he was to serve as Coffin's inspecting officer. In this role, it was clear, Pole would need a means of getting rapidly from place to place. That was why, as the Treasury informed the Admiralty, the Commissariat team in Oban had to have 'at [their] disposal . . . a small steamer'. This turned out to be HMS *Firefly* on which George Pole, as indicated earlier, was to spend a lot of time in the months ahead.[30]

Pole's tour of inspection began, not far from Oban, on Lismore. There, he reported, he had 'walked over the northernmost half of the island, visiting several of the dwellings of the poor, and conversing with them whenever we could mutually understand each other. Of the potato crop there is nothing left fit for use; the root is rotting in the ground where it was planted.' Pole's subsequent visits to several more islands and some mainland localities were to result in similar findings, and, by mid October, Coffin was confirming to Charles Trevelyan that, as the Free Church and others had been warning for some weeks, 'the failure is all but universal and complete'.[31]

This almost total loss of the 1846 potato crop was not confined to the British Isles. Blight was a Europe-wide phenomenon and its impact was almost everywhere aggravated by a weather-hit grain harvest that (other than in the Scottish north) was one of the poorest in living memory. On the Continent, however, disaster was staved off by vigorous action on the part of a range of public authorities. Town councils reduced the price of foodstuffs to consumers by means of generous subsidies. Governments outlawed food exports, flooded local markets with supplies from army stores and underwrote grain imports from Russia where the harvest had been comparatively good. But to British civil servants like Charles Trevelyan, and to the Whig or Liberal ministers to whom Trevelyan answered, all such measures were anathema. While it was generally (though not universally) agreed, as Trevelyan insisted, that it was the UK government's duty to ensure that 'people cannot, under any circumstances, be allowed to starve', it was equally the case, or so Trevelyan asserted, that this objective had to be attained by means that 'avoid[ed] interfering more than [was] absolutely necessary with the retail trade in the sale of grain or meal'. The catastrophe that was to engulf Ireland as a result of cack-handed attempts to square this unsquarable circle was not yet apparent. But the government's initial response to the findings communicated to London by Edward Pine Coffin and George Pole was not such as to inspire confidence that the Highlands and Islands were destined to fare much better.[32]

'It has been proved to demonstration,' Trevelyan was to observe, 'that local distress cannot be relieved out of national funds without great abuses and evils, tending, by a direct and rapid process, to an entire disorganisation of society.' 'There is only one way,' Trevelyan continued, 'in which the relief of the destitute ever has been, or ever will be, conducted consistently with the general welfare, and that is by making it a local charge.' If people were going hungry in the Highlands and Islands, in other words, the cost of providing them with food was not one that could be permitted to fall on taxpayers across the country as a whole. That cost had to be met from within the affected area. In practice this meant, as government made clear from the outset, that the primary responsibility for coping with the unfolding crisis in the Highlands and Islands lay with the region's lairds – whose approach to land management Andrew Rutherfurd was by no means alone in thinking one of the principal causes of that crisis. While ministers were ready to 'facilitate the efforts of landed proprietors to lessen the distress which is apprehended', a Highland MP was duly informed by the home secretary as early as 5 September, 'they [could] not encourage the expectation that by any direct system of pecuniary advances they can relieve . . . proprietors from the obligation . . . to take upon themselves the charge of providing for the wants of the people'.[33]

Charles Trevelyan was confident that Highlands and Islands landowners would do as government urged. Edward Pine Coffin and George Pole, Trevelyan's men on the spot, were less certain. Not long after his arrival in Oban, Coffin had gone to Mull to meet, among others, the local representatives of one of the island's more substantial proprietors, the Duke of Argyll. Those men acknowledged the imminence of famine, Coffin reported. 'But it does not appear,' he added, 'that they are either taking, or have in

contemplation, any measures adequate for the relief of it'. His further enquiries, Coffin commented in mid October, had convinced him that lots of other
estate owners and land managers were equally lackadaisical. This 'serve[d] to
show,' Coffin warned, 'that the moral obligation supposed to attach to landowners cannot be relied on to secure the people from destitution.'[34]

George Pole offered a forensic analysis of what could, or could not, be
expected from Highlands and Islands lairds. In the course of his travels, Pole
wrote, he had met 'proprietors of various dispositions'. These fell into a
number of broad groupings: 'the proprietor who was able to provide for his
tenants and was doing so'; 'the proprietor who was willing to provide for his
people' but whose financial difficulties deprived him of 'the ability to do so
efficiently'; 'and, lastly, the proprietor who [despite having no lack of cash]
was neglecting to provide for his people'.[35]

Pre-eminent in Pole's first category were the Duke of Sutherland and Sir
James Matheson. Both were immensely rich. The duke, whose Highland
estate – at well over a million acres – was the most extensive in Britain, had a
great deal of inherited wealth at his disposal. Matheson, a man of comparatively modest background, had made a fortune from shipping opium from
British India into China and had expended a part of this fortune on his 1844
purchase of the entire island of Lewis. There he was to spend heavily on
famine relief – winning praise from the Free Church, which was of the view
that, during the winter of 1846–47, Matheson's 'generous liberality' kept
Lewis's 18,000 or so inhabitants 'out of reach of danger'.[36]

The Duke of Sutherland, whose aid to his hunger-threatened tenantry was
every bit as generous as Matheson's, attracted equivalent plaudits from both
churchmen and politicians. Less impressed were the duke's estate managers,
the most senior of whom, James Loch, was of the opinion that his employer's
'benevolence' and 'kindness of heart' were taking the Sutherland Estate in a
direction that would 'turn out to be injurious to the people [the duke was
endeavouring to assist] and fatal to their future progress'. At the heart of this
dispute, just as it was at the heart of so much of what had gone wrong in the
Highlands and Islands, was the legacy of clearance. The duke, whose parents
had ordered the transfer of thousands of people from Sutherland's interior to
coastal crofts where potato-dependence was the only option, well understood
the damage done by that policy to his family's reputation. He wanted, therefore, to avoid actions – such as refusing help to the starving – which might
result in renewed criticism of himself and, still more, his wife who, because of
her closeness (as already seen) to Queen Victoria, was particularly susceptible

to press scrutiny. Loch, on the other hand, was the clearance policy's architect and, despite its having resulted in exactly the sort of poverty and suffering he had once claimed to have brought to an end in Sutherland, he continued to defend – not least in his latest role as a Highland MP – what had been done. If the duke's crofting tenants were in trouble, Loch argued, the cause was to be found in their being 'most wonderfully idle'. 'I do not think that some pressure of distress will not reach these people,' Loch wrote of the folk the Duke of Sutherland wished to assist. 'I think it will and I think it ought. It is the only thing that will induce them to work.'[37]

Irrespective of how much they spent on food aid, neither the Duke of Sutherland nor James Matheson risked bankruptcy. That could not be said of landlords in George Pole's second category, men who were anxious to do right by their tenants but who lacked the necessary means. Two of these were Walter Frederick Campbell, who owned all of the Isle of Islay, and Norman MacLeod of Dunvegan, whose estate, in the north-western corner of Skye, was one of the largest on that island. At a time when most Highlands and Islands lairds were absentees, MacLeod and Campbell resided on their properties. 'I live among my people and I constantly watch over their wants,' Campbell told Edward Pine Coffin. There was truth in this. In comparison with localities like Sutherland or Morvern, clearance on Islay, though it occurred in the course of Campbell's ownership, had been minimal. Instead Campbell had set out, with consequences still to be seen, to make Islay – described in 1842 as 'the richest and most productive island of the Hebrides' – a place of arable farms and carefully laid-out villages. That is why John Murdoch, who grew up on Islay and who was to become one of late nineteenth-century Scotland's leading land reformers, always exempted Campbell – 'a fine looking man with a ruddy complexion', Murdoch recalled – from charges of the sort he levelled against virtually every other member of the proprietorial class. But Campbell, while anxious, as he put it, to 'save a brave . . . race of people from starvation', was, he informed the home secretary in October 1846, no 'capitalist'. By this, Islay's owner meant that he had no source of funds other than his rents 'with which [to] . . . meet the famine caused by . . . the total loss of the potato crop'. Adding to his problems, Walter Frederick Campbell went on, was the fact that his rental income was itself shrinking drastically because so many of his tenants had been 'left absolutely destitute' by the effects of blight. While Campbell's own eventual insolvency – arising from debts of perhaps £75 million at today's values – was by no means wholly due to his efforts to help the many Islay people in a worse

plight than himself, there is no doubt that the 1846–47 famine was the immediate cause of his going under financially. Much the same was true of Norman
MacLeod.[38]

Unlike Campbell's, MacLeod's estate had been subjected to extensive
clearance. But for a time in the closing months of 1846 and the early months
of 1847, it was as if the MacLeod family's long-standing and hard-edged
attempts to raise rents, expand sheep farming and otherwise boost their cash-
flow had been abandoned. Instead Dunvegan Castle became again a source of
the sort of protection it had offered to surrounding communities in the long-
gone era when Norman MacLeod's forebears were clan chiefs rather than
landlords. 'The famine years,' MacLeod said afterwards, 'found me at
Dunvegan. Every morning . . . hundreds of people awaited my appearance at
the castle door. I had at the time large supplies of meal for my [estate] work-
people . . . These were soon exhausted and I went to Aberdeen for more.'
Why, MacLeod was asked, had he undertaken the feeding of so many people
at a cost so great that it led to his estate being placed under the control of his
creditors? 'I only did what every other man similarly circumstanced would
have done,' he replied. 'They were my people. It was my duty to assist them.'[39]

In fact, virtually none of MacLeod's 'similarly circumstanced' counterparts
matched his endeavours – certainly not Skye's other leading laird, Lord
Macdonald of Sleat, who was also the owner of North Uist. On sailing into
Armadale, not far from Macdonald's principal residence, in early October
1846, George Pole found no lack of evidence that Skye's 25,000* inhabitants,
a majority of whom lived on Lord Macdonald's estate, were already finding it
hard to obtain enough food. When talking with a local minister, whom he
thought 'a pious and intelligent man', Pole heard that 'the state of five-sixths'
of the minister's parishioners was 'very bad' – something 'confirmed,' Pole
wrote, 'by the visits I personally made to the poor . . . in the neighbourhood'.
At nearby Armadale Castle, Pole commented in his official report, he was
'hospitably received' by Lord Macdonald. A private letter from Pole to Coffin,
however, told a different story. Because Macdonald was much taken up with
entertaining a number of house guests, Pole told Coffin, 'I found some difficulty in obtaining his lordship's close attention to the real object of my visit.'
He was 'doing everything in [his] power to alleviate the condition of the
tenantry on [his Skye and North Uist] estates', Lord Macdonald would

---

* The 1841 census put Skye's population at 23,074. By 1846–47, it was estimated by various observers to have grown to between 25,000 and 26,000.

subsequently assure a government minister, 'but it [was] hopeless for [him], from [his] own resources, to attempt to cope'. This would remain Lord Macdonald's position – which makes it no accident that it was on his estate, in December 1846, that Oban doctor Andrew Aldcorn encountered the scenes of hunger, illness and death that so appalled him. As far as the provision of famine relief on Skye was concerned, one of George Pole's Commissariat colleagues noted in February 1847, Norman MacLeod remained 'the only thoroughly active and good landlord of the larger class'. Well over half the population of Skye, the same man estimated, had to get through the famine winter 'without the least assistance from the [island's] proprietors'.[40]

Financially, to be sure, Lord Macdonald, who had inherited his properties from his father in 1832, was in some difficulty at the point when famine took hold. From North Uist in particular the immediately preceding generation of his family had been in receipt of massive revenues from kelp. Instead of being invested productively, however, these – as happened throughout the Hebrides – were spent as soon as, or indeed before, they were received. This, according to one contemporary journalist, was because the hugely inflated incomes that came their way during the kelp trade's heyday encouraged lairds like the Macdonalds to believe they could emulate the lifestyle, and expenditure patterns, of 'the English aristocracy'. 'The effect,' this journalist continued, 'was the same as when a hawker of the [North American] backwoods spreads out his toys and trinkets . . . The vanity of the [island] chiefs was intoxicated, and the solid advantages which the new tide in their affairs had opened up to them were bartered for the merest baubles. There is a staircase window in Lord Macdonald's mansion in Skye which is said to have cost £500.'[41]

That window, its value equivalent to several hundred times the then average weekly wage, accounted for no more than one tiny component of the spending associated with the construction – just as kelp prices began to fall precipitately – of Armadale Castle,* the grand home where George Pole was given something of a cold-shoulder by an otherwise engaged Lord Macdonald. This spending, and more of the same sort, went a long way to accounting for debts which, by the later 1840s, were in excess of those accumulated by Campbell of Islay. So extensive were Lord Macdonald's landholdings, however, that he was able to retrieve the position, in part at least, by selling some of them – most notably North Uist. This severed an ownership link that had endured for centuries.

---

* Armadale Castle is today mainly a ruin.

Elsewhere in the Outer Hebrides there were identical developments. The MacNeil family, who owned Barra, and the MacDonalds of Clanranald, proprietors of Benbecula and South Uist, had become even more addicted than the Macdonalds of Sleat to inflated receipts from kelp sales. This made more or less inevitable the Clanranald and MacNeil bankruptcies that were to lead to Benbecula, South Uist and Barra being acquired by the man whose conduct, for reasons explored in a previous chapter, was to be censured so severely by George Pole.

There was more than a dash of Charles Dickens's Scrooge – that 'squeezing, wrenching, grasping, clutching, covetous, old sinner' – in the attitudes and actions of John Gordon of Cluny. Gordon inherited the Aberdeenshire estate which provided him with his territorial designation from a father said to be 'scrupulously careful as to his expenditure'. The son exhibited identical traits and – by never marrying but setting up home with a housekeeper – added a blithe disregard for nineteenth-century convention to the mix. 'The remark was frequently made of [John Gordon],' according to an extraordinarily frank obituary in one of north-east Scotland's newspapers, 'that if anyone was cheating him out of a penny he would not stick at spending £100 in recovering it'. Gordon's 'main objective', that same obituary asserted, was the accumulation of money and property. In this characteristic, verging on obsession, is probably to be found the reasoning behind otherwise inexplicable acts on Gordon's part. How else to account for his having expropriated, by means touched on already, a legacy meant to benefit Barra's poor? But what is harder to explain, because it made little sense financially, is Gordon's purchase of islands which, for the most part, brought him nothing but bad publicity.[42]

Gordon, who had interests in sugar plantations in Tobago and who was a beneficiary of the remarkably generous compensation payments made to slave-owners when slavery was abolished in Britain's West Indian possessions, may simply have been looking to invest that windfall in properties available at what were, in comparison with the going rate for land in Aberdeenshire, knock-down prices. It may be too that Gordon came to regret his Hebridean speculations. He certainly did none of the things that Highlands and Islands landlords of the time were expected to do. Thus meetings of the Inverness-shire Commissioners of Supply, which Gordon should have attended in his capacity as one of the county's more substantial landowners, were consistently boycotted by him – with the result, Sheriff William Fraser-Tytler complained, that Barra, South Uist and Benbecula were 'now almost separated from Inverness-shire, the proprietor never being seen amongst us'. Nor was Gordon glimpsed, other than once and briefly, on his island landholdings where, well before potato blight took hold, it became all too apparent that 'on any point demanding an outlay of money it [was] vain to appeal to him'. There was little that was unexpected, therefore, in John Gordon's response, or lack of it, to the beginnings of famine. 'His character is so well known,' remarked Sir John MacNeill who chaired the Board of Supervision and whose older brother owned the island of Colonsay, 'that his conduct will surprise no-one.'[43]

Gordon, from the perspective of Whig premier Lord John Russell and his cabinet, was an embarrassment. While the prime minister, his colleagues and Charles Trevelyan had long since lost patience with Ireland's landlords, whose neglect of their tenantries was notorious, Highlands and Islands landowners were said repeatedly by government to be men of a different stamp. John Gordon's stance, the home secretary told the House of Commons, 'was an exception to the general conduct of [Highlands and Islands] proprietors'. This, however, was not a unanimous view. While Edward Ellice, Liberal MP for St Andrews, was more than happy to acknowledge the merits of what was being done by Norman MacLeod and others, he was insistent that 'there were not wanting instances of an opposite nature'. While that was certainly the case, as Ellice went on to demonstrate, it was left to an English MP, George Poulett Scrope, to point to the key weakness in the government's entire approach to famine relief. 'It was highly praiseworthy of these landlords who had taken care of their poor,' said Scrope, 'and it was equally reprehensible of these landlords who did not support their poor. But what was still more reprehensible was for government to allow the poor to remain at the mercy of any landlord.'[44]

By mid October, in response to Edward Pine Coffin's insistence that, without such a move, the population of the Highlands and Islands might not have access to adequate supplies of emergency aid, it had been decided in London that food depots of the sort provided in Ireland during the previous winter would be established in the Hebrides. Because there was no adequate warehousing in the islands, these were to take the form of redundant frigates built in the closing stages of the Napoleonic Wars. Two such vessels, Charles Trevelyan reported, were being 'fitted out' for their new duties as rapidly as possible. Several naval mills were meanwhile 'employed in grinding [the] barley with which they [were] to be laden'. From the Thames, by way of Portsmouth and Plymouth where they took on maize as well as barley, the two ships, the *Belvidera* and the *Aeolus*, made their way north. By the beginning of December, the first of them, the *Belvidera*, was on station at Tobermory. The second, the *Aeolus*, bound for Portree on Skye, was delayed by the bad weather characteristic of much of that winter. By the year's end, however, it too had reached its destination.[45]

The *Aeolus* and *Belvidera* were to remain at anchor off Portree and Tobermory for several months. Coffin and George Pole, the Treasury announced, would 'exercise a general superintendence' over the issuing of the food stocks they contained. Each floating depot – its holds replenished regularly with the help of chartered steamers sailing out of southern ports – was also to be supplied with its own small staff of Commissariat officers. Those men, it was made clear, would operate in accordance with Treasury-imposed rules intended to ensure that government-provided food supplies were distributed in ways that 'interfere[ed] as little as possible with private trade'. Prices charged would be pegged to prevailing rates in Liverpool and Glasgow markets; and there would be no sales of small amounts of barley-meal or maize to individual consumers. 'These depots,' the public were told, 'are formed for the purpose of assisting landed proprietors and others in providing for the wants of the people in districts where local markets may prove insufficient.'[46]

The Treasury, then, was still looking to West Highland and Hebridean lairds to take a lead in alleviating hunger at the local level. Landlords or their factors, it was stated, would find ways of employing crofters – funding job creation, if need be, with the help of loans advanced by government under the provisions of the Peel administration's Drainage Act, which the Commissariat was under constant pressure to bring to proprietors' attention. People given work in this way, it was hoped, would receive payment in the form of maize or barley, which landlords, in turn, would buy from the Tobermory or Portree depots. The difficulty with this plan was that it grossly overestimated the willingness of estate owners to do what was expected of them. It had been anticipated, Edward Pine Coffin was afterwards to reflect, that 'food should be brought home to the doors of the people by the intervention of [landed] proprietors, but the latter [had] for the most part declined this task, and left the people to find their own way to the depots'. Receipts for food sold by the Commissariat from the *Belvidera* and the *Aeolus*, Coffin noted, totalled £36,000. Of this amount, no less than two-thirds or £24,000 (a sum approaching £2.5 million at present-day values) had been received not from lairds or their agents but from the wider population – 'a number [of crofters and others] from the same district,' Coffin reported, 'usually clubbing their money to purchase the minimum quantity which the depot regulations allowed to be sold'.[47]

This money came from a variety of sources. In part, according to Coffin, it consisted of 'the accumulated savings of bygone years'. But savings, seldom more than meagre to begin with, had to be supplemented with cash from the sale of the few cattle still in crofting ownership and by the earnings of the many younger men who moved south temporarily to take paid jobs – mostly on railway construction projects then underway in the Scottish Lowlands. Some families of course found it easier than others to scrape food together in this way. Most such families, however, did not keep all such food to themselves. During the 1846–47 winter nothing earned more 'unfeigned admiration' from the Free Church than 'the conduct of the small tenantry . . . towards their . . . neighbours'. Families who had food were in no way averse, it was reported, to 'sharing their own little stores most liberally' with people who had none.[48]

In this 'readiness with which they brought such resources as they possessed to bear upon their condition', Edward Pine Coffin detected among the Highlands and Islands population 'a feeling of independence not commonly ascribed to them'. What Coffin there took issue with perhaps was the widespread, indeed almost universal, tendency of land managers like James Loch to attribute Highlands and Islands difficulties to alleged character deficiencies on the part of the region's inhabitants. What the commissary-general may also have had in mind were some of the dispatches compiled by the special correspondents – 'commissioners' they called themselves – posted north by the editors of national and Scottish newspapers.[49]

The first of these, a man from the *Morning Chronicle*, voyaged down the Caledonian Canal from Inverness. Stopping off at Drumnadrochit, on the shores of Loch Ness, he found nearby Glen Urquhart as 'picturesque' as it was 'romantic'. 'Yet within the confines of this magnificent panorama,' he told *Chronicle* readers, 'we have witnessed perhaps a greater contrast of splendour and misery . . . than the grandeur and wretchedness of even London can parallel.' At the opulent end of this spectrum was 'the splendid mansion of Balmacaan' where Lord Reidhaven, heir to the Earl of Seafield, Glen Urquhart's owner, was hosting a set of 'noble guests' who had joined him for the deer-stalking season. But not far from Balmacaan,* the *Chronicle* man continued, a blacksmith, his wife and their seven children occupied a meagrely

---

* Balmacaan House, on rising ground near Drumnadrochit, was demolished in the 1970s.

furnished house or hut 'constructed of the bark slabs* of the fir [or Scots pine] tree'. With her potatoes gone and oatmeal rising steadily in price, 'the mother of the family' told the visiting journalist that 'she did not know how she could take on the winter . . . She felt sorry most of all that [to have the cash needed to feed her family] she must take three of the children from school.'[50]

The *Chronicle* reporter, who would see worse housing as he travelled further west, had only sympathy for famine's victims. His counterpart from the *Times*, Thomas Campbell Foster, sympathised with neither the hungry nor their landlords. A typical example of the latter, Foster wrote while in Lochaber, was one of that district's principal proprietors, 'a gentleman named [Donald] Cameron of Lochiel'. 'By reputation,' *Times* readers were informed, 'this gentleman is . . . amiable and benevolent . . . He, however, chooses to live absent from his estate. His factor lives at Inverness, 60 miles off. Two-thirds of [Cameron's] estate are let [as sheep farms] in immense tracts to two tenants, who pay him about £4,000 a year rental, and both these tenants are south-country men and absentees. Now is it in the nature of things to expect . . . improve[ment] under such circumstances? You have here an absentee laird, an absentee factor and absentee farmers, leaving none but a few shepherds and . . . peasants in the country.'[51]

But if Cameron of Lochiel merited harsh words from the *Times* commissioner, Cameron's crofting or 'peasant' tenants – many of whom had been moved out of areas given over to the sheep farmers mentioned by Foster – were reckoned to be deserving only of contempt. Foster had been earlier in Ireland where he had found, he commented, 'the laziest people on the face of God's earth'. 'Their extreme poverty,' Foster wrote of the Irish, 'is simply the natural result of their extreme laziness.' As for Highlanders, 'a kindred Celtic race', their sufferings too stemmed from 'their want of industry'.[52]

There was little that was new in what the *Inverness Courier* called Thomas Campbell Foster's 'disquisitions on the inferiority' of the Highlands and Islands population. As far back as the fourteenth century, Lowland writers had been contrasting their own 'docile . . . civilised . . . polite and peaceable' behaviour with that of Gaelic-speaking Highlanders who were 'fierce and untameable, uncouth and unpleasant, much given to theft [and] fond of doing nothing'. By Foster's time, however, prejudices of this sort had been reinforced by the then

---

* Slabs are the bark-covered boards sawmilled from the exteriors of logs that are being turned into building timber. A good deal of Scots pine was then being extracted from Glen Urquhart and nearby Glen Affric.

widespread practice of dividing humanity into 'races' and giving each race a place in a pecking order which always awarded top billing to 'Saxons' or 'Anglo-Saxons' while assigning a significantly lower slot to 'Celts'. Categorisations and characterisations of that sort were seldom absent from Thomas Campbell Foster's dispatches to the *Times*. They were to be still more prevalent in the reporting of a third commissioner, James Bruce of the *Scotsman*.[53]

Bruce's excursion into the Highlands and Islands began on a steamer that took him from Glasgow, by way of Oban, to Tobermory. On that same steamer, bound ultimately for Armadale and Portree, were Skyemen who, for the preceding six months, had been employed by railway contractors in Ayrshire, Lanarkshire and Fife. 'They were men neither ignorant nor unintelligent,' Bruce noted of this group, 'men with a good inclination for work and some confidence in their own ability to make their way through this world and to provide for their families.' 'These men,' Bruce went on, 'all joined together in reprobating the renting of vast tracts of country to sheep farmers . . . "The ruin of the poor people in Skye," said one of them, "is that there are whole miles of country with nothing but sheep . . . upon them."' Nor were such complaints confined to Skye, Bruce wrote. In Mull, where 'there were some cases of nearly absolute starvation the very week [he] arrived' in Tobermory, Bruce heard it said repeatedly that people had everywhere been 'driven into corners too small to raise a subsistence from'.[54]

This was matter-of-fact journalism, a product of interview and observation. Soon, however, it gave way to a series of explicitly racist diatribes, which appear to have had their origin in the *Scotsman* commissioner having 'not calculated' that he was bound to meet in the Highlands and Islands with people who spoke no English. Bruce, though he thought 'the Saxon language' to be 'the language of civilisation', had a wide knowledge of classical and modern European languages and afterwards, when in India, would attempt to communicate with people there in their vernaculars. But for Gaelic, a 'jargon of ignorance and barbarism', he had zero tolerance. The fact that this 'ugly and offensive language' had not been abandoned by the 'Celtic' inhabitants of the Highlands and Islands, *Scotsman* readers were told, was proof that, 'morally and intellectually', its speakers were 'an inferior race to the Lowland Saxon'. Nor was there any scarcity of other such proofs. Women everywhere in the Highlands and Islands had far too many children; 'want of enterprise' was endemic; 'extraordinary filthiness' was commonplace; and the 'wretchedness' commonly attributed to the 'temporary calamity' of potato blight was actually a consequence of 'moral degradation'.[55]

Many of the men James Bruce encountered in the Highlands and Islands were, by mid nineteenth-century standards, unusually tall. Today this is believed to have been owed, as were similar characteristics in Ireland, to the fact that a potato-based diet was more nutritious (as long as potatoes were to be had) than were typical urban diets of the time. The *Scotsman* commissioner, however, had an alternative explanation. The fact that the male population of the Highlands and Islands lacked 'the bent backs and rounded shoulders . . . so common in the Lowlands' was a product, he wrote, of this population's refusal to engage in 'laborious and earnest employment'. And while it was 'undeniable' that Highlanders had 'shown themselves to be very good soldiers', this too was a pointer to their innate 'indolence': 'In time of peace the soldier's life is pre-eminently an idle life.'[56]

Charles Trevelyan, to his credit, had no time for what he called 'foolish cackle' about the supposed hopelessness of Celts. Nor, the evidence suggests, did material of the sort published by the *Times* and *Scotsman* impact to any marked extent on famine relief fund-raising which, by the close of 1846, was ceasing to be a Free Church monopoly. In both Edinburgh and Glasgow, interdenominational committees – well supported and highly organised – were soon to have immense sums to spend on getting aid to people James Bruce thought undeserving of what he called 'the charity of the Saxon'. Much of this money came from the Lowland middle class – as is indicated by an Edinburgh committee circular advising prospective donors who might 'not be at home' on the day of a house-to-house collection 'to leave their contribution with a servant'. But cash came in too from England and from overseas. Press hostility notwithstanding, people struggling for survival in the Highlands and Islands were, it seems, viewed widely with goodwill.[57]

During the opening weeks of 1847, just enough external aid reached the Highlands and Islands in just enough time to prevent a repetition of the cataclysm then overwhelming Ireland. But this became evident only with hindsight. All through December and into January and February, as persistent frost and heavy snow added everywhere to people's miseries, there was little reason to do other than fear the worst. Why this was so is apparent from the tenor of a report from Tobermory carried by the Christmas Day* edition of the *Greenock Advertiser*, a paper that maintained a network of

---

* Christmas Day was not then a holiday in Scotland. This would remain the case into the second half of the twentieth century.

spare-time correspondents all along the steamer routes linking the Clyde with the Hebrides.

'We mentioned lately that a government vessel [the *Belvidera*] was in the bay [at Tobermory] and loaded with provisions,' the *Advertiser* commented by way of preface to what came next. 'But from this source the unemployed and destitute creatures to whom the following letter relates derive no advantage as the officers in charge of [the] ship are only authorised to *sell* the food on board. We do most earnestly hope that this and many similar appeals will open the hearts and minds of all who have it in their power to render [a] suffering and patient people prompt and liberal assistance.'[58]

'I would have written sooner,' the *Advertiser*'s Tobermory correspondent began, 'but the state of our poor people prevents my thinking of or doing anything else . . . There are hundreds now in this little village who have not a morsel of food except what is given them by those who still have some; many who never begged before are almost famished before they leave home to ask for food . . . One person known to us had been from Saturday morning till Monday afternoon without a mouthful. Three of a family subsisted two days on a very little milk given by a half-starved cow which inhabits the same room as themselves. A household of four grown persons had nothing but one . . . biscuit divided among them for a day, and [they] most respectable [and] well-behaved people. The children may be heard outside crying for food which the miserable parents have not to give . . . At present the snow aggravates our distress as it prevents draining in which a few . . . could get employment . . . Human lives are at stake. They will be perishing about our doors ere long if something is not done.'

Tobermory, not long before the famine, had been described as a 'well built' little town. But now, with a number of Mull's landlords responding to famine by evicting its victims, the place had become desperately overcrowded. What he saw in Tobermory moved even James Bruce of the *Scotsman* to pity. Equally affected was another journalist, Robert Somers of the *North British Daily Mail*, a Glasgow paper. Somers, who made it his business 'to visit as many of the poor as possible' in the single rooms, sheds and cellars that had become their homes, heard over and over again how Tobermory was often the only refuge available to people 'ejected', as he put it, from crofts in different parts of Mull. 'The results of these evictions,' Somers wrote, 'are injurious in the extreme. They accumulate poverty and destitution in heaps. Instead of the poor being spread over their respective parishes, they are thrown together in villages where there is no property, no agency, no resources adequate to cope . . . and where [as a result] . . . there is nothing but the most appalling and unmanageable destitution.'[59]

Tobermory's predicament was shared by every other village or small town in the islands and on the mainland's west coast. Nor were conditions in the countryside any better. 'I become more and more alarmed at our prospects,' Edward Pine Coffin commented at the start of February, 'and [I] fear that the period is not distant when the Highlands will present almost as disastrous a picture as Ireland.' 'It is a mistake,' Coffin warned Charles Trevelyan, 'to suppose that all the proprietors are yet doing what we consider their duty . . . It becomes apparent, as our inquiries proceed, that many, even of these proprietors who make a show of employing their people, are in reality doing nothing equal to the exigency of the situation.'[60]

Coffin's apprehensions were reinforced by the outcome of a visit made in January to Moidart, Arisaig, Morar and Knoydart by Andrew Fraser, Fort William's sheriff-substitute and the man who, not long before, had been called on to deal with the soldiers who had attacked maidservant Mary Cameron. Having ridden hard through Ardgour and Strontian, Fraser entered Moidart by way of the bridge that spans the River Shiel a mile or so north of Acharacle. What he met with just across the river on the Lochshiel Estate, where crofters had to get by on the few acres left to them after the bulk of the property had been put under sheep, was typical of much else the sheriff was to encounter in the days ahead. On calling at 'every house' on the Moss of Shiel, Fraser was especially affected, much as Andrew Aldcorn had earlier been in Skye, by the plight of a family trying to cope with typhus as well as with hunger.[61]

'The mother was the first person attacked,' Fraser reported of this family, 'and she fell a victim to the disease. She died about a month ago, leaving an infant four months old and six other bairns. [Other people in the vicinity] were so much afraid of catching infection that they would not visit this unfortunate family who must have perished but for the humanity of Kate MacDonald, aged 23, one of the neighbours, who volunteered to nurse the fever patients.'[62]

Before leaving Fort William, Fraser went on, he had been entrusted with the sum of £250 by the newly formed Central Board for the Management of the Fund Raised for the Relief of the Destitute Inhabitants of the Highlands and Islands of Scotland – an umbrella organisation intended to unify, and give direction to, what had previously been a set of separate groupings in Glasgow, Edinburgh and other centres. Drawing on this sum, the sheriff 'rewarded'

Kate MacDonald for her efforts. He also arranged for 'some supplies' to be sent to the family assisted by 'this humble but true heroine' as Kate was dubbed by the *Inverness Courier*.[63]

On the Lochshiel Estate as a whole, Andrew Fraser calculated, there were no fewer than '483 individuals in a state bordering on starvation'. Further north, matters were equally dire. His meticulous enquiries on the Arisaig Estate led Fraser to conclude that 671 of its 868 residents were in need of immediate help. Arisaig's owner, Lord Cranstoun, lived in Devon and, according to Fraser, 'completely neglected' the population of his Highland property. But for what the sheriff called 'the untiring exertions' of a local priest, William MacIntosh, a part of this population, Fraser was convinced, would have perished.[64]

The 'great bulk' of the several hundred people living in Knoydart, Fraser found on getting to Inverie, that locality's principal settlement, were as hard-pressed as their Arisaig counterparts. Knoydart's owner, Alexander MacDonell of Glengarry, headed a family that had owned the estate since medieval times but, despite this, he took little or no interest in what happened there. 'The most remarkable feature in the case of Knoydart,' Andrew Fraser wrote, 'is that, amidst all the privations of the people, the proprietor has about 15 bolls [nearly a ton] of meal in a store at Inverie which might as well be in China.' This store had been 'shut up about Christmas' and, since then, 'a single pound [could] not be [got from it] for love or money'.[65]

'I have not a doubt,' Fraser stated when summarising the results of his west coast trip, 'that, but for the relief afforded [to Knoydart, Arisaig and Moidart] in December by the Free Church, many would have died of starvation in all these districts.' Before his return to Fort William, the sheriff explained, he had been able to arrange – thanks to the funds made available to him by the Destitution Fund's central board – that all the places he had visited would receive new stocks of food from the government's Tobermory or Portree depots. These would have the effect of pulling Moidart, Arisaig and Knoydart back from the brink of disaster. Elsewhere, however, deaths from hunger continued to occur.[66]

Two of those, at Morvich in Kintail, were investigated by George Pole just prior to his early February departure for England. One of the dead, survived by her husband, was a mother of six children. The other, a further member of the same household, was the children's grandmother. Pole, who landed from the *Firefly* near the head of Loch Duich and then walked 'a few miles' into Morvich was impressed, as so many other visitors to this area have been, by 'the magnificent scenery' he found himself among. But the 'sickness' and the 'want of proper nourishment' apparent everywhere he went in this 'thickly peopled' locality – its population swollen by families turned out of the area's inland glens to make way for sheep – caused Pole to conclude that the place had been 'wretchedly neglected' by its proprietor, Keith William Stewart-MacKenzie, who lived in some style at Brahan Castle on the other side of the Highlands.[67]

When Pole's findings (based partly on what he learned from the 'weak and emaciated' husband of the younger of the two dead women) reached Edward Pine Coffin, the commissary-general wrote to Stewart-MacKenzie and asked him to do more for his Kintail tenantry. This was not well received at Brahan Castle, Stewart-Makenzie taking exception both to what he called Pole's 'unfounded charges' and to 'the tone' of Coffin's letter – this tone not being in accord, the Brahan laird complained, with what was to be expected from 'a public servant'. 'You must permit me,' Stewart-MacKenzie informed Coffin, 'to tell you that my family and its tenants in Kintail have been connected now for more than 600 years.'[68]

Coffin, who appears by this stage to have had more than enough of the pretensions of Highland Scotland's landed gentry, was unrepentant. 'I am neither ignorant nor regardless of the consideration due to the position of your family,' he told Stewart-MacKenzie, 'but I cannot admit that it ought for a moment to have stopped me in the discharge of an irksome but necessary duty. The relation in which you stand to the property and population which formed the subject of my letter might render the imputed neglect of them more inexplicable but not, if justly imputed, the less open to animadversion.' George Pole's assessment of conditions in Kintail, Coffin went on, had been substantiated by others – notably Sheriff Andrew Fraser who had also spent time there. 'I have no desire to exaggerate the present or prospective distress of the country,' Coffin told Stewart-MacKenzie. 'But I assuredly will not, out of personal regard of any kind, suppress or extenuate facts which I have reason to consider well substantiated.'[69]

From his Oban office, during the opening weeks of 1847, Edward Pine Coffin mailed several such letters to Highlands and Islands landlords. Some had no effect. Others, especially after Charles Trevelyan arranged for much of Coffin's correspondence to be published, produced some movement. By the winter's end, for instance, there were signs that even John Gordon of Cluny was beginning to yield at least a little to Coffin's urgings. These were given added force by the outcome of inquiries made by Lochmaddy's sheriff-substitute, Charles Shaw, into the death in South Uist at the beginning of March of a woman called Ann O'Henley or Gillies – Gillies being the surname of Ann's husband who had died some time previously.

Ann's home, which she shared with her four children, was one of several houses in Gugary,* a little settlement on rising ground a mile or two east of the larger community of Smeircleit at the southern tip of South Uist. Ann's family, Sheriff Shaw was told by Donald Gillies, only 12 but now the family's oldest surviving member, had lacked food throughout the winter – 'having had no crop in the ground but potatoes which failed'. They had eaten 'their few poultry long ago', Donald said, and had then, in Shaw's words, 'subsisted on begging'. Even this had become impossible during February, Shaw learned. For much of that time South Uist, like the rest of the Highlands and Islands, had been affected by heavy snowfalls; and because the children had 'no shoes' and very little in the way of clothes, said Marion, Donald's ten-year-old sister, they 'could not [then] go out'.[70]

'During the snow,' Marion went on, 'they were three days without food.' On the third day, she added, 'they got a bowl of meal from a neighbour . . . made gruel of it and drank it all at once.' Even before the snow and cold had kept the children at home, Shaw heard, their mother had eaten almost nothing 'in order', Donald said, 'that she might give them [himself, his brother and his two sisters] any little food she could collect'. Neighbours, it seems, had done what they could to help. But their own resources being next to non-existent, this was not a great deal. 'On the day of [Ann O'Henley's] death,' Sheriff Shaw was told by one of those neighbours, Flora Johnston, 'one of [Ann's] children came to [her] home and said to her that his mother was dead.' She had run 'into the house', Flora continued, and found Ann 'lying on some straw at the fireside, her head on her eldest boy [Donald's] knee'. Because the house contained only one blanket, 'and that one in tatters', there had been nothing with which to cover Ann's body, Flora said, until she herself 'got linen for that purpose'.[71]

On one of the several days in February 1847 when the Isle of Mull was swept by squalls of snow, a Commissariat officer serving on the *Belvidera*, then

---

* Gugary no longer exists. It is likely to have been located in the vicinity of a burn, Abhainn Dubh-ghearraidh, readily anglicised to Dugary, which flows into Loch Aiseabhat not far from Smeircleit. The author is grateful to Cailean Maclean and other contributors to the South Uist Facebook page for help in fixing Dugary's position.

anchored in Tobermory Bay, set out to walk, by his own account, 'some miles over the hills . . . with a gun in his hand'. He did not expect to shoot any game, said this officer, a Captain Rose. But he took his gun with him to make his true purpose less obvious to people who might otherwise have wondered why he and the Gaelic-speaking colleague accompanying him were out and about in such bitter weather. His real aim, Rose explained, was to 'satisfy . . . [himself] of the condition of some families who had been represented to [him] as very destitute'. That these reports were accurate he was soon in no doubt. In the course of his walk, Rose wrote, he 'witnessed . . . misery' of a sort he hoped 'never . . . to see again'.[72]

'In one cottage,' Rose continued, 'there was a poor woman, quite a cripple from paralysis, with a family of no less than eight young children, with starvation on their countenances, cowering over a wretched turf fire in the middle of the cottage floor, who, though it was late in the afternoon, described themselves as not having tasted a particle of food that day, and their looks left no doubt of the truth of the assertion. The father had been out since morning seeking for work, though in a most infirm state of health, and the frost and snow gave him little hope of finding any. The storm was finding its way in through every crevice of the roof, and there was neither food nor covering [meaning bedclothes] in the house . . . It was a picture of wretchedness . . . My sister had raised, and sent me, some money to be applied to cases of this kind, so I was fortunately able to relieve them.'

In his formal role as the *Belvidera*'s enforcer of Treasury rules and strictures, Captain Rose had little freedom of manoeuvre. On that snowy day in Mull, however, the cash collected by his sister, coupled with his wish to see at first hand what Mull people were going through, enabled Rose, for a few hours at least, to give full rein to more generous impulses than the Treasury permitted. That winter there would be other instances of individuals in other official positions doing something similar. Of these, none is more striking than the way Inverness-shire's sheriff principal, William Fraser-Tytler, chose to respond to a criminal case involving families living on the Harris Estate.

Harris, at this point, was owned by the seventh Earl of Dunmore, Charles Murray, whose grandfather, a Lowland laird, had bought the island (from yet another landed bankrupt) in 1834. The earl, however, was a boy of five and management, therefore, was in the hands of his widowed mother, Countess Catherine, and her close adviser, an ex-military man by the name of William Sitwell. Both Sitwell and the countess were anxious, they insisted, to set Harris on a path very different from the one that had for years been followed there and elsewhere in the Highlands and Islands. What they wanted, Sitwell told Lord Advocate Rutherfurd, was to give the generality of Harris people some sort of stake in the enormous acreage (Sitwell reckoned it amounted to well over 95 per cent of the estate) tenanted by just four farmers. His problem, Sitwell went on, was that the farmers in question (the most prominent of whom had amassed his huge landholding when serving as estate factor) were 'standing out upon their rights as granted by their leases'. This meant that not so much as a square inch could be restored to people who, as Sitwell put it, had been 'huddled into corners to make places for the flocks and herds of these rich men'. The four farmers, William Sitwell wrote, occupied in its entirety Harris's Atlantic coast, the part of the island that was by far the most productive agriculturally. The rest of the population, which Sitwell put at more than 4,500,* had been left with nothing but patches of 'rocky soil' that were 'wholly unsuited to their sure support even when potatoes were to be relied on'. With potatoes gone, it came as no surprise that, during the closing weeks of 1846, Harris's population was declared by Sheriff Charles Shaw to be 'on the eve of starvation' – a state of affairs that goes a long way to explaining what happened when, towards the end of November, a cargo ship ran aground on one of the many reefs in the shallow sound separating Harris from North Uist.[73]

This ship, the Greenock-owned *Superb*, inward-bound to Glasgow from New York, was carrying more than 6,000 barrels of flour. Although too badly damaged to be refloated, the grounded ship was, to begin with, in one piece and, the crew having been rescued, there were hopes that much of its cargo might be transferred to other vessels sent from the Clyde with this aim in view. But by mid December, when the now storm-battered *Superb* began to come apart, that plan had to be abandoned. The ship's copper sheathing, its masts, bowsprit and anything else that might someday be salvaged were advertised for sale to anyone foolhardy enough to buy them; and, since the safety of the 'watch' or guard that had been 'kept on board all night' could no longer be guaranteed, this watch was now withdrawn. The predictable result, Sheriff Shaw reported, was that, under cover of darkness, barrel after barrel of flour began to be taken off the *Superb* by men to whom the ship's grounding must have seemed a God-given opportunity to supply themselves and their families with desperately needed food.[74]

'The discovery of the guilty parties,' Shaw informed William Fraser-Tytler, 'was attended with great difficulty because [prior to the *Superb* being

---

* Harris's population, at the 1841 census, was 4,429.

abandoned] a vast number of broken barrels [were] thrown overboard, some of them having a peck or two of flour in them, and thus any person with whom flour was found accounted for it by saying it was part of . . . [the] flour contained in these broken barrels.' While Shaw was certain that others from both the North Uist and Harris sides of the sound had taken part, the folk who mounted most raids on the wrecked vessel, Shaw understood, came from the island of Berneray – the place nearest to what was left of the *Superb*. Although close to the coast of North Uist, to which it is has been linked by a causeway since 1999, Berneray was a part of the Harris Estate and, in December 1846, its people were as hard-pressed as everyone else on that property. 'I believe the greater part of the population of Berneray, 800 in number, are involved in the business,' Shaw wrote. Altogether, he was sure, they had 'stolen hundreds of barrels'. But for lack of evidence, he had been able to arrest just eight men who were honest (or foolish) enough to admit to having gone one night to the *Superb* and, between them, taken away 16 barrels of flour. Those men, Shaw reported on 11 January, had now been formally accused of theft. Because so serious a charge meant, in his opinion, that they should at once be imprisoned – and because there was no nearer jail where they could be held – he had sent all eight to Inverness where he expected them to be kept in custody until their trial.[75]

The eight came from two Berneray townships, Ruisgarry and Borve. On getting to Inverness, they were installed in a just-completed prison block in the town's newly built 'castle' or courthouse. At the insistence of Fraser-Tytler, who thought they should have been tried and 'leniently dealt with' by Shaw in Lochmaddy, the eight (whose fellow prisoners included the two 76th Regiment soldiers, Dennis Driscoll and James Ball, awaiting trial for attempted rape) were promptly granted special privileges. Within a day or two of their arrival, they also received a visit from the sheriff principal. 'Your poor fellows from Berneray are as comfortable as their anxieties for their families can allow them to be,' Fraser-Tytler told Charles Shaw. 'I found them busy at work yesterday, making nets in a large room with a good fire. Pray let their families know this.'[76]

A day or two before, as it happened, Fraser-Tytler had received 'from a benevolent friend', as he put it, the then very considerable sum of £50 which the friend, 'a clergyman in the Church of England', wanted spent on famine relief measures in the Hebrides. This cash was now forwarded by Fraser-Tytler to Shaw with the instruction that a part of it was to be used to ensure that 'none of [the Berneray men's] families suffered any additional privation from their absence'.[77]

Informing Lord Advocate Rutherfurd of his meeting with the eight prisoners, Fraser-Tytler commented: 'I took occasion to learn from [them] . . . something of the statistics of their country.' Notes arising from the resulting interviews – necessarily conducted with the help of an interpreter because most of the Berneray men spoke little or no English – were subsequently forwarded by the sheriff principal to Rutherfurd and to Lady Dunmore. To read these notes is to understand why William Fraser-Tytler, who is unlikely to have been exposed previously to first-hand accounts of deprivation and hunger, 'could not,' as he wrote, 'get [these] poor fellows out of [his] head'.[78]

From Donald Campbell whose croft 'of about four acres' was home to himself, his wife, his baby girl, his mother and four of his sisters, Fraser-Tytler heard that Campbell's annual rent, together with other charges levied by the estate, was in excess of £6 annually – a figure which, allowing for the massive fall in money values that has taken place over the last 170 or so years, is extraordinarily high by present-day standards. Rent demands of this sort always made for difficulties. But those difficulties, subsequent to blight's arrival, had become acute. Since the autumn, Donald Campbell said, he and the other members of his household had been 'obliged to eat their [two or three] sheep and consume most of the grain which they should have kept for seed'.[79]

So it continued. William MacDonald shared his small croft with his widowed mother, his three sisters and two orphaned nieces. Donald Paterson, who had 'no croft of [his] own', lived with his brother whom Paterson described as 'a tailor in bad health'. For months past, Paterson said, his brother and himself had been reliant on their mother who, being 'a pauper' and entered as such on the local poor roll, was eligible for aid from the Harris Parochial Board. On this aid, consisting of 'one half stone [or seven pounds] of meal per week', all three had somehow contrived to get by: 'There [was] no money in the family. It was all done.'

Malcolm MacLeod, a single man, worked a croft – its rent as high as Donald Campbell's – with his father, a man of about 70. This croft was also home to Malcolm's mother, his brother and his sister. Since he was the 'principal support of the family', Malcolm said, he was desperately worried as to how, in his absence, his kinsfolk were making out on an island where, as Fraser-Tytler was told by another prisoner, Angus Morrison, 'nothing but starvation' was to be seen 'on every side'.

William Paterson, at 23 the eldest son in a family of ten, helped his father and mother on a croft where he had 'killed the four sheep they had' for food.

His parents, himself, his brothers and his sisters 'did not see a potato of last year's planting', he told Fraser-Tytler. 'It was hunger and famine staring himself and his father's numerous family in the face,' William said, that had 'induced him' to take flour from the *Superb*. With this, it seems, the whole Berneray contingent agreed. Apart from their saying that 'they thought all the flour would be lost [to] the sea' and that they thus saw nothing wrong in taking it, the eight men, when speaking with Sheriff Fraser-Tyler anyway, 'made no attempt to deny their guilt'. The 'sight of their starving families,' more than one man said, 'drove them' to do what they had done.

The meeting at which Fraser-Tytler jotted down those statements took place on Sunday 17 January. On leaving the prison, the sheriff, a man of no small personal wealth, sought out the Inverness lawyer who acted for him on matters having to do with the Fraser-Tytler family's ownership of the Aldourie Estate at the north end of Loch Ness. On the following morning, this lawyer was told, he was at once to bail the eight Berneray prisoners and, on getting them out of jail, have them conveyed at once to the sheriff's home, Aldourie Castle. That was done. On the Monday, Donald Campbell, Malcolm MacLeod, Angus Morrison and the five other Berneray men were, in effect, set free. By the Thursday following, as William Fraser-Tytler told the lord advocate, 'they [were] busy employed with [the sheriff's] other labourers' on landscaping and drainage projects then ongoing at Aldourie.[80]

In that same letter, Inverness-shire's sheriff principal asked the lord advocate to sanction what he now proposed – this being to have the former prisoners formally admonished and sent home. Andrew Rutherfurd's assent to this suggestion reached Fraser-Tytler on Thursday 28 January. Next day, the eight men were 'sent for' – as was Ewen MacKenzie, a Church of Scotland minister whose parish included Aldourie. MacKenzie, who came from the Fort William area, was a Gaelic-speaker. 'With the help of [that] good minister,' Fraser-Tytler informed Charles Shaw, '[I] gave [the Berneray men] a most serious admonition before communicating to them that I was now enabled to let them go home to their families on their solemn promise of future good conduct. They seemed much impressed, and several of them shed tears of gratitude for the leniency that had been shown them.'[81]

Days later, and presumably at William Fraser-Tytler's expense, the eight men were put aboard a steamer that took them down Loch Ness and on to Oban where they were able to connect with a further steamer for the Outer Isles. No record was made of their homecoming. But by Charles Shaw, and to Fraser-Tytler's evident chagrin, a notably sour note was struck. The

Berneray eight, Shaw pointed out, had been guilty of 'stealing the value of upwards of £20 of property . . . Yet they are allowed to go unpunished'. This, Shaw argued, sent an unfortunate signal. Already, he informed Fraser-Tytler, he had heard word of plans being made to take 'forcible possession' of 500 barrels of flour which had been salvaged successfully from the *Superb* and were now in storage at Lochmaddy. It was unclear if anything would come of this, Shaw wrote. But that there was such talk was worrying; and it arose, he felt, from what had been done in Inverness and at Aldourie. 'There is no-one who has the slightest particle of human pity in his bosom,' Shaw continued, 'but must deeply feel for the state of these poor people, and to the fullest extent I admit the propriety of taking . . . [their] destitution . . . into consideration [when] dealing with [the Berneray] case, but I am humbly of opinion that this ought rather to lead [to] leniency in . . . punishment than to the course which has been adopted.'[82]

Perhaps Shaw, who felt that his authority had been undermined by the sheriff principal's actions, exaggerated the risk of trouble breaking out in North Uist. Certainly that island, like the rest of the area for which Charles Shaw was responsible, remained quiet for the remainder of the 1846–47 winter. Nor is this surprising. Where life-threatening hunger already has a population in its grip, mass protest happens rarely. But as Sir George Sinclair observed of the Pulteneytown disturbances, and as Elizabeth Waters would afterwards tell Sarah MacPherson of Cluny, matters are different in places where starvation, though not actually occurring, is thought imminent. In these circumstances, people fearing for themselves and for their families might well do whatever they think necessary to stave off disaster. At the start of 1847, this was very much the position, not in North Uist but at the other end of Inverness-shire. It was there, and in places further east, that violence of the sort feared by Charles Shaw was now to erupt.

4

'A pointed pistol in each hand'

Grantown-on-Spey • Fort William • Aberdeen • Fraserburgh
St Combs • Inverallochy • Cairnbulg • Pitullie • Cullen
Macduff • Portgordon • Portknockie • Findochty
Portessie • Buckie • Garmouth • Fochabers

Two or three weeks into January 1847, while William Fraser-Tytler was dealing with the fall-out from Berneray people's seizure of flour from the *Superb*, he learned of further food-related crimes in a different part of his sheriffdom. The focus of these was Grantown. Located just north of the Spey and near the spot where that river flows out of Inverness-shire into Moray,* Grantown, like Pulteneytown, is a place that owes its existence to efforts to grow the Highland economy. Planned by a development-minded laird towards the close of the eighteenth century, Grantown, by the 1840s, consisted of a large central square surrounded by regularly laid-out streets containing, not just row after row of well-built homes, but inns, banks, shops and other commercial premises. This, then, was a prosperous settlement and one whose 1,000 or so people, according to their Church of Scotland minister, were 'sober, honest and industrious'. Now those same people, it was reported, had made their normally quiet community 'a scene of tumult and disturbance'. This uproar's cause, it seemed, was the arrival in town of a little convoy of horse-drawn wagons from Fort William.[1]

Throughout December and into the new year, Edward Pine Coffin had been getting warnings that a number of Fort William's inhabitants, many of them refugees from clearances elsewhere in Lochaber, were 'in actual starvation'. Cash had been collected locally in an attempt 'to supply the immediate

---

* Local authority boundaries in Strathspey and Speyside have changed repeatedly over the last 200 years. Here the boundaries mentioned are those of the mid nineteenth century.

wants' of the hungry. But with food costs going up fast, Fort William's numerous poor – concentrated in hovel-like homes strung out along the town's waterfront* – were clearly in dire straits. 'There is neither barley nor pease-meal to be got in this place,' Coffin was told by one of Fort William's more prominent residents on 13 January. '[The] supply of oatmeal at the present time is small and the price extravagantly high'. So steeply were prices rising, in fact, that it became worthwhile for Fort William merchants to hire carters to transport fresh supplies from Grantown where, it was reported, the 1846 oat crop had 'greatly exceed[ed] the produce of ordinary years'.[2]

The 75-mile trek from Fort William to Grantown, by way of Kinlochlaggan and Newtonmore, became a little easier in January when a temporary rise in temperature thawed some of December's snows and made overland travel more feasible than it had been. In Grantown, however, the beginnings of this new trade with Lochaber were viewed with suspicion by townsfolk who, though previously the beneficiaries of the good grain harvest in their own locality, worried that they might now become victims of scarcity. Those anxieties were heightened by what Sheriff Fraser-Tytler afterwards called the 'misconduct' of Grantown's meal-dealers. Until January, those men had been happy to supply what Fraser-Tytler called 'the lower classes' with, as the sheriff put it, 'meal per stone'. But 'in consequence of the demand from Lochaber', Fraser-Tytler went on, this practice had been abandoned, Grantown dealers now refusing 'to sell in less quantity than per boll'. Although dealers thought it 'more convenient', and certainly more profitable, to thus 'dispose of . . . stock wholesale', their local customers, formerly able to purchase meal in 14-pound bags, now found themselves barred from buying less than 140 pounds at a time. With per-pound prices also rocketing, this 'so incensed the populace', the *Inverness Courier* observed, that on Wednesday 20 January, a day that saw no fewer than eight Fort William wagons roll into Grantown, 'a meeting of the inhabitants was convened by tuck of drum† to consider what steps should be taken'. No more meal, this meeting resolved, should be sent from Grantown to Lochaber.[3]

---

* During the later nineteenth century, those homes were demolished to make way for the railway linking Fort William with Glasgow. Towards the close of the twentieth century, this railway's terminus was moved out of the town centre, making it possible for a now redundant section of rail track to be replaced by a dual carriageway.

† Rousing a town to action by means of sending a drummer through the streets was a long-standing practice in Scotland.

That evening 'several hundred' people 'congregated' in the town square with the intention of putting this resolution into effect. From the square the crowd 'proceeded to the lodgings of the Lochaber men and carried off [their] carts'. These, it was announced, would not be returned until their owners agreed to depart without meal. No such concession being forthcoming, the carts were promptly 'unwheeled' and the wheels taken away to be hidden. Next evening, with the Fort William carters still declaring their willingness 'to give a high price' for such meal as Grantown dealers had in store, a crowd again assembled – with the stated aim, this time, of forcing the Fort William men to go home with neither meal nor carts. On the locality's two policemen trying to quieten things down by taking a protest leader into custody, 'the mob,' commented the *Inverness Courier*, 'rescued him and a scuffle ensued in the course of which both officials were struck to the effusion of blood'.[4]

Renewed confrontation occurred on Monday of the following week when William Colquhoun, another of Fraser-Tytler's sheriff-substitutes, reached Grantown from Inverness at the head of a posse of constables. Several men who had been prominent participants in the previous Thursday's fracas were at once tracked down and arrested. 'But when the prisoners were about to be driven off to Inverness,' the *Courier* reported, 'a mob [attacked] the authorities and rescued [them].' The one thing that had been accomplished, Sheriff Fraser-Tytler noted ruefully, was that Grantown's meal merchants had belatedly 'seen their folly . . . and now advertise in their windows meal per stone'. From the Grantown community's perspective, the sheriff acknowledged, this was something of a victory. But it was 'most unfortunate', he commented, that it had been 'gained by popular . . . violence'. Nor, to Fraser-Tytler's chagrin, was what had happened in Grantown to be a one-off occurrence. There would be plenty more such episodes in the days ahead. One of the first took place in Aberdeen.[5]

In that fast-growing city, on the Friday of the week that saw the start of Grantown's troubles, there were said to be 'apprehensions of a riot taking place' in response to 'the present high prices of provisions'. Those fears stemmed from 'a number of people [having] assembled here and there' in shopping thoroughfares like Union Street, Castle Street and Marischal Street. Still more 'ominous', it was thought, was the way those gatherings were augmented by 'about 200 . . . railway labourers' who had marched into the city with, at their head, 'a black flag' – a banner much favoured by protest marchers until it was supplanted, in the later nineteenth century, by the red flags adopted by socialist groupings. The newly arrived labourers, it appears, had walked from Kincardine where they were constructing the railway that, two or three years later, would connect Aberdeen with Dundee and points south. But for all that railway navvies like them had something of a reputation as habitual battlers with the forces of law and order, neither they nor the Aberdonian crowds they linked up with engaged in any immediate violence. Although one contingent began 'yelling and causing a considerable disturbance' outside the city council's headquarters in what was called the town house, most of the people on the streets moved off to the Links, an area of open land between the city centre and the sea. There, according to the *Aberdeen Journal*, 'distressing details were given of the state to which many [had] been reduced' by January's sudden rise in the cost of basic foodstuffs.[6]

One key grievance voiced at the Links stemmed from a widespread suspicion that meal prices were going up because more and more grain was being shipped south from the city's harbour. This, it was agreed, was a point that should be put to Aberdeen's lord provost, Thomas Blaikie, by a deputation elected from among the 900-strong Links crowd. Blaikie, for his part, had already shown himself willing to engage in dialogue with protesters by quitting his town house office to talk with some of the people milling about outside. Despite his having told those people that it was 'folly . . . to disturb the public peace', the provost, a local industrialist, was by no means out of sympathy with them. At a council meeting he called four days later, Blaikie would 'allude . . . in very feeling terms to the condition of many parties who, though earning fair wages, must yet have their comforts greatly abridged, and their wants but scantily supplied, at the present time from . . . the dearth of provisions'. Now, speaking at the town house with delegates sent there from the Links, he told them he and council colleagues were already arranging to meet 'with the principal grain merchants in Aberdeen' – men who, when pressed by the lord provost, 'expressed an earnest desire to co-operate with the [council]' and 'agreed in the meantime not to purchase more grain for shipment'.[7]

Prior to this news becoming generally known, attacks were mounted on cartloads of meal being taken to the harbour, while in Castle Street and Marischal Street shop windows were smashed. The weekend, however, passed without incident and, at the start of the following week, Thomas Blaikie was able to report to the home secretary in London that 'tranquility [had] been restored' by measures taken to address 'symptoms of discontent . . . manifested among the working classes'. Prominent among those measures were the concessions that Blaikie, in the course of the preceding Friday, had managed to secure from his city's grain traders. On that same Friday, although nothing of this was then known in Aberdeen, identical concessions were being noisily demanded some 40 miles to the north in the fishing port of Fraserburgh.[8]

At Fraserburgh, Baillie Lewis Chalmers, the local businessman who was the town's counterpart to Thomas Blaikie, found himself confronting 'some hundreds of fishermen . . . and other people', many of them reportedly 'armed with bludgeons' and all of them 'determined on violent measures . . . to stop shipments of grain'. In an attempt to restore order, Chalmers set about swearing in a number of special constables. But on several of the tradesmen and merchants whom he summonsed for this duty refusing to take the necessary oath, the baillie decided to send an 'express' – by which was meant a mounted messenger – to Aberdeen to ask for help from the military. When, early on Saturday morning, this man reached the city, there was some delay in complying with Chalmers's request – the Aberdeen authorities being reluctant to deprive themselves of any of the few troops quartered in the city's Castlehill Barracks until they were sure that Friday's unrest was truly at an end. Eventually, however, 40 soldiers were packed into requisitioned stagecoaches and sent north – only to be met, 5 miles south of Fraserburgh, with the news that their services were no longer required because Baillie Chalmers had meanwhile entered into 'a sort of truce with the fishermen'. Much as in Aberdeen, this truce consisted principally of an agreement on the part of Fraserburgh grain merchants to halt shipments from the harbour for a period – eight days in the Fraserburgh case – during which Chalmers undertook, as Aberdeen's town council had also done, to find ways of 'securing a supply of meal for the poorer classes'. Although there would be renewed trouble in Fraserburgh when a further shipment was attempted by an out-of-town merchant who claimed he knew nothing of the baillie's deal, Lewis Chalmers was reckoned, even by people critical of the speed with which he gave in to street protest, to have averted a conflict that might easily have ended, or so it was feared, in bloodshed.[9]

In Fraserburgh, on Friday 22 January 1847, local residents had been joined, and very possibly urged into action, by people from nearby villages like St Combs, Inverallochy, Cairnbulg and Pitullie. These were fishing communities where, that winter, conditions were grim and every day, it seemed, getting grimmer. In each of the four villages as well as in Fraserburgh itself, the *Aberdeen Herald* reported, 'a good deal of murmuring' had 'for some time past' been heard 'among the seafaring and labouring classes . . . on account of the high prices of food' – high prices 'doubly felt,' the paper continued, 'on account of the total failure of the potato crop'. Here in Aberdeenshire, to be sure, dependence on potatoes was much less absolute than in the West Highlands and Islands. But fishing families, for all that, relied to no small extent on their potato plots. Loss of those plots' output would thus have caused difficulties at any time. But because blight's arrival, as the *Herald* pointed out, had coincided with a severe downturn in incomes from fishing, those difficulties had become acute.[10]

Like Wick and Pulteneytown, Fraserburgh and the coastal villages in its vicinity had been hard hit towards the close of 1846 by collapsing demand for herring. Curers in Aberdeenshire, as in Caithness, were no longer giving cash advances to crews and, knowing this, meal-dealers and shopkeepers were refusing credit to fishing families. This might not have mattered so much had Aberdeenshire fishermen – who, unlike most Caithness fishers, went to sea all year round – landed reasonable amounts of the whitefish they counted on in winter. But whitefish catches, because of incessant bad weather, had been poor. In the Fraserburgh district, or so the *Aberdeen Herald* estimated at the end of January, 'fishermen [had] not averaged [earnings] much above 30 shillings, certainly not to the extent of £2 per man, [during the previous] five months'. When unavoidable expenses were deducted from these meagre sums, the paper calculated, fishermen, that winter, had been 'losers to a great extent'. Hence the spread of hunger: 'The condition of nearly three-fourths of the population is deplorable. To our knowledge, [some] families have been living on turnips . . . with a handful of meal cast in among them. Others have been without meal or bread in their houses for days. Want in many cases is to be seen depicted on their countenances and it is reported, on good evidence, that two deaths have occurred [from], or at least been hastened by, want of sufficient nourishment.' Given these bleak circumstances, the *Aberdeen Herald* concluded, it was scarcely surprising that Fraserburgh streets had filled with fishermen 'demanding relief for themselves and their families'.[11]

Nor was the Fraserburgh area's plight in any way unique. Between that area, at the eastern end of the Moray Firth's south coast, and Inverness, at the same coast's western end, were lots of settlements whose fisher families, at the start of 1847, were doing little or no better than people in St Combs, Inverallochy and Cairnbulg. Among those settlements were, from east to west, Macduff, Banff, Portsoy, Sandend, Cullen, Portknockie, Findochty, Portessie, Buckie, Portgordon, Garmouth, Lossiemouth, Hopeman, Burghead, Findhorn, Nairn and Ardersier. Some of these places were more populous than others; some had existed for less than a century; others were age-old. All, however, were involved, often heavily, in fishing. And though each had its own identity of which its inhabitants were insistently proud, all such communities had a good deal in common – something apparent in their shared tendency to have little in the way of close contact with nearby, but inland, localities. 'They form a society quite distinct,' a Banffshire clergyman noted of the fisherfolk among his congregation. But despite their keeping themselves to themselves socially, culturally and in other ways, those same fisherfolk – most of them more than willing to innovate, experiment, take risks – were happy to participate in Victorian Britain's fast-growing economy.[12]

Fishermen based on the Moray Firth's southern coast had for generations depended for the most part on baited-line fishing for haddock, cod, ling, halibut and other species – resulting catches being sold largely into local markets. In the course of the nineteenth century's opening decades, however, this pattern changed radically. With southern ports now accessible by means of new and ever more rapid steamship services, whitefish began to be smoked for sale in urban centres as far away as London. At the same time, summer drift netting for herring was taken up on a scale that quickly challenged Caithness's initial dominance of the cured herring trade. Together, those developments had the effect of boosting incomes to unprecedented levels. That was why Cullen's Church of Scotland minister, writing in 1842, had 'no hesitation in stating it as his decided conviction that there are comparatively few of the working-classes in Scotland whose labours are so amply remunerated as those of the fishermen on this coast'.[13]

Prior to the mid 1840s, then, what most commentators were inclined to stress about Cullen and equivalent communities was their growing prosperity. Fishing families, it was said, dressed well, lived in 'mostly slated' homes and, as could be seen from 'the style of their . . . furniture', were invariably better off than 'their forefathers'. All of this contrasted markedly with the penury so prevalent in Highlands and Islands crofting districts. It contrasted too, as clerical and other observers noted, with the nearer-hand hardships commonly experienced by Moray, Banffshire and Aberdeenshire farm labourers – hired by their farmer employers for no more than six months at a time, poorly paid, worse housed and forever on the move.[14]

Fishing, for all that, remained a perennially dangerous occupation – a point made strongly by Maggie Mucklebackit, the fish-seller who is one of Walter Scott's more memorable creations, when, on the morning following a storm, a local laird questions the price Maggie is charging for her menfolk's catch. 'Div ye think,' says Maggie, 'that my man and my sons are to gae to the sea in weather like yestreen . . . and get naething for their fish . . . It's no fish ye're buying – it's men's lives.' The exchange is a powerful one; not just because Maggie so forcefully drives home the hazards fishermen confronted; but in the way she dares to take issue with a social superior. A fictional character Maggie Mucklebackit may have been. But all along the Moray Firth coastline, in the middle years of the nineteenth century, it would have been possible, one senses, to come across women just like her – women who, in the case of Mary Jack, Isabella Main and Margaret Main from Hopeman, had the self-assuredness it took to seek an audience with Queen Victoria.[15]

One Banffshire clergyman described the typical fisherwoman as 'handsome, good-looking and the very picture of health'. Another, Alexander Anderson, minister at Boyndie near Banff, thought that, in fishing communities, 'the wife occupie[d] a far more important position in the family' than her counterparts elsewhere. A fisherman's wife, Anderson conceded, did not have things easy. 'In addition to the ordinary domestic duties,' he wrote, 'she is subjected to the daily labour of baiting lines and preparing fish for sale.' Aided perhaps by her daughters, the same woman was then expected to undertake 'the formidable task of carrying fish to market' – something that might involve a walk 'of many miles' into the surrounding countryside or to some inland town where fish could be exchanged for cash or for other goods like meal, butter or cheese. In any fishing community, then, women's role was nothing if not demanding. But it was also basic to the community's success. Hence the common saying that 'no man [could] be a fisher and want a wife'. Hence too Revd Alexander Anderson's disapproving observation that, in fishing families, wives 'adopt[ed] a tone and [were] allowed an influence which, in another condition of life, would appear little consistent either with feminine propriety or domestic order'. Women of this sort – women who had lately taken to attending church dressed in 'white muslin caps or straw bonnets' and with 'red cloaks or tartan scarfs' thrown over their shoulders* – were unlikely to be passive in the face of the threat posed to their own and their menfolk's newfound affluence by the crisis that gripped so many fishing communities in the winter of 1846–47.[16]

Aberdeenshire, Banffshire and Moray farmers were doing better in January 1847 than were those counties' fishermen. Five or six months earlier, admittedly, the potato crop in all three areas had been 'utterly destroyed'. But cereal

---

* When they met with Earl Grey at Ardverikie, it is more than likely that Margaret Main, Isabella Main and Mary Jack were wearing 'Sunday best' outfits of this type.

yields had been good, and farmers were understandably anxious to cash in on spiralling demand for wheat, oats and barley in the Scottish Lowlands and in England where upward price pressure caused by the loss of potatoes had been intensified by a poor grain harvest. In principle, Corn Law repeal should have led to Britain's cereal shortfalls being made good by imports from overseas. But bad weather in the Atlantic, combined with winter freezing of the rivers and canals that were the means of getting North American wheat to US and Canadian ports, meant that cereal shipments from overseas appeared, for the moment at least, to be as scarce as ever. Hence the opportunity that now opened up to the north of Scotland's arable farmers. As far back as November, there had been reports of 'a considerable export of grain' from the region's east coast harbours. By January, when 'no fewer than 15 vessels' took on grain at one such harbour in just a few days, shipments to the Lowlands and to England were on a previously unmatched scale. During the 1845–46 winter, outflows of this sort from Fraserburgh, for example, had totalled 2,459 bolls in the four months to February. In 1846–47, in the course of the same four months, the total was three and a half times greater – at 8,690 bolls or some 550 tons.[17]

Increased grain movements of this sort were, in one sense, no more than a classic instance of the price mechanism at work. When there is famine and scarcity, more is paid for such foodstuffs as are available. This, in turn, means that producers and stockists who might normally sell only into nearby markets find themselves able to cover – indeed more than cover – the transport costs associated with getting those foodstuffs to increasingly faraway places where prices may well be higher than in their own communities. This was why, in January 1847, it made sense for Grantown's meal merchants to begin disposing of big quantities of meal to carters from Lochaber. This was also why it made equal sense, at much the same time, for farmers and grain-dealers in Aberdeenshire, Banffshire, Moray, Caithness and other areas to do something similar – by dispatching cartload after cartload of both meal and unmilled cereals down the roads leading to the nearest ports. Farmers had everywhere been 'tempted to part with a more than ordinary quantity of their grain' to shippers, Banffshire's sheriff was told at the beginning of February 1847. In other years, the sheriff's informant went on, those same farmers had been perfectly willing 'to sell small quantities of meal' to consumers or shopkeepers in their own vicinities. But the 'high prices' being offered in the south meant that this now 'did not pay as well as selling the grain in bulk'.[18]

As far as farmers were concerned, then, it was good business to send more and more grain south. From the perspective of hard-pressed working families in Aberdeen or still harder-pressed fisherfolk in a place like Fraserburgh, however, matters seemed very different. The spectacle of harbour-bound grain carts rumbling through their streets was, to them, a cause of fury. With potatoes no longer available, oatmeal – turned, with minimal effort, into bannocks, oatcakes or porridge – had become those people's dietary staple. But increasingly, as in Grantown and lots more centres, it could no longer be got in amounts – whether a stone or a pound or two – that cash-strapped households could afford. And even where it could still be bought, meal's cost, by January, was rising day by day. Might this be a prelude to out-and-out famine of the kind already gripping Ireland and the Hebrides? Might it make sense, therefore, to stop district after district being denuded of grain and, by means of price controls or other mechanisms, ensure that oatmeal was brought within everyone's reach? By January 1847, there was no lack of people in the Scottish north who thought the answer to such questions should be yes. And especially in fishing communities, where things were particularly bad and where the harbours used by traders were invariably within easy reach, those people were well-placed to do themselves what they felt needed to be done. Nor was there anything novel about the direct action they now took. Protest and riot of the sort that, in January and February, was to occur in communities all around the Moray Firth – from Fraserburgh, by way of Inverness, to Wick – had a long history.

When, in the 1690s, a series of harvest failures brought nationwide scarcity to Scotland, grain carts were seized, ships boarded and their holds emptied by people opposed to interregional trading in grain. Much the same thing happened, for much the same reason, in the 1740s, the 1790s and the early 1800s. Many of the places affected by those outbreaks – places like Fraserburgh, Macduff, Inverness, Dingwall and Cromarty, for example – would again experience disturbance and disorder in 1847. On the ground, much of this new disorder would be very similar in character to what had gone before. Varying rather more across the 150 years between the 1690s and the 1840s was the nature of officialdom's response.[19]

During what were to be recalled as the 'seven ill years' that brought starvation and death to much of 1690s Scotland, the Scottish Privy Council – in effect the country's government – set a 'common price' for grain and, north of the Tay, made it illegal to remove grain from the counties where it had been grown. This was because those counties, or so the Privy Council stated, were 'in hazard to be brought to great extremity by persons carrying victuall out and from these parts to other places where they expect to have higher prices'. What had been banned in the 1690s, however, was never going to be made unlawful in 1847. Plenty of 'persons' might once more have been 'carrying victuall' out of Aberdeenshire, Banffshire and Moray. But while late seventeenth-century Scottish politicians had been willing to deploy the state's powers in order to curtail such practices, the men who ran mid nineteenth-century Britain were in no way disposed to do likewise. That would have been to interfere with market forces, which, as Charles Trevelyan and others kept insisting, were always now to be treated as sacrosanct.[20]

But if national government's commitment to what was starting to be called laissez-faire economics was unshakeable, the men in charge of several north of Scotland localities were to prove more flexible. In 1847, Aberdeen's town council did not do what its predecessor had done in 1696 – buy grain in order to guarantee supplies of food to the city's population. But Thomas Blaikie, the council's head, first listened to what protesters had to say and then, by securing at least a temporary halt to grain shipments, made a significant concession to them. Lewis Chalmers in Fraserburgh acted similarly. So did the authorities in Macduff, scene of the first of 1847's many riots.

Macduff, separated by the estuary of the River Deveron from the nearby and much older burgh of Banff, was one of several harbour towns or villages – Portgordon and Hopeman were others – established in the years just before and after 1800 by landed proprietors looking to boost both commerce and fishing. The place was a success and, by the late 1830s, its harbour, described at the time as 'commodious', was attracting more than 200 cargo ships annually. These brought in lime (used extensively by farmers to improve yields from sour soils), coal, salt (required in quantity by fish-curers) and manufactured goods. Outward-bound freight, taken south by the same ships, consisted mainly of agricultural products – not least grain. But for all that grain had thus been going south from Macduff for some years, the 'enormous shipments' leaving the port in the first two weeks of 1847 were said to be 'unexampled'. It was with a view to calling a halt to those shipments that on Friday 15 January – five days before the Grantown protests and a week before trouble began in Aberdeen – 'a formidable mob' gathered in the town centre with a view to 'barricad[ing] the quays' and thus stopping carts getting to the harbour.[21]

During one of that month's many storms, somewhere out at sea, a southbound ship had shed a cargo of wooden railway sleepers – items in huge demand in 1840s Britain – and, in the days that followed, lots of these had floated ashore in the bay between Macduff and Banff. Now dozens of sleepers, each one of them heavy and hard to move, were used to block off all the streets leading to the harbour. At the harbour itself, meantime, the latest ship to start taking on grain was boarded by people who, to forestall its departure, removed its mainsail which was then carried ashore and concealed. Next day, in order to close the harbour completely, booms or barriers were floated into place across its entrance by 'a number of lads' – acting doubtless with the connivance of, and maybe in accordance with instructions from, their elders. For the moment, then, Macduff's grain trade had been brought to an end.[22]

Co-ordinated effort of this sort must have required a good deal of pre-planning. Who the planners were is unknown. But they are bound to have been gratified by what happened next. When Captain George Davies, the officer in charge of the well-armed coastguard unit based at Banff, offered to use such force as it might take to reopen the harbour, his offer was turned down. Instead Macduff's provost, Alexander Carny, owner of a local rope-works, made it known on Saturday that on Monday he would convene a public meeting 'for the purpose of considering the best means of aiding the labouring poor in procuring meal for support of their families at a rate more in accordance with their means than the prices at which it is now sold'. At this meeting, it was revealed that one of Macduff's corn merchants was prepared to supply the town with 500 bolls of oatmeal at 24 shillings a boll – still above the 20 shillings that would have been charged in December but well below the 32 shillings that had been demanded just a day or two before. Still more welcome was what was said by estate managers representing James Duff, Earl of Fife, much the most significant landowner in the immediate vicinity and a man whose uncle, more than half a century before, had organised and financed the construction of Macduff harbour. The earl, his agents announced at Provost Carny's public meeting, had agreed to make meal available to anyone in need of it. This meal would be issued from Fife Estate stores at 'three grades of prices'. These would all be below market rates – the charge per stone to particular individuals being fixed in accordance with 'their weekly income and the number of their family'.[23]

Well pleased by this outcome, the people whose Friday and Saturday actions had brought it about, removed their booms and barricades from the harbour. That got trade flowing again. But the resumption of normal business notwithstanding, there was now some questioning of what had been done to make this possible. Perhaps the most influential source of such questioning was Thomas Balmer.

From an office in Fochabers, just west of the Banffshire–Moray border and on the main road from Aberdeen to Inverness, Balmer ran the hugely extensive properties – consisting of around 250,000 acres in several northern counties – amassed by successive Dukes of Gordon. In 1836, when the last of those dukes died, his landholdings had been inherited by his nephew, Charles Gordon-Lennox, fifth Duke of Richmond, whose home was in Sussex and whose over-all outlook could scarcely have been more at odds with that of the Banffshire-based Earl of Fife. The earl's politics, though more than a little idiosyncratic, were reformist. The duke's were reactionary. A bitter opponent of the 1829 measure which ended centuries of officially enforced discrimination against Catholics, he was still more fervent in his condemnation of Robert Peel's deci-sion to repeal the Corn Law – denouncing this decision in the House of Lords and becoming president of the Central Agricultural Protection Society set up in 1844 to press for Corn Law retention. Given this history, neither Richmond nor his Fochabers-based commissioner,* as Thomas Balmer was styled, were likely to endorse placatory responses to disorder. And so it proved.

Balmer, whom Richmond had sent north to reorganise and sort out estates thought to have been neglected or mismanaged by their previous owners, was not unaware that times were hard. In early January, recognising that, 'with meal at the present price', the wages paid to the Richmond Estate's own labourers had become 'totally insufficient to keep a family living', he had authorised a temporary uplift in those wages.† But this had been done at Balmer's own initiative and was, to his mind, a better way of dealing with high food costs than Macduff-style price cuts. Instead of supplying protesters with cheap meal, Balmer felt strongly, the Macduff authorities should instantly have crushed their protest. Especially at fault, Balmer believed, was Banffshire's sheriff-substitute, John Pringle. On the day or two following the commence-ment of the harbour blockade at Macduff, Pringle had been happy to go along with the conciliatory approach taken by Provost Carny. This, in Balmer's view, had been a mistake. It was 'deeply to be regretted', Balmer told the Duke of Richmond, that Pringle had not accepted his, Balmer's, advice 'and applied for two or three companies of military at the commencement of the

---

* Also the title given to the Duke of Sutherland's leading land manager, James Loch.

† This was a less generous gesture than might at first sight appear. Richmond Estate wages went from eight shillings to nine shillings and sixpence a week – an increase of under 20 per cent at a point when meal prices were at least 50 or 60 per cent higher than they had been.

riots at Macduff'. As it was, the sheriff, like the provost, had 'insisted on . . . making concessions' – a stance which, Balmer believed, served simply to encourage 'new demands' in other places. It was thus no coincidence, in Balmer's opinion, that, on Monday 18 January, the day the Macduff people's gains became known, he found himself dealing with an outbreak of trouble in one of the coastal villages for which, as Richmond's commissioner, he was himself responsible.[24]

This was Portgordon. A little over 20 miles west of Banff and established, as its name indicates, by one of the Dukes of Gordon, it was a much smaller place than Macduff. But though no more than 500 people lived here in 1847, Portgordon, like Macduff, possessed a harbour capable, as was noted in 1842, of accommodating 'ships of considerable burden'. Again like Macduff, it had thus become one of Banffshire's key outlets for grain earmarked for southern markets. It was this trade that was now targeted, not just by Portgordon's own residents but by fishermen and their families from nearby communities like Portknockie, Findochty, Portessie and Buckie. Of these, Buckie, with a population of around 2,000, was much the largest, and it was there, just as peace was being restored to Macduff, that several hundred fishermen gathered prior to marching on Portgordon harbour. Since Portgordon is not much more than 2 miles from Buckie, this march, headed by men equipped with flags and placards, did not take long. But it was conducted, or so said the area's solitary policeman, 'in a riotous manner' by men who voiced 'threats of a serious nature' – threats directed principally against grain shippers, whose vessels they promised to scuttle, and a local corn-dealer whose home, it was declared, would shortly be set ablaze. In the event, no ships were sunk and no house burned that Monday. But Portgordon, for as long as prices kept rising and for as long as its grain trade continued, seemed likely to experience further protest. That was why, on Tuesday, Sheriff John Pringle went to Fochabers to speak with Thomas Balmer.[25]

Theirs was no meeting of minds. Pringle, an active member of the Free Church and a man who had for several years been a vice-president of the Aberdeen Anti-Slavery Society, in no way shared the Richmond commissioner's authoritarian outlook. According to Balmer, the sheriff pressed him to do much as had been done in Macduff by subscribing, on the Duke of Richmond's behalf, to a fund 'for the purpose of purchasing meal to be sold [to fishing families in places like Portgordon and Buckie] at 20 shillings a boll'. This was far below the then market rate and Balmer, who could 'see no good reason' for such gestures, 'positively refused' to do as Pringle suggested.

Fishermen, he said, were 'not worse off' than anyone else and it was, in any case, 'perfectly impossible . . . to keep the price of meal low [in Banffshire] when it [was] higher in other places'. His 'decided opinion', Balmer informed his employer within hours of Sheriff Pringle's visit, was that 'if . . . fishermen, without any good reason, attempt again to overawe the country, they ought to be punished and, if the civil power is not sufficient [to enforce such punishment], the military ought to be called in'. With this, Richmond was fully in agreement. 'I am quite clear that the law should be put into force if fishermen attempt to prevent the export of grain,' he replied. 'With this class of men, firmness must be shown . . . Giving them meal below the market price would be fatal.' There was to be no repeat in Portgordon, then, of the conciliatory measures adopted in Macduff.[26]

In taking this hard line, Thomas Balmer was not without allies. One of them was none other than Uist and Barra laird John Gordon of Cluny. Although based in Aberdeenshire, Gordon had for some time been acquiring properties in Banffshire – and in Buckie in particular. Now he made clear that, in his capacity as a Buckie landlord, he was every bit as hostile as Balmer and Richmond to any suggestion that others should follow the Earl of Fife's example and make oatmeal available at less than the prevailing price. What finally stymied John Pringle's attempt to reduce the cost of meal in the Portgordon–Buckie area, however, was unease in Edinburgh about the way Pringle and Provost Carny had responded to the Macduff protests. The Edinburgh authorities, it emerged, were at one with Thomas Balmer in thinking that John Pringle had come close to capitulating to lawlessness. That is why the sheriff was reminded by one of the lord advocate's senior officials that 'in any district [where] there [was] any reason to apprehend disturbance' the proper response was to have 'special constables . . . instantly sworn in' with a view to their keeping such disturbance firmly in check. The letter containing this directive – and directive it was – reached Pringle's Banff home some three or four days after the failure of his Fochabers attempt to bring Thomas Balmer round to his way of thinking. The sheriff accordingly instructed two of Banffshire's Justices of the Peace to go to Portgordon on Monday 25 January and there begin swearing in a force of special constables.[27]

The JPs in question were Alexander Marquis and John Bennett. They were put in charge of the swearing-in process because, between them, they knew exactly who was who in Buckie and Portgordon. But this was because Marquis was one of Thomas Balmer's subfactors and because Bennett acted as factor for John Gordon of Cluny in Buckie. This was not calculated to be helpful. Few estate factors in Scotland, then or later, were well regarded by the people they dealt with. Bennett and Marquis – whose local unpopularity was later admitted by the authorities – were no exception. This doubtless gave an added edge to what followed. So did the fact that the two factors had been provided by Sheriff John Pringle with an armed escort. This consisted of a coastguard unit headed by Captain George Davies. The captain and his men had been mobilised by Pringle because, it seems likely, the sheriff was well aware that, by following Edinburgh's orders and trying to raise a force of special constables, he was likely to precipitate a fresh furore in and around Portgordon. This was certainly what occurred.[28]

Davies, a man in his late forties, came from Somerset. He had joined the Royal Navy when barely a teenager and, after seeing a good deal of action during anti-piracy campaigns in West Indian and Algerian waters, had been transferred to the then recently formed coastguard service. Stationed initially at various points on the English coast, Davies had been posted to Banff in 1842. He was, it appears, a bit of a fire-eater; for, despite his offer to clear Macduff harbour of protesters having been rebuffed, he evidently remained as keen as ever to make clear to Banffshire's fishermen – with whom, as coastguard commander, Davies must have had all sorts of regular dealings – that they could not, with impunity, obstruct marine trade.[29]

George Davies left Banff with one of Sheriff Pringle's local colleagues, a clerk called William Grant, on the early morning of Monday. Travelling overland by way of Portsoy and Cullen, he reached Buckie at about 2 p.m. There the captain ordered six of his Buckie-based subordinates to equip themselves with muskets and, boarding a locally stationed coastguard cutter, sailed with these men to Portgordon. At Portgordon, the six Buckie coastguards were instructed to hold themselves in readiness at the harbour while their commander made his way to a nearby inn where, he had been told, Marquis and Bennett, who had meanwhile been joined by William Grant, would be swearing in Buckie and Portgordon men they had summonsed to do duty as special constables. The JPs' efforts, Davies learned, had been 'almost a total failure'. Scarcely anyone had put in an appearance at the inn, and one of the few who did, a man by the name of John Thompson, had told Bennett and Marquis exactly what he thought of them in 'violent and unlawful language'. That was why George Davies was now asked by the two JPs to 'bring up' his men from the harbour and 'execute a warrant' for Thompson's arrest.[30]

This was done and Thompson duly taken into custody. His arrest, however, at once led to a crowd gathering outside the inn where, with much 'strong language', they made clear their 'determination to rescue the man'. To keep Grant, Marquis and Bennett safe, Davies would write next day, he 'found it necessary to order bayonets to be fixed and muskets to be loaded with ball and cartridge'. Perhaps not wishing to be the cause of the shooting that now seemed possible, Thompson, at this point, agreed to take the oath demanded of a special constable. But his subsequent release, it instantly became apparent, had come too late to pacify local feeling. Thompson had scarcely left the inn, William Grant reported afterwards, 'when a person came in . . . and stated to the justices and myself that an immense concourse of fishermen were on the march . . . to Portgordon and that our only safe [course of action] was to leave the place'. 'Upon this,' Grant went on, 'orders were given to get conveyances ready'. But before this could be accomplished, 'the yells of the . . . multitude [now] at the further end of the village had become terrific' and departures by carriage were accordingly deemed too risky. 'Mr Marquis escaped on horseback and Mr Bennett on foot,' Grant wrote, 'while I myself [had] a narrow escape from the mob who were not many yards behind me [and] swearing most awful oaths.'[31]

As all this was going on, word had reached George Davies from Alexander Hepburn, the Portgordon corn merchant who had been handling most of the port's outgoing grain traffic, that, like Bennett and Marquis, he feared for his safety. Davies, who had no intention of taking to his heels in the way the JPs were doing, accordingly left four of his men to cover their flight while, with the other two, he made his way to Hepburn's home. Streaming into the village, meantime, were 'vast companies . . . from Buckie, Findochty, Portessie and [from] even as far as . . . Portknockie' – the last being eight or nine miles distant. That this force had been got together so speedily, and that, in Davies's words, 'it . . . embodied order', was a further indication that, in part at least, the Moray Firth uprising of 1847 was no chaotically spontaneous outbreak. As there had been in Macduff, and as there would be afterwards in Wick, there was method and direction to be glimpsed in what took place at Portgordon.[32]

Something of this was evident in the military-like way that horns or bugles began to be sounded in order to direct several hundred men, backed by 'a vast collection of women and children', to Alexander Hepburn's house. There, with the winter dusk now thickening, the crowd was brought to a halt by Davies and his men, their backs to the grain merchant's door, their weapons levelled at the people confronting them. This stand-off, Davies later informed Sheriff Pringle, lasted 'for two hours'. Flanking Davies were his two rank-and-file coastguards 'with [their] loaded muskets and fixed bayonets' – he himself, he wrote, gripping 'a pointed pistol in each hand'.[33]

From among what Davies called 'the mob' came shouts to the effect that he and his companions should be killed. But those threats, the captain added, were 'occasionally qualif[ied]' by a 'spokesman and leader' who kept repeating, in Davies's hearing, 'that it was not us they came for but the buggers who [had] sent for us'. Was it thought, then, that John Bennett and Alexander Marquis, on whose instructions the coastguard unit had been fetched from the harbour, were hiding in Alexander Hepburn's home? And did it gradually become known that in fact the JPs had long gone? Perhaps. At all events, and with darkness now total, the coastguard trio's ordeal was at last brought to an end by an announcement from the crowd's spokesman that what he referred to as 'the committee' had agreed that no further action would be taken against Hepburn and that Davies, as a result, was free to return to his vessel. This Davies did. But to guard against any renewed attack on the grain-dealer's house, he ordered his two men to remain there overnight.[34]

While the dramatic events of the afternoon of Monday 27 January were unfolding in Portgordon, an Aberdeen-bound coach was leaving Edinburgh with, among its passengers, a man who had been instructed by Lord Advocate Rutherfurd's civil servants to go north. This was Alexander Currie. He was Banffshire's sheriff principal. Much like his Caithness counterpart, Robert Thomson, however, Currie relied on a locally based depute, John Pringle in his case, to look after things in his faraway sheriffdom while he himself got on with the business of managing a well-paying legal practice in the Scottish capital. But now, or so it was felt in Edinburgh, the situation in Banffshire was so threatening that the county's sheriff principal ought to be there in person. And so, from Aberdeen, which he reached on Tuesday morning, Currie pushed on at once to Banff where, that same day, he was brought up to date with Portgordon developments by Pringle and several others.[35]

Currie's first action was to ask for soldiers to be sent to the Portgordon area. His second was to prepare a 'proclamation' that, as well as being circulated in handbill form, was printed prominently on the front page of the local newspaper, the *Banffshire Journal*.* Currie, whose proclamation was meant in part to show that he had taken charge of local law enforcement, began by

---

* That Banff-published weekly, its politics the reverse of Wick's *John O'Groat Journal*, had up to this point 'purposely abstained . . . from taking any notice' of the riots occurring on its doorstep on the grounds, as its editor explained, that to cover them might be to encourage further protests.

touching on the various 'assemblages' that had 'of late ... disturb[ed] the public peace'. These had culminated, the sheriff went on, in the previous week's events in Portgordon when what Currie called a 'meeting of Her Majesty's Justices of the Peace' had to be abandoned because of 'the outrageous conduct of a lawless multitude'. It was his 'firm determination', Currie next declared, 'to suppress' all such 'wicked and flagitious [meaning criminal] practices' and he therefore called on 'all Her Majesty's liege subjects within the County of Banff to guard against every attempt to violate the law and to abstain from every act inconsistent with the peace and good order of society'.[36]

His stern language notwithstanding, Alexander Currie was soon persuaded – partly perhaps by his deputy; partly, it may be, by what he saw for himself – that Banffshire fishers were in real and serious difficulty. 'There can be no doubt that there is a great deal of misery among the population of the fishing villages,' he informed the lord advocate. 'The people are, in some places, in a state of desperation.' Among the most hard-hit communities, the sheriff added, was Buckie where, he understood, there was next to no oatmeal to be got. 'I believe some of the [landed] proprietors are now refusing to sell any more grain until they see that the people on their own estates have sufficiency of food,' Currie concluded. 'I hope this will become more general.' Much to the sheriff's relief, there was indeed to be movement in exactly that direction.[37]

The Earl of Fife may have been in the vanguard of what gradually became a widespread commitment on the part of Banffshire agriculturalists to put local need ahead of profit. Not far behind, however, was John Wilson, factor on the Seafield Estate, another of the area's larger properties and one that included a number of fishing villages, among them Cullen, Sandend and Portsoy. In letters mailed to Seafield, then in Rome, Wilson kept the earl informed about Banffshire's serial outbreaks of 'riot and disturbance' – all of which, in his opinion, were rooted in the 'panic' caused by 'the price of meal having suddenly risen from 20 shillings to 30 shillings a boll'. Cullen and Portsoy 'had not been altogether free of [this] spirit of clamour and alarm', Wilson wrote, but he had managed to prevent any 'breach of the public peace' in those communities by 'agreeing to let [their] fishermen be supplied with a certain quantity of meal ... upon credit'.[38]

The pacifying impact of those measures was especially evident in Portsoy. Grain shipments from its harbour were reputedly 'greater than shipments from any other place of the same size along the whole shores of the [Moray] Firth'. But though these shipments would be said later to have caused

'considerable excitement', there was no overt protest or violence. This, a
Banffshire Journal correspondent reckoned, was owed not just to the steps
taken by John Wilson but to initiatives organised by 'grain-dealers, merchants
and farmers' who, perhaps at Wilson's prompting, 'came forward and . . .
provided a supply of meal at a moderate price'.[39]

Gestures like these, Alexander Currie stressed, offered much the best
chance of 'quieting the people'. This was why he welcomed the extent to
which, in late January and into February, a growing number of landed proprietors and tenant farmers, responding it may be to Currie's urgings, began to
follow the example set on the Seafield Estate – some farmers going so far as
to donate significant amounts of oatmeal to the many local groupings (one
was in Portsoy) that sprang up to channel foodstuffs to people experiencing
what John Wilson described as 'a great deal of real distress'. Among eventual
converts to this cause, Currie learned, were John Gordon of Cluny and, more
surprising still, Thomas Balmer – the Richmond commissioner's change of
heart having had to be helped along, admittedly, by a final mobilisation on the
part of Banffshire's fishermen.[40]

On the Tuesday that brought Currie to Banff, Balmer, John Wilson and
several other land managers were due to meet at an inn on the outskirts of
Buckie. But their meeting, called to facilitate an exchange of views on food
supply issues, had been fixed in advance of the previous day's unrest in nearby
Portgordon and, fearing a new incursion of the sort that had wrecked
Monday's swearing-in session, the meeting's attendees agreed to switch its
location to Fochabers. There, 8 miles from Buckie and 5 miles from the sea,
they would be out of reach, they thought, of renewed protest. This calcula-
tion proved wrong.

There is no way of knowing how news of the Fochabers gathering reached
members of the committee mentioned to George Davies in Portgordon. But
it is more than likely to have been this shadowy group, best envisaged maybe
as an informal network of leading fishermen, that co-ordinated the call to
action that was now transmitted all along the coast. An hour or so after dawn
on Tuesday, signal flags were run up at the Buckie pierhead. Within minutes,
a chain of such flags was seen to stretch from Portknockie in the east to the
up-to-now quiescent community of Garmouth, some way to the west. The
outcome was the mustering in Buckie, within an hour or two of those flags'
appearance, of some 1,500 men. Having first 'marched in order' round the
town's coastguard station, by way of thumbing a collective nose at the station's
occupants, this force, more sizeable than some army regiments of that time,

next set off up the road to Fochabers. There it was discovered that the meeting the fishers had intended to lobby was already over. But Thomas Balmer – his home as well as his place of work in Fochabers – agreed, perhaps because he had little choice in the matter, to speak with some of the men now drawn up in the square where the Richmond Estate office was located. Whether or not in response to a threatened 'razing' of his house, Balmer now promised to make meal available on credit to fishing families resident on Richmond land. 'I should have liked much better to have made no concession at all,' an aggrieved and somewhat humiliated Balmer wrote subsequently, 'but placed as I was in the midst of an infuriated multitude of several hundreds, the greatest caution was necessary, as the least unguarded word [would] have set the whole aflame.'[41]

Next day the 50-strong troop detachment Sheriff Currie had requested arrived in Buckie at the end of a two-day forced march from Aberdeen. This detachment's availability put the Banffshire authorities in a much stronger position than they had been. But the ease with which Currie was able, on Thursday and Friday, to preside over the reopening of Portgordon harbour, where trade had been at a standstill for more than a week, very possibly owed as much to Thomas Balmer's enforced climbdown as it did to fear of military intervention. Fishermen in and around Portgordon and Buckie had by this stage got exactly what they wanted.

It remained only for Currie to deal with queries from Edinburgh as to why, given the extent of recent disorder in Banffshire he had managed, by the start of February, to take only two men into custody. This, the sheriff replied, was because it was impossible to be clear about who should be charged. 'The fishing people,' Currie wrote, 'are all united together in what they consider a matter of life and death.' This being the case, it was 'very difficult to get evidence from any of themselves or their families'.[42]

That was true. But it was not the whole truth because some at least of the necessary identification evidence could surely have been provided by the coastguards who had been deployed in Portgordon and who, since they would have had no lack of local knowledge, are bound to have recognised some of the people confronting them. It is tempting, therefore, to suspect that Alexander Currie simply did not want to run the risk of making arrests that might well have triggered more disruption. By this point, after all, he would have been well aware that when his Moray counterpart had taken actions of the sort that Edinburgh was calling for, those actions had provoked ferocious violence.

5

'The sheriff of Elginshire is overpowered'

Edinburgh • Burghead • Hopeman • Elgin • Inverness
Forres • Lossiemouth • Findhorn • Garmouth

John Lindsay, as can be seen from his surviving correspondence, had never before dealt with so challenging a situation as the one confronting him in the closing days of January 1847. Lindsay was Scotland's crown agent. As such, he was in charge of the country's prosecution service – represented, at city and county level, by procurators-fiscal who supervised investigations into criminal activity of all kinds. Answering formally to Lord Advocate Andrew Rutherfurd, Lindsay also advised on the content of any Scottish legislation and acted as Rutherfurd's chief executive – managing and directing the Edinburgh-based team whose members gave effect in Scotland to the policies of Britain's government. This meant that when the lord advocate's political duties took him to London, where he was unavoidably out of touch with day-to-day developments north of the border, John Lindsay was expected to deal with any crisis that might arise. Hence his key role in the events of late January 1847. When Rutherfurd had gone south for the start of the parliamentary session opened by Queen Victoria on 19 January, all of Scotland – the Highland and Hebridean famine notwithstanding – had seemed at peace. By the weekend following parliament's state opening, however, it had become clear to Lindsay that protests of the sort launched in Macduff on 15 January were posing a threat to the maintenance of law and order across an ever wider area. This, he wrote, was why he had instructed Sheriff Alexander Currie to 'go down immediately' to Banff and there take control of efforts to restore peace to places like Portgordon.[1]

Since there was thought to be every chance that unrest might spread from Banffshire to still unaffected parts of the Moray Firth coast, John Lindsay ordered a second sheriff to go north at the same time as Currie. This was

Cosmo Innes, sheriff principal of Moray, a county then known officially as Elginshire. Not least because his father's family had originated in Moray, Innes had welcomed his 1840 appointment to the Elginshire sheriffdom – an appointment he combined with an Edinburgh legal practice and with historical researches that had earned him a professorship* at the city's university. But it was one thing to make leisurely summer trips to Moray; quite another to travel there in haste in winter. Although said by John Lindsay to have 'assented cheerfully' when told that 'it was advisable and proper that [he] should go at once' to Elgin, Cosmo Innes is unlikely to have been enthusiastic about quitting his Edinburgh home and setting out on a difficult journey – a journey that started when, with Alexander Currie, he boarded an overnight coach for the north just as dusk was gathering on Monday 25 January.[2]

'I saw them off on the Aberdeen mail at four,' Lindsay commented of Innes and Currie's departure. 'Mr Innes [whose booking was a late one] had to go outside as far as Perth.' For a full five hours, then, Elginshire's sheriff, his 'tall, thin figure' doubtless swathed in a greatcoat and in travel rugs, would have been obliged to perch alongside his coach's driver as, by the flickering glow of his vehicle's lanterns and the light of a waxing moon,† this driver made as much speed as was possible – first to the Forth ferry and then on across Fife.[3]

That evening, in one of the first of what would become a stream of letters to the lord advocate, John Lindsay reflected on the day's events. 'I never saw men go off more bent on their duty,' he wrote of Currie and Innes. It had been his initial inclination to accompany the two sheriffs, the crown agent went on: 'It does not suit my nature to [send] other men out and stay behind.' But it had been put to him strongly by his senior colleagues and by High Court judge Henry Cockburn, a man close politically to Rutherfurd, that he 'should not go' but should instead remain in Edinburgh where it would be his task to organise an effective response to the growing turmoil in the north.[4]

One of Lindsay's first actions was to tell fiscals in Aberdeenshire, Banffshire, Elginshire and Inverness-shire that, because he needed to be kept informed about both scarcity and disorder, he expected 'a daily report from each'. The disquieting content of some of the resulting updates, together with the still more alarming dispatches that were to reach Lindsay from Sheriff Innes, made

---

* Innes's professorship was an honorary one. Edinburgh University then possessed no history department and Innes's lectures on Scottish history were unpaid.

† The moon on 25 January 1847 was three-quarters full and, even if the weather was cloudy, the night would have been a lot less dark than it might have been.

it essential, in the crown agent's opinion, to deploy troops in localities like Moray. This, however, was difficult to accomplish. There were few soldiers available; and, in Scotland anyway, there were next to no means of getting them quickly to where they were required.[5]

Since Britain in 1847 was the world's most powerful state, this might seem odd. But the country's military dispositions were organised around its having to safeguard (whether from external or internal threats) the widely separated components of its global empire. Much of Britain's navy, it followed, was based overseas. The army too was scattered across a host of colonial possessions, there usually being more need to have soldiers on hand in territories like India or South Africa than in any part, with one exception, of the United Kingdom. The exception, perhaps needless to say, was Ireland. Not only did civil unrest break out more frequently there than elsewhere in the British Isles, there was in Ireland, or so it was feared, a real possibility of armed rebellion* against rule from London. That is why, in 1847, the British authorities in Dublin Castle had at their disposal some 30,000 troops and, in addition, a 10,000-strong and gun-carrying police force. This was in marked contrast to the position in Scotland. Here no policemen were armed and, despite a County Police Act of 1839 having enabled commissioners of supply to establish local constabularies, these were by no means universal – while such forces as did exist were invariably small. This reflected the low likelihood, as it seemed until 1847, of widespread disorder. Equally reflective of there being no expectation of large-scale riot and protest was an army presence that, by Irish standards, was tiny. Just how tiny became apparent to John Lindsay when, a day or two after he had said his goodbyes to Innes and Currie, he went to Edinburgh Castle for an urgently convened meeting with General Henry Riddell, Commander-in-Chief Scotland, and Colonel John Eden, the C-in-C's adjutant.

It had been 'a pleasure to meet Colonel Eden and the general', Lindsay informed the lord advocate. It had been less of a pleasure perhaps to hear what they had to say. In all of Scotland, the crown agent now discovered, there were barely 1,850 rank-and-file soldiers. Of these, around 300 were accounted for by a cavalry unit of a kind that governments had been reluctant to unleash against rioters ever since mounted troops had killed 15 members of a

---

* This was not an exaggerated threat. There would be just such an uprising, albeit one that was easily crushed, in 1848.

protesting crowd in Manchester in 1819.* Available infantrymen, then, totalled just over 1,500. Most of them, moreover, were in the Scottish Central Belt. In all of the north, there were fewer than 300 soldiers – 240 in Aberdeen and 55 at Fort George. It was that last contingent, Fort George being the only military base in the Moray Firth area, that John Lindsay was especially anxious to strengthen. But there were, it emerged, a variety of logistic and other obstacles in the way of doing this. Among them was an understandable reluctance to reduce troop numbers in cities and towns that might themselves be about to erupt in anger about rising food prices. Only 150 soldiers could safely be moved north, it was decided. All of them were to be drawn from a 450-strong detachment of the 76th Regiment – the regiment then providing most of the infantry presence in Scotland – stationed at Edinburgh Castle.[6]

But how to get 150 men, their weapons, ammunition, baggage and other gear shifted speedily from Edinburgh to Fort George? Railway links to the north still being some years in the future, this could only be accomplished by sea. Since troop movements of that kind had long been a Royal Navy speciality, there should, in principle, have been no great problem about making the necessary arrangements. Nor would there have been had John Lindsay been looking to get 150 soldiers from Hong Kong, say, to Shanghai. In the South China Sea at this time, there was no lack of British naval vessels. On the east coast of Scotland in 1847, however, there was just one – a steam-powered gunboat called the *Cuckoo*. Commanded by Lieutenant Abraham Parks and based at Newhaven, the port used by the fishing fleet serving Edinburgh, the *Cuckoo* had the job of ensuring that fishermen adhered to the rules and regulations, concerning net mesh sizes and the like, governing their industry. Now its captain, a man whose naval career had begun during the Napoleonic Wars, found himself embroiled in anxious talks with John Lindsay, General Riddell and Colonel Hope. 'We have all felt deeply indebted to the . . . cheerful readiness of Lieutenant Parks to do all the service in his power,' Lindsay reported to Andrew Rutherfurd. 'Unfortunately the *Cuckoo* is but a small ship . . . not fit for the comfortable transport of troops.' That was indubitably the case. But in the absence of the 'powerful war steamer' Lindsay would have liked to have had at his disposal, the *Cuckoo*, as he told Rutherfurd, was going to have to suffice. 'I earnestly hope to be able to report tomorrow,' the crown agent wrote on 28 January, 'that [the] *Cuckoo* is off with 50 soldiers . . . [for]

---

* Those deaths, occurring as a result of the forcible dispersal of a demonstration at St Peter's Fields, became known as the Peterloo Massacre.

Fort George or some . . . point in Morayshire.' Making good that wish would become all the more necessary when, early on Friday 29 January, it became known in Edinburgh that Cosmo Innes had, in Lindsay's words, 'been entirely overcome by the mob'.[7]

Innes's overnight coach trip from Edinburgh by way of Perth to Aberdeen had been followed by a further journey to Elgin, which the sheriff reached not long after midday on Tuesday 26 January. At Elgin, Innes learned that his Moray-based sheriff-substitute, Patrick Cameron, had earlier that day gone off to confront rioters in Burghead. 'I got a gig,' Innes was later to say of what came next, 'and went down there immediately.'[8]

Since a gig – a light and two-wheeled carriage pulled by a single horse – was capable of a reasonable turn of speed, the sheriff would have covered the 9 miles between Elgin and Burghead in well under an hour. His destination was the town's harbour, which, like the warehouses, business premises and homes around it, was then no more than 40 years old. As indicated by its grid-like set of streets, Burghead was the product of careful planning on the part of the several businessmen who, in 1805, had acquired ownership of the land on which their new town took shape. The most prominent member of this 1805 consortium was William Young who, in 1819, bought out his partners and set about adding to the capacity of a harbour first opened to shipping in 1810. Between 1811 and 1817, Young, while still taking an interest in Burghead's development, had been factor of the Sutherland Estate and, in that role, had helped organise the estate's clearance. In Sutherland, then, William Young was not well regarded. In Moray, however, he was described shortly after his death in 1842 as a 'benefactor . . . who had done more for this part of the country than any person of his day and generation'. Tributes of that sort stemmed mainly from Young's commitment to Burghead where his proprie-torial role had been inherited by his nephew, also William Young, who thus took over one of the busiest harbours on the Moray Firth coast.[9]

Inland from Burghead, on the low-lying and sheltered plain known as the Laigh of Moray, were some of the most productive farms in the Scottish north. Almost all these farms grew grain. When a part of this grain went south, as happened on an extensive scale in the winter of 1846–47, it did so mainly by way of William Young's harbour, from which ships left regularly for places like Leith, Newcastle and London. Much of this trade was handled by an Elgin corn merchant, John Allan, who, on Monday 25 January, the day Cosmo Innes left Edinburgh, was arranging, he said, for 'a couple of hundred bolls' of oatmeal, already in store at Burghead, to be put aboard a locally owned cargo vessel, the *James and Jessie*, scheduled to sail that week for the Firth of Forth port of Grangemouth.[10]

Had Allan been shipping unmilled barley or wheat, trouble might have been averted. But at a time when fishing families in Burghead and nearby localities were finding it harder and harder to buy the oatmeal on which they depended during that potato-less winter, the sight of so much ready-to-use meal being sent elsewhere was calculated to produce, at the minimum, a great deal of outrage. This outrage was most acute in Hopeman, a village no more than an hour's walk from Burghead and a place where, perhaps because it was entirely fisheries-reliant in a way that Burghead itself was not, the downturn in cash returns from fishing had hit especially hard. Given this circumstance, it was perhaps predictable that, on news of John Allan's planned shipment reaching Hopeman, there would be backing in the village for an attempt to keep his 200 bolls of oatmeal in Moray. This attempt took definite shape on the Monday immediately preceding the planned departure of the *James and Jessie*. That afternoon, it was reported, 'a great many . . . fishermen' marched out of Hopeman and headed in procession for Burghead.[11]

The Hopeman marchers, said Burghead's harbour-master, Peter Christall, 'congregated about my office'. 'They had come over,' they told Christall, 'to stop the shipment of meal until they were satisfied [that] there was plenty in the county.' On Christall trying to convince the crowd, soon joined by a growing number of Burghead people, that there was in fact no shortage of oats in Moray, he was peremptorily informed that, if this was indeed the position, meal should be retailing not for 32 or more shillings a boll but for 20 or 24 shillings at most. 'Not allow[ing] meal to be shipped,' someone remarked, would bring the price down. Obstructing lawful shipments, Christall retorted, might well result in the military being called in to restore order. 'He did not care a farthing for the military,' said Daniel Sutherland, a fisherman whose wife and mother would afterwards walk from Hopeman to Ardverikie to press for his release from prison. Even if 'some of them might be shot,' Sutherland insisted, 'they would have . . . meal at their own price'.[12]

Before first light next morning, and in response to the previous day's demonstration, a number of men – all of them holding positions of some influence in Moray – met in the Elgin office of William Grigor, a lawyer who acted for Burghead's proprietor, William Young. Attendees included grain merchant John Allan, Sheriff-Substitute Patrick Cameron and Moray's procurator fiscal, Alexander Brown, a man who also served, in his private capacity, as factor to Archibald Duff of Drummuir, a Banffshire and Moray laird whose properties included much of Hopeman.

Just after dawn, while these men were still in session, they were lobbied by several Hopeman and Burghead fishermen who had come to Elgin to find out what, if anything, the authorities might be prepared to do by way of responding to demands for cheaper meal. Having first made clear to the newly arrived delegation that 'he had not the power [to] . . . fix the price of . . . grain', Cameron went on to say that he was urging Moray farmers and landowners to get together, in just three days time, with a view to their guaranteeing that 'plenty' meal would be available for local purchase. Allan, for his part, stressed that, while he was contractually obliged to press on with that week's shipments, 'he would not purchase more oats . . . for exportation' until 'irritation was allayed' by assurances that meal supplies would be forthcoming. With this, or so Alexander Brown felt, the Burghead–Hopeman 'deputation' seemed 'perfectly satisfied'. But both on Brown's part and on the part of his colleagues, there remained some doubt as to whether enough had been done to head off interference with the loading of the *James and Jessie* – loading due to get underway that day. To check on this, it was decided, Brown and Patrick Cameron should go at once to Burghead where they would be joined by William Hay, superintendent of Moray's still minuscule police force, and one of Hay's few constables, John McIntyre.[13]

On reaching Burghead in mid morning, said Superintendent Hay, he learned that, though there had been 'great difficulty [in getting] people to assist with the shipping', all was otherwise going 'pretty quietly'. But just as the final two cartloads of meal were en route from John Allan's quayside 'granary' to the *James and Jessie*, Hay went on, he heard 'a bell . . . rung, seemingly as a signal'. The bell-ringer was a ten-year-old boy, Alexander Main, who had been asked by Burghead shoemaker, James Falconer, to fetch a handbell from a household known to have one and then 'to go round the town', sounding the bell as loudly as possible while 'call[ing] out to the women that there was cheap meal to be got' at the harbour. Falconer, the lad said, had promised him 'a halfpenny to [himself] for going round'. But this, the boy added angrily, had never been forthcoming.[14]

Down at the harbour, meanwhile, Police Superintendent Hay became aware of an approaching crowd consisting of 'a great many men and women' led, or so Hay reckoned, by two individuals whom he recognised, one of them the shoemaker James Falconer and the other Angus Davidson, a Burghead cooper. This 'mob', said Hay, set about 'prevent[ing] the meal being put on board' the *James and Jessie*, a first group 'throwing stones at a great rate', a second, mostly women in this instance, trying to halt the carting operation by unhitching carters' horses from their carts. In consequence of this disruption, Hay explained subsequently, the loading of the *James and Jessie* had to be taken over by himself, Sheriff Cameron, Procurator Fiscal Brown and Constable McIntyre – the vessel's crew, most of whom are likely to have been Burghead men, having '[given] up working when they saw the people assembled about the ship'.[15]

Exposed as they were to 'threatening language', stone-throwing, 'pushing and jostling', it took William Hay, Patrick Cameron and their colleagues some time to get the last few sacks of meal hoisted on to the *James and Jessie*. Nor was this the end of their difficulties. While the loading of the *James and Jessie*, moored at the harbour's north quay, was being completed, four more cartloads of meal – 100 bolls in total – were seen to be on their way to another ship, the *Ceres*, which had not long before tied up at the south quay. On seeing these carts, said Superintendent Hay, 'the mob ran round the harbour' to attack not just the newly arrived carters but John Allan who was with them and who had been hoping to get his new consignment of meal, this one earmarked for Leith, stowed aboard the *Ceres*. 'With the assistance of [some of] the carters,' Hay said, 'we got a few bags . . . put on the deck of the vessel but the mob was taking [the meal] off as fast as we got it on . . . [I] was struck a . . . blow with a stone on the left cheek which cut and wounded me very much . . . My hat [symbolic of its wearer's status] was taken off and thrown away . . . A whip I had in my hand was taken from me and . . . with the handle of it . . . I was struck several severe blows on the back.'[16]

Seeing 'numbers' of people rushing towards the *Ceres*, John Allan, as he said, 'got up on the top of a cask to reason with them, but [this] was in vain as they insisted I should agree to supply them with meal for the season [until the 1847 harvest in other words] at 24 shillings a boll and grant bond [by which was meant a signed undertaking] . . . to do so, otherwise they would not allow a particle of meal to be shipped . . . The cask [was pulled] . . . from under me. I then got on to the parapet of the quay and tried to speak with them, but they would not hear me and . . . laid hold of me by the bottom of my trousers to pull me down.' 'The mob,' said Superintendent Hay, '[now] became so infuriated at [Allan] that he was obliged to take shelter in the [*Ceres*'] cabin, the mob [shouting] . . . that if they had a hold of him they would kill him, the women calling out that they would open him [meaning gut him] like a haddock'.[17]

Fearing for the corn merchant's life and powerless to disperse the crowd besieging the *Ceres*, Sheriff Patrick Cameron decided that the only course open to him was to seek help from Burghead's clergymen: David Waters of the Free Church, the Church of Scotland's Alexander Leslie and Alexander Tillie who preached to adherents of a minority denomination known as the Secession Church.* Waters, who ministered in Hopeman as well as Burghead and who had much the biggest congregation of the three, was known by Cameron to command a great deal of respect in the communities he served. It was to the Free Church manse on Burghead's outskirts, then, that Moray's sheriff-depute first went in search of aid – Waters at once agreeing to do as Patrick Cameron requested.

David Waters was shocked by the scenes awaiting him at the harbour. 'I did not believe they were capable of it,' the Free Church minister wrote of stone-throwing members of his congregation. Nothing he saw intimidated him, however. At Sheriff Cameron's bidding, though with little expectation of getting a hearing, Waters attempted, as he put it, to 'say a few words . . . to [the] great crowd on the quay'. This had 'little effect', he admitted. But such was his local standing that the minister was permitted, without interference from the crowd, to rescue John Allan from his hiding place on the *Ceres* and usher him on to the quay. From the quay, Allan – flanked not just by Waters but also by Leslie and Tillie who had now put in an appearance – was led away by Patrick Cameron and taken to an inn in Granary Street, no more than a minute or two's walk from the harbour. There the grain merchant, having been spirited through a back door and provided with a horse, was told to ride at once for Elgin.[18]

As John Allan left Burghead, Cosmo Innes's hired gig clattered into town. The sheriff made at once for the Granary Street inn where – all hope of getting Allan's cargo on to the *Ceres* having been abandoned – Patrick Cameron had been joined by Superintendent Hay, by Hay's solitary constable and by Alexander Brown, the procurator fiscal. Hay, his wounds still untreated, had 'blood running down his cheek' while Brown and Cameron, in Innes's recollection, came to greet him in 'coats and hats [that were] disordered and covered with [the] meal' that had been thrown over the two officials when, in the course of their efforts to get sackload after sackload put aboard the *Ceres*, one or more sacks had broken open. Outside the inn, Cosmo Innes said, was

---

* The Secession Church was the product of an eighteenth-century breakaway from the Church of Scotland.

the victorious 'mob'. Its now largely silent ranks, the sheriff added, were composed of hundreds of men and women who, though no longer engaging in violence, 'laughed at all attempts to reason with them'.[19]

In the face of this hostility, Innes and his colleagues, being hopelessly outnumbered, felt themselves to have no alternative but to retreat, as John Allan had already done, to Elgin where the newly arrived sheriff principal was briefed on the background to what he had just witnessed. The Burghead crowd, it was agreed, had neither gathered nor acted spontaneously. There had been leadership on view. Among the women who had been 'particularly active' in mobilising others, 'in throwing stones . . . and in endeavouring to [bring meal carts to a halt by] lead[ing] away . . . horses', said William Hay and Alexander Brown, were Elizabeth Grant and Janet MacIntosh, both of whom, it was felt, ought to be arrested. Also needing taken into custody, in Brown and Hay's opinion, were three young fishermen from Hopeman. One was Daniel Sutherland who had tangled with Burghead's harbour-master, Peter Christall, the previous day. The others were John Young and John Main. All three were thought by Procurator Fiscal Brown to have behaved extremely violently. He had accordingly told Main, Young and Sutherland that he 'had marked them out and that if they persisted they would assuredly get them-selves into trouble'. But the men he most wanted to see jailed, the procurator fiscal went on, were Angus Davidson and James Falconer, especially the latter. They, it appeared, had got people together, told them where to go and what to do. Falconer, moreover, had used all sorts of radical and revolutionary language, talking of 'liberty and equality [and] stating that the rich had too long had it their own way'.[20]

That the foremost organiser of the Burghead protests should have been a shoemaker – or, in Scots, a souter – would have come as no surprise to the French writer who, in 1856, produced a history of the cobbler's craft. It was, 'a very curious thing,' this man observed, 'that each trade develops, in the artisans practising it, a specific character, a particular temperament. The butcher is generally serious and full of his own importance, the house painter is thoughtless and a rake, the tailor is sensual, the grocer stupid, the porter curious and prattling.' But it was to shoemakers one had to look for enthusi-astic engagement in political agitation: 'The makers of . . . shoes are always distinguished by a restless, sometimes aggressive spirit and by a . . . tendency to loquacity. Is there a riot? Does an orator emerge from the crowd? It is without doubt a cobbler who has come to make a speech to the people.'[21]

GOD SAVE THE QUEEN!

PROCLAMATION

WHEREAS Outrages and Wanton Destruction of Property have taken place in Inverness and its vicinity in the course of the present week, the PROVOST and MAGISTRATES of the BURGH, and the SHERIFF of the COUNTY, Hereby call upon all and sundry, not only to avoid participation in acts of violence, but to aid the constituted authorities in repressing the same should they further occur, certifying to those who may, either directly or indirectly, connive at breaches of the public peace, that they shall be dealt with as the law and constitution of the country may warrant.

The PROVOST and MAGISTRATES take this opportunity of reminding the Inhabitants that the consequences of disorder and misrule cannot be otherwise than disastrous to the community, particularly to those classes who require the assistance of others, in a greater or less degree, for support. Happily, in this part of the country the quantities of Corn and Provisions available are much more than the thoughtless conceive; but obstructions to commerce and destruction of property will unavoidably result in scarcity and disappointment; for such acts of insubordination not only involve severe punishment, but are calculated to prevent beneficial dealing and those IMPORTATIONS of Provisions and Seed required in this district in seasons of plenty, as well as in seasons of partial failure; while at the same time it is obvious that the enormous expense attending outrages and crime will not increase but greatly diminish the means at the disposal of public bodies and private individuals for the relief of distress. That the poor and needy, therefore, will be the principal, if not comparatively the only sufferers from violence, is a self-evident proposition.

The Provost, Sheriff, and Magistrates further intimate, that subscriptions have been entered into of this date, at a Public Meeting, for purchasing Grain and Meal, at the lowest possible prices, to be sold in the Inverness market without profit, and in any quantities not exceeding a quarter of a Boll.

WILLIAM SIMPSON, *Provost.*
W. H. COLQUHOUN, *Sheriff-Substitute.*

Inverness Castle, 6th Feb., 1847.

INVERNESS; PRINTED AT THE JOURNAL OFFICE.

Inverness authorities circulated this Proclamation, a mix of threats and promises, at the height of the 1847 disturbances in the town. (Crown copyright, National Records of Scotland, AD56/308/2, no. 33)

In famine times children were often said to be 'in rags'. What was meant by that description can be seen in this early photograph from Harris. (Reproduced by permission of the National Records of Scotland and the Society of Writers to Her Majesty's Signet)

A SKYE COTTAGE.

A house of the sort to be seen throughout the Hebrides at a time when thousands of islanders were starving.

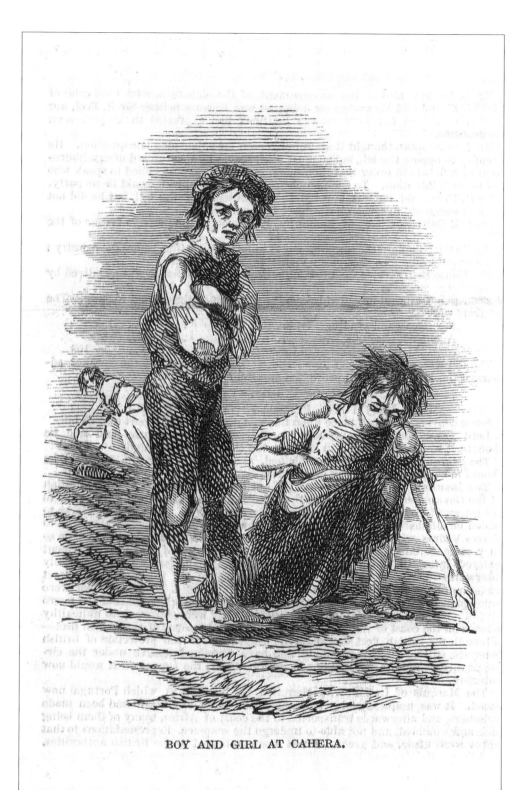

BOY AND GIRL AT CAHERA.

Irish famine victims in the hunger-devastated countryside around Skibbereen, West Cork.
(The National Library of Scotland CC-BY 4.0)

Ardverikie Lodge by Loch Laggan as it was in August 1847, when three Moray 'fisherwomen' came here to ask Queen Victoria, then holidaying at Ardverikie, to exercise her prerogative of mercy in the case of Hopeman fishermen whose part in a Burghead riot led to their being sentenced to transportation to a penal colony in Australia. (The National Library of Scotland CC-BY 4.0)

Fishing boats in Pulteneytown Harbour, Wick, at the height of the summer herring season. (Wick Society, Johnston Collection)

A procession in Pulteneytown's Union Street. Here, on 24 February 1847, troops opened fire on a stone-throwing crowd occupying the rising ground to the left. (Wick Society, Johnston Collection)

Bridge Street, Wick. Scene of repeated protests in the opening weeks of 1847. (Wick Society, Johnston Collection)

Inverness Town Hall. Scene in February 1847 of largely unsuccessful attempts to recruit special constables whose role would have been to confront protesters whose demands for cheaper food had caused all sorts of disruption. Today's Town House occupies the same site.
(By Pierre Delavault, Highland Libraries, courtesy of Am Baile)

Herring gutters at work. Women played key roles in the fishing industry and in the protests that convulsed so many Moray Firth fishing communities in 1847. (Wick Society, Johnston Collection)

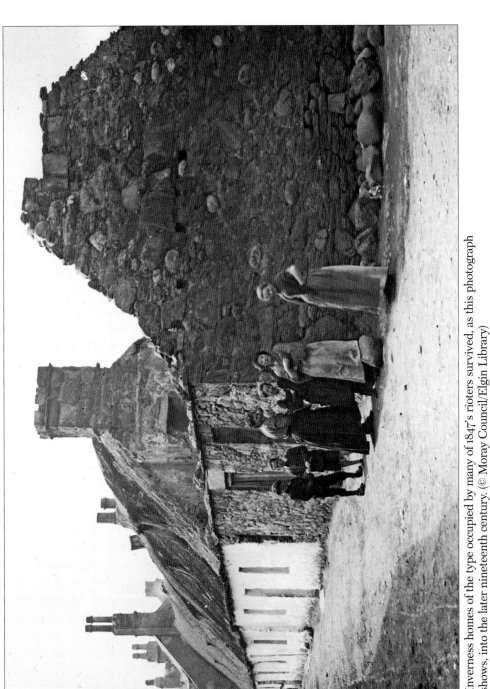

Inverness homes of the type occupied by many of 1847's rioters survived, as this photograph shows, into the later nineteenth century. (© Moray Council/Elgin Library)

Street scene in Cromarty, one of several Black Isle villages where, during the hunger winter of 1846–47, people took to the streets in protest at the soaring price of food. (Willie John Smith Archive courtesy of Am Baile)

Rhynie Farm, Easter Ross. In early 1847, grain from this farm had to have a military escort to get it safely to Invergordon Harbour for shipment south. (© National Museums Scotland)

Findhorn Harbour. Military intervention was required to reopen the harbour after it was blockaded by the local fishing community. (© Moray Council/Elgin Library)

A Lossiemouth fishwife. Women like her tramped for many miles through Moray's towns and countryside in search of buyers for their fish. (© Moray Council/Elgin Library)

A grain storehouse at Foulis Point near Dingwall. Today housing a popular restaurant just off the A9, this storehouse complex was the scene of several of 1847's mass protests. (© HES/John Hume Collection)

Hopeman, Moray. This fishing village was home to many of the people involved in the Burghead riots of January 1847. (© Moray Council/Elgin Library)

Why shoemakers should have been so markedly militant in their politics is a question that, despite a lot of effort having been put into resolving it, has yet to be answered definitively. Did it have to do with the nature of a cobbler's work; with his self-employed status enabling him to express his opinions without fear of what an employer might say or do; with his job being less demanding physically than that of, say, a miner, a ploughman, a factory operative; with his thus having opportunity for reading, thought, reflection; with the extent to which he came in contact (because everyone needed boots and shoes) with a wide cross-section of society? Or was it due to something else entirely? The one thing that is certain is that any challenge to established order from the eighteenth century onwards, in France, in Britain and in lots of other countries, appears always to have featured cobblers in leading roles. To this extent, James Falconer – a man described in 1847 as being '34 years of age [and] . . . a shoemaker by trade' – was conforming to type when he set about 'exciting' Burghead people by telling them the time had come for 'the poor [to] . . . have equal justice'.[22]

Was Falconer alone in Burghead in holding views of that sort? It seems unlikely. James Loch's conviction that there was no end of 'radical and levelling' sentiment to be found on the north coast of the Moray Firth has already been cited. Similar opinions were expressed by commentators with an interest in communities on the firth's other shore. The press, which Loch thought a source of especially dangerous ideas, was as omnipresent in Banffshire and Moray, it appears, as in Caithness. 'Newspapers,' one Banffshire minister noted, 'are circulated as long as the texture of the paper holds together.' This, the same minister observed, led working folk to take an interest in 'political excitements' of which they might otherwise have known nothing. Were those same folk thus rendered more susceptible, as Revd David Waters suspected, to the influence of what Waters called 'radicals and designing demagogues'? Thomas Balmer, the Duke of Richmond's commissioner and the man targeted by the fishermen who occupied Fochabers on 26 January 1847, would certainly have given an affirmative answer to that question. 'The feelings of the people are much changed within the last 12 or 15 years,' Balmer informed the duke in the aftermath of his having had to give ground to the Fochabers protesters. 'There is now a strong desire among the working population to bring all above them down to their own level, and when it is considered that many of the measures of government . . . have been forced upon it by popular clamour and agitation [a reference to Corn Law repeal], we need not be astonished at the *mobility* thinking that all power is vested in themselves and that they have the right to dictate to every other class.'[23]

If, as Thomas Balmer asserted, 'levelling' notions gained a foothold in the Moray Firth area during the 1830s and early 1840s, they are likely to have done so as a result of the region having been caught up, as virtually all of Britain was then caught up, in a clamour for political and constitutional change. This clamour, which the country's ruling elite had hoped to quell by means of what came to be called the Great Reform Act of 1832, had not in fact been quietened by that measure. The 1832 Act had eliminated all sorts of earlier abuses and given more people the opportunity to participate in parliamentary elections. In Scotland, for example, the (then wholly male) electorate went up from 4,500 to 65,000. Proportionately, this was a bigger advance than was made in England where the franchise had been less restrictive to begin with. On neither side of the border, however, was the scale of political exclusion much reduced by a reform that, for all its undoubted significance, left most folk as disenfranchised as before. There continued to be pressure, therefore, for voting rights – still limited to a comparatively affluent minority – to be extended further. This pressure was given focus by a People's Charter drawn up by radical groups in Birmingham and London. The charter, embodying demands for universal suffrage, secret ballots and much else that is today taken for granted, was at once denounced in Westminster. By many of the voteless, however, it was backed enthusiastically – the charter acting, in effect, as the manifesto of what became one of the world's first working-class or labour movements. To be supportive of this movement was to be a Chartist and, by the late 1830s and early 1840s, there were substantial Chartist groupings to be found in virtually all of Britain's larger population centres. In northern Scotland, much the most populous such centre was Aberdeen. There Chartism was organised around the Aberdeen Working Men's Association, which was formed in 1838 and which soon had enough support for it to be possible for the association to publish its own (admittedly short-lived) newspaper.[24]

Early Victorian Aberdeen, with its burgeoning papermills, textile mills, shipyards and foundries, was a working-class city. Even the biggest settlements to its north – Fraserburgh, Banff, Elgin, Inverness, Wick – were a lot smaller and far less industrialised. But all around the Moray Firth there was, for all that, a good deal of Chartist activity. In Caithness, for instance, a man referred to by the Chartist press as 'Mr G. McBean' was reported to have 'delivered in all 27 lectures on the principles of Chartism' during the winter of 1840–41.

This was followed, in May 1841, by several hundred Wick Chartists rallying behind a plan to run a Chartist against James Loch, the town's sitting MP, in that year's general election. The chosen candidate was John Swanson, a local joiner or carpenter. As was common Chartist practice, Swanson, though nominated for election, did not actually contest the poll – because, given the heavily restricted nature of the franchise, there would have been little point in his doing so. But where he stood politically in relation to James Loch is clear from John Swanson's take on food prices. If the cost of living was high in the north, he said, then this was in part attributable to Wick's MP who, in his role as the Sutherland Estate's management supremo, 'had been the means of rendering corn dear by exterminating the corn-producing population of Sutherland by every barbarous means that tyranny could suggest'.[25]

Swanson's candidacy in the Wick Burghs seat had its counterpart on the opposite side of the Moray Firth where Archibald MacDonald, an Aberdeen activist, was named Chartist candidate for Elgin Burghs – a constituency comprising towns like Banff and Cullen as well as Elgin itself. From MacDonald's perspective, his 1841 nomination is likely to have served principally as a means of spreading the Chartist message. This was something on which the wider Chartist movement, as can be seen from the activities of its 'missionaries' in Cornwall, rural Wales and similar localities, set a great deal of store. Hence the visit made to Inverness in the summer of 1839 by another Aberdeen Chartist, Alexander MacKenzie, a tailor by profession. Dismissed by the *Inverness Courier* (no fan of franchise reform) as 'brazen-faced . . . raw and uneducated', MacKenzie was received more positively by what the *Courier* called 'young men and women of the humblest class' – a number of whom gathered to hear him speak. The same 'humblest class' would loom large in the audiences that turned out in town after town in the Scottish north towards the end of 1840 when a man then emerging as one of Chartism's foremost – and boldest – spokesmen undertook a speaking tour of the area.[26]

This was Julian Harney. A 'thorough-going Londoner' who had been brought up in poverty and who was largely self-educated, Harney, afterwards a close friend of Friedrich Engels, was just 23 when he set out on what turned into a seven-week tramp through Aberdeenshire, Banffshire, Moray and Inverness-shire. An admirer of Jean-Paul Marat, one of the more radically inclined leaders of the French Revolution, Harney made his name on the 'physical force' wing of Chartism – backing men who thought, as Marat had done, that democracy would never be gained by anything other than violence. 'Time was when every Englishman had a musket in his cottage,' Harney told a Chartist gathering in Derby in early 1839, 'and along with it hung a flitch of bacon. Now there was no flitch of bacon for there was no musket. Let the musket be restored and the flitch of bacon would soon follow. You will get nothing from tyrants but what you can take.' This was to risk arrest on a charge of sedition, and it was partly with a view to dodging a jail sentence by dropping out of sight in England that Harney took to spending more and more time in Scotland – not least in Aberdeen where he addressed demonstrations and mass-meetings reckoned (by Chartist sources anyway) to have drawn crowds numbered in thousands. 'We the trampled upon people,' Harney said on one of those occasions, 'we the plundered and long-suffering people, we the tyrannised and insulted people . . . have gathered ourselves together . . . and, in firm phalanx formed, [we] have shown the appalled and affrighted aristocrats the moral might and physical strength of [our] democracy.'[27]

This key piece of Chartist doctrine – that working folk, if organised, were irresistible – was to be Harney's constant theme in the course of the long trek he embarked on in mid November 1840. First, he hiked through Aberdeenshire, addressing meetings in, among other places, Ellon, Turriff and Peterhead. Then came Banffshire. Often, as Harney discovered in Macduff on 8 December, 'no hall wherein to hold [a] meeting could be procured'. Describing how he had to settle in Macduff for what he called 'a moonlight meeting', Harney wrote: 'I summoned the good people to meet me in the marketplace at six o'clock. The result was the largest gathering I have held since leaving Aberdeen. I was heartily pleased with the . . . attendance and [the] . . . good humour of [the crowd] . . . A good number of females were present who . . . [took] a lively interest in the evening's proceedings.'[28]

From Macduff, Harney walked on to Portsoy, Cullen and Elgin. Attendance at a meeting in the Trades Hall, Elgin, 'was comparatively numerous considering it had been anything but timely and properly announced'. The following evening in Forres was 'passed . . . with a few good men and true'. Then it was back on the road for an 18-mile tramp to Ardersier where Harney stayed 'at the house of a worthy Highlander of the Cameron clan'. Was this man a relative of Adam Cameron, the Ayrshire weaver whose daughter, Mary, the young Chartist had married some months previously? And was it to his father-in-law that Harney owed the tweed plaid,* which provided him with

---

* Plaids of this type were commonly worn by men such as shepherds and drovers who worked for long hours out of doors.

some protection from November and December cold and wet? Perhaps. What is certain is that, irrespective of the weather, Harney encountered much – politics aside – that took his interest. More than 50 years later, he would write about the 'specialities' of the Scots speech (today called Doric) he heard in Aberdeenshire, Moray and adjacent districts. Now what caught Harney's attention, on leaving Ardersier for Inverness, was the fact that he had crossed a linguistic boundary and entered a locality where farm labourers he met with on the road were to be heard 'addressing each other', as he put it, not in Scots but Gaelic. This was the sort of thing that, from journalists like James Bruce of the *Scotsman*, might have drawn a sneering comment. Harney's response was different. 'Gaelic,' he wrote, 'sounded not a little strange, yet interesting, to my southern ear. In reply to my Sassenach compliments, "A fine day, sir'', was the courteous answer given in good Saxon by the passing Gael.'[29]

In Inverness, strenuous efforts had been made in 1839 to ensure that Alexander MacKenzie, the Aberdeen Chartist, could find no indoor venue. Harney, whose arrival was preceded by news of his activities in places like Macduff and Elgin, ran into the same difficulty. 'Refused the Trades and other Halls,' he reported, 'I at length managed to get [the use of] a room attached to a temperance coffee house* in Castle Street'. Here, yards from Inverness's then newly built courthouse, Harney spoke on the evening of Monday 21 December 1840. His address, according to the *Inverness Courier*, 'consisted of the stale and hackneyed topics which form the staple of . . . Chartist harangues'. Maybe so. But Harney's remarks were nevertheless considered worthy of organised disruption by a number of people intent on denouncing any thought of an expanded franchise. In charge of this group was an Inverness businessman by the name of Munro.[30]

From Munro, Harney wrote, he had to endure 'lengthy tirades of abuse'. 'To enlist the working men on his side,' Harney went on, '[Munro] descended to the low artifice of appealing to their national prejudices; lauding the working classes of Scotland as being an intelligent, industrious, loyal and contented people; and abusing the English working men as being an ignorant, dissolute, intemperate and rebellious race.' Munro's interventions, according to the *Courier*, 'exposed the utter fallacy and mis-statements of the Chartist orator'. But the meeting, for all that, resulted in a motion in support of the People's

---

* Temperance coffee houses were a product of the Victorian crusade against 'strong drink' in all its forms. Chartists and other labour activists were often hostile to the drinks trade, which, they felt, caused a great deal of misery among the working class.

Charter being moved by 'a working [stone]mason' and seconded by 'a working shoemaker'. It resulted too in Munro and his backers drawing criticism from a member of Inverness Town Council, William Forbes. 'A Whig as regards my own political sentiments,' Forbes remarked, 'I would desire to obtain fairness and toleration towards those holding different opinions.'[31]

At the close of his Castle Street meeting, Harney wrote, he 'partook of coffee with a number of the working men' who had attended. His conversation with those men, he added, convinced him 'that a second [and better advertised] meeting would have completely established Chartism in the Highland capital'. But Harney, now needing to retrace his steps to Aberdeen, was pledged to speak in Forres on the evening following his Inverness engagement – and in Elgin, for the second time, on the evening after that. Those Moray meetings went well, and, within weeks, Elgin possessed a Working Men's Association whose founders attributed its existence to the 'lasting impression' Julian Harney had made 'upon . . . his hearers'. Others of those hearers had meanwhile been organised into a pro-Chartist network extending from Peterhead, through Macduff, to Inverness. This network's existence is a pointer (others are the emergence of the Elgin association and the nomination of Chartist candidates in the Wick and Elgin parliamentary constituencies) to Chartism having obtained a following in much of the area affected by the disturbances of early 1847. That is not to imply that this area's exposure to Chartist ideas made it more prone to rebellion. It is to suggest, however, that the radical thinking spoken of by men like Thomas Balmer and James Loch was something that definitely existed.[32]

James Falconer, the cobbler so much to the fore in the Burghead troubles of January 1847, was not one of the half-dozen shoemakers whose names feature in the Chartist network put in place six years previously. But his noisily expressed conviction 'that the rich had too long had it their own way' may well have owed something to his having come in contact – directly or indirectly – with Chartist beliefs of the sort Julian Harney helped implant in Moray. A further factor in Falconer's radicalisation is likely to have been his exposure to pressures of the sort then propelling many skilled craftsmen – not just shoemakers but weavers, tailors and others – into left-leaning politics. Foremost among those pressures was the rapid growth in factory-based manufacture of items such as shoes, boots and garments – items formerly turned out by individual artisans whose products (in the face of mass-produced alternatives) were becoming harder and harder to sell. James Falconer, a married man with a family to support, could thus have been finding it hard to meet household expenses even before the price of meal began to spiral upwards in the hunger winter of 1846–47.[33]

Be that as it may, there is certainly no lack of testimony – from participants in riot as well as from the law enforcement side – to the effect that James Falconer did more than anyone else to shape the pattern of protest in Burghead. Falconer had a loyal lieutenant in Angus Davidson, eight years the shoemaker's senior and a man whose work had for some time taken him from his Burghead home to Hopeman where, Davidson explained, he was employed 'in making haddock barrels'. But it was James Falconer who was reported to have been 'particularly prominent' in the events of Monday 25 and Tuesday 26 January; going to Hopeman to rouse its residents to action; negating the efforts made by Hopeman's older skippers 'to keep [their] men,' as one of them said, 'out of any harm'; 'urging every man . . . he met' to do whatever it took to stop John Allan shipping oatmeal on the *Ceres* and *James and Jessie*. It may be, of course, that even if Falconer had done none of these things, Sheriff Cosmo Innes, on his arrival in Burghead, would have found himself coping with the aftermath of violence. The scale and intensity of this violence, however, appear to have owed a good deal to James Falconer.[34]

Returning to Elgin from Burghead on the late afternoon of Tuesday 26 January, Cosmo Innes, still just 24 hours out of Edinburgh, soon found himself encountering more unrest. This was unexpected. Elgin – with its well-paved streets, gas lighting, piped water supply and impressive public buildings – was already taking on the appearance of the 'tidy little city' described in a guide of 1868. As such, it was not, and had not been for a long time, a place accustomed to disorder of the sort that occurred that Tuesday evening when, as the *Elgin Courant* reported, 'a concourse of people assembled on the streets . . . and exhibited much turbulence at the residence of a gentleman extensively concerned in the grain trade'. The gentleman in question was John Allan whose home was in Elgin's King Street. His day had begun terrifyingly at Burghead Harbour. Now it ended no less frighteningly – Allan's house being 'assailed . . . with stones' prior to its being 'put in danger of being burned' when flaming material was 'thrust . . . in at the fanlight over the door'.[35]

Elgin's rioters, unlike their Burghead predecessors, were quickly dispersed by the authorities – leaving Innes free to concentrate, in consultation with others, on how best to get grain exports moving again. It was his intention, the sheriff made clear, to provide himself with such force as might be needed to bring Burghead to heel. This, Innes thought, would entail the swearing in and mobilisation of at least 100 special constables – something, it was agreed, that would take up much of the next morning. But while this was being attended to in Elgin, it was further agreed, William Young and William Grigor – Young being Burghead Harbour's owner and Grigor his lawyer – 'would go down to Burghead,' as Grigor explained, 'and [there] endeavour to persuade the people not to interfere with the shipment of meal'.[36]

Well before daybreak on Wednesday 27 January, then, Grigor and Young left Elgin for Burghead, getting there by 7 a.m. They began by calling on William Brown who owned the *James and Jessie*. His news was not encouraging. To safeguard the meal loaded on to his vessel on Tuesday, Brown said, its hatch covers had been padlocked. During the night, however, the covers had been stove in – by way of preparation, Brown suspected, for a Wednesday morning attempt to have his ship's cargo returned to John Allan's quayside warehouse. On hearing this, Young and Grigor told Brown that 'it [was] of great importance to get [his] vessel to sea' before any illegal unloading could commence. Both William Brown and his son, who skippered the *James and Jessie*, were – or appeared to be – in agreement that this should indeed be done. 'We . . . had every preparation made for the vessel going to sea by that [morning's] tide,' William Grigor said of what came next, 'when we discovered that Brown's son was [after all] unwilling to go, making the excuse that his crew [perhaps under pressure from their Burghead neighbours] had deserted him.'[37]

This, from Young and Grigor's standpoint, was a setback. But Burghead was still quiet and, the two men were informed, was likely to remain so as long as 'the Hopeman people . . . kept away'. By way of reassuring themselves on that point, Grigor said, 'we sent a person to the top of [a] hill which overlooks the road [from] Hopeman'. On this person '[coming] back and report[ing] to us that he saw no people on the road,' the lawyer continued, 'we went . . . for breakfast'. This they obtained in the Granary Street inn where John Allan and his escorts had sought refuge the day before. Managed by a young man called Lewis Grant, the inn, then the only such establishment in Burghead, was reputed to be a place where 'a good salmon, as well as more substantial fare, [could] always be had on the shortest notice'. Grigor and Young, who had been up since long before first light, are thus likely to have ordered a sizeable meal. It would soon be interrupted.[38]

This was because of what was then occurring in Hopeman where 'a rapping . . . to the doors' had signalled James Falconer's return to the village. Soon the shoemaker, now 'blowing a horn', was getting together 'a body' of men with a view to their staging a further march on Burghead where, Falconer insisted, it had again become essential to take action to 'stop . . . meal from being shipped'. Hence the enforced abandonment of Young and Grigor's breakfast – 'the innkeeper,' Grigor said, '[entering] the room [to tell] us that a great many of the Hopeman fishermen were . . . coming into the town'.[39]

Those fishermen's arrival, Grigor went on, 'had the effect of rousing the Burghead women' who were soon hard at work 'hoist[ing] the meal out of the [*James and Jessie's*] hold . . . and . . . carting it to Mr Allan's granary'. Both he and William Young went down to the quayside and spoke to 'several' of the women assisting with these operations, Grigor said, 'but we found . . . that it was vain for us to attempt to reason with them as they seemed determined to have meal . . . at a price to be fixed by themselves'. Young and Grigor accordingly returned to their breakfast, Grigor 'despatch[ing] a note to Sheriff Innes [to let him know] what was taking place'.[40]

In Elgin, meanwhile, Innes was having to engage in what he called 'some whipping and spurring' in order to get special constables signed up. 'The shopkeepers and tradesmen are either against us or are lukewarm and timid,' he informed Crown Agent John Lindsay. Equally unhelpful were Moray's landed proprietors – despite their being the ultimate beneficiaries of the grain trade Cosmo Innes was aiming to restart. 'No country gentlemen have looked near us,' the sheriff complained. By the time he received William Grigor's note, however, Innes had managed, with the help of Police Superintendent Hay, to get 'about 60' men mustered, sworn in, issued with batons and loaded into 'conveyances'. Climbing into one of these carriages, the sheriff, along with Hay, a couple of Hay's constables and Procurator Fiscal Alexander Brown, set off once more for Burghead.[41]

At Burghead, Cosmo Innes and his party made at once for the inn where William Young and William Grigor were already installed. Outside, the sheriff wrote later, 'a large mob [had] assembled, perhaps from 400 to 500 . . . and for the most part fishermen armed with bludgeons or boat-stretchers'.* Inside, Hay said, Innes 'called [everyone present] into a large room and stated that the meal which had [earlier] been put on board [the *James and Jessie*] had that morning been taken off by the mob and lodged in Mr Allan's granary'. Since it would thus 'be in vain to attempt . . . to put it [back] on board,' Hay went

---

* Boat-stretchers are detachable spars against which rowers rest their feet to increase their purchase on their oars.

on, 'our business would be to endeavour to get hold [of] and secure some of the ringleaders of the riot of the previous day'.[42]

Innes's entire force duly exited the inn to confront a 'mob' that was every moment being joined by new recruits – women as well as men. 'We . . . had not proceeded far,' William Grigor said, 'when the fiscal pointed out one of the Hopeman men [who] . . . was seized hold of'. This was Daniel Sutherland whom the fiscal, Alexander Brown, had 'marked out' in the course of Tuesday's disturbances. 'Instantly,' said Superintendent Hay, 'there was a general rush at rescue.' Hay was thrown to the ground, the special constables surrounding Sutherland were 'overpowered' and Sutherland himself spirited away into the crowd, which – enraged rather than cowed by the attempted arrest of one of its number – promptly launched a massed assault on Sheriff Innes and his men.[43]

'Immense showers of stones [collected from a nearby beach] were thrown at us,' Hay said, '[and] the [special] constables . . . broken in rank.' While a larger group withdrew into the inn, a smaller contingent, unable to gain the inn's interior, were 'driven down a lane' towards stables at its rear. 'The mob then attacked the inn [itself],' said William Grigor, 'broke the whole windows in front . . . destroyed the door and [by pounding the building with stones] knocked large chips off the freestone [surrounding] the door and windows.'[44]

Among the special constables who tried to take Daniel Sutherland into custody was James Grant, manager of the Caledonian Bank's Elgin branch. While trying to prevent Sutherland's rescue, Grant said, he had received 'a tremendous blow on the right arm'. 'The blow was aimed at my head,' the banker continued, 'but I held up my arm and the blow cut me severely through my greatcoat, undercoat and shirt. I then got a blow with a stone in the chest which knocked me down . . . I was . . . for a few seconds quite insensible and . . . if a woman, on hearing me call out *Murder*, had not inter-fered, I do believe I would have been killed.'[45]

Another of Innes's special constables was James Gillan who had retired to Elgin from Jamaica where he had practised as a surgeon. He had helped carry James Grant into the shelter of a hayloft above the inn's stables, Gillan said: 'He [Grant] was in a very weak state . . . I got some water and washed his face which was covered with blood. I also got a little brandy and water for him and he began to rally . . . Mr Grant is a very strong, stout-built person and I am satisfied [that], if he had not been so, he would not have got the better of his injuries.'[46]

Also assisting James Grant was another special constable, Alexander Forteith, who farmed at Newton, two or three miles west of Elgin. 'The mob were most violent,' he said. 'I never saw people in such a state of frenzy.' So heightened were rioters' emotions, Forteith believed, that they had ceased to respect, or fear, even the most senior officials on the receiving end of their onslaught. Everyone involved in the rescue of Daniel Sutherland and the subsequent beating up of Grant and others was wholly 'disregardless', the farmer thought, of the authority supposedly possessed by Superintendent Hay, Procurator Fiscal Brown or, for that matter, Sheriff Cosmo Innes.[47]

Inside the inn, Innes himself had arrived at much the same conclusion. Order in Burghead, it was evident, would never be restored by however many special constables he might deploy. Military aid would be required. Seeking out Lewis Grant, the sheriff accordingly asked the innkeeper for 'writing materials'. On these being produced, Innes scribbled a quick letter to the commander of the Fort George garrison. It was imperative, this letter stated, that as many troops as could be made available should at once be sent to Moray.[48]

The sheriff's letter was entrusted to one of Hay's full-time constables, John Cumming, whose instructions were to borrow, or commandeer, a horse and then ride 'express' to Fort George, just under 30 miles away. 'I got out of the inn by a back way,' Cumming explained. All went well, he continued, until on Burghead's outskirts he was set upon by four men who appear to have had the task of monitoring approaches to the town. 'They demanded my baton,' the policeman said, 'and then took off my coat, tore my cap and took my [note]book from my pocket and tore the leaves out of it.' Cumming was not detained, however. Nor was Innes's letter discovered by his assailants – Cumming, anticipating trouble, having hidden it inside his shoe.[49]

It would be a day or two, Innes knew, before military assistance could reach Moray from Fort George. In the interim, he also knew, it would be necessary for him to organise the withdrawal of his battered and demoralised special constables from Burghead. The means of doing this were provided by the arrival on the scene of a man described as 'a senior fisherman in Hopeman'. This was John MacPherson. Having failed that morning to dissuade Hopeman's younger men from falling in with James Falconer's plans, MacPherson had walked into town to discover, he said, 'stones flying in all directions and the windows of the inn smashed into pieces'. By speaking with the people massed around the inn and 'endeavour[ing] to pacify them', MacPherson managed to gain access to the sheriff and, in effect, open negotiations with him. These talks centred on two demands voiced from among the crowd outside. The first was that Innes guarantee that meal would be put on sale in Burghead at a price no higher than 24 shillings a boll. The second concerned the fate of two rioters who had been snatched, more or less at random, by a small group of Innes's special constables in the course of this group's earlier retreat to the safety of the inn. Those prisoners, the crowd insisted, must now be set free.[50]

While again taking care to stress that he 'had no control over prices', the sheriff told John MacPherson and – through him – the hundreds of now quieter people in the streets that every effort would be made to have Burghead and Hopeman supplied with oatmeal. This, though it may have helped MacPherson to ease tensions, was to do little more than repeat an earlier promise. Much harder for Innes to approve was the liberation of men he and his colleagues had formally taken into custody. But only if this were done, MacPherson advised the sheriff, would he be able, to 'prevent . . . further mischief'. The two prisoners were accordingly released and, through John MacPherson's good offices, Innes and everyone else sheltering in the inn and in its adjoining stables were shortly afterwards permitted to leave Burghead for Elgin – though not before the sheriff's special constables were made to comply with what one of them called 'very violent and insolent demands' that they hand their batons to men they had battled just an hour or two before.[51]

Shortly after he got back to Elgin, Cosmo Innes, summarising events in Burghead for the benefit of John Lindsay in Edinburgh, wrote: 'We have been well licked and beaten off [in] disgrace.' Nor was the sheriff at all confident that his humiliations were at an end. 'My constables have lost heart and some of them are badly hurt,' he informed the crown agent. 'I have not much confidence of keeping the peace . . . or protecting property.' That these forebodings were well-founded was proved by renewed disturbances in Elgin that same Wednesday evening.[52]

Two or three hours after dark, people began to gather outside the Elgin home of Sheriff-Substitute Patrick Cameron with whom Innes was lodging. 'The mob,' Innes commented of the crowd that thus took shape, '[was] a determined one of 300 or so men with the usual accompaniment of women and children.' Clearly influenced by Innes's earlier surrender of his Burghead prisoners, those people had taken to the streets, as their 'leader' or spokesman made plain to the two sheriffs, to demand the handing over to them of a man who had earlier been arrested as a result of his having had a leading role in the previous evening's attack on the home of grain merchant John Allan.[53]

This man, John Lawrence, was being held in Elgin's jail. Located just beyond the western frontage of St Giles Church in the town's High Street, the jail was a 200-year-old building in very poor condition. Even had it been possible to defend such a place, Innes commented, he and Cameron 'had no means' with which to do so. 'The [special] constables who . . . returned fatigued from Burghead were in bed or had disappeared.' There was, moreover, a real possibility that the Elgin crowd, if 'exasperated' by a refusal to submit to their ultimatum, might mount 'an attack upon the houses of the town as well as upon . . . [grain] mills in the neighbourhood'. There was thus no alternative, in Innes's view, but to agree to the jail doors being unlocked and Lawrence being 'given up'. The sheriff's anguish, however, was plain. 'I feel mortified much more than I can say,' he wrote.[54]

Dispatches containing details of this new reversal – dispatches compiled by Cosmo Innes just prior to midnight on Wednesday – reached John Lindsay's Edinburgh office first thing on Friday morning. Having already 'worked night and day' to convince military commanders to send troops north, the crown agent was now more than ever persuaded of the need to expedite such a deployment. What had taken place in Moray, Lindsay advised Lord Advocate Rutherfurd, was nothing other than 'one of the heaviest disgraces that can occur to the civil power – [a] sheriff stoned and then forced to open [a] county jail . . . I see no end of the flame if it is not smothered effectually and at once . . . The larger the force sent, the quicker will be the desired result – complete submission [of all rioters] and the seizure of the ringleaders for punishment.'[55]

By way of ensuring that the military were fully in accord with this thinking, the crown agent had a letter conveyed by messenger to Colonel John Eden at Edinburgh Castle. 'The Sheriff of Elginshire is overpowered and the county without support,' this communication informed the C-in-C's adjutant. It had therefore become imperative, Lindsay added, that Eden finalise any outstanding arrangements and at once issue orders for the prompt departure for Moray of at least an initial detachment of troops. The crown agent's letter reached the colonel at around 10 a.m. on Friday 29 January. That afternoon, 50 men of the 76th Regiment left Edinburgh Castle, marched to Newhaven and boarded the *Cuckoo*, which then sailed for Burghead. Next day 100 more men followed – this second contingent taken north by a passenger steamer, the *Bonnie Dundee*, which normally sailed between Aberdeen and Edinburgh* but which John Lindsay, in order to get round the scarcity of naval vessels, had chartered two or three days previously.[56]

*   *   *

---

* Coastal passenger services of this type would soon be made obsolete by the expansion of the railway network.

Although obscured by the ferocity of what occurred in Burghead during the afternoon of 27 January, one of the more striking aspects of that day's events is the highly disciplined behaviour of the women who, prior to the fracas at the town's inn, unloaded more than 12 tons of oatmeal from the hold of the *James and Jessie*. Many of those women must have been hard-pressed to find food for their families. But they kept none of the meal they handled. Instead, they returned every ounce to John Allan's premises in one of the stone-built warehouses still to be seen today at Burghead Harbour. Much the same had happened in Macduff and Portgordon – just as it would in other Moray Firth communities in the weeks ahead. For a time, riot and disturbance were endemic in those communities. Theft was not. Lots of the rioters he confronted, Cosmo Innes noted, 'were in considerable distress'. But, he added, they stole nothing: 'There has been no plundering or pilfering of the grain or meal which was in their power.'[57]

That was because scarcely any of the thousands of people who took part in the Moray Firth protest movement of early 1847 thought it legitimate to help themselves to food. Their grievances centred on oatmeal's soaring cost. Price hikes, they suspected, came about in part because of scarcities caused by grain being sent south – which is why so much effort was put into halting ship-ments of the sort being undertaken so profitably by Allan and other corn merchants. But still more basic to the outlook of many of the people who brought grain trading to a standstill was their belief that a meal price in excess of 30 or 32 shillings a boll was in breach of what was right and acceptable in the ethical sense of those terms.

To think about cost in this way in 1840s Britain was to be at odds with capitalist economics of a sort that had taken on, in the minds of most opinion-formers, the status of an unchallengeable truth. Price levels, it was reckoned in the country's ruling circles, were entirely a function of supply and demand. And for anyone to interfere with, let alone overturn, this market mechanism – even in the context of combating famine in Ireland or in the Highlands and Islands – was considered to be not just unwise but impossible.

The Burghead and Hopeman rioters, however, adhered to pre-capitalist approaches to price determination. Victorian Britain's politicians might have abandoned thinking of the sort that led their seventeenth-century predeces-sors to prohibit grain exports from the Scottish north. But just such thinking, as mentioned in relation to events in Aberdeenshire and Banffshire, continued to make perfect sense to hungry crowds who set about banning by force what the Scottish Privy Council had once banned by edict. Nor were those same crowds at all persuaded by arguments to the effect that commodity costs were outside human jurisdiction. The selling of food, from the perspective of people who found it hard to purchase that same food, was something that ought to be governed, as much of the rest of life was governed, by moral, as well as financial, considerations. What this meant in practice, or so Hopeman and Burghead residents said over and over again in January 1847, was that meal should retail for around 20 shillings a boll. Prices at this level were fair. A price of 30 or 32 shillings, in contrast, was unfair. More than that, it was unjust, iniquitous, wrong.[58]

As the *Elgin Courier* took some delight in pointing out, fishing families, when advancing arguments of this kind, were susceptible to accusations of hypocrisy. People who expected to be free to 'export fish', the paper commented, wished to be equally free to engage in 'lawless proceedings' intended to 'prevent the exportation of grain'. But the *Courier*, for all its denunciations of riot and disorder, accepted that something had to be done to tackle the causes of discontent: 'We are convinced that the present high prices have created much suffering among the industrious classes. It is high time that the more highly favoured of every town, village and parish were taking measures to alleviate the sufferings of the poor.' What was required, then, was for landlords, farmers and others in Moray to do what had already been done by their Banffshire counterparts and find some means of making oatmeal available at prices fixed in accordance, not with what the market would bear, but with what the generality of people considered reasonable.[59]

Moves in that direction were initiated within hours of the riot that culminated, on Wednesday 27 January, in the expulsion of Cosmo Innes and his special constables from Burghead. That evening, Burghead's proprietor, William Young, and Young's legal adviser, William Grigor, called on John Allan whose Elgin home still bore the scars – scorch-marks and broken windows principally – left by the previous night's attack on it. The time had come, Young and Grigor told the grain-dealer, for him to make some concession to feeling in Burghead and Hopeman. Allan agreed. He would immediately release 100 bolls of meal for sale at below market rates, he said. An hour or two later, Grigor and Young were in Burghead and addressing a hurriedly organised meeting. Who, their listeners were asked, should be entrusted with the promised meal? The people present, said Grigor, 'pointed at . . . [one] Jaffray, a baker, whose mother dealt in meal, and . . . they [the baker and his mother] agreed to take charge of the meal [from John Allan] and to retail [it] at a fair price'.[60]

Ways of cutting oatmeal's cost were also exercising Sheriff-Substitute Patrick Cameron. On Tuesday 26 January, as he informed the Hopeman and Burghead delegates who lobbied him that morning, he had invited Moray farmers, landowners and corn merchants to meet with him in Elgin on the following Friday. His meeting, Cameron's circular stated, was being called 'for the purpose of considering the existing supply of oats and oatmeal in the county . . . and adopting measures to allay . . . excitement on that subject'. So big was the resulting turn-out, the *Elgin Courier* reported, that Cameron's chosen venue, Elgin's courthouse, was 'crowded to excess'. What he wanted, Cameron told the 'very numerous and influential' audience he had attracted was an 'assurance' from grain-growers present 'that they would not sell more of their . . . oat crop for exportation'. A resolution to this effect was promptly approved overwhelmingly – John Allan, described by the *Courier* as 'one of the most extensive corn shippers [in] the county', going so far as 'to bind' himself 'to buy no more grain of any kind for exportation [and] . . . to supply the provision dealers of Burghead with whatever quantity of oatmeal they [might] require for the next six months'. Next on the sheriff-substitute's agenda was the possibility of funds being raised with a view to subsidising the cost of meal to working people in every part of Moray. 'They were all bound together by one common interest,' it was said of this proposal by Archibald Duff, the Drummuir laird who was also Hopeman's principal proprietor, 'and it was the duty of [the] . . . more wealthy [among them] to look to the interest and welfare of other classes.' Cash, it was duly resolved, should begin to be collected at once.[61]

An enthusiastic backer of this initiative was Elgin's provost, James Wilson. On the day preceding Sheriff Cameron's courthouse gathering, Wilson and his fellow councillors had issued an appeal for calm – this appeal coming hard on the heels of Tuesday's violence at John Allan's home and Wednesday night's forced opening of Elgin's jail. 'We are deeply concerned,' Wilson and his colleagues declared, 'to find that the anxiety of the community to secure to themselves and their families a sufficient supply of food . . . has so much excited even the peaceable and well-disposed as to induce them to look on with favour, or at least with indifference, while a lawless mob were engaged in riotous proceedings. We earnestly request that all heads of families, tradesmen and others, will be careful to prevent their children, apprentices . . . and servants from being on the streets, or out of doors, after nine o'clock at night.' If Elgin's peace was thus preserved, the town council's 'address' to townsfolk continued, remedial action on food prices would follow: 'We shall do all that men can do to secure . . . an abundant supply of food; and . . . we can, with the assistance of the humane and charitable, provide a fund out of which to assist those who are unable to provide, by their industry, for themselves and their families in the way that has been so generously and effectively done for . . . the destitute inhabitants of the [Hebridean] islands.'[62]

The people Provost Wilson was particularly keen to help were not the poorest of the poor. They, he felt, could look to Elgin's Parochial Board for the aid to which they were entitled. Most at risk and thus most prone to engage in protest and disturbance, Wilson considered, were labourers and others for whom the parochial board, forbidden legally from helping anyone capable of taking paid employment, could do nothing. An Elgin workman with a wife and four children, the provost calculated, was likely to require at least six pounds of meal a day* to provide himself and his family with adequate nourishment. At the then market price, Wilson pointed out, such a family's weekly meal bill would be well over eight shillings. This would have to come out of weekly earnings that were unlikely to exceed nine or ten shillings – leaving next to no cash for other essentials like rent, fuel and milk. Hence the discontent that so quickly turned into runaway disorder.[63]

James Wilson's thinking was persuasive. In the closing days of January and the early weeks of February, not just in Elgin but in other towns in its vicinity, immense efforts were made to raise the cash needed to facilitate the provision of meal, 'at such prices,' it was said, 'as could be afforded'. The speed at which contributions came forward is extraordinary. In Forres, for example, a sum equivalent to £20,000 at present-day values was raised in a single day in a place with a population not much above 3,000 – the town's provost, Robert Urquhart, himself donating no less than a tenth of that total.[64]

Although strongly supportive of all such measures, Cosmo Innes, for his part, remained set on stamping out the 'riotous and turbulent spirit' that was all too discernible, he believed, not just in Elgin, Hopeman and Burghead, but in 'the whole district' for which, as Elginshire's sheriff, he was responsible. In endeavouring to do this, Innes was helped greatly by his having been provided, by the start of the first week in February, with the better part of 200 troops.

When Police Constable John Cumming got to Fort George on the evening of Wednesday 27 January and handed to the base commander, Colonel

---

* This amount is roughly equivalent to what the organisers of famine relief in the Highlands and Islands considered a minimum allocation to a family of this size.

Alexander Findlay, Cosmo Innes's appeal for help, Findlay's response was immediate. At five the next morning, 40 soldiers – around three-quarters of the Fort George garrison – set off for Elgin, which, courtesy of 'special conveyances' provided for them at Nairn, they reached just nine hours later. The pacifying impact of this development, which Innes thought considerable, was strengthened by the arrival, over the next four days, of the two detachments, amounting between them to a further 150 soldiers, Crown Agent Lindsay had managed to get sent from Edinburgh.[65]

HMS *Cuckoo*, the Newhaven-based gunboat commanded by Lieutenant Abraham Parks, hove to off Burghead just after nightfall on Saturday 30 January – at the end, Parks reported, of 'a very stormy passage'. Thinking 'the surf too heavy to effect a landing', Parks contented himself with firing his vessel's heavy guns in order to make it known ashore, despite it now being dark, that the military was about to take a hand in what had been occurring in Moray. Parks then sailed on to more sheltered waters near Fort George where, on Sunday morning, he landed the 50 troops – all 'much exposed to the weather' – he had brought north.[66]

The shattering sound of naval gunfire off Burghead produced exactly the result Parks hoped for. 'A report of its coming,' Innes noted of the *Cuckoo*'s noisy arrival on the scene, 'spread like wildfire and the effect has been marvellous.' That was written towards midnight on Saturday. The rest of the weekend passed uneventfully and, on Monday, Innes, accompanied by some of the soldiers who had reached Elgin on Thursday, went to Burghead to 'superintend', as he put it, the 'reloading' of the meal 'unshipped' from the *James and Jessie* at the height of the previous week's troubles. That same morning 100 soldiers were disembarked at Burghead from the *Bonnie Dundee* – the *Cuckoo* delivering its quota of 50, rested by a night's sleep at Fort George, in the course of the afternoon.[67]

A sizeable troop contingent was left in Burghead, which Innes reckoned 'quiet but sulky'. Most of the newly arrived soldiers, however, were marched to Elgin. From there, on Tuesday and over several days following, the sheriff led a series of expeditions, each one consisting mainly of heavily armed troops, to the various harbour towns and villages in his Elginshire sheriffdom – Lossiemouth, Findhorn and Garmouth as well as Burghead – where trading in grain had been obstructed.[68]

Lossiemouth, where a 'mob composed chiefly of women' had compelled prospective shippers to return meal to storage, was speedily dealt with. Findhorn, west of Burghead, proved more time-consuming. Because ships sailing into or leaving Findhorn Bay had to hire local pilots acquainted with the shifting sandbars at the bay's junction with the Moray Firth, it had been easy to stop grain shipments from the village. The pilots, most of whom were also fishermen, had simply gone on strike. This 'illegal conspiracy', as the authorities termed it, had been organised by a 12-strong committee of whom the 'promoter' or 'ringleader' was reportedly John MacKay, a local shop-keeper. On it becoming evident to Cosmo Innes that MacKay and his colleagues had, in effect, taken control of Findhorn – calling community meetings by 'tuck of drum' and ordering people to ensure that no carter could access the village or its harbour – the sheriff ordered the shopkeeper's arrest. On Thursday 4 February, he was duly detained and, under military escort, conveyed to Elgin. Also seized and jailed that Thursday was another Findhorn resident, Elizabeth Hadden, described by Innes as 'a very mischievous [and] turbulent woman who was first in all the attacks on corn carters'.[69]

Hadden and MacKay were joined in prison by several people apprehended in the course of repeated sweeps through Burghead and Hopeman. Among them were the two women, Elizabeth Grant and Janet MacIntosh, earlier earmarked for eventual arrest by Procurator Fiscal Alexander Brown. Also conveyed to jail in Elgin at Brown's instigation were Hopeman fishermen John Main, John Young and Daniel Sutherland. Not found, however, were the two Burghead men the authorities most wanted to lay hands on, cooper Angus Davidson and shoemaker James Falconer. On Sunday 31 January, perhaps alerted to the likely reimposition of Sheriff Innes's authority in Burghead by the previous evening's discharge of the *Cuckoo*'s guns, Falconer and Davidson had left their homes and had not returned. A reward of £5 apiece – equivalent together to more than most labourers then earned in five months – was at once offered for information leading to the shoemaker and cooper's arrest.[70]

Davidson and Falconer's disappearance was one obstacle in the way of Cosmo Innes's stated intention to bring 'the whole county [of Moray] again under the law'. Another was the continuing intransigence of people in Garmouth. Today separated from the tidal waters of the Spey estuary by changes in the river's course, Garmouth in the 1840s was, as it had been for many years, a harbour village and shipbuilding centre – turning out sailing ships constructed from timber floated down the Spey from Highland forests. Occupying a little piece of rising ground on the western bank of the river, which divided Innes's Elginshire sheriffdom from its Banffshire neighbour, Garmouth was just four or five miles from the Banffshire fishing communities of Portgordon and Buckie – which is why it had been easy for Garmouth folk to join the Portgordon-organised march on the Richmond Estate's head-quarters in Fochabers.[71]

That march took place on 26 January. In Garmouth it marked the commencement of a period characterised, according to the *Elgin Courant*, by 'utmost excitement . . . among the working classes'. 'Order and regularity were set at nought,' the paper continued, 'by the unruly proceedings of a number of women . . . Guards were kept during the night to warn . . . of the approach of any carts with grain for the [riverside] stores [or granaries], and in daytime the most perfect surveillance was observed. Farmers' [carts] . . . have been repeatedly attacked [and their] drivers abused . . . In several cases grain has been taken possession of, conveyed to the granaries, and the keys [of those granaries] kept by the mob.'[72]

Had Cosmo Innes tried to enter Garmouth with only special constables for support, the chances are that he would have had to withdraw every bit as ignominiously as he had been forced to withdraw from Burghead. Knowing this, the sheriff, now well-supplied with military backing, launched a care-fully co-ordinated and multipronged invasion of the village. First the *Cuckoo* was sent into the river estuary with orders to once more discharge its guns. Next, and in accordance with arrangements made with Richmond Estate managers, a set of grain-loaded carts from farms in the vicinity of nearby Fochabers trundled into Garmouth in the company of Cosmo Innes and no fewer than 140 armed troops. At this point, Innes reported, 'a horn was blown and the whole female population mustered'. On attempts being made to halt the advancing carts, the sheriff continued, 'we formed lines for their protec-tion. This was met with great shouts and violent language . . . the people [men as well as women] pressing in multitudes upon the soldiers and using the most violent expressions.'[73]

Soon grain was being put aboard a waiting ship. This resulted in several individuals from among the crowd trying to cut its mooring ropes and in the sheriff ordering 'two of the most noisy women to be apprehended'. The two in question, Margaret MacDonald and Isabella Bowie, were placed in a cart, Innes wrote, and 'escorted by [an army] sergeant's party to Elgin jail. The effect was miraculous. Whenever a woman afterwards saw me pointing her out . . . she slunk off.' It took two days together with further arrests – this time of two men, James Shand and James Guthrie, 'who had been very violent in talk' – to restore Garmouth to a semblance of normality. But by the evening of the second day, Innes felt it possible to describe the village, where 50 soldiers were under orders to remain for some time, as being at last 'quiet'. Much the same, by this point, was true of Moray as a whole.[74]

In Edinburgh, John Lindsay received news of this development with some relief. Overall, however, the situation in the north continued to cause the crown agent the most acute concern. Foremost among his anxieties, Lindsay informed Lord Advocate Rutherfurd, were dangers arising from there still being no worthwhile troop reserve at his disposal. Between them, to be sure, Sheriff Alexander Currie in Banffshire and Sheriff Innes in Elginshire were now in control of nearly 250 infantrymen. But none of these soldiers, the two sheriffs claimed, could be spared for service elsewhere. Currie, for his part, insisted on his 50-strong contingent being kept on hand to deal with any fresh disorders in either Portgordon or Macduff. Innes's 190 men had meanwhile been dispersed across his sheriffdom – with a view to their garrisoning, in effect, Burghead and Elgin as well as Garmouth. In all of the Moray Firth area, it followed, the only uncommitted troops to be had consisted of the dozen or so soldiers left behind at Fort George when their comrades marched off in response to Cosmo Innes's original plea for aid. That would not have mattered if the rest of the north was as peaceable as Banffshire and Moray now appeared to be. But this, as John Lindsay well knew, was not the case. The encouraging communications he had begun to get from Cosmo Innes were more than offset by ever more alarming dispatches reaching him from Inverness.

6

'Acts of the most disgraceful character'

Inverness • Nairn • Beauly • Rosemarkie • Fortrose • Avoch
Cromarty • Urray • Invergordon • Evanton • Foulis Point
Thurso • Castletown • Alness • Dingwall

On the afternoon of Saturday 30 January 1847, the day that ended in Burghead with naval gunfire out at sea, three of Inverness's key decision-makers met with John and William Chisholm, brothers who owned a grain-selling business. The officials taking part in what was a hurriedly arranged meeting at Inverness Castle were William Simpson, the town's provost, William Colquhoun, one of Inverness-shire's several sheriff-substitutes, and John MacKay, the county's procurator fiscal. He and his brother, John Chisholm said, had contracted to send 400 quarters, or five tons, of barley to Leith aboard a cargo ship they expected to reach Inverness over the weekend. 'But . . . he had reason to believe,' the grain merchant added, 'that the shipment would be violently obstructed.' What he wanted, John Chisholm went on, was an assurance that he, his brother and their suppliers would be shielded from attack. No such assurance could be given, Chisholm was informed. Neither Inverness nor Inverness-shire possessed worthwhile numbers of policemen, it was explained; and because 'the few soldiers stationed at Fort George [had] been called to Elgin', there was no immediate possibility of troops being made available. In these circumstances, the Chisholms were advised, it would be best if they put any shipping plans on hold.[1]

At Inverness Castle, the Chisholm brothers, according to John MacKay, 'agreed to suspend [their] shipment'. Within hours, however, they had changed their minds and 'intimated their intent to ship on Monday unless the sheriff and the provost would guarantee them from all loss or damage they might be found liable [for] through delay in fulfilling their engagements'. What the Chisholms wanted in return for deferring grain shipments, then, was a promise that the Inverness authorities would indemnify them against losses arising from breach of contract. When told that no such indemnification could be granted, the brothers duly dug in their heels and made known that, in the absence of the compensation they had requested, they would start on Monday to load the ship that, by Saturday night, had docked at Thornbush Quay on the lower, and tidal, reaches of the River Ness. The Chisholms' stance, Procurator Fiscal MacKay informed Crown Agent John Lindsay, was likely to have serious consequences. 'Up to this we are all quiet [here],' runs a letter MacKay wrote on the morning of Sunday, 'but appearances [now] indicate an outbreak ... Various persons have ... hinted to the Chisholms that it will be in vain to attempt [shipment]; that their persons and property will be [at] imminent risk; and that 400 persons have signed an obligation [or undertaking] to prevent [grain reaching the quay] ... Last night the streets were unusually crowded and ... there is an evident feverishness in the minds of the people.' Where such 'feverishness' could lead had become all too apparent to John MacKay exactly 12 months before when, for a day or two, public order in Inverness had been brought close to collapse. Now, the procurator fiscal feared, much the same thing was going to happen again.[2]

Among the hundreds of Inverness folk involved in the 1846 disturbances that, a full year on, still troubled John MacKay was a 12-year-old boy called John Fraser. 'On the night of Thursday last [5 February],' John said of his part in the events of that evening, 'two [older] boys ... came into my mother's house, when I was going to bed, and asked me to come out with [my] drum.' In partnership with three friends, John continued, he had some time previously set up 'a musical band in the Merkinch where I live'. One of his pals, John said, played a triangle; the other two played flute-like fifes of the sort favoured by the army's marching bands; he himself was his band's drummer. This, John was told by the callers at his mother's home, was why his services were required by people wishing, in effect, to rouse Merkinch and neighbouring localities by means of tuck of drum – a long-standing procedure which, as mentioned earlier, would be employed again in several north of Scotland localities in the opening weeks of 1847.[3]

He had not wanted to go with his visitors, John said, and his widowed mother Margaret had been still more opposed to his making any kind of night-time excursion from the upstairs room they shared in Merkinch's Grant Street. But for John, it seems, refusal to do as he was asked was not an option.

'The boys,' he said, 'pulled me out to the door and downstairs where there was a number of persons collected . . . They all insisted on my getting the drum [which was stored elsewhere] and going with them.' It was to be his role, the boy now learned, to head a march which, from Merkinch or 'the Merkinch' as the district was then called, would head first for the Green of Muirtown, like Merkinch an area occupied largely by labouring people, before turning towards the town centre. This march, its organisers were clear, had to be a big one. Only by getting a lot of people to join them could they demonstrate that there was, in Merkinch and more widely, a great deal of opposition to exports of a basic foodstuff.[4]

Twelve months later, the foodstuff at the centre of similar protests would be oatmeal. But this was 1846, not 1847, and Merkinch people were taking to the streets in an attempt to keep in the north a crop which, during the late summer and autumn of 1845, had been diseased in every part of the British Isles except the Highlands. This crop was potatoes. And though many Merkinch and Green of Muirtown residents possessed, as will be seen, their own potato patches, there were plenty of families reliant, in part at least, on the potato market held twice weekly in the town's Academy Street. Towards the end of January, an Academy Street trader said, potato prices had shot up (much as meal prices would do in 1847) and it had become harder and harder (as would also happen in the case of meal) to buy potatoes in small quantities. 'I have seen the market with so scanty a supply,' this same trader commented, 'that . . . people who came to purchase could get none . . . I know that there are several wholesale buyers in the district at present who are shipping potatoes [southwards] and the farmers in general prefer selling them that way [to] bringing them into the market to retail.'[5]

Resulting discontents boiled over on Tuesday 3 February 1846 when, as the *Inverness Courier* reported, 'a mob composed principally of women and boys . . . turned back carts on their way to the Thornbush [Quay]' where 'two vessels [were] . . . loading potatoes for the London market'. Next day, Wednesday, still bigger crowds occupied the quay while, elsewhere in town, other groups began to halt harbour-bound carts. On hearing of this lawlessness, said Inverness's provost, James Sutherland,* he made his way to Church Street, a principal thoroughfare, 'and [there] saw several carts with . . . a mob around them'. 'I addressed [members of this mob] on the impropriety of their

---

* Sutherland would be replaced by William Simpson (mentioned above) towards the end of 1846.

conduct,' the provost went on, 'but they hissed and hooted and closed in upon the carts and would not allow them to proceed.'[6]

A funeral held that same day had brought Inverness-shire's sheriff principal, William Fraser-Tytler, into Inverness where, he said, he 'was strongly urged on all sides instantly to send off for the military'. Initially reluctant to take such a step, Fraser-Tytler changed tack on going personally to Thornbush Quay, not far from Merkinch, and seeing carter after carter sent packing. 'Upon this,' the sheriff principal remarked, 'I wrote to the commanding officer at Fort George for the assistance of the military, sending off three [horse-drawn] omnibuses for them.' By Wednesday evening, the fort being only 12 miles distant, 70 soldiers had arrived in town where they were billeted in the castle.[7]

Thursday was one of Inverness's 'sacramental fast days' – meaning that all commercial and other activity came to a standstill to allow as many people as possible to attend church in advance of the communion services due to be held on the ensuing Sunday. No carts, it followed, entered town and all was quiet – until, two or three hours after nightfall, the several hundred people who by this stage had gathered in Grant Street moved off with, at their head, John Fraser, beating energetically on his drum and, despite his initial reservations, surely enjoying the applause that came his way from what must have been his largest ever audience.

To begin with, John said, he and his fellow marchers did nothing other than parade through Merkinch with the aim of adding to their numbers. Then, keeping the River Ness to their left, they made for the Green of Muirtown, on the same side of the river as Merkinch but closer to the town centre. Here John Fraser was approached by one of Inverness's ship-owners who, the boy said, 'came and caught hold of [my] drum to prevent me from playing and desired me to go home. But the crowd,' John went on, 'gathered round him and struck his hat [a top hat of some sort] down over his face.' The night, this confrontation suggested, was not destined to end peacefully – something that became all the more evident when, from the Green, the crowd, which the *Inverness Courier* put at 'fully 1,500', crossed the Ness by way of the bridge just downstream from Inverness Castle and made its way into the town's more upmarket districts.[8]

He knew from the moment he left Grant Street, said one Merkinch youth among the marchers, that 'it was their intention to go to the houses of different persons . . . and to break their windows'. The individuals thus targeted, it became apparent, were involved in the potato export trade or, if not so involved, were thought complicit in efforts made by the town council and others to keep that trade flowing. Among the latter group was John Nicol, a councillor and medical man who had been James Sutherland's predecessor as provost and whose property was first to suffer damage.[9]

Once across the Ness, the Merkinch and Green of Muirtown crowd, now turning right, surged towards Nicol's home in a recently established residential area adjacent to the river. Here men and women jointly 'tore down a wooden paling at the end of [the councillor's] house and commenced breaking the windows with stones'. This accomplished, everyone swept back towards the town to make a noisy and drum-accompanied circuit of Inverness's shopping and business quarters. By onlookers, among them John Nicol and Provost Sutherland who were attending a function in the centrally situated Caledonian Hotel, the 'able-bodied young men and labourers' in the crowd's front rank were seen to be equipped with heavy, club-like stakes they had taken from Nicol's wrecked fence. That was alarming. Still more alarming, said James Sutherland, was news that now reached him – this news being that the marchers striding past the Caledonian Hotel on Church Street 'had [already] broken Dr Nicol's windows and . . . were on their way to break mine'. It was also rumoured, the provost learned, that some among the hundreds on the streets wanted 'to set fire' to the distillery he had not long before established on the town's outskirts.[10]

In the event, the provost's distillery, on a site adjacent to the northernmost stretch of the Caledonian Canal, escaped destruction.* His house, however, was indeed attacked. It stood on Telford Street. Named for the man who had masterminded the nearby canal's construction, this street, still to be fully developed in the 1840s and thus flanked by just a handful of buildings, linked the town centre with James Sutherland's distillery and other commercial concerns that had taken shape around the Canal Basin, a harbour-like facility not far from the point where Thomas Telford's trans-Highland waterway enters the sea.

Provost Sutherland's home was occupied that evening by his two sons, his daughter and two servants. Because she had been warned by a quick-thinking town council employee that 'there was a mob coming to the house', said one of those servants, Catherine MacKenzie, she had pulled interior shutters

---

* Sutherland's distillery, the Glen Albyn as it came to be called, survived until the 1980s when it was closed and demolished. Its site is occupied today by retail outlets and associated carparks.

across each window. These protected carpets and furnishings from stone-shattered window glass. But so intense was the bombardment unleashed from the street that, as James Sutherland found when it was judged safe for him to return, 'almost every pane of glass in the front of the house was broken'.[11]

Also in Telford Street but a little further out of town was Pine Cottage, which, despite its modest-sounding name, was the imposing residence* belonging to James Masson who was both a timber merchant and a farmer – his farmland (today built over) lying just south of his home. Masson, because he was believed to have supplied some of the potatoes meant for London, was reckoned by most folk involved in the events of that Thursday evening to be every bit as deserving of their attentions as Councillor Nicol and Provost Sutherland. From Sutherland's wrecked home, then, the people thronging Telford Street began to advance on Pine Cottage – their approach witnessed by John Cameron, a 16-year-old member of Masson's domestic staff.

'I was in my master's house,' Cameron said, 'and heard the sound of a drum at a distance and I and the [household's] two servant girls went to the door to see what it was about, and I [saw] a crowd of people at Provost Sutherland's house, which is but a short distance from Mr Masson's, making a great noise.' Soon came sounds of breaking glass and not long after, John Cameron said, the Masson home too was approached by men who 'all appeared to have sticks which they were holding over their heads'.[12]

Those people were confronted both by James Masson and by Daniel Rose, a young man who assisted with the administration of Masson's timber business. On Masson demanding to know what the crowd wanted with him, there came repeated roars of 'Potatoes! Potatoes!' Struggling to make himself heard, Masson insisted he had sent no potatoes south. But this, while strictly accurate, was more than a little disingenuous – because, as was known widely or at least suspected, Pine Cottage's owner had sold consignment after consignment of potatoes to William Fraser, one of the Inverness-based dealers who had entered into supply contracts with merchants in London. None of James Masson's protestations, therefore, served to do more than delay for a minute or two the rain of stones soon unleashed on him, on Rose and on the home behind them.[13]

Masson now retreated into his house. But 'when . . . stones came through the windows', he said, he stepped out again, 'taking my gun in my hand'. 'The stones rattled about us,' Masson continued, 'on which I loaded my

---

* Today the Pine Guest House at 60 Telford Street.

gun . . . and told [the people in the street] that the first one that should fire a stone would be a dead man.' Joined by Daniel Rose, also brandishing a fire-arm, Masson next advanced down the flight of steps giving access to Pine Cottage's front door. At this, Rose said, 'the crowd . . . retreated and we followed them for a short way'. But guessing – correctly – that James Masson would not actually fire on them, the hundreds of men, women and young folk occupying much of Telford Street began again to rush forward, forcing Rose and Masson back and, by so doing, isolating Rose from his employer. 'Several of them,' Rose said of the people surrounding him, 'struck me on the head with sticks and fists . . . I was knocked down. I had [a] gun in my hand and struck some of them with it in self-defence, [but] the stock of the gun broke . . . and I was obliged to fly into the house.'[14]

The siege of Pine Cottage, where more than 40 panes of glass were broken that evening, was lifted only by the inexplicably belated intervention of the soldiers quartered in Inverness Castle. But the peace thus imposed did not last. Next day, when Sheriff Principal William Fraser-Tytler and 100 or so special constables he had mustered came under attack at Thornbush Quay, the military had to be called out once more – though not before the sheriff and his constables had been forced to evacuate the quay and seek refuge in a nearby brewery. From the brewery's windows, Fraser-Tytler said, he watched 'the mob [take] possession of [a] potato cart . . . empty the potatoes on the [quay] and throw the cart . . . into the sea'.[15]

'The history of all hitherto existing society,' Karl Marx and Friedrich Engels commented at the start of the *Communist Manifesto* they compiled in 1847, 'is the history of class struggles.' The Inverness events of that year and the year before, it is safe to say, were not foremost in the thoughts of Marxism's founders when they agreed those words. But the unrest which broke out in the Highland capital in February 1846, and which was to recur 12 months later, was shot through, for all that, with tensions of the sort Marx and Engels had in mind. Hence the pleasure Inverness's rioters obviously took in inflicting damage on the fine homes of people who, if not excessively wealthy, were far more comfortably placed than themselves. Hence too the apprehension that gripped the many better-off folk living east of the Ness when their streets began to echo to what the *Inverness Courier* called 'the most discordant shouts and yells' of people not normally seen en masse on that side of the river.[16]

'Every great city,' Engels observed in his 1845 report on social conditions in England, 'has one or more slums where the working-class is crowded together. True, poverty often dwells in hidden alleys close to the palaces of the rich; but, in general, a separate territory has been assigned to it, where, removed from the sight of the happier classes, it may struggle along as it can. These slums are pretty equally arranged in all the great towns . . . the worst houses in the worst quarters . . . usually one or two-storied cottages . . . almost always irregularly built. These houses . . . form . . . the dwellings of the working-class. The streets are generally unpaved, rough, dirty, filled with vegetable and animal refuse, without sewers or gutters, but supplied with foul, stagnant pools instead.'[17]

Inverness in the 1840s was by no means a 'great city' of the sort Engels wrote about. But it was divided socially in much the same way. In and around the town centre, streets were paved, 'well lighted' and equipped with drains and sewers. Piped water was beginning to be general in this area – as it was in the still being built-on localities where the town's businessmen, lawyers, doctors, teachers and other professionals were more and more taking up residence. Here, on rising ground to the south of the central district or on the Ness's eastern bank and upriver from the castle, there could be seen 'some of the newest houses and most beautiful villas' in the Highlands. No such affluence was to be glimpsed west of the river in areas like Merkinch or the Green of Muirtown – areas accessed either by the 200-year-old stone bridge below the castle or by the more recent Waterloo Bridge, which was constructed largely from timber and located half a mile nearer the sea.[18]

Over there, it was observed in an 1841 *Report on the Sanitary Condition of the Labouring Classes in the Town of Inverness*, the 'inhabitants' were mostly poor. Here gas and water supplies were unknown, streets unpaved and pavements non-existent. 'Rainwater and other accumulations [by which was meant sewage] pass[ed] away only by means of surface or open drains' that ended, very often, in 'stagnant pools' of the sort Engels mentioned. Nor were the houses alongside these reeking ponds anything other than dismal. Though some homes, like the one in Grant Street where John Fraser lived with his mother, ran to garret rooms accessed by stairs, most were 'only one-storey high and covered with straw thatch'. Often families occupied no more than a single apartment. And because lots of people kept pigs, while some kept dairy cows and one or two owned horses, it was by no means unknown for 'the pig, the horse and cow all [to] live under the same roof [as] their owners'. Where there were animals there was of course manure. But this, as the Poor Law Commission heard in 1843, was treated less as a health hazard, more as a valuable asset.[19]

The commission's informant on these points was Dr William Forbes, the person who, three years before, had defended Chartist Julian Harney's right to speak in Inverness. Forbes, the Poor Law Commission heard, had 'planned and set on foot' a 'dispensary' where the town's poor could access affordable or even free medical care. His charitable endeavours, Forbes told the Poor Law Commission, had provided him with 'many opportunities' of seeing for himself how matters stood in Inverness's less prosperous areas: 'In the Merkinch and the Green of Muirtown where the larger portion of the poor are to be met with . . . the floors [of the houses] . . . are earthen . . . The windows generally are small and there is a want of ventilation.' Most Green of Muirtown and Merkinch families, Forbes went on, 'have dunghills about their houses and a great want of cleanliness in and about them . . . They are very ill-off as respects bedding. Generally they [sleep on] a little straw or [on] ferns gathered from the hillside' – the hillside in question being the lower slopes of Craig Phadrig just beyond the Canal Basin.[20]

'The poor,' said William Forbes, 'live chiefly upon potatoes and a little milk . . . They raise their potatoes from manure collected from the woods and roadsides; and they live, in a great measure, on the potatoes grown from this manure; consequently, they accumulate quantities of manure about their doors, which tends very much to the production and diffusion of fevers.' As is evident from statements made to the Poor Law Commission by Forbes and others, the 'manure' of which so much mention was made consisted of animal droppings mixed with what would later be called compost. The droppings came from the livestock to be found throughout Merkinch and similar localities; the compost was made mainly from leaves; and the resulting concoction was carried or carted each spring to plots made available on farms within walking distance of the town. Those plots, in the vicinity of Inverness at least, were laid out in six-yard-wide strips. Close to the town, where demand was highest, a shilling secured an eight-yard length of such a strip. Further out, farmers might charge nothing – because a field divided in this way, dug over by hand and well fertilised would yield, during the following year, more oats, barley or wheat than might otherwise have been forthcoming.[21]

Arrangements of this kind were not peculiar to Inverness. Farmers in the neighbourhood of other urban centres made similar deals with townspeople. In Inverness's more disadvantaged districts, however, families appear to have relied more completely than elsewhere on the potatoes they harvested and stored away each autumn. Partly, perhaps, this was because many such families – described as 'poor tenants and cottagers' in one contemporary account – had moved into town following their eviction from rural localities where they had been crofters or smallholders. In this category, it seems likely, were those members of Inverness's 'poorer classes' by whom 'the Gaelic language [was] exclusively spoken'. People of that sort – some of them prone to 'the depression of mind' that William Forbes thought prevalent in places like Merkinch – may have derived some comfort from engaging in what would, to them, have been the long familiar tasks involved in cultivating a little piece of land. But when, in the late summer of 1846, potato blight reached every corner of the Scottish north, this group's dependence on potatoes left a substantial segment of Inverness almost as vulnerable to hunger as were crofting districts in the Hebrides and the West Highlands. That vulnerability, which became all the more acute as meal prices went up, was to mean that many families from Merkinch and the Green of Muirtown took once more to the streets.[22]

Inverness-shire's procurator fiscal, John MacKay, took a perverse pleasure in having been proved right about the likely outcome of grain-dealers William and John Chisholm's insistence on sticking with the planned loading of the Leith-bound ship, the *Morayshire*, which, by Monday 1 February 1847, lay at Thornbush Quay. This is evident from the tone of one of MacKay's reports to Crown Agent John Lindsay, a report the procurator fiscal sat down to write at around six that Monday evening. 'I . . . have to intimate that at an early hour this morning the Chisholms succeeded in shipping some grain,' MacKay began. 'But at length, as I anticipated, a mob consisting of women and young lads put an end to it by turning back one of the carts [making for] the Chisholms' storehouse and breaking the [storehouse] window with stones.' Sheriff-Substitute William Colquhoun and Provost William Simpson had gone down to the quay to 'remonstrate' with the crowd, the procurator fiscal wrote. This, predictably, had been 'in vain'. 'The mob proceeded through the town, increasing in number, and smashed the windows of several . . . mealmongers.' 'Tonight,' MacKay added at around 8 p.m., 'a large mob has congregated on the street in front of the Town Hall,* evidently bent on more mischief . . . The mob now consists of trades lads and labourers and amounts to several hundred.' 'The authorities,' John MacKay informed the crown agent, 'are . . . utterly helpless and can do nothing until aided by a strong military force which they trust will soon make its appearance.'[23]

---

* This was not Inverness's present-day Town House on which work would not start until 1878 but an earlier building on the same site.

No such appearance, however, was imminent. Sheriff Cosmo Innes, still engaged in efforts to pacify communities like Findhorn, Burghead and Garmouth, was determined to hang on to the 200 or so troops at his disposal until all was quiet in Moray. Fort George, it followed, was now more or less ungarrisoned. And though the crown agent and the lord advocate (who was still in London) were trying to have several hundred more troops shipped north from England, this was proving difficult to arrange. In the interim, it was felt in Edinburgh, John MacKay, Provost Simpson and Sheriff Colquhoun should concentrate on conscripting the strongest possible force of special constables. As had been shown in Elgin, however, attempts to bolster law enforcement by this means tended to founder on a general conviction that the stone-throwers and window-breakers, deplorable though their violence might be, had a good deal of right on their side. 'While we regret that such a spirit should manifest itself,' the *Inverness Courier* noted of the events of 1 February, 'we are afraid that the blame does not always rest with the crowd.' Equally if not more responsible for manifestations of unrest, the paper commented, were farmers and traders who had found it more profitable to export 'large quantities' of grain than to supply 'the retail market'. That the usually conservative, not to say reactionary, *Courier* should have given voice to these opinions is a pointer to their having been widely held. Other such pointers are to be found in the correspondence of Inverness's procurator fiscal. 'I understand that the general feeling of the community is in favour of preventing the shipping of grain,' John MacKay warned his Edinburgh superiors, 'and that the inhabitants [of Inverness] are not disposed [therefore] to act as special constables.'[24]

This was shown to be the case when some 300 men selected from among Inverness's 'more respectable' residents were ordered to present themselves at the town hall 'to be sworn in as special constables'. 'With few exceptions,' MacKay noted, 'they all attended. But it was evident from the speeches made by some of them, and the applause [those speeches] met with, that [many] . . . of them [are] strongly disaffected . . . Nearly half of them left the meeting [after] refusing to take the oath, [and] even of those who did take the oath a large proportion are not to be relied on.'[25]

Inverness, Provost William Sutherland informed Lord Advocate Rutherfurd, was experiencing 'violence and disturbance . . . of a very alarming nature'. Farmers and other 'holders of grain' had been forcibly 'deter[red]' from 'delivering' this grain to southern buyers and 'considerable injury [had been] done to private property'. But so prevalent was 'the feeling that the grain of the district should be kept within it' that, until military aid could be made available, any attempt to protect shippers like the Chisholm brothers was bound to be 'defeated'. Special constables, insofar as they could be recruited, were unlikely to go into battle on behalf of Inverness's grain-dealers, and there could be no 'certain reliance' that members of the regular police force – who were anyway few in number – would do so either.[26]

For much of the first half of February 1847, then, control of Inverness's streets was surrendered to well-organised groups of people who set up and manned a series of roadblocks all around the town. At those barriers every approaching cart was stopped and inspected. Carts found to be taking wheat to an Inverness bakery were 'allowed to pass', Procurator Fiscal MacKay reported. So was a cart 'laden with turnip seed'. But the drivers of carts thought to be making for Thornbush Quay were told to turn back; and when one carter disregarded an order to halt and tried to push on, his horse was seized and unyoked, his cart's contents tipped out and the cart itself dragged through Merkinch to the Waterloo Bridge where it was 'pitched . . . into the river'.[27]

But actions of this sort did not have to be repeated. Recognising the futility of attempting to get southbound grain through the blockade that had been put in place, farmers and traders simply gave up all notion of supplying the Lowland and English markets. There was, in consequence, no need for further violence. 'All has remained quiet here,' Sheriff Principal Fraser-Tytler informed the lord advocate on 9 February, 'but only from no shipments having been made; not, I fear, from any improvement . . . in the temper . . . of the people.' This, however, may have been an unduly gloomy reading of the popular mood. The 1 February protesters, after all, had won more than a suspension of sales of grain to faraway purchasers. Like their counterparts in Banffshire and Moray, they had gained widespread recognition of the urgent need to make food available to the many families who could not afford to buy it. The upshot was a concerted effort to ease the plight of people in places like Merkinch.[28]

As far back as October, the Inverness Parochial Board, suspecting that oatmeal prices were bound to rise in the course of the ensuing winter, had bought several tons of meal – for a much smaller outlay than would have been required some three months later. Because the meal distributions thus made possible were additional to the cash payments already being made to people in receipt of poor relief, they had the effect of cushioning those people – who were also provided with supplies of coal – from the worst effects of food scarcity.

Inverness's experience of the reformed Poor Law, then, was the reverse of Barra's. There, as seen earlier, the government's decision to make the administration of poor relief an entirely local responsibility had resulted in virtually no assistance reaching those entitled to aid. In Inverness, in contrast, the clergymen who dominated the town's newly established parochial board cited biblical authority* in support of their insistence that 'allowances be arranged on a liberal scale'. Nor were they alone in so doing. While the administrative structure put in place by the Poor Law Act of 1845 would come in time to be associated with grimly inadequate responses to poverty, the Act's immediate impact – certainly in the Highland capital and its vicinity – was beneficial. Just how marked was the change for the better is evident in the outlook of the parochial board serving Kirkhill, a wholly rural locality a little to the west of Inverness.[29]

When, in 1843, the Poor Law Commission interviewed William Gunn, the man in charge of distributing poor relief on behalf of the Church of Scotland's Kirkhill kirk session, his answers to the questions put to him were as revealing as they were terse: 'What are your usual allowances to the poor?' 'Sometimes 10 shillings a year; sometimes a little more.' 'Does the 10 shillings maintain them?' 'No.' 'How are they maintained?' 'That is more than I can say.'[30]

Two or three years later, when care of the Kirkhill poor had been taken over by a parochial board empowered to levy a rate on the parish's property owners, this situation had been transformed – the 50-plus individuals on the board's poor roll now getting, not 10 shillings a year, but 5 shillings a week. Like its Inverness counterpart, moreover, the Kirkhill board, in the run-up to the 1846–47 winter, laid in a stock of meal drawn on in such a way as to enable the board's inspector to supply each recipient of poor relief with a monthly oatmeal allowance of 2½ stones – an amount which, by January, was worth six or seven shillings.[31]

Nor was the Kirkhill board unsympathetic to appeals for aid received from people who, though formerly resident in the parish, had moved into Inverness. One such person was William Callum, a farm worker who, with his wife and family, had quit Kirkhill in 1839 when a recurrent illness made it impossible for him to remain in employment. By the end of 1846, the four oldest of

---

* The text quoted by the board was Deuteronomy 15:11. 'For the poor shall never cease out of the land: therefore I command thee, saying, Thou shalt open thine hand wide unto thy brother, to thy poor, and to thy needy, in thy land.'

Callum's seven children – who would have found it easier to get casual jobs in Inverness than in Kirkhill – were, between them, bringing in weekly earnings of 8s 6d. This was roughly equivalent to an adult male labourer's wage – which is why, on receipt of a January 1847 application for assistance from Callum, the Kirkhill board 'doubt[ed] whether the claimant [was] a fit object for parochial relief'. Exercising discretion of a kind denied to present-day Britain's rule-bound welfare agencies, the board nevertheless went on to grant William Callum a weekly payment of 1s 6d on account of 'the inclemency of the season and the high price of provisions'.[32]

Support of this sort, however, was unavailable to the many Inverness people who, though in work and thus unable to turn for help to the parochial board, found it increasingly difficult to buy enough meal to feed themselves and their dependants. One response to their predicament came in the form of a late-January and early-February effort to raise funds for the 'immediate relief of the presently prevailing destitution amongst the poor and labouring classes in the burgh and parish of Inverness'. Donors to this fund were drawn overwhelmingly from the shopkeepers, tailors, gunsmiths, bakers, blacksmiths, lawyers, teachers and others who were simultaneously refusing, in many instances, to serve as special constables. Unwilling to rally to those trying to put down unrest by force, they were happy to combat by financial means the principal cause of that unrest – this being the looming threat of hunger. Soon a sum well in excess of £50,000 at present-day values had been raised. By mid February, as a result, some 3,000 people, none of them entitled to poor relief, were being 'supplied with meal, soup, bread and coals'. Recipients of this aid, it was noted by way of countering charges that not all of them were as hard-pressed as they made out, had been selected 'with the greatest care and circumspection'.[33]

By mid February, a number of soldiers, including many of those sent north from Edinburgh at the end of January, had begun to be transferred from Moray to Fort George. From there some troops were marched to Inverness. But possibly because food aid had started by this point to flow into Merkinch and the Green of Muirtown, the most pressing calls for military intervention were now coming from elsewhere. This had been anticipated by Inverness's provost, William Simpson, in a letter sent to Lord Advocate Rutherfurd in the immediate aftermath of the 1 February outbreak. 'I would respectfully submit,' Simpson wrote, 'that the spirit which has exhibited itself here exists all over the northern counties and is not confined to the larger towns.' In even the 'smallest villages', the provost warned, there was likely to be trouble for as long as people remained exposed to 'the destitution and calamity' resulting from the absence of potatoes and the ever-climbing price of meal.[34]

This certainly proved true of several communities, notably Nairn, Avoch and Beauly, in the wider Inverness area. Only one of these, Nairn, on the Moray Firth coast to the east of Inverness, managed to avoid an army presence on its streets. That was because of the prompt, and markedly conciliatory, action taken by its town councillors in response to the appearance of 'inflammatory placards' said to have led to 'a crowd attack[ing] a corn-dealer and pelt[ing] him with stones'. Within a day or two of that episode, and instead of trying to reimpose order by force, the Nairn authorities had established a 'retail store' where meal could be got cheaply – its price subsidised from a locally collected, and soon substantial, cash reserve. This development, it was reported, had produced 'the most gratifying results' – disorder having been 'checked in the bud'. There was to be no such success in Beauly, 9 miles west of Inverness. Here, as in so many places that winter, an attempt to ship grain provoked mass protest.[35]

Beauly, in the 1840s was growing rapidly as new homes were constructed in and around a central square. These 'building operations,' a visiting journalist commented in 1847, 'gave employment and afforded room for an increased population'. Activity of this sort had been promoted and encouraged by the village's principal proprietor, Lord Lovat, whom that same journalist, Robert Somers, described as one of the few truly progressive lairds to be found in the Highlands and Islands. All around Beauly, Somers wrote, were highly productive farms that had taken shape, over the preceding half-century, on 'the rich and extensive plain' known as the Aird. Much of this area too was in Lovat's ownership, with Beauly being developed as its service centre. 'Situated in . . . a country capable of high cultivation . . . and washed by a river that is navigable to goodly-sized vessels to its doors,' Somers observed of Beauly, 'there are few villages which possess so many elements of prosperity.'[36]

The river Somers mentioned is the Beauly. Flowing into the Beauly Firth, a westward extension of the Moray Firth, it was then considered 'navigable at high water' to a point just below the village. During the opening weeks of 1847, in part perhaps because grain cargoes could no longer be got out of Inverness's blockaded harbour, Beauly's riverside wharf handled a series of cereal shipments. This caused resentment. Because of its being seen as a place where there might be work to be had, Robert Somers noted, Beauly had been 'inundated with the victims of ejection from less-favoured parts of the [Highlands]'. Lots of those people, together with a number of longer-established Beauly families, were finding it increasingly impossible to feed themselves. Hence their anger when it became known, on Sunday 31 January, that a ship which had moored in the river the day before was there to load oatmeal of a sort many Beauly folk could no longer afford. 'A vessel which was taking on meal at Beauly ... was obliged to sail last night with half [its] cargo,' Inverness-shire's procurator fiscal, John MacKay, noted on 1 February, 'as intimation was received that the people of the village were only waiting till Sunday was over to unship the meal.'[37]

On that occasion, Beauly experienced no actual violence. Just short of a fortnight later, however, the village became the scene of yet another clash between a normally peaceful population and the still beleaguered forces of law and order. 'I have this day received a letter from Lord Lovat's factor at Beauly stating that the shipping of grain was interrupted there yesterday,' John MacKay reported on 12 February. 'Two carts were turned back ... The person who was shipping was assaulted and obliged to take refuge in the factor's house [from which he] ... durst not venture out to go home.'[38]

The foiled shipper, MacKay learned, was a farmer by the name of Henderson. Next morning, with a view to rescuing him and making it possible for his grain to reach its intended destination, the procurator fiscal sent John MacBean, Inverness-shire's superintendent of police, to Beauly. On getting there, MacBean, who was accompanied by two or three of the county's few full-time policemen, told Henderson that he and his constables would ensure that the farmer's grain-laden carts were able to pass safely through the village and on down to the river. This, it turned out, was seriously to underestimate the intensity of Beauly's opposition to the trade in which Henderson was engaged.

The weather having again turned wintry, Beauly that day was 'several inches' deep in snow. This made it easy for the crowd that met Henderson's two carts to set about 'pelting both the drivers and [their] horses with snowballs'. Those snowballs, made from pebble-studded snow gathered from gravelled streets, were capable of inflicting serious hurt on both people and animals. Horses reared in fright. One cart came close to overturning. The driver of the other cart fled and had to be replaced by one of MacBean's constables. MacBean himself, meanwhile, was 'expostulat[ing] with the mob' and stressing 'the danger they incurred by violating the law'. But this produced nothing other than shouts of derision – those much encouraged by a local shoemaker, Hugh Wishart, who noisily made clear his determination 'to prevent [Henderson's] shipment'.[39]

With difficulty, the two carts were got on to a street leading to the river. There, however, 'the attack was renewed so fiercely', John MacBean said, that he and his subordinates were 'compelled' to retreat towards the centre of the village and there take refuge in an inn. Here they were joined by Sheriff-Substitute William Colquhoun who had meanwhile made his own way from Inverness with the aim of swearing in a Beauly-based set of special constables. Men approached in this connection, it transpired, were 'unwilling to act until told of the consequences [which could include jail terms as well as fines] of refusal'. Their reluctance to do as instructed, the sheriff was informed by such constables as he managed to recruit, originated in its being their firm view that 'the excited state of the people' made it 'impossible to ship grain'.[40]

At this juncture, as if by way of confirming what Colquhoun had just been told, 'intelligence was brought that the mob had taken one of the carts [which had been left outside the inn] and had gone towards the pier'. Colquhoun, MacBean and such uniformed constables as were available set off hurriedly in pursuit only to find that 'the cart had been pitched . . . into the water'. 'Mr Colquhoun,' MacBean said, '[now] endeavoured to address the rioters but was severely struck by a snowball in the face.' Next the police superintendent was himself assaulted 'and severely bruised'. There followed an attempt by Colquhoun to read the Riot Act. But no sooner had the sheriff launched into the proclamation the Act insisted on than the paper containing the requisite wording 'was snatched away and destroyed'.[41]

Hemmed in and rendered powerless by a crowd MacBean reckoned to number at least 600, William Colquhoun and his colleagues had no option but to return to the inn where they had earlier sought sanctuary. There they remained until rescued by a 70-strong troop detachment the sheriff had summoned from Fort George. This detachment's arrival made it possible for the police superintendent to arrest three men considered to have been especially prominent in the earlier fracas at the Beauly water-front. But of Hugh Wishart, the person the authorities most wanted to take into custody, there was no sign. Like that other shoemaker, Burghead's James Falconer, Wishart had left home and, despite an extensive search, could not be found.

The week that brought soldiers to Beauly also saw the military deployed in the Black Isle. Bordered on three sides by the sea – in the shape of the Beauly,

Moray and Cromarty Firths – that peninsula, like the nearby Aird, had been transformed agriculturally in the course of the preceding four or five decades. There was, then, no lack of oats or oatmeal to be had in the Black Isle, a part of Ross-shire. But neither was there any scarcity of individuals happy to cash in on the opportunities opened up by oatmeal's escalating cost. One such was Sir James MacKenzie, owner of the Rosehaugh Estate on the Black Isle's southern coast.

When, during the first week of February, Sir James made known that stocks of oatmeal in his possession were not to be sold for less than 32 shillings a boll, his grand home was visited by what John Jardine, Ross-shire's sheriff principal, called 'a mob of from two to three hundred persons'. Those people came from the nearby villages of Rosemarkie, Fortrose and Avoch. They were more than willing to buy his meal, they told Rosehaugh's laird, but only at 'their own price' – this being 24 shillings a boll. 'They distinctly intimated,' Sheriff Jardine reported, 'that they would come [again] in a body to insist on this demand . . . and, unless it was complied with, [they said], they would take [the meal] by force.' A panicked Sir James at once sent a message to Fort George – separated from Fortrose and Rosemarkie by no more than a mile or two of sea – asking for military protection. But because such soldiers as had been stationed there were mostly still in Moray at this point, Sir James was told he would have to fend for himself.[42]

Next day was Sunday. At services in Avoch, Fortrose and Rosemarkie, Ross-shire's procurator fiscal noted, 'people were . . . warned by the ministers of all denominations against committing any breach of the peace'. That may have helped – temporarily as it proved – to calm matters. But of greater significance in this regard was the outcome of a meeting held the following day, 8 February. At that gathering, 'proprietors . . . and farmers' resident in the southern part of the Black Isle agreed to make available 'a supply of meal to be retailed in small quantities to the poorer classes'. 'Members of this meeting,' it was further resolved, 'bind and oblige themselves not to export either grain or meal until [local] requirements . . . shall have been fully ascertained and provided for.'[43]

What was unappreciated initially was that not every grain-producer in the area was party to those arrangements. Hence the uproar that broke out on Thursday 11 February when a Rosemarkie farmer (who had not participated in the Monday gathering) tried to have a cereal consignment put aboard a ship moored at Chanonry Point near Fortrose. On learning that 'a large mob' had collected with a view to preventing this, Roderick MacKenzie, Fortrose's provost, 'attempted,' as he told Sheriff Jardine, 'to swear in special constables but failed' – the men he summoned 'all going away as soon as they found out the reason they were sent for'. By this stage, however, Fort George was again garrisoned and, in response to an urgent appeal from Provost MacKenzie, 50 soldiers were ferried across the narrows between the fort and Chanonry Point. Once ashore, the troops dispersed a loudly protesting crowd 'of boys and women'. They then headed off along the mile-long track connecting the point with Rosemarkie – where a Fortrose shoemaker, Robert Munro, had organised 'an attempt . . . to stop [grain] carts and to cut open the sacks [they contained]'.[44]

Because Chanonry Point possessed no pier or landing stage of any kind, it was customary there to use relays of small boats to take cargoes to larger vessels anchored a hundred or more yards out to sea. This was as inconvenient as it was time-consuming. But at the start of February 1847, Black Isle grain shippers are likely to have thought it safer to keep cargo ships offshore than to bring them into the nearest harbour, at Avoch, where such ships, it was feared, would be at risk of being boarded, or otherwise interfered with, in a place where hunger was known to be widespread.

Avoch, a fishing community, was experiencing difficulties of the kind afflicting all such communities on the Moray Firth coast. As elsewhere, no advances were available that winter from herring curers – while, again as elsewhere, the winter fishing for haddock and whiting had been disrupted by ceaseless bad weather. In an 1840 account of his parish, Avoch's Church of Scotland minister, James Gibson, had commented that, 'though destitute of many comforts', the folk he served 'seem[ed], upon the whole, contented with their situation and circumstances'. But this, in the opening weeks of 1847, had ceased to be the case. 'The Avoch fishermen and their families,' Gibson now wrote, 'are at present real objects of charity. In times past they lived almost entirely upon potatoes and fish. But . . . last season, instead of having their 12, 14 or 16 bolls of potatoes, few of them have one bushel' – an amount equivalent to just one-fifth of a single boll. This, together with the dwindling away of cash incomes from fishing, had left many Avoch people, their minister thought, 'on the brink of starvation'. Those same people, it followed, felt themselves provoked beyond endurance when, on Friday 19 February, a ship put into their harbour to pick up a cargo of grain being sent south by George More who farmed at nearby Muiralehouse.[45]

Anticipating trouble, More had written in advance of this ship's arrival to Sheriff John Jardine who, in response to the farmer's appeal for protection, requested the aid of the Fort George military. He himself, Jardine thought, should be on hand at Avoch when troops reached there. Early on Friday, therefore, the sheriff left his Dingwall base — only to discover, on getting to Avoch, that the soldiers he had expected to join him were stormbound on the far side of the firth. Loading operations were accordingly postponed until the following day.

Next morning, backed now by '50 men and two officers of the 76th Regiment', John Jardine returned to Avoch where, as he put it, 'we found the people most determined for resistance'. During the night, it emerged, fishermen had 'unmoored' the waiting cargo ship, which, the tide having meantime gone out, had been left grounded in the middle of Avoch's harbour. 'As the tide did not permit the vessel to approach the [quay] for a couple of hours,' the sheriff reported, we could take no steps to put the grain on board.' There duly ensued a lengthy stand-off. On one side were the sheriff, George More, More's accompanying carters and a long line of musket-carrying soldiers. On the other were several hundred people who, by way of adding to Jardine's difficulties, had 'barricaded' the main access to the harbour by hauling fishing boats across it. 'No expostulations or threats,' Jardine commented, 'made the slightest impression on the mob who said they might as well die by being shot as of starvation'.[46]

Next came a development which left the sheriff as infuriated with George More as with the crowd confronting him. 'We were informed by the people and the fact is undoubted,' Jardine wrote, 'that the person shipping this grain [More in other words] had attended a meeting of the farmers in the neighbourhood [this being the meeting of 8 February] . . . and [had] there subscribed certain resolutions binding [himself and others] not to ship any grain but to reserve it for sale in the [Avoch, Fortrose and Rosemarkie] district. This shipment, the people said not without reason, was in direct violation of that agreement . . . the terms of which one of them read aloud.'[47]

More's violation of his promise notwithstanding, Jardine felt himself to have no alternative but to order the military into action against the crowd. First, however, he had to attend to the necessary formalities. Accordingly, he read the Riot Act. But scarcely had he done so than More 'came forward,' as Jardine put it, 'and said [that], if he was secured against all expenses, he would give up his shipment'. 'To which I replied,' the sheriff went on, 'that we could come under no conditions whatsoever; that we were there to protect [his] shipment and would do so to the best of our ability if he wished [this] . . . Upon which [and] after some delay . . . [he] said that, rather than run the risk of bloodshed, he was resolved not to persist.'[48]

'I cannot help regretting the result,' John Jardine informed Lord Advocate Rutherfurd, his regret stemming, it seems, from his sense of having been placed by George More in an entirely false position. But it was nevertheless a source of some satisfaction to the sheriff that, in the event, there had been no need for the army to move against the hundreds of people milling around the harbour. 'I was satisfied from their determined aspect,' his dispatch to Rutherfurd concludes, 'that the mob . . . would have resisted the military and, if there had been loss of life, it would have been peculiarly distressing [for that loss] to have arisen from a shipment of grain apparently made in violation of an agreement entered into by the [shipper].'[49]

In Cromarty, at the northern end of the Black Isle, there were equivalent disturbances. The most serious resulted from the town's provost, who was also a farmer, having bought 20 bolls of oatmeal from a Cromarty dealer. 'The people attributed [this] purchase . . . to an intention to hoard up meal in the expectation of getting a [higher] price for it by and by,' reported Robert Taylor, one of Ross-shire's sheriff-substitutes. Speculation of this sort, Taylor wrote, was calculated to provoke fury. 'A number . . . of half-grown lads, girls and women [accordingly] . . . collected together and, after perambulating the streets in a very disorderly and noisy manner, proceed[ed] to the [provost's] farmhouse, to which the meal . . . had been conveyed, and broke several of the windows . . . with stones.' 'I conceive it would be very imprudent at present to apprehend any of the rioters,' Sheriff Taylor commented, 'for the public feeling is undoubtedly in their favour.' Recognising this, the provost, George MacDonald, returned his newly purchased meal to its seller – while several of his fellow agriculturalists, maybe fearing that they too might be targeted, assured a hastily called public meeting that what remained of their oat crops would be retained in Ross-shire 'and that supplies of meal would be [provided] for the town'.[50]

Criticism of Provost MacDonald was all the more ferocious because his Newton Farm, a mile or so south of Cromarty, resulted from the amalgamation of four smaller landholdings whose occupants had not long before been evicted. This was just one instance of a process that, in the course of the preceding half-century, had resulted in the reshaping of settlement patterns across much of the Black Isle and almost all of nearby Easter Ross. This latter district's southern boundary is not far from Beauly. Its northern boundary is the Dornoch Firth. In between, both west and north of the Cromarty Firth which separates Easter Ross from the Black Isle, is a great deal of low-lying, sheltered and productive countryside. Prior to 1800, this countryside had been 'chiefly occupied,' an Easter Ross clergyman said in 1843, 'by small farmers'. During subsequent decades, however, that had ceased to be the case. 'All the good land,' a second minister commented, 'has been thrown into large farms.' 'The improvement of the soil was much required,' a third observed. 'But its improvement may be carried on at an expense . . . which no pecuniary advantage can counterbalance. Many families were driven from their homes.'[51]

The small farms of the past had been worked by their tenants. The new farms needed workforces. These consisted mainly of single men hired for no more than six months at a time and accommodated in tumbledown hovels known as bothies. *Witness* editor Hugh Miller, when a young man, spent several months in just such an Easter Ross bothy where the breakfasts and dinners he and his workmates prepared for themselves at the start and finish of each day consisted of nothing other than 'a little hot water poured on a handful of meal with a sprinkling of salt'. 'It was a dingy, low, thatched build-ing,' Miller wrote of this bothy, 'bulg[ing] in the sidewalls in a dozen different places, and green atop with chickweed and stonecrop. One long apartment, without partition or ceiling, occupied the interior from gable to gable. A row of undressed deal beds ran along the sides. There was a fire at each gable, or rather a place at which fires might be lighted, for there were no chimneys . . . The roof leaked in a dozen different places; and along the ridge the sky might be seen . . . We learned to know what o'clock it was, when we awoke in the night-time, by the [position of] the stars which we saw glimmering through the opening.'[52]

If an Easter Ross farm labourer's life was not to be envied, neither was that of the area's crofters. Most of them were folk removed from good land to be resettled on worse – often in places where they had no alternative but to carve fields out of bogs or moors that had never before been cultivated. A *Morning Chronicle* journalist, visiting Easter Ross and the Black Isle in the autumn of 1846, spoke with several such crofters whose potatoes, like everyone else's, had been wiped out by blight but whose cereal harvest, that year, had been better than usual. 'It was no relief to tell them that they had a larger crop of oats than formerly,' this journalist reported, 'the answer in every case being, we need all the oats for the factor.' As in Ireland, then, Ross-shire's small-scale agriculturalists could only meet their landlord's rent demands by selling all their grain. Hence the *Morning Chronicle* man's discovery that 'the constant anxiety of these people is to grow as much oats or barley as will pay the landlord' – they themselves, together with their families, subsisting on the output of potato plots that, in 1846, were largely bereft of potatoes.[53]

Easter Ross crofters, then, went hungry in the winter of 1846–47. Hungrier still were the thousands of Easter Ross people who had no landholdings of any kind. Many of them, according to their clergymen, had long since been reduced to 'poverty and degradation' by 'the breaking up of the small farm system'. Some had moved into long-established towns like Tain and Dingwall. Others found homes in settlements that were established, or grew rapidly, at this time – places like Portmahomack, Barbaraville, Saltburn, Invergordon, Alness, Evanton and Conon Bridge. None of those communities offered much in the way of secure and well-paid employment. All that was available, in many instances, was casual or seasonal work (mostly at harvest-time) on neighbouring farms or estates. And in the hunger winter of 1846–47 even someone with a full-time job could struggle – a point made repeatedly in representations to the Edinburgh-based Central Board for the Management of the Fund Raised for the Relief of the Destitute Inhabitants of the Highlands and Islands. A typical such representation, this one from Urray in the southern part of Easter Ross, highlighted the case of 'an able-bodied man' earning as much as two shillings a day, then a good wage. Because this man had a wife and several children, it was 'altogether impossible for him to earn what, at [then prevailing] prices, [was] sufficient for their support. It gave him quite enough to do when he had potatoes from one end of the year to the other and could purchase meal at 16 shillings per boll. It is . . . evident [that], when he has no potatoes and must pay 30 shillings per boll for meal, he cannot support his family however industrious he may be.'[54]

In Urray alone there were calculated, in the opening weeks of 1847, to be more than 100 families who were 'unprovided with food [or] the means of procuring it'. Nor were conditions any better in the rest of Easter Ross. 'The starving people all come to me,' Invergordon's Free Church minister, David Carment, noted in a letter to his son, 'and I am giving meal and money, more than my income will warrant, but what can I do? I cannot see the people starve . . . Your mother has been out all day in Invergordon and Saltburn and found people who had been a day and a half without food.'[55]

When, towards the end of December 1846, a committee was set up in Dingwall with a view to helping 'the many families' thought to be 'suffering severely', its members were shocked by how bad things had become: 'The visits and inquiries of the committee have [shown] . . . that there is a fearful amount of poverty at our very doors, even among the able-bodied . . . The ill-furnished dwellings, the want of fuel, and [everywhere] the strong smell of turnips, indicate the privations to which the people are subjected and the wretched food by which they ward off starvation.'[56]

In Evanton, as early as November, millers and meal-dealers ceased trading in small amounts of meal – 'many needy persons, [even when] with money in their hands, [being] obliged to return [home] . . . without a supply'. There as elsewhere, difficulties were aggravated by the 'frost and snow' brought by 'one of the hardest seasons' seen for many years – the bitter weather leading to lay-offs among even the minority of men who had managed to find work. The outcome was summarised in a petition sent to Ross-shire's Commissioners of Supply by 'the labouring class in the village of Evanton'. 'Owing to the total failure of the potato crop, the severity of the winter and the entire want of [demand for] labour,' commissioners were informed, 'your petitioners are reduced to the lowest degree of poverty and distress. Many, having had no meal in their [households] for weeks, have subsisted entirely on boiled turnips and such other vegetables as they could with difficulty from time to time procure.'[57]

Similar findings were reported by several of the local committees the Destitution Fund's Edinburgh organisers asked clergymen and others to set up. 'Generally speaking,' commented members of the committee that took shape in Rosskeen parish, '[our] community is deplorably destitute of remu-nerative employment.' Rosskeen's principal settlements, they went on, were Invergordon and Saltburn: 'While it is unimportant here to enquire into the origin of these villages, it is not out of place to remark that the source both of their growth and poverty is very mainly attributable to the clearance from estates of the small tenantry.'[58]

This was to echo remarks made by Invergordon's David Carment when, prior to his quitting the Church of Scotland for the Free Church, he warned that agricultural advancement came at a price: 'The depopulation of the [countryside] by large farms is a serious evil and is likely to bring along with it consequences which the landed interest seem not to have anticipated. There is no longer an independent peasantry. The morals of the people are deterio-rated by the loss of independence, and their spirits embittered by what they deem oppression.' Violence of some sort, Carment reckoned, could readily ensue – a prognosis shown to be correct when, towards the end of January 1847, protest erupted in almost every part of Easter Ross.[59]

Those Easter Ross troubles were similar in origin to comparable disorders in Banffshire, Moray and elsewhere. But for reasons rooted in tensions of the sort identified by David Carment, there was an especially acrimonious edge to Easter Ross people's efforts to bring grain shipments to a stop. This was because the farmers seen to be profiting from such shipments were the same farmers that lots of Easter Ross folk blamed for their having been left landless, workless, poor and now hungry.

The upheavals that forced so many Easter Ross families from the land had produced a highly commercialised arable agriculture given over mainly to cereal production. Starting not long after 1800, therefore, barley, oats and – increasingly – wheat were shipped from the area to Leith, London and other southern centres. Some shipments left from Balintraid, towards the northern tip of the Cromarty Firth, or Foulis Point, nearer Dingwall. These were places where cargo vessels could be beached at high water, loaded at low water and then floated off when the tide came in again. Most central to the Easter Ross cereals trade, however, were Portmahomack and Invergordon – Portmahomack serving the area around and to the east of Tain, Invergordon handling grain from farms closer to the Cromarty Firth. For ages, that firth's principal port had been Cromarty. But the jetties, quays and other facilities that took shape at Invergordon during the 1820s had the effect of ending the older town's dominance. In 1843 Cromarty was described as 'a miserable place in the last stages of decay' – Invergordon being seen, in contrast, as somewhere 'rising very fast into importance'.[60]

Invergordon, then, became a principal focus of what turned into a series of successful efforts to curtail exports both of grain and other foodstuffs. Those efforts started on Saturday 30 January 1847 when people marched through the town to urge 'lovers of their country to turn out on [the] Monday [following] to prevent the shipment of corn . . . fish and eggs'. This was readily achieved. On the Monday in question, Tain's procurator fiscal reported, 'a mob consisting of some hundreds [of] persons met at the pier of Invergordon and forcibly prevented the shipment of a large quantity of fish [and other commodities] by the *North Star* steamer for the London market'. This crowd, consisting of people from Saltburn, Alness and Evanton as well as from Invergordon itself, turned out again the next day when, as the procurator fiscal put it, 'a Leith trader, the *Inverness*, arrived . . . at Invergordon to take on grain and another Leith trader, the *Favourite*, [put in] at the same time [to] Balintraid. In consequence,' the procurator fiscal went on, 'there was a large assembly of people . . . at both places determined to oppose any attempt to ship corn and, there being no force to give protection to the intending shippers, they did not make the attempt. The *Inverness* has sailed . . . without her cargo and I believe the *Favourite* is likewise to do so ... Some of the Invergordon mob went to the private houses in which they supposed some of the shippers were, threatening them with personal violence.'[61]

When Tain's sheriff-substitute, Robert Taylor, tried to reason with the organisers of those proceedings 'the clamour and noise of the people' was said to have 'got up to such a great height that [he] could not be heard'. The sheriff, then, was left with little alternative but to head home while, in Invergordon, the triumphant 'rioters' lit a bonfire on the beach and, well into the evening, danced 'on the rough shingle' to music provided by a piper.[62]

From Evanton, meanwhile, came reports of 'a party of ill-disposed persons ... parading through the village ... with a view to incit[ing] the inhabitants to outrage'. This was in response to 'several cargoes of barley [having been] shipped for the south' from nearby Foulis Point. No more such shipments, it was resolved in Evanton, should be permitted and, with a view to enforcing this resolution, several hundred people promptly gathered in the vicinity of the point's 'storehouse' complex* – a complex capable of housing a great deal of grain.[63]

To guard against the possibility of a ship being loaded at Foulis Point during the hours of darkness, a 24-hour watch was maintained, 'a large bonfire [being] kept burning on the beach' in order to keep the watchers warm. As in Invergordon, Robert Taylor turned up 'to expostulate with the people'. But they, for their part, made clear 'in the strongest terms' that 'they would allow no barley or oats to be shipped [for as long] as they could get no meal'. Taylor accordingly withdrew and, when a cargo vessel eventually put in an appearance, 'the result ... was that she sailed ... without grain'. On this 'object [being] accomplished', the Foulis Point 'mob', according to the *Ross-shire Advertiser*, 'marched back to Evanton with flags and a piper' prior to 'quietly dispers[ing]'. 'The coast,' the paper added, 'may now be literally said to be blockaded.'[64]

So things continued for the next four or five weeks – to the fury of a Ross-shire Justice of the Peace who, on 27 February, penned a letter to the *Scotsman*. 'Sir,' this JP wrote, 'You have of late had many accounts of riots in the north of Scotland, but I suspect that neither you nor the public are at all aware of the state in which the county of Ross has been for a month past. Within 15 miles of each other there are three shipping places – Balintraid, Invergordon

---

* The Storehouse of Foulis has survived into the present. Today it houses a restaurant, shop and exhibition centre that together constitute a popular stopping off point on the A9 a mile or so north of the Cromarty Bridge.

and Foulis – all of which have been under mob dominion during that time, so as to prevent the shipment of a single quarter of any kind of grain . . . Sheriffs have several times been deforced [or attacked] . . . No fewer than five vessels have been sent away empty . . . Matters have risen to such a pitch in our hitherto peaceful county that no person connected with the trade in corn or meal is safe either in person or property.'[65]

Ross-shire's sheriff principal, John Jardine, shared that letter-writer's frustrations. Sent north by Crown Agent John Lindsay, as his Banffshire and Moray counterparts had been some days previously, Jardine reached Dingwall on Thursday 4 February. To begin with, he was by no means out of sympathy with the protesters he had been ordered to bring into line. 'I have . . . every reason to suppose,' the sheriff wrote on the day following his arrival, 'that the late disturbances have originated from no lawless or mischievous disposition . . . but from a serious [meaning genuine] apprehension of there not being sufficient food reserved for the maintenance of the people.'[66]

What disheartened Jardine was his helplessness. 'I am pretty much alone in this large county without advice or assistance of any sort,' he told Lord Advocate Andrew Rutherfurd, 'while I have almost daily applications from the shippers of grain for protection which I have . . . been unable to afford them.' 'We have no regular constabulary,' the sheriff continued, 'and the services of any persons sworn in as special constables are . . . little to be depended on, they not being hearty in the cause but rather disposed to side with the people, many of whom are really in distress for want of food.' What he needed, Jardine insisted, was military assistance. In its absence, he warned Rutherfurd, 'the disposition to resist the law will continue to gain ground'.[67]

But no soldiers could be sent to Easter Ross because, as the lord advocate was informed by his officials, there had begun to be 'more demands for aid . . . than there [were] troops to answer'. This problem seemed solved when, in response to urgent lobbying from Rutherfurd, the War Office agreed that a large contingent of men from the 27th Regiment, newly returned from South Africa, should be sent to Scotland. Again, however, there were logistical difficulties. This latest consignment of troops for the north should have left Portsmouth on a steam-powered troopship, HMS *Birkenhead*, in early February. But the *Birkenhead*, despite its having been launched not much more than a year before, was plagued by engine troubles that held up its departure not just for days but for weeks.* To farmers and others on the

---

* The *Birkenhead*, an unfortunate ship, was wrecked off South Africa in 1852.

receiving end of the Easter Ross protests, this 'extraordinary delay', as one exasperated official called it, made it appear as if the authorities in Edinburgh and London cared little for their plight. 'It is said,' remarked the author of that irate letter to the *Scotsman*, 'and has been so [said] for the last fortnight, that troops are coming from Portsmouth, but . . . none have appeared and we know not when they may.'[68]

By mid February the gradual return to Fort George of soldiers deployed in Moray in late January had made it possible, as already seen, to have troops deal with unrest in places like Beauly and Avoch. But partly because the 'want of proper accommodation' was said to have led to the spread of 'sickness' among Moray-based soldiers, continuing manpower shortages made for difficulties in finding troops for Easter Ross – those difficulties becoming insuperable when, on 22 February, the greater part of what remained of the Fort George garrison had to be dispatched, for reasons explored earlier, to Wick.[69]

In Wick, where peace of a sort had been restored to the burgh and to neighbouring Pulteneytown in the wake of the musket volley resulting from Sheriff Robert Thomson's much criticised orders of the night of 24 February, both Thomson and the military felt free by the end of the month to turn their attention to the other parts of Caithness where trading in grain was at a standstill. There were two of these, Thurso and Castlehill, both on the county's north coast.

Thurso, Caithness's principal town until it was overtaken in population and economic importance by early nineteenth-century Wick, was said to have experienced 'a great deal of wretchedness' since the onset of the 1846–47 winter. A local Benevolent Society, the Destitution Fund's central board learned, was supplying the 'labouring classes' with oatmeal 'at the rate of 15 shillings per boll, the society paying the difference between that amount and the actual price' of 30 shillings or more. Those charitable endeavours, however, had done little to mitigate what William Manson, the burgh's procurator fiscal, described as 'a pretty general feeling . . . against the purchasers of grain for exportation'. This feeling exploded into direct action when, on 3 February, a cargo vessel put into Thurso's harbour to take on oats. At once the ship was boarded by local fishermen who, according to the *John O'Groat Journal*, 'so threatened the [cargo boat's] captain that he was glad to make off very speedily'. Two days later, it was the turn of Thurso grain merchants to be targeted by 'an immense crowd', which, after 'marching through the town', set about making as much noise as possible outside 'the houses of those [individuals] who had rendered themselves obnoxious by [their] purchase of grain and meal'.[70]

By way of dealing with those disorders, William Manson swore in some 40 special constables. But in the face of what he called 'the excitement . . . [arising] from a fear of the want of food', those men, Manson felt, 'would form but a very inefficient force even could they be depended upon – of which there is considerable doubt'. The harbour had effectively been closed, Manson reported. 'Should any attempt be made to ship grain or meal,' he added, 'I firmly believe the shipment could not be effected as there is every probability a mob would turn out which any force we have here could not put down.'[71]

All this changed on Monday 1 March when Sheriff Robert Thomson and 70 of the soldiers he had earlier sent into Pulteneytown arrived in Thurso at the end of a forced march from Wick. Next day, when a vessel arrived in the harbour to load grain, a stone-throwing crowd found themselves confronted by bayonet-wielding troops. Cartload after cartload of grain was taken under military escort to the harbour and, despite the 'showers of shingle' that came soldiers' way, it was clear that the prolonged period during which 'not a boll of grain [could] be shipped from Thurso' had been brought to an end.[72]

Thomson's one remaining task was to deal with people who, a week or so earlier, had forced their way on to a ship at Castlehill, 6 miles east of Thurso. The harbour there had been constructed to facilitate the export of flagstones quarried from a local estate belonging to Caithness's MP,* George Traill. Until superseded in the twentieth century by concrete paving slabs, flagstones of the sort shipped out of Castlehill were laid in immense numbers throughout Britain; and such was the success of the industry he had helped pioneer that Traill convinced himself that his workforce, housed mainly in the nearby village of Castletown, were so loyal to him as to be immune to any suggestion that they should take action of the kind that had convulsed both Wick and Thurso. 'No interruption [of grain shipments] will be given by my people,' Traill maintained on 15 February. This, he wrote, was because they were 'completely provided for'.[73]

A week later, on Monday 22 February, Traill's confidence was shown to have been misplaced. That evening, the captain of the *Fisher*, a Leith cargo boat which had come to Castlehill to take on grain, was menaced by 'several

---

* Traill represented all of Caithness except Wick, which, with a number of other Highland burghs, was represented in parliament (as noted earlier) by James Loch.

hundred' people whose stated aim, the *John O'Groat Journal* reported, was 'to compel [him] to leave the port'. Among this crowd were men – some from Castletown, others from further afield – seen to be 'armed with sticks and bludgeons'. By chance, Caithness's Wick-based sheriff-substitute, James Gregg, had arranged to spend the night in the vicinity of Castlehill. Together with George Traill, whose home stood just above the harbour, Gregg 'proceeded to the scene of the action'. But with neither the MP nor the sheriff able to make themselves heard above 'the noise and confusion' and 'in the entire absence of any police or other force', nothing could be done to stop 'the mob' boarding the *Fisher*. Neither was it possible to prevent an ensuing scuffle which resulted in the *Fisher*'s mate, Colin Colquhoun, who 'attempt[ed] to defend himself with a knife', being 'felled to the deck' by one of the ship's invaders.[74]

Colquhoun, rumoured initially to have been killed, was quickly to recover. Within days, however, Sheriff Principal Thomson had been provided with the names and addresses of three Castletown men said to have directed the protest that had led to his injuries. One morning towards the end of the week that had begun with Thomson's arrival in Thurso, therefore, a military platoon swept into Castletown before dawn and took all three* – one still in bed when soldiers entered his home – into custody.

On the early afternoon of Tuesday 2 March, a large iron-hulled, twin paddle-wheeled ship of a sort no one in Ross-shire had seen before steamed into the Cromarty Firth. This was HMS *Birkenhead*, which, four or five days previously, had at last been declared seaworthy. Aboard the *Birkenhead* when the troopship pulled out of Portsmouth were Colonel Samuel Goodman and 450 men of the army's 27th Regiment. Around 200 of the 450 had been landed at Fort George. A further 150 had been transferred to the *Pharos*, the lighthouse supply ship, mentioned earlier, which had taken them on to Caithness. The remaining 100 or so soldiers, together with their colonel, were earmarked for Invergordon where, as soon as the Birkenhead docked, they were disembarked and put into marching order.

---

* One of the men taken prisoner at Castletown was John Swanson, a joiner. The man nominated to stand as Chartist candidate for Wick Burghs in the general election of 1841 was (as already noted) also John Swanson and also a joiner. Swanson was, and is, a fairly common name in Caithness. It does not follow, then, that the two were one and the same. But nor can this possibility be ruled out.

The Ross-shire authorities, who had been kept abreast of the *Birkenhead*'s movements and who had arranged for a cargo ship to reach Invergordon that same afternoon, immediately alerted one of the many farmers who had for some time found it impossible to get grain moved south. The farmer in question was Andrew Baxter of Rosskeen Farm, not far out of town. What had been intended was that the newly landed troops should march to Rosskeen, take Baxter and his carters under their protection, and head back to the harbour with a first consignment of grain for the waiting cargo vessel. The understandably nervous farmer, however, misunderstood his instructions. Before Goodman and his soldiers had got themselves properly ashore, he ordered the men in charge of the six fully laden carts lined up in his farmyard to set off along the shore road leading to Invergordon. On that road they were met by what the official account of those events would describe as 'a mob . . . of evil-disposed and disorderly persons' who, by grabbing hold of each set of carthorse bridles, managed to turn Baxter's carts around and to compel their drivers to return to their starting point.[75]

The Rosskeen-bound troops, meanwhile, were being followed out of Invergordon by people 'threatening,' it was said, '[to] knock the daylights out of [them]'. Those people, on getting to Rosskeen Farm, at once linked up with the group which, shortly before, had forced Baxter's carters to retreat. There was, as a result, a crowd of several hundred people at Rosskeen; some members of this crowd heaving heavy sacks of wheat from the now-abandoned carts; other folk slashing open those sacks in order to ruin the wheat they contained by spilling this wheat on to mud and into puddles.[76]

The military had been accompanied to Andrew Baxter's farm by one of Ross-shire's sheriff-substitutes, George Cameron, who had reached Invergordon from Dingwall earlier that day. On being confronted by the chaotic scenes unfolding at Rosskeen, Cameron felt himself to have no alternative but to read the Riot Act and to order the arrest of as many people as could be snatched and held. One of the first to be seized was Donald Holme, an Alness man who, prior to his being grabbed, managed somehow to attack the sheriff and knock him off his feet.

Among others taken into custody were Kenneth Robertson, Lachlan Ross, Elizabeth Munro, Bathia MacKenzie, Jessie Munro and Barbara MacLean. MacLean, an Invergordon widow, maintained she had committed no crime. Munro contended that her only offence had been to object to a soldier 'seizing hold of a girl'. But Lachlan Ross, who, like Donald Holme, was one of many Alness* men involved in the Rosskeen Farm disturbances, was more defiant. 'I am a shoemaker by trade,' he said. 'I told Mr Cameron, the sheriff-substitute, that it was hard [for me to see farmers] sending grain out of the country. I have three children and when I left home today I had nothing for them to eat.'[77]

Once the military had reimposed order of a sort at Rosskeen Farm, Andrew Baxter's carts, again filled with wheat, left his farm for a second time. But the moment the carts and their escorts reached Invergordon, they came under renewed attack. Carters, horses, soldiers and sheriff were pelted with stones, and, with the convoy brought to a halt, a number of young men darted forward and succeeded in knocking from one or two of the carts the linchpins that held their wheels in place. This meant that, when those carts finally moved off, wheels began to come loose – one cart overturning and its driver being dragged 'for some distance along the . . . road'.[78]

Those carts that were not disabled were in the end got down to Invergordon harbour. But Baxter's carters, thanks to a piece of carelessness on the part of Sheriff George Cameron and the military, were permitted to leave the harbour, at the point when night was falling, without any accompanying troops. On the coast road, somewhere between Invergordon and the turn-off to Rosskeen Farm, the carters were ambushed and their horses cut from each cart's traces – two carts being systematically broken apart to make it easier for their component timbers to be chucked into the sea.

Back in a now dark Invergordon, Cameron and a number of local JPs who had turned out in his support moved into the Commercial Inn in the town's High Street. There they were joined by the 27th Regiment's Colonel Samuel Goodman who had been commandeering houses, 'four or five doors from the inn' as he put it, where his rank-and-file soldiers were to be billeted over-night. 'The prisoners [meaning the people arrested at Rosskeen Farm] were taken to the inn,' Goodman reported, 'and lodged in a room there.' This, it soon transpired, was to be a source of further trouble.[79]

Outside, several hundred folk – from Alness and other communities as well as from Invergordon itself – were debating what they might do next. Soon, it was said, 'one of [their] ringleaders got up and made a speech to the people proposing that they should go . . . to the inn in a body and demand [the release of] the prisoners'. 'I had not long been in [the Commercial Inn],' Colonel Goodman wrote of what followed, 'when the mob collected in

_____

* Rosskeen is as close to Alness as it is to Invergordon.

front . . . [and] began throwing in stones. The door was shut against a party of pressing women [who had been trying to gain entry] but, after it had been closed, the attack on it became violent and its panels were broken in.'[80]

While one part of the crowd had been shattering the Commercial Inn's windows with stones that rained into its front rooms, a second group, it emerged, had got hold of a battering ram in the shape of a heavy pole. With this, the inn's front door was rapidly stove in completely. In charge of that particular operation, or so it was afterwards asserted, was a young man called John Munro who had earlier been 'exciting the mob' and who may well have been the person who suggested that the inn should be attacked. Munro lived at Newmore, two or three miles north of Invergordon, and his principal aim, it appears, was to engineer the release of Donald Holme, the Alness man who had assaulted Sheriff Cameron and who was thought by the authorities to be one of the key organisers of the Easter Ross protest movement.[81]

Munro's objective was easily accomplished. Its door gone, the inn was rushed and, in the course of the melee that followed, Donald Holme vanished into the night. Neither Sheriff Cameron nor Colonel Goodman, it appears, could do much to prevent this because Goodman was unable to get a message to his troops. 'The house [meaning the inn] stood as if besieged,' he explained, 'and there was much difficulty in getting out.' Eventually, however, communications were re-established between the colonel and his junior officers. Soldiers were roused and, with fixed bayonets, came hurtling up the street. 'The mob,' said a witness, 'dispersed . . . in an instant'. As people scattered, however, there was opportunity for a new round of arrests – one of the several folk taken into custody being, ironically, a woman formally identified as 'Catherine Munro, wife of Donald Holme, labourer'. Holme's freedom, then, had been obtained at the expense of his partner's.[82]

Morning brought fresh confrontation. At dawn or even earlier, some 75 men of the 27th were seen to be heading out of town in a direction opposite to the one taken the previous day. Their mission, it became known, was to protect a set of 30 or more carts that had been put together with the aim of transporting grain to the harbour from farms as far away as Rhynie and Calrossie – 10 or 12 miles north-east of Invergordon. By way of assisting with this scheme, a nearer-at-hand farmer sent two cartloads of empty sacks into town. That was unwise. 'Before you could say "Jack Robinson",' commented a reporter from the *Ross-shire Advertiser*, 'the carts were in smash and, together with the bags, were thrown into the sea.' On word of this reaching the approaching convoy, the *Advertiser* journalist went on, the military men in charge of it took appropriate precautions: 'They put the carts two abreast* and . . . [positioned] soldiers [with] screwed bayonets on either side. They were preceded and followed by an immense mob who were howling [and] yelling . . . I saw [the troops and carts] coming into the [town] and certainly it was the most imposing spectacle . . . They marched west as far as the post-office [in the middle part of the High Street] and there turned down [King Street] to the pier. When the cavalcade had got about half-way down, some wicked one in the crowd threw a stone. Before you could look about you, the soldiers wheeled round, levelled their bayonets and charged. I happened to be looking on with the rest, and I need hardly tell you that we all took leg-bail† and made ourselves scarce, running into houses and shops wherever we could go.'[83]

That same day, when the troops were otherwise engaged, there was renewed evidence of the extent to which Easter Ross's farmers were loathed by much of area's still hard-pressed population. At Invergordon, Foulis Point and elsewhere, barns, granaries and warehouses were broken into by bands of people who stole nothing but who set about mixing systematically the various types of grain stored in these places. 'Wheat, oats and barley [were left] all in one heap'; and, where this was possible, coal, lime and other materials were flung on top. The effect, the lord advocate's Edinburgh office was informed by Tain's sheriff-substitute, was to 'render [grain] unsaleable'.[84]

In Dingwall, where earlier attempts to ship grain south had had to be suspended when the farmers involved in these attempts were 'threatened with violence', there was identical activity. On the evening of Tuesday 2 March, that week's *Ross-shire Advertiser* informed readers, 'the streets became crowded . . . while a horn was blown by one evidently employed for the purpose of collecting a mob. Having met at the east of the High Street, [this] mob proceeded to [a] . . . granary on the Greenhill [towards Dingwall's southern outskirts] where there were about 60 quarters of grain, wheat, oats and barley, in order to mix the same . . . The crowd then went, in a highly excited state and making [a] prodigious noise, to [a] vessel in the canal [which then linked the town with the Cromarty Firth] and, having awakened the master and crew, some went on board and the rest towed the vessel to the [foot] of the canal where, the tide having lifted her, the vessel grounded and so . . . could not put to sea.'[85]

---

* This was made possible by the fact that Invergordon's High Street was, and is, unusually wide.
† To take leg-bail: to escape; take flight; run away.

Trouble of this sort persisted into Wednesday and Thursday, attempts to counter it foundering, as was the common experience, on most local men's point-blank refusal to serve as special constables. Not until Friday 5 March, when Colonel Samuel Goodman marched into town at the head of a new troop detachment brought from Fort George by the *Birkenhead*, did life in Dingwall return to something like normal – as it had also done, by that Friday, in Invergordon and in Easter Ross more generally.

'I am glad to say that good order appears to have been re-established in this part of the country,' Tain's procurator fiscal reported on Monday 8 March. 'No new outbreaks have been reported [over the weekend] and large ship-ments of grain are being made at the various ports.' This news was received with a great deal of relief in Edinburgh – as were equivalent dispatches from law officers in Caithness, Inverness-shire, Moray and Banffshire. The Scottish north's descent into what the *Spectator* had described as 'nearly . . . a state of insurrection' had at last been decisively checked.[86]

It was now more than seven weeks since access routes to Macduff harbour had first been barricaded. Quelling the unrest this event had triggered had been no straightforward task. It had required the deployment of more than 700 soldiers, a gunboat, a troopship and two further vessels. Several sheriff-principals – not just Ross-shire's John Jardine but Banffshire's Alexander Currie, Moray's Cosmo Innes and Caithness's Robert Thomson – had had to abandon legal practices in the south and travel to their sheriffdoms. Thousands of men had been ordered to take the oaths required of special constables. Trade had been badly disrupted. Building after building had been damaged. Officials of all sorts had been assaulted and intimidated. There had been bloodshed.

At the close of the first quiet week the north of Scotland had experienced in nearly two months, the *Inverness Journal* reflected on what had occurred. The *Journal*, a rival to the *Inverness Courier*, had begun the year by reporting – sympathetically – on the plight of Easter Ross's many struggling families: 'This district forms a series of contradictions which are neither easy to recon-cile nor understand. A finer country than is presented to the view – richer in the quality of its soil – possessed by farmers of greater opulence – subjected generally to better systems of cultivation – more abundant in its crops – more convenient to markets – affording greater facilities for exportation – is nowhere to be found. Yet from it we have frequently heard of people wanting bread, of starvation and famine stalking through its length and breadth, and want, in its worst and gauntest forms, dwelling in the cottages of the poor and labouring classes.'[87]

Subsequent developments produced an abrupt change of tone. The *Courier* had responded to the Inverness riots of early February with some attempt to understand their causes. The *Journal* was having none of that. 'The late disturbances in this part of the kingdom,' runs the paper's editorial of 12 March, 'are more disgraceful to it than anything connected with its history for the last half century . . . These riotings appear monstrous and unjustifiable. [Nor have they] been confined to isolated spots. No county in the north has avoided − scarcely a village − their contamination . . . The scenes in Ross-shire last week were truly frightful − those at Invergordon surpassing any that preceded them . . . [This was clear] from the violence which [people] were prepared to commit against persons and property. Their acts were of the most disgraceful character . . . The riots at Dingwall were . . . the same . . . We were informed by a gentleman who took a very prominent part in suppressing the outbreaks at both places that a more demoniacal appearance never was exhibited by any assembly.'[88]

How widespread were views of this sort? It is impossible to say. Before March 1847 drew to a close, however, it would be evident that the *Inverness Journal*'s opinions were shared by Scotland's High Court judges.

7

'Chains of degradation'

*South Uist • Dunnet • Hopeman • Burghead • Scotland's
High Court • Pulteneytown • Wick • Fort William
Millbank Prison • Skye • Barra • North Uist • Knoydart*

On a summer's day in 1847, nearly 12 months after the destruction of the previous year's potato crop, Norman MacLeod, a man who had worked tirelessly to raise funds for Highlands and Islands famine relief, saw for himself what prolonged hunger does to people. MacLeod, then in the Outer Hebrides, had spent a weekend in North Uist. Now he and one or two companions were moving on to South Uist by way of Benbecula and by way of the fords which, at low tide, connected those three islands.* 'We started on Monday morning for South Uist,' MacLeod reported. 'The scene ... which we witnessed, as we entered the estate of Colonel Gordon [of Cluny], was deplorable, nay heart-rending. On one beach the whole population of the country seemed to be gathering the precious cockles, hundreds of people with creels – men, women and naked children all at work. We met a crowd of people at the fords. I never witnessed such countenances – starvation on many faces – the children with their melancholy looks, big-looking knees, hollow eyes, swollen-like bellies. God help them! I never did witness such wretchedness.'[1]

Norman MacLeod, a Church of Scotland clergyman, had grown up in Morvern where his younger brother John, like the two men's father before them, was parish minister. A popular and well-regarded public speaker, Norman, whose home and church were in Glasgow, spent much of the winter of 1846–47 travelling from meeting to meeting across Britain – urging

---

* During the middle decades of the twentieth century these fords were replaced by road-carrying causeways.

audiences to dig deep in their pockets on the grounds that cash in big amounts was needed to help combat the mounting crisis in the north. 'It is indeed an unnatural and unhappy state where the population of a whole country depends upon the potato crop alone,' Norman MacLeod told a January gathering. 'Society in the Highlands,' he went on, 'has for many years past been in a very hollow and rotten state . . . And why is it so? Because vast sections of that country have been given . . . to sheep graziers . . . and from [their] grazings the population have been driven to . . . comparatively useless corner[s] . . . where they are allowed to build their huts in the middle of an uncultivated waste and seek subsistence as best they may.'[2]

'The facility of raising a crop of potatoes was the prop and stay of this crazy edifice,' MacLeod said, 'and [potatoes] having . . . totally failed, want and starvation must be the necessary consequence.' In December, he went on, he had written to parish ministers, schoolmasters and others in every part of the Highlands and Islands. The scores of letters he had received by return '[told] of men and women living for four and twenty hours on the value of three-halfpence of barley meal – of families seeking . . . shellfish along the shores – of children confined to bed . . . to keep them quiet – of little ones asking bread of their parents and [there being none] to give'.[3]

Pleas of this sort resulted, as already noted, in enormous sums of money being put at the disposal of what became the Central Board for the Management of the Fund Raised for the Relief of the Destitute Inhabitants of the Highlands and Islands. The support programme thus made possible, in combination with what was done by the Free Church, by the Commissariat and by those landlords who responded positively to government urgings, did much to limit deaths from starvation in the Hebrides and on the Highland mainland's west coast. But even when winter had given way to spring and summer, plenty of communities in these areas still teetered on the brink of dire calamity. This was most apparent in a continued deterioration in the health and appearance of children. So extreme was the poverty of their parents – all of whose little cash went on rent and food – that many of those children could not be provided with replacement clothes when the clothes they had been wearing fell apart. More and more children too were seen to have the 'melancholy looks, big-looking knees, hollow eyes [and] swollen-like bellies' described by a shocked Norman MacLeod. He had no name for this condition. Today it is known as kwashiorkor* and is described by Britain's National

---

* The name derives from the Ga language spoken in coastal areas of Ghana.

Health Service (NHS) as 'a severe form of malnutrition' whose effects include 'loss of muscle mass', 'an enlarged tummy' and all the other symptoms MacLeod described. In the twenty-first century, according to the NHS, kwashiorkor is confined to 'developing regions of the world where babies and children have a diet that lacks protein and other essential nutrients'. In 1847, however, it was common, as Norman MacLeod discovered, in places like South Uist.[4]

Nor was there anything transient about this ghastly state of affairs. Year after year, into the early 1850s, potatoes in practically every part of the Highlands and Islands were wiped out by blight. Year after year, it followed, whole populations continued to be dependent on external aid. After August 1847, when naval store ships were withdrawn from Tobermory and Portree, this aid was administered largely by the Destitution Fund's central board, which, with encouragement from Charles Trevelyan and the Treasury, now took on functions previously entrusted to Edward Pine Coffin and his Commissariat colleagues. In its new role as a quasi-official agency, the board, very much in accordance with streams of instructions from Trevelyan, operated a regime characterised by an insistence that 'relief should only be given where labour is got in return'. Because local committees of the sort the board first relied on were thought insufficiently rigorous in their enforcement of such rules, they were abolished and replaced by salaried officials tasked with enforcing the hardest of hard lines. The outcome, one critic observed, was that 'a huge staff of stipendiaries on liberal pay' was employed to supervise an endless series of make-work schemes on which crofters and others were compelled to put in eight, ten or more hours a day in return for what the same critic called 'a modicum of meal'.[5]

Among the principal beneficiaries of the central board's operations were crofting landlords. With the board carrying most of the cost of fending off starvation, their poor rate bills were significantly lower than they otherwise would have been. Lairds worried, however, about what might happen when the board ran out of money. Might the poor rates levied on their properties then rise steeply?

Since the collapse of the kelp industry, which could not have existed but for the crofting families who provided its workforce, landlords had taken to calling those same families 'a redundant population' – a term, Norman MacLeod said, he was 'sick of hearing'. This same population, estate owners and managers now felt, needed to be reduced. The outcome, on almost all the islands and in much of the western mainland, was a renewal of clearance.

Some of the people who now began to be evicted were to fetch up on the streets of Lowland cities. But this caused controversy. Hence the growing tendency to have family after family shipped, at their landlords' expense, to Canada. From Lewis, Sir James Matheson, having given up on his earlier commitment to feeding the hungry, got rid of more than 2,000 people in this way. From Barra, South Uist and Benbecula, John Gordon of Cluny sent nearly 1,700 folk to join them. 'These parties,' a senior immigration officer noted of people reaching Quebec from Gordon's estate, 'presented every appearance of poverty and . . . were without the means . . . of procuring a day's subsistence for their helpless families on landing.' George Douglas, the medical man in charge of the Grosse Île quarantine centre in the St Lawrence River, was equally caustic. Douglas had dealt with many thousands of refugees from Ireland's famine. None of them, however, had been so ill-provided for as deportees from Benbecula, South Uist and Barra. 'I never, during my long experience at the station, saw a body of emigrants so destitute of clothing and bedding,' Douglas reported of these people. 'Many children of nine and ten years old had not a rag to cover them.' When, a little later, the Quebec authorities tried to recover from John Gordon a proportion of the cost of caring for his former tenants, he – predictably – refused to reimburse them.[6]

Mass evictions of the Gordon and Matheson variety were confined to crofting areas. But among landed proprietors whose more easterly estates had been affected by 1847's riots there was some feeling that participants in protest and disorder should lose their homes by way of punishment. 'I regret much that the fishermen have been so unruly,' the Duke of Richmond informed his Fochaber-based commissioner in the immediate aftermath of the Portgordon troubles, 'but I hope that the names of [rioters] residing on my property may be ascertained, that we know those who will violate the law and take measures accordingly.' 'I feel the people should know that landowners will not sanction the proceedings which lately have disgraced . . . the fishing villages,' the duke added in a subsequent letter. That was why he wanted people involved in these proceedings to be identified with a view to his commissioner, Thomas Balmer, at once 'giv[ing] them notice to quit'.[7]

Balmer, perhaps fearing that evictions might result in renewed protest, seems to have left former rioters well alone. More unaccommodating was Caithness landlord William Sinclair of Freswick. Smallholding tenants on one of Sinclair's properties, at Dunnet on Caithness's north coast, were known to have been involved in the late-February disturbances at Castlehill. Days after those disturbances, Sinclair's Dunnet tenants were informed that, because of their having been at Castlehill, they were to vacate their homes and their smallholdings by the end of May.

The Dunnet tenants attempted to appeal to Sinclair's better nature by means of a petition. His 'petitioners,' the Freswick laird was assured, '[were] extremely sorry to learn that in thoughtlessly going to Castlehill to prevent the shipment of grain they [had given] offence' to their laird whom they addressed as 'your honour'. 'That . . . we acted in a very foolish and improper manner, we are, upon reflection, fully sensible,' the petitioners continued, 'but in a moment of excitement [and] under the alarm of a scarcity of food . . . we were easily misled . . . We . . . now, in the most humble manner, beg your honour's pardon . . . [and hope to be] permitted to remain in the possessions which we have so long occupied.'[8]

On this producing no change of heart on William Sinclair's part, the Dunnet people's case was taken up by their Church of Scotland minister, Peter Jolly. 'Though the people in this quarter have been acting a very foolish part of late,' Jolly told Sinclair's factor, 'I certainly sympathise with them in their present alarm [about] a scarcity of food.' He had made enquiries into the circumstances of the six tenants in receipt of eviction notices, the minister went on. They included Donald Allan, a married man with eight children, and James Dunnet whose wife, as well as looking after her seven children, was caring for her 'aged' mother. If families like these were indeed evicted, Jolly felt, 'wretchedness', 'misery', 'poverty and starvation' was bound to await the 41 adults and children who would thus be made homeless.[9]

Sinclair of Freswick, however, proved unyielding. 'I must say,' Jolly wrote, 'that I deeply regret the determination at which he has arrived . . . The very idea of turning out 41 individuals in such a year as this is very far from being agreeable in contemplation and will appear almost inhuman in realisation.' But Sinclair, the minister acknowledged, '[had] a right to act with his property as he shall see cause'. This being so, there was no more to be done.[10]

No other rioters shared the Dunnet people's fate. But a number, as already described, found themselves in custody. Several people in this category, especially the women among them, were simply held briefly before being released without charge. Some, however, faced trial, mostly in sheriff courts. One or two, such as John Lawrence, the young man who led the attempt to set fire to Elgin grain-dealer John Allan's home, were accused of serious crimes. But neither he nor the Grantown, Inverness, Beauly and Easter Ross people tried on mobbing and rioting charges in Moray, Inverness-shire and Ross-shire sheriff courts were sentenced to more than 60 days in prison. A punishment of this type, whether by contemporary or present-day standards, was by no means draconian.* It certainly bore no comparison with the sentences passed on rioters who – because they were said to have had prominent roles in the violence directed against Moray's sheriff principal, Cosmo Innes, and his Caithness counterpart, Robert Thomson – stood trial in Scotland's High Court. The first such trial involved three men from Hopeman and two from Burghead.[11]

The Hopeman three – fishermen Daniel Sutherland, John Young and John Main – were picked up, as mentioned earlier, in the immediate aftermath of the troubles that had convulsed Burghead during the closing days of January. But the Burghead pair – shoemaker James Falconer and cooper Angus Davidson – were then, as also mentioned, nowhere to be found. Both, it emerged, had left on Sunday 31 January, the day after the noisy arrival of HMS *Cuckoo* off Burghead and the day before the troop landings that followed. Their departure, Davidson was afterwards to reveal, took place under cover of darkness. 'Falconer came to my house,' he explained, 'and said he had been advised to go away and that he had been told I should go also, for that we would both be taken up next morning . . . I set out that night and Falconer followed and overtook me . . . and we slept that night at his mother's house in the parish of Birnie and then went to his father's house in the parish of Dallas . . . [before going] again to Birnie which we left on [the] Tuesday evening to go to Aberdeen.'[12]

From Birnie, just south of Elgin and some 13 or 14 miles from Burghead, it would have taken little time to reach the high road (today's A96) leading, by way of Fochabers, to Aberdeen. Since itinerant labouring men 'on the tramp' between jobs were common enough sights at that time, the two fugitives would have attracted little attention as they trekked south. But if Davidson and Falconer were to eat, they needed work. This they found by moving on into Kincardine where they were hired by one of the contractors handling the construction of the Dundee–Aberdeen railway line. Days later, however, they were identified – whether by a fellow navvy or someone else is not clear – and arrested. After a brief interrogation in Stonehaven, where both admitted their involvement in the Burghead disturbances, the two men,

---

* Many of the hundreds of people arrested in connection with rioting in London and Manchester in 2011 were jailed for at least four or five months – some for much longer.

now under escort, were taken to Elgin where they joined Main, Young and Sutherland in jail.

At their trial, held in Edinburgh on 22 March, the five prisoners were charged with 'mobbing and rioting' and with 'assault committed to the effusion of blood and serious injury' – this assault being of an aggravated character because of its having been 'committed upon the sheriff of a county . . . and officers of the law . . . while in the execution of their duty'. The mobbing and rioting charge, it was made clear, related to the generality of what had taken place in Burghead. The assault charge, however, arose from the events of Wednesday 26 January – when Sheriff Cosmo Innes, his colleagues and their special constables had come under sustained attack in and around the inn where they had been forced to seek shelter.[13]

James Falconer, who had not been a member of the crowd that had besieged the inn, pleaded guilty to mobbing and rioting but not to assault. Because Falconer was known to have been elsewhere during the hours in question, this was accepted by the prosecution. The remaining prisoners, however, had no such defence. Partly because of the weight of evidence against them and partly, it appears, because they had been advised that this might minimise their eventual sentences, they pleaded guilty to both charges.

Two advocates acted for the prisoners: Patrick Fraser for the three fishermen; Hugh Tennent for Davidson and Falconer. Both entered pleas of mitigation on behalf of their clients. The court, Fraser and Tennent urged, should be lenient because of the Burghead outbreak having been rooted in 'a very general panic in regard to a scarcity of food'. Written submissions from David Waters, Burghead's Free Church minister, were next produced – these being to the effect that all the prisoners were of good 'moral character' and that the three fishermen in particular were regular attenders at Sunday service. This was endorsed by Alexander Brown, Moray's procurator fiscal, who testified in person to the previous good behaviour of John Young, John Main and Daniel Sutherland – men known to Brown in his capacity as factor to Hopeman's laird, Archibald Duff of Drummuir. Sutherland, though 'sometimes loose with his tongue', was, according to Brown, 'a sober man' who had never been caught up in 'any quarrel'. Young was 'quiet and peaceable'. Main, too, was of 'good character'.[14]

All this was heard in silence by the High Court's presiding judges, Lords Hope, Medwyn and Moncreiff, who then retired to discuss their verdict. On their return, Moncreiff addressed the prisoners. The charges against them, he said, added up to an indictment 'of a most formidable nature. He might say that he had seldom read an indictment . . . that made him more ashamed of his country.' It was sad to find men 'who had had the benefits of a Scottish education' taking 'the law into their own hands' and persisting over a long period 'with their atrocious and violent proceedings'. 'What was to become of the country if such outrageous acts were to be permitted? They had been told that three of [the prisoners] were regular attenders at divine service; and it was lamentable to think that such gross ignorance, and such awful and cowardly selfishness, should have so imbued the minds of men with these advantages.' James Falconer, Moncreiff said, would be jailed for 18 months for mobbing and rioting. This was to imply that Davidson, Sutherland, Main and Young, guilty of assault as well as of mobbing and rioting, would be treated more severely. So it proved. 'Whenever a case of this kind was brought before the court,' Moncreiff continued, 'he apprehended that it must be [the court's] duty to the public, and to the country, to visit the persons involved in such . . . proceedings with a punishment proportioned to the measure of their deeds.' This was why 'he could not reconcile it with his duty to propose to their lordships [his colleagues indicating their assent] any other sentence than that of transportation for a period of seven years'.[15]

In what was described as a 'crowded' courtroom, this announcement produced a 'sensation'. No such sentence had been anticipated and, as news of it spread, initial astonishment quickly gave way to anger. Soon the responsible government minister, Home Secretary Sir George Grey, was in receipt of the first of a series of requests that he take steps to have the transportation verdict set aside. This took the shape of a letter from defence lawyers Hugh Tennent and Patrick Fraser, the latter of whom would himself go on to become a High Court judge.[16]

'We venture to think that this is a sentence of extreme rigour and disproportionate to . . . the offence,' the two lawyers wrote. Medwyn, Moncreiff and Hope, they acknowledged, might have opted for the harshest of punishments in order to 'intimidate those districts of the country which were lately in a disturbed state'. But the time for intimidation had passed. 'Not only in the county of Elgin, but also in every other part of Scotland, the country is in a state of perfect tranquility and submission to the law.' 'The disturbances at Burghead,' Fraser and Tennent went on, 'appear to have originated under the influence of [a] universal panic which seized the people [and led them to] imagine . . . that, if the shipment of grain continued, the district might be left totally destitute of food.' The four men scheduled for deportation had been 'led away' by this 'delusion'. 'They [had] hitherto been irreproachable characters and [had], for the most part, families entirely dependent upon them for support.' Because Young, Main, Sutherland and Davidson had pled guilty, there had been no opportunity to put these points to a jury. But they were now being drawn to the home secretary's attention with a view to persuading him that the 'whole circumstances of the case' were such as 'to make the prisoners fit objects for the exercise of the royal clemency'.[17]

Other representations followed. Revd David Waters, in a letter to Grey, was especially anxious to put in a good word for John Main, John Young and Daniel Sutherland. 'As pastor of [those] three unfortunate young fishermen,' Waters wrote, 'I take the liberty of stating that, previous to the late unhappy riots, no fisherman from Hopeman ever had been within the walls of a prison or had ever appeared as a delinquent in a criminal court.' He had been 'intimately acquainted' with Sutherland, Young and Main 'almost from their infancy', Burghead's Free Church minister continued 'and I know that they have been affectionate and obedient to their parents' who, 'like the whole village of Hopeman', were 'in a state of complete prostration'. While he knew less of Angus Davidson than of the others now destined for an Australian penal colony, Waters added, he believed Davidson to be a 'steady, quiet and inoffensive man' and 'the father of a numerous young family'. He hoped, therefore, that the home secretary would advise Queen Victoria that all four men under sentence of transportation were deserving of 'Her Majesty's mercy'.[18]

In this, as in several more of the communications George Grey received from Moray, there was an undercurrent – or more than an undercurrent – to the effect that Main, Young and Sutherland had been led astray by others. It was with this interpretation of events in mind that, as far back as 10 February, David Waters had written to Sheriff Cosmo Innes in the hope that he might 'put in a quiet word . . . in their favour' with the appropriate authorities. The same contention surfaced at the High Court in representations made by the three fishermen's lawyer, Patrick Fraser. The 'outbreak' in which Sutherland, Young and Main became caught up, he said, 'arose from certain individuals from Burghead coming to Hopeman and telling the inhabitants that unless they assisted them in stopping the exportation of grain . . . famine would soon overtake them'. The individuals in question were Angus Davidson and James Falconer. Davidson, the High Court had decreed, should suffer the same penalty as the Hopeman three. But Falconer – despite its being agreed on all sides in Moray that he had been the foremost promoter of the Burghead protests – had escaped with a relatively light sentence. This rankled.[19]

Whether Cosmo Innes did as David Waters requested cannot be known. Commenting more than quarter of a century later, however, Innes's daughter recalled that the sheriff visited the Hopeman and Burghead prisoners prior to their trial and 'supplied their families with money'. 'Many must still remember,' she wrote of her father who was by then dead, 'his passionate and uncontrollable grief, his tears and sobs in open court, on [Sutherland, Young, Main and Davidson] being sentenced to what seemed to him cruelly severe punishments.'[20]

Innes's feelings were shared by many people in Moray. This is evident from the backing attracted by the organisers of a petition urging clemency for Main, Young and Sutherland – men described by those same organisers as 'industrious, meritorious and peaceful'. Adding to the petition's significance was the fact that signatories included numerous individuals whose lives and businesses had been impacted adversely by what had occurred in Burghead. Among them were farmers, bankers, fish-curers and, not least, Burghead's principal proprietor, William Young. His Moray petitioners, the home secretary was informed, '[could] not but lament a sentence which would consign [three young fishermen] to all the miseries and the degradation and the vice of a penal colony'.[21]

There was much press comment to the same effect. A *Witness* leader, almost certainly the work of Hugh Miller, the paper's editor, began by noting 'the sensation visible in the [High] Court in the case of the Burghead rioters'. 'Riot,' the *Witness* stated, 'is wrong in any circumstances, very wrong.' But there was a pressing need for some judicial understanding of why people from Burghead and Hopeman had done what they did: 'The three Lords of Justiciary who sat in the case of the Burghead rioters are unquestionably honourable and upright men; but men they are, husbands and fathers too . . . Let us suppose them divested of their offices, stripped of their legal and general knowledge, transposed from the higher to the lower levels of society, in poverty and without food . . . and then say whether even they might not come, in such circumstances, to occupy the place of the poor misguided [prisoners] at their bar.'[22]

The Chartist newspaper, *Northern Star*, based in Leeds, was still more unforgiving of the High Court verdict. Edited at this point by Julian Harney who, as a result of his 1840 excursion from Aberdeen to Inverness, was one of the few Chartist leaders to have set foot in Moray and adjacent areas, the *Northern Star* described the High Court verdict as an 'infernal mockery of justice'. Judges of the Hope, Medwyn and Moncreiff variety, the paper declared, were 'wealthy executioners of the pitiless will of the property-holders'. The 'working men of Scotland' should at once 'demand . . . the free pardon' of all five convicted men.[23]

Some reform activists were to do just that. At what its Chartist co-ordinators described as 'a large and respectable meeting of the citizens of Glasgow', letters from relatives of the prisoners were read aloud prior to all present putting their names to a submission that called the High Court verdict 'far too severe' and 'pray[ed] for a free pardon' to be granted to everyone sentenced in connection with the Burghead disturbances.[24]

Nothing of this had any effect on Lord Hope, the most senior of the three judges presiding at the 22 March trial and a man who, because he held the office of lord justice clerk, was close to the top of Scotland's judicial hierarchy. Hope, according to one summary of his career, was 'regarded as having contempt for public opinion'. That view is reinforced by the correspondence the lord justice clerk now entered into with the home secretary.[25]

Hope began this correspondence by emphasising 'the very alarming character' of troubles that had culminated at Burghead in the forces of law and order being 'completely vanquished and overcome'. It was also important to keep in mind, the lord justice clerk felt, that the rebellious tendencies so evident in Burghead had 'pervaded the whole north . . . of Scotland'. During January, February and March, he pointed out, riots had occurred in localities as far apart as Aberdeenshire and Caithness. 'This was one of the first of these riots,' Hope commented of the Burghead disorders, 'and the triumph of the mob in this instance instantly led to greater disturbances elsewhere.' Nor was he impressed by the line taken by the accused men's lawyers. When pressing for leniency, Hope felt, Patrick Fraser and Hugh Tennent 'treat[ed] the spirit in which [the Burghead] rioting originated as a very excusable, if not commendable, feeling on the part of the poor people'. In their post-trial letter to the home secretary, Hope went on, Tennent and Fraser had made the point 'that the north is now quiet'. But this, in the lord justice clerk's opinion, was not because the populace had 'become sensible of the guilt and folly of their outrages'. It was entirely owing to 'the presence of the military'; and, because troops sent from Edinburgh and Portsmouth remained in the north, there was 'no proof,' Hope contended, 'that the people are as yet kept in order by any other check than that of an armed force'. With an eye to the future, and given the possibility of continued food shortages, it was essential to avoid creating an impression that riot and illegality could, in times of scarcity, be excused. This, Hope wrote, was why he and his colleagues had concluded that 'the public peace and order of society . . . required the sentence of transportation'.[26]

The lord justice clerk's views were to become all the more implacable when, on 14 April, two Pulteneytown men, James Nicolson and John Shearer, came before the High Court – sitting, on this occasion, in Inverness. Nicolson, one more of the many shoemakers involved in the 1847 protests, was 24; Shearer, a carter, was still a teenager. Both had been arrested during the Pulteneytown disorders of 24 February – disorders which had culminated in the soldiers taking the two men to jail being ordered by Caithness's sheriff, Robert Thomson, to open fire on a crowd whose stone-throwing, Thomson thought, had jeopardised both his and the military's safety.

Perhaps because the guilty pleas entered by Shearer and Nicolson's Hopeman and Burghead counterparts had not resulted in light sentences, the Pulteneytown pair – whose single trial judge was Lord Hope – pleaded not guilty to the mobbing, rioting and assault charges they faced. This meant that their trial was conducted before a jury. By the prosecution, much was made of the violence in which both accused had allegedly taken part. But James Nicolson's role in what unfolded in Pulteneytown, it was insisted, had been especially reprehensible.

When the troop detachment guarding the *William Bowers*, the cargo ship at the centre of the Pulteneytown disturbances, had set about removing everyone in the ship's vicinity, Nicolson, it was said, had been to the fore in the furore that followed. He had begun by attempting to find a way round the troop cordon put in place at the head of the quay where the vessel was moored. Then, according to statements taken from witnesses, 'he tried to get [further along] the quay by going into a fishing boat'. Having steered this boat 'under the bows of the *William Bowers*', Nicolson began to shin up the ship's anchor chain. Beaten off by soldiers, he had next been seen at the forefront of 'a mob' whose members subjected troops to a great deal of 'abusive language' before going on to bombard them with stones.[27]

Hence Nicolson's arrest. Subsequent to this, however, he had caused further trouble. When en route to jail and under guard, Nicolson had fallen to the ground in what appeared to be a faint or collapse of some kind. Although the shoemaker was later to assert that he had indeed lost consciousness, the authorities were unconvinced. Nor was this an unreasonable reading of what had occurred. Set down briefly by the soldiers given the job of carrying him, Nicolson had at once leaped to his feet and sprinted off – only to be apprehended all over again.

All this, and more besides, was rehearsed in Inverness on 14 April – Hope indicating, at the close of evidence given by Sheriff Robert Thomson, exactly where he stood on the matters before him. Thomson, at this point, was still facing calls for some sort of inquiry to be mounted into his activities on the evening of 24 February. Just days before the Inverness trial, in fact, William Miller, the Wick lawyer acting for John Shearer and James Nicolson, had 'proposed a resolution deprecating the conduct of the sheriff' at what was described as 'a public meeting of the merchants, traders and householders of Wick and Pulteneytown'. That resolution had been embodied in a submission sent to the home secretary. What the lord justice clerk thought of Miller's efforts in this regard, he made obvious to everyone in his Inverness courtroom. 'Mr Thomson,' Hope said as the sheriff prepared to leave the witness box, 'the evidence you have given is most clear and satisfactory; and the conduct you displayed throughout an arduous and important duty, [was] such as entitles you to the thanks of the country. You showed forbearance as long as that was proper . . . [and] when decisive action was necessary to curb the violence of the mob you showed the requisite firmness . . . Had you failed to give the order under which the soldiers fired, you would have failed in what I conceive was your duty. In short, your entire conduct was such as a long acquaintance with you . . . would have led me to expect.'[28]

It would have taken a bold jury to disregard this steer as to where Hope's sympathies lay. As it was, Nicolson and Shearer were each found guilty – though the jury mustered enough courage to recommend leniency in the younger man's case. This was deemed acceptable by the lord justice clerk who, after telling Shearer that everyone 'join[ing] in a mob' became 'liable for all' that then took place, sentenced him to 'imprisonment for eight calendar months'.[29]

James Nicolson, it at once became apparent, was going to fare less well. 'Your case,' Hope informed him, 'is very flagrant and calls for a very severe punishment . . . The crime of mobbing and rioting is one of the most . . . serious that can occur. The character of the mob in this case was most determined and alarming; its object most illegal; and, looking at all the facts against you, your case is most serious indeed.' However, he would not pass sentence there and then. That would be delayed until a further High Court sitting in Edinburgh towards the end of May – because, Hope said, he wanted to take time to consider and 'to consult [his] brother judges'.[30]

This was not the real reason for postponement. As the lord justice clerk explained in a new letter to Sir George Grey, he had deferred sentence on Nicolson because 'he did not know the decision come to by [the home secretary] in the [Burghead case]'. It would have been unfortunate, Hope indicated, if he had pronounced 'another sentence of transportation' days in advance of its perhaps becoming known that it had been agreed in London to mitigate the Burghead sentences. He had decided, therefore, not to run that risk. Nicolson, meanwhile, would remain in custody.[31]

The home secretary, Hope went on, needed to be aware of just how perilous was the situation in the north: 'I feel it to be my duty to bring under your consideration the proofs generally which appeared at . . . Inverness of the spirit of resistance to the civil authorities . . . and of the extent and determination of attempts to interfere with the supply [of grain] to the markets.' Pulteneytown, Hope was convinced, had been the scene of 'the most serious riot which [had] occurred in Scotland since 1820' – a year when, in and around Glasgow, widespread strikes and other disorders had culminated in efforts to organise an armed uprising. The violence that broke out in Pulteneytown on 24 February had 'lasted for five hours'. Such was the ferocity of the attack mounted on Sheriff Robert Thomson and his accompanying troops, moreover, that there could be no doubt that, in instructing soldiers to open fire, the sheriff had done the right thing. 'I have never seen a case in which the circumstances more clearly . . . called for the measure which was adopted.' Because of what he had learned 'of the . . . determination of the lower orders to prevent . . . the shipment of provisions', Hope added, he was more than ever 'persuaded that only very serious punishment, producing a salutary awe of the law, will keep the [northern] district in restraint'.[32]

The lord justice clerk need not have worried about a weakening of resolve in Whitehall. Within days, Hope had been assured 'that it was not [George Grey's] intention to advise any immediate commutation' of the sentences arising from the Burghead trial. Nor was he disposed, the home secretary told the Caithness people pressing for an inquiry into Robert Thomson's actions, to order any such inquiry. Evidence heard at the 14 April High Court hearing in Inverness, Grey wrote, 'appear[ed] to him to render any further [investigation] unnecessary' – not least because, in light of what had been 'disclosed' at Inverness, he 'fully approve[d] of the conduct of the sheriff'.[33]

Lord Hope, it followed, was now free to do as he pleased with James Nicolson who, on 31 May in Edinburgh, was brought before the lord justice clerk and two further judges, Lords Moncreiff and Cockburn. He and his colleagues, Hope told Nicolson, took the view that his was 'a case of the most aggravated kind and . . . they were unanimously of opinion that he should suffer transportation for ten years'.[34]

It is hard to interpret this sentence as anything other than a disdainful dismissal of all those people who, whether in the press or by means of representations to the home secretary, had lambasted the High Court's decision to have four Moray men transported. Not only was James Nicolson, too, to be transported. As compared with the Hopeman and Burghead prisoners he was to join in Australia, he would endure three additional years of penal servitude in a harshly disciplined work gang. This, from Hope's perspective, served to make three points. First, it signalled his determination to treat violent protest, irrespective of the background to it, as a heinous crime. Second, it underscored the lord justice clerk's belief that the Pulteneytown disturbances had been even more shameful than those which took place in Burghead. Third, it served as a deterrent, or so Hope thought, to further such disturbance by showing that participants in disorder could expect to receive sentences that, short of their being condemned to death, were the most punitive available to the courts.

The severity of the sentence passed on James Nicolson is underlined by the outcome of another of the trials Lord Hope conducted when in Inverness. This trial arose from the attempted rape of Mary Cameron, the Fort William woman who, following the dance she attended on a November evening in 1846, had agreed to be escorted home by two soldiers who were jointly to attack her. For reasons touched on earlier, a charge of 'assault with intent to ravish' could be brought against just one of those soldiers, Dennis Driscoll. Because the detail of what had been done to Mary Cameron was deemed too sordid for public exposure, Driscoll's High Court trial, which took place a day or two after James Nicolson's, was held behind closed doors.* On his being found guilty, Hope sentenced him to transportation for seven years. By the lord justice clerk, in other words, Driscoll's crime of attempted rape was deemed a lesser offence than James Nicolson's involvement in efforts to prevent the shipping of grain from Pulteneytown.

On 3 June 1847, three days after he had been sentenced, Nicolson was permitted to write a letter to his mother, his father and his sister. 'You can

---

* As mentioned previously, another 76th Regiment soldier, James Ball, had been arrested in late 1846 in connection with the attempted rape of a woman who lived near Ardersier. In April 1847, Ball too was sentenced to seven years in a penal colony. The Victorian practice of holding trials of this sort in private might seem odd from today's perspective. But it had the indubitably beneficial effect of sparing victims of rape or attempted rape from the ordeal of a public examination by defence and prosecution lawyers.

consider my feelings,' he began, 'when I must inform you that I am now sentenced to ten years transportation.' Because he had been granted bail by the Wick authorities during the weeks following his arrest, Nicolson, who was unmarried and lived with his parents, had spent those weeks at home – bidding farewell to his family only when put aboard the ship that took him to Inverness for trial. 'Poor Mother and Dear Sister,' he wrote, 'I little thought that, when I parted from your affectionate hand at the harbour, it was never to meet again.' 'We may meet,' the young man acknowledged, 'but ten years is a long time. Death will make a great alteration before it expire.' 'If it was God's will,' Nicolson continued, 'I would be thankful if he should call me by death before I should be bound in chains of degradation . . . O! I am lost for time and for eternity . . . Pray for me that the Lord will strengthen me in this sad state.' During his court appearance, Nicolson added, a lawyer had shown him several documents that had been supplied by his father and others in the hope that their contents might help secure a lesser sentence. But this, he explained, had been in vain. 'Poor Father, I got your letter, and the letters of character, from a counsel in the court. But they were for no good. The judges would not allow them to be read.'[35]

Because James Nicolson's 3 June letter found its way into the press, it helped create sympathy for him. Nicolson, commented the *Morning Advertiser*, a London daily, 'was religiously brought up [and] was well conducted and industrious. He was the chief support of his aged parents, and had been led to take part in the [Pulteneytown] riot, not from any turbulence or malignancy of feeling, but [because he was] carried away by the dread of an approaching famine.'[36]

And from what had been done to James Nicolson, the *Morning Advertiser* drew a wider lesson as to the damage inflicted on Britain's justice system by men like Lord Hope. 'So extreme a punishment for an offence committed under so many extenuating circumstances,' the paper commented, 'has not only created a feeling of surprise but produced emotions akin to horror from one end of Scotland to the other. There is not a [person] in that country that does not revolt at the idea of such a sentence for such an offence. The most intense sympathy is everywhere felt for the unfortunate prisoner. In this way the great ends of an enlightened criminal jurisprudence are defeated. No sentence should be so severe as to induce the people to withhold their condemnation from the prisoner and direct it against the judicial bench. This has been the effect of the sentence in question. The prisoner is pitied while the judge is condemned . . . The consequence is that the ends of justice are defeated. The law ceases to be respected because, administered by the judge who presided on this occasion, it is arrayed in vindictive garb.'[37]

Also engaging actively with the Pulteneytown man's case was the *Manchester Times*, which had been strongly supportive of the ultimately successful campaign to have the Corn Law repealed. Who, the paper wondered, was guilty of 'the greatest moral crime'? James Nicolson or those who, over many years and even in 'periods of deep distress', had 'excluded . . . all foreign corn' from Britain? Many of its readers, the *Manchester Times* implied, would be in no doubt as to the answer to that question. But 'the men who supported the . . . exclusion are in high office and honour, and the poor young fellow who obstructed the exportation of a boatload of corn, when his neighbours had the horrors of starvation before their eyes, is *sentenced to ten years transportation*.'[38]

In newspaper after newspaper, there was much to the same effect. Over the summer of 1847, then, Sir George Grey found himself under mounting public pressure to secure the early release of all five Pulteneytown, Hopeman and Burghead men. Soon politicians too were weighing in – the Nicolson case, in particular, being taken up by Charles Cowan, an industrialist who had not long before been elected Edinburgh's MP in preference to the long-standing incumbent, Thomas Babington Macaulay. Politically radical in a way that Macaulay, an old-style Whig, was not, Cowan was sure that James Nicolson had been done a serious injustice. Enquiries he had made in Wick, Cowan informed Grey, had convinced him that the Pulteneytown protests had resulted from a 'not ill-founded dread' that 'the exportation of most of the corn grown in Caithness' might easily lead to famine. Nor were the riots in which James Nicolson had taken part anything like as threatening as Lord Hope maintained. 'No serious damage was done either to person or property,' Charles Cowan insisted. Nor was Nicolson any sort of habitual offender. That the young man was of good character, Cowan wrote, he had been told by none other than the governor of the Edinburgh prison where Nicolson had been held for some weeks. 'The governor . . . was highly pleased with him,' Cowan advised the home secretary, 'and stated that he was of a very different disposition from the usual description of prisoners under his care.'[39]

From Caithness, meanwhile, came a petition organised by Wick's Free Church minister, Charles Thomson, with whom Charles Cowan had been in communication. The 'exportation' of so much grain from Caithness, Thomson commented, had caused 'absolute terror' that 'dreadful famine was approaching'. This, more than anything else, explained James Nicolson's actions – actions which, however ill-advised, had not been such as to merit 'the fearful sentence . . . pronounced upon him'.[40]

This claim attracted support from an unexpected quarter in the person of James Loch. Ever since the widespread outcry arising from the clearance of much of the Sutherland Estate, a clearance he planned personally, Loch, as indicated previously, had nurtured an obsessive suspicion of anything that smacked of a challenge to the established order. But now, in his capacity as Wick's MP and by means of a letter to the home secretary, he threw his weight behind Revd Charles Thomson's petition – a petition, Loch told Grey, which had been 'very numerously and, to my knowledge, most respectably signed'.[41]

Urging clemency for James Nicolson, Loch, like Thomson and Charles Cowan, majored on what he called 'the condition of the north of Scotland' during the opening weeks of 1847. In Caithness, Loch wrote, this condition had been 'of a complicated character'. 'The local failure of the potato crop affected directly a considerable proportion of the population.' Making the consequent crisis more acute, however, was 'an entire stagnation in the trade of the principal manufacture of the place' – that 'manufacture' being cured herring. The outcome – because of the way the slump in demand for herring impacted negatively on boat-builders, coopers and others – had been a 'casting out of employment' of practically 'every class' in both Pulteneytown and Wick. 'Under such a state of things,' James Loch went on, 'with the [cost of] provisions rising' and demand for labour 'scarce', 'was it wonderful that an uneasy feeling should have prevailed when an extensive shipment of corn was apprehended?' 'This,' Loch stressed to the home secretary, 'is not stated as any justification of a breach of the law, but it is submitted as the groundwork for mercy.'

If, as James Loch suggested, there should be clemency for James Nicolson, then, in logic, there needed also to be clemency for Burghead's Angus Davidson and Hopeman's John Main, John Young and Daniel Sutherland. Following their conviction, these four men had been taken from Edinburgh to London where they were incarcerated at Millbank, the Thameside waystation for prisoners headed ultimately for Australia. But a final ruling as to when, or if, they should join an Australia-bound convict ship was still awaited. In late August and September, the need for such a ruling became more pressing as a result of the trek made to Ardverikie by Margaret Main, Isabella Main and Mary Jack. There was much that was newsworthy in that trek. The young wife of a Millbank prisoner had walked more than halfway across Scotland in the hope of raising his plight with Queen Victoria. She had been accompanied by her husband's mother and by the mother of another prisoner; and, though none of the three 'fisherwomen', as Mary, Margaret and Isabella were described in the press, had obtained an audience with the queen, they had been invited to meet with Earl Grey. This had given Isabella, Margaret and Mary an opportunity to outline, in conversation with a member of the British cabinet, the reasons why, in their opinion, Daniel Sutherland, John Young and John Main should be spared transportation and, indeed, set free.

Those reasons were set out in the petition the earl urged Mary, Margaret and Isabella to submit to Victoria. Daniel Sutherland, John Young and John Main, that document stated, had been 'induced through . . . dread of famine' to take the actions they took in Burghead. Each of them was 'deeply sensible' of having done wrong and all were 'heartily contrite for their fault'. Almost certainly compiled in Burghead's Free Church manse with the help of David and Elizabeth Waters, this latest petition ended by appealing to the queen not as monarch but as mother and wife: 'The prayers of your petitioners will be that Your Most Excellent Majesty may long enjoy the society of your beloved consort and children.' No such enjoyment was available, it was hinted, to the women now petitioning the head of state. Their sons in the case of Isabella and Margaret Main, her husband in Mary Jack's case, remained 'prisoners in Millbank Penitentiary': 'Their families are, by their absence, subjected to great hardship and privations, as well as bitter sorrow.'[42]

Did Earl Grey raise directly with Sir George Grey, the earl's cousin as well as his cabinet colleague, the points made by the Hopeman fisherwomen at Ardverikie? If so, no note was kept of their discussion. But Home Office records show that, at Fallodon, a Northumberland country mansion he had not long before inherited, Sir George spoke about 'the case of the northern rioters' with one of his house guests, Andrew Rutherfurd, Scotland's lord advocate. Soon the two government ministers had planned a way forward. James Falconer, the Burghead shoemaker who had 'managed [things] cunningly', in Rutherfurd's opinion, and had thus 'escaped with [the] slight punishment' of 18 months in jail, would be released, nine months early, at the end of 1847. His Burghead associate, Angus Davidson, together with Daniel Sutherland, John Main and John Young from Hopeman, would not be transported but would remain in prison for a period of one year from the date of their trial. James Nicolson would not be transported either. But he, perhaps in a nod to Lord Hope's belief that the Pulteneytown riot had been especially shocking, would serve a full two years.[43]

Although the home secretary and the lord advocate agreed those matters in early October 1847, news of their decision was not released. This was because, before announcing any relaxation of the sentences arising from the Burghead and Pulteneytown protests, Grey and Rutherfurd wanted to be confident that there was little chance of the 1847–48 winter bringing renewed scarcity – with an attendant risk of further rioting – to the Moray Firth area. In this regard, price trends were reassuring. Although potato yields around the Moray Firth were little, if any, better in 1847 than they had been in 1846, a good grain harvest there and elsewhere had the effect – reinforced by imports made possible by Corn Law repeal – of exerting downward pressure on the cost of meal. In Easter Ross, for example, its purchase price was reckoned 'less than half' that of the year before. During December, therefore, it was judged safe to inform affected prisoners and their relatives of what had been settled at Fallodon.[44]

Because his revised sentence still had more than 15 months to run, James Nicolson, who had been sent south to join Davidson, Young, Main and Sutherland in Millbank, was transferred from there to Portsmouth where he was held, as were many other convicts at this time, in a prison hulk. Like other such hulks, this one, the *Stirling Castle*, was a decommissioned warship stripped of its rigging and masts and anchored just offshore. Despite the long-standing view that the typical hulk was a disease-ridden 'hell on water', conditions on these vessels (soon to be done away with) were, by the 1840s, a lot less gruesome than they had been – certainly no worse than those in Millbank where complaints about its governor's conduct had led, during 1846, to an official inquiry into the prison's disciplinary practices. Accounting for, if not excusing, the harshness of the Millbank regime was the problem of maintaining order in a place that was little more than a transit camp for prisoners en route to Australia. Thousands of such prisoners passed through Millbank each year. 'Among those thousands,' commented one of Millbank's later governors, 'were the choicest specimens of criminality, male and female, ripe always for desperate deeds and at times almost unmanageable.'[45]

Nothing is known of how the Burghead cooper, Angus Davidson, or the Hopeman fishermen, John Young, John Main and Daniel Sutherland, got through the months they spent in Millbank. All of them are likely to have found those months difficult. But for the three young men from Hopeman – none of whom had previously left their home village other than to go each day to sea – confinement in so bleak an establishment must have been especially hard to bear.

Sutherland, Main, Young and Davidson were released from Millbank on 29 March 1848. How Davidson got home is unclear. But on Wednesday 5 April, Young, Main and Sutherland disembarked at Burghead from the *Duke of Richmond*, a steamship named, a little ironically in the circumstances, for one of the north of Scotland's tougher-minded landlords. 'They were received with joy by their friends,' the press reported of the three men's homecoming, 'and the people of Hopeman, as well as themselves, feel gratitude for the royal clemency which has been extended towards them.'[46]

That left only James Nicolson still serving a sentence arising from the 1847 troubles. In the spring of 1848 renewed representations, including a 'memorial' signed by Caithness clergymen of several denominations, were made to the home secretary on his behalf. These representations, again endorsed by James Loch, requested a further reduction in Nicolson's sentence. In July 1848, however, this was refused, and so Nicolson did not get back to Pulteneytown until June 1849. 'He does not appear to have suffered in body from his lengthy confinement,' the *John O'Groat Journal* remarked.[47]

What, in the end, had been accomplished by James Nicolson, Daniel Sutherland, John Main, John Young, Angus Davidson and the thousands of other men, women and children who, between January and March 1847, succeeded – even if temporarily – in putting a stop to grain shipments from harbour after harbour all around the Moray Firth? Their biggest and most immediate victory consisted of a marked and very welcome improvement in the food supplies available to their communities. This improvement took various forms. Meal-dealers who had been so tempted by high prices elsewhere that they had given up on sales of small amounts of meal to local customers now resumed such sales. Prices also fell, often substantially, as farmers and landlords, as well as dealers, were persuaded to give greater priority to closer-at-hand purchasers – and as councillors, business people and others in towns like Elgin, Inverness and Dingwall launched fund-raising efforts that made it possible for meal to be sold cheaply to those most in need.

Might cost-cutting moves of this sort have happened anyway? Not according to Crown Agent John Lindsay, no friend of protest and the man primarily responsible for the troop deployments that played a big part in bringing disorder to an end. Merchants and landlords, Lindsay felt, were guilty of 'harshness if not injustice' in their dealings with folk in their neighbourhoods. What might seem good business to the typical laird or dealer – cashing in, for instance, on southern demand for grain – could all too readily look to others like sharp practice or, as Lindsay put it, 'oppression'. Nor was it at all helpful to good governance, in the crown agent's opinion, that next to nothing had been done to tackle discontent about high prices in advance of these high prices becoming a cause of serious unrest. 'The large grain dealers,' John Lindsay informed the lord advocate, 'have refused to retail [meal in their home markets] . . . till forced by terror; [and] the rich landlords have shut their ears and their purses till racked [or compelled] by alarm.'[48]

John Lindsay's criticisms of landowning and commercial interests did not imply sympathy for, let alone approval of, people of the sort who battled with the army in Pulteneytown and forced Sheriff Cosmo Innes to stage an igno-minious retreat from Burghead. What Lindsay described as 'the tendency . . . by the working classes to use force for the preventing of shipment of grain' was something he deplored. It was his duty, Lindsay believed, 'to maintain the rights of private property and free commerce'. Hence the crown agent's unre-lenting determination – evident in the effort he put into having more and more troops sent north – to meet force with force until what had evolved into a Moray Firth protest movement was beaten back and ultimately crushed.[49]

But while it is clear that the disturbances dealt with so vigorously by John Lindsay posed, from his standpoint, a very real threat, did they also constitute a *movement* in the sense that this word, with its connotations of planning and design, is used here? Eric Richards, the one historian to have investigated these events, did not think so. 'The forms of collective action employed [in the Scottish north] by the many different crowds [who undertook such action],' Richards concluded, 'were, on the whole, unsophisticated and unco-ordinated. Little organisation or leadership emerged.' That, as indicated on previous pages, is not this writer's view. The placing of booms across the harbour entrance at Macduff; Buckie and Portgordon people's use of signal flags to communicate with the various coastal settlements between Garmouth and Portknockie; the maintenance, for a week or two, of checkpoints on roads leading into Inverness; the blockades kept in place, for a month or more, at Cromarty Firth harbours and loading places like Foulis Point and Invergordon; the handing out of leaflets and the nailing up of placards or posters in Pulteneytown and Wick: these surely show, as do lots of similar occurrences, that organising ability was by no means lacking among men and women drawn from what John Lindsay called 'the working classes'.[50]

Nor, or so this book contends, was grassroots leadership absent either. Given the circumstances in which that leadership emerged, it was necessarily secretive, clandestine, elusive. But the mention made by rioters in Portgordon of their answering to a 'committee' hints at such leadership's existence – as does the emergence of a similar committee in Findhorn and the discipline so evident, whether in Banffshire, Moray, Inverness-shire, Ross-shire or Caithness, in an almost total absence, even when rioting was at its height, of any kind of theft or looting.

But if, in February 1847, northern Scotland could be said by the *Economist* 'to be nearly in a state of insurrection', this was an insurrection with, as Eric Richards was right to observe, 'limited and specific objectives'. In Continental Europe, less than 12 months after the Moray Firth area's troubles wound down, disturbances which started in much the same way as the Moray Firth uprising were to escalate so rapidly that governments were endangered and, in some cases, toppled. Nothing like that was contemplated in the course of Scotland's famine winter. Concessions were demanded, and obtained, from landowners, councillors and others in authority. But no consideration was given, as it certainly was by Continental revolutionaries, to overturning the country's entire social structure. Here and there – as when Burghead shoe-maker James Falconer spoke of 'liberty' and of 'the rich [having] too long had it their own way' – there were echoes of the Chartist thinking to which localities like Moray had been exposed. By and large, however, the 1847 rebels had no aim beyond that of countering what was thought to be a press-ing risk of famine. They possessed, in other words, little or nothing by way of a wider political agenda. It is this which most differentiates the 1847 upheavals from those that broke out some 35 years later when, for the first time since John Lindsay authorised the dispatch of troops to Banffshire, Moray, Inverness-shire, Ross-shire and Caithness, the military had to be called on to deal with unrest in the northern half of Scotland.[51]

This new unrest – characterised by widespread rent-strikes and equally widespread land seizures – would last far longer than the 1847 upheavals. Unlike their 1847 predecessors, moreover, people who participated in it were to develop a set of well worked-out and far-reaching demands which, for the most part, they succeeded in getting government to meet. By so doing, they transformed greatly for the better the prospects of the localities hardest hit by famine in 1846, in 1847 and in the years that followed. Those localities, for reasons explored in earlier chapters, were crofting districts in the Hebrides and on the Highland mainland's western seaboard.

No such upturn seemed probable when, in 1852, Lady Anne MacAskill visited Skye. Lady Anne's soldier husband had been born there and, subse-quent to his death in action in India in 1845, she had been drawn into charitable efforts on behalf of his native island. What she witnessed in Skye, where food shortages were as prevalent as ever, left Lady Anne appalled. 'At the appointed time and place,' she commented of one distribution of emergency supplies, '[the] poor creatures troop down in hundreds, wretched and thin, starved and wan. Some have clothing, some almost none, and some are a mass of rags. Old and young, feeble and infirm, they take their station and await their turn – not a murmur, not a clamour, not a word – but they wept aloud . . . as they detailed their miseries.'[52]

Even in the face of suffering of this sort, however, the crofting population remained quiescent. Nor, for the most part, did crofting families resist the clearances and deportations which, in the late 1840s and early 1850s, became the landowning class's common means of dealing with their tenantries' hunger and poverty. On Lord Macdonald's North Uist estate, admittedly, several hundred people battled in July 1849 with the estate managers and sheriff-officers attempting to evict them. But there were few other such episodes.

When, in the summer of 1853, its owners set out to depopulate Knoydart, a grand total of 332 people were shipped to Canada. But 100 or more tried somehow to cling on – mostly on grounds that age, ill-health or family responsibilities made it impossible for them to leave. Their homes were at once demolished, and when some of them tried to provide themselves with temporary shelters made from boat sails and the like, these too were destroyed. Weeks later, Donald Ross, a man who would be described today as an investigative journalist, made the long journey from Glasgow to Knoydart (a place that has never been accessible by road) to see for himself what had happened and to speak with as many clearance victims as he could arrange to meet. What Donald Ross learned he put into print.

'John McKinnon,' Ross recorded of one of his interviewees, '[is] aged 44, is married and has a wife and six children [aged between two and 11] . . . When McKinnon's house was pulled down he had no place to put his head in; consequently himself and his family, for the first night or two, had to burrow among the rocks near the shore.' Moved on from even that miserable refuge, the McKinnons, like others in the same predicament, were left to make what shift they could. 'McKinnon's wife,' Donald Ross wrote, 'was pregnant when she was turned out . . . In about four days thereafter she had a premature birth; and this, and the exposure to the elements, and the want of . . . a nutritious diet, has brought on consumption [tuberculosis] from which there is no chance whatever of her recovery.'[53]

Neither Donald Ross nor any other pressman was on hand in Barra, South Uist and Benbecula in 1851 to witness the expulsion of the hundreds of people herded on to the five Quebec-bound ships their landlord, John Gordon of Cluny, had chartered with a view to ensuring those people's permanent departure from his property. In the 1880s and 1890s, however, two commissions of inquiry would hear accounts of Gordon's 1851 evictions from men whose memories of that awful time had stayed with them throughout their lives.

Among the Barra communities left derelict by Gordon's evicting parties was Bruernish. Here George Pole of the Commissariat had landed from the *Firefly* in January 1847. Here Sheriff Charles Shaw, that same month, had listened while Archibald MacMillan spoke about his teenage daughter Catherine's death from hunger. 'Twenty-seven families were cleared away from that township in one day,' it would be said of the place* where Catherine MacMillan once lived.[54]

'As regards emigration,' an 1883 commission heard from one of South Uist's parish priests, 'we may frankly tell . . . that we are in no way inclined to emigrate . . . We desire not to see revived cruel and forced evictions as carried out in . . . 1851, when many were bound, hand and feet, and packed off like cattle on board the vessel to [North] America.' 'I saw . . . people sent to the emigrant ships by violence,' a 60-year-old South Uist crofter commented by way of corroboration. There followed further confirmation that South Uist and Barra's 1851 emigrants – folk whose plight would afterwards cause so much concern in Quebec – had, in some instances, been shackled or tied up to prevent their going into hiding before they could be sent away.[55]

Why were so many so steadfastly passive in the face of viciousness of the kind perpetrated in Knoydart, in Barra, in South Uist and – such cruelties being by no means localised – in plenty other parts of the Highlands and Islands? Lady Anne MacAskill offered a persuasive explanation. 'I glanced at their countenances,' she wrote of people she met with in Skye, 'and thought, if ever the Highlanders were a handsome race . . . they are so no longer: cadaverous . . . thin . . . diminutive, listless, supine-looking, quiet and grave.' Highlanders and Hebrideans, Lady Anne went on, had long been said to be proud and independent-minded. But if that had been the case, she felt, it had manifestly ceased to be so. 'Half-starved for years . . . [and confronted by] failing crops [and] diseased potatoes, their characters of necessity become

---

* Bruernish would later be resettled.

affected: their spirits sunk, their minds depressed, their energies cramped, their intellect clouded and their hopes gone.'[56]

But if, in 1852, Skye's crofting population was downtrodden, despairing and demoralised, as it surely was, then how did it come about that in 1882, just 30 years later, this same population had become so self-assured as to be capable of initiating protest action that, within months, would spread from Skye to much of northern Scotland? There is no single answer to that question.* But one key contributor to the crofting community's improved morale is to be found in the extent to which, in the 1860s and 1870s, the economic circumstances of crofting localities – not just in Skye but everywhere in the Highlands and Islands – began, at last, to improve. This newfound prosperity ought not to be exaggerated. But it was nevertheless real; and it resulted, in no small part, from crofting families having managed to obtain a share of the still more striking uplift in incomes experienced, during those same decades, by residents of the Moray Firth port towns and harbour villages that had been at the centre of the 1847 revolt.

The origins of that revolt were bound up, as underlined already, in an 1846 collapse in demand for cured herring. Even by the summer and autumn of 1847, however, demand had started to pick up and, for the next 30 years or more, as new buyers and new consumers were found in Germany, Poland, Russia and elsewhere, cured herring exports expanded exponentially. In Moray Firth fishing communities this meant that the 1847 crisis, when a steep fall in incomes coincided with soaring food prices, was soon no more than a memory.

Even in the 1840s crofters from the west coast and the Hebrides were picking up jobs as hired hands on herring boats fishing out of Pulteneytown – while women from the same crofting areas could be found among gutters and packers at work in Caithness curing yards. From the 1850s onwards, however, opportunities of this sort began to multiply as ways were found of extending the herring season by opening up new fishing grounds. Soon the Scottish herring fleet was at sea from spring until late autumn – a development made possible by the realisation that herring could be taken in quantity at different times in different places. Herring fishermen, as a result, became migratory

---

* For a full account of post-famine developments, the Skye disturbances of 1882 and the wider struggle that followed, see J. Hunter, *The Making of the Crofting Community*, first published in 1976, since updated and presently available in paperback from this book's publishers.

– with fishing effort of a sort once concentrated around Caithness now extending from the Hebrides to waters off the eastern and south-eastern coast of England.

By the 1870s, it followed, the herring fishing season was commencing in May when boats gathered at the southern end of the Long Island. Initial landings were made in Barra. But from there the fleet moved gradually north, to Lewis and to Shetland, before turning south for Caithness, Moray, Aberdeenshire and, eventually, East Anglia. Although most herring boats continued to be owned by families resident in ports like Wick, Avoch, Fraserburgh and Peterhead, their skippers now started the annual fishing season by taking on additional crewmen whose homes were in Hebridean and West Highland crofting communities. Those men then stuck with their employers until paid off in the autumn – much the same pattern being followed by women who might begin the season in one of the curing yards established at this time in Barra and end that same season, hundreds of miles away, in Lowestoft or Great Yarmouth.

Although cash thus earned helped greatly to make crofting families better off, there could still be setbacks. One of the most severe occurred in the early 1880s when the effects of a temporary slump in herring catches were aggravated by the weather-related loss of both grain and cereal crops. Suggestions that conditions in hardest-hit localities were such as to merit a renewal of external aid provoked predictable scorn in predictable quarters – the *Scotsman*, for example, reverting to its long-standing conviction that crofters, said to be 'men who love to live without work', needed to be 'disabused' of any notion that they might be deserving of help from outside. But if the prospect of crofting areas receiving such assistance was alarming to *Scotsman* leader-writers, still worse, from their standpoint, was what actually happened – the emergence of a crofter protest movement given, as the paper put it, to 'setting all law at defiance' by staging, for example, well-publicised reoccupations of land lost to crofting in the course of the many clearances that had taken place during the famine era of 30 or so years before.[57]

Those clearances – in Knoydart, Lewis, the Uists, Barra and elsewhere – occurred at a time when, as Lady Anne MacAskill pointed out, crofting families, shattered physically and psychologically by famine, lacked both the will and the capacity to mount a worthwhile fightback. By the 1880s, however, the crofting population was in a different place. Its younger generations in particular – the generations at the forefront of the protest campaign now unleashed – had come to maturity with an expectation that, year by year on average, their material circumstances would improve. There would be no reversion on their part to a past when it seemed to very many crofters that, no matter how bad things might be, next to nothing could be done to put them right.

Underpinning and enforcing this changed outlook was the fact that levels of education and literacy were everywhere higher than they had been. This made for greater openness to new ideas. These, in turn, contributed to a wholly novel willingness – again especially on the part of younger people – to consider the possibility of embarking on actions of a sort that, because of their associations with Irish insurgency, many crofters had previously thought it right, and indeed virtuous, to reject.

Nowhere is that older attitude more evident than in what was said to Sir John MacNeill, Scotland's principal Poor Law administrator, when, in 1851, he toured crofting areas. 'It is due to the working classes in the parishes I . . . visited,' MacNeill reported, 'to state that their deportment was uniformly civil and obliging, even in circumstances that might have produced feelings of discontent.' The circumstances MacNeill mentioned arose from the imminent winding up of the Destitution Fund's central board. The board's planned withdrawal from the Highlands and Islands scene, MacNeill heard, made it imperative to have renewed intervention of the type undertaken by the Commissariat in the winter of 1846–47. That, MacNeill made clear to everyone he spoke with, would not happen. But even on being told this, crofters evinced no anger. Instead they 'contrasted their own loyalty and respect for the laws with occurrences in [Ireland] . . . and asked whether it was possible that the Queen, after doing so much for a rebellious people, should refuse all assistance to a people who had been constantly loyal and orderly'.[58]

There would be no recurrence of sentiments of that sort in the 1880s – certainly not on the part of a group of Skye crofters who, in the summer of 1881 went to Ireland where, capitalising on skills picked up on Scottish herring boats, they hired their services to skippers operating from Kinsale. This was the part of Ireland where, in December 1846, Cork magistrate Nicholas Cummins had witnessed the horrors – 'such as no tongue nor pen can convey the slightest idea of' – he had drawn attention to by means of the letter he had sent to the *Times*. But by 1881, in part because of the Great Hunger's lingering legacy, the same area had become one of the foremost strongholds of the Irish Land League – an organisation which, by winning a huge following in the Irish countryside, forced the British government to grant a series of concessions, most notably security of tenure, to Ireland's farming tenants. On having had the opportunity to see something of this development, and of the methods by which it had been brought about, the visiting Skyemen, on getting home, did exactly as the Irish Land League had advised its membership. They stopped paying their rents. Soon lots of other crofters did the same.

When Highlands and Islands landlords tried to evict rent-strikers, crofters retaliated by taking over sheep farms and by battling with the authorities in much the same way as Moray Firth fishing folk had done in 1847. Nor were rebel crofters without allies. In cities like Glasgow and London, professional men (usually of crofting background) were quickly to set up pro-crofter groupings that coalesced into a Highland Land Law Reform Association (HLLRA). This new body's key role was to insist that parliament should at once make available to the Highlands and Islands the various rights and protections now standard in Ireland.

Although the HLLRA, afterwards renamed the Highland Land League, began as an urban pressure group, it did not long remain so. In August 1883, more than 2,000 crofters, all of them herring boat crewmen, met in Fraserburgh to discuss how they might most effectively obtain security of the Irish type. On returning home, they agreed, they would establish HLLRA branches 'in their various parishes'. 'The object of the HLLRA,' reads a leaflet circulated just after the Fraserburgh gathering, 'is to effect by unity of purpose and action such changes in the land laws as will promote the welfare of the people . . . The cause has many friends . . . But the success of the movement must necessarily depend upon . . . unity and determination . . . Unity is might and, with might on their side, the people will soon succeed in obtaining their rights.'[59]

In pressing for that outcome, the HLLRA was helped hugely by its emergence having coincided with reforms that entitled most crofters, and some working men,[*] to vote. Hence the HLLRA's decision, in the run-up to the general election scheduled for December 1885, to field candidates in Highlands and Islands constituencies. Among those candidates was Gavin Brown Clark. A Scots-born but London-based medical doctor who had had a leading role in the HLLRA's formation, Clark, at the invitation of the association's Caithness members, became HLLRA flag-bearer in that county.[†]

---

[*] Votes for women would be delayed until 1918.

[†] Because MPs were then unpaid, only men with independent incomes of the sort Clark's medical practice delivered, could afford to stand for parliament.

Gavin Clark's politics were radical. While a student he joined the International Working Men's Association,* one of whose guiding lights was Karl Marx, and, prior to his Caithness candidacy, he had been for some time on good terms with future Labour Party founder James Keir Hardie. Affiliations of that sort, together with his less-than-strict religious beliefs and his sponsorship of anti-imperial causes, enabled Clark's Caithness critics to brand this 'obscure London physician', as they called him, a 'socialist', a friend of Britain's enemies, a 'Sabbath-breaker' and a man given to placing 'Popery on an equality with Protestantism'.[60]

But as shown by the dozens of well-attended public meetings he conducted during the autumn and early winter of 1885, Clark was not short of backers. The Caithness constituency was one where, as in Easter Ross, grain-growing arable farms had been created at the expense of small-scale agriculturalists. Many of them had been displaced to crofts or smallholdings on marginal land. They or their descendants now rallied behind Gavin Clark. So did the larger number of people whose grandparents or great-grandparents had moved into Caithness when evicted from neighbouring Sutherland. Some families in this category had managed to get crofts. Others lived in towns or fishing villages. Either way, they were happy to sign up to Clark's agenda. 'They had been driven from their . . . straths and glens,' the HLLRA candidate said of these folk's forebears, 'because landlords thought sheep and deer paid better than men.'[61]

Because the Conservative Party had agreed to let Gavin Clark's Liberal opponent have a clear run against him, the HLLRA man confronted just one rival. This was Clarence Sinclair whose father, owner of Caithness's biggest estate, had been the county's MP for the previous 16 years. By most suppos-edly informed observers, a Sinclair victory was taken for granted. But when, two days after polling† closed on the evening of Tuesday 8 December, ballot papers were tallied in Wick's courthouse, it was found that he had been heav-ily defeated – by 2,110 votes to 1,218. Outside, in a snow-covered Bridge Street, this result, according to one press report, 'was received with cheers' by 'a large crowd'. Addressing that crowd from an upstairs window in his elec-tion agent's Bridge Street office, Gavin Clark said: 'I thank the people [of Caithness] for the work they have done for me, and [I promise] I shall do all I can to fight the battle for them when I get into parliament.' This pledge was

---

* Better known today as the First International.

† In Britain open and public voting by show of hands gave way to the secret ballot in 1872.

kept. Within months of Clark's success, and the equal success of other HLLRA candidates, Britain's government did as crofters and their MPs were demanding and enacted legislation which provided crofting families with the security so long denied them. There would be no more clearances.[62]

Might there have been among the Bridge Street crowd, on the day when Gavin Clark became MP for Caithness, at least one or two people – in their fifties or sixties now – who were in that same street, on an equally snowy day in February 1847, when the Riot Act was read and a harbour-bound grain cart brought forcibly to a halt? Might those same people, or others among Clark's hearers, have been in the vicinity of nearby Union Street when, in the darkness, soldiers opened fire on them? And might such people – when cheering a man elected with the help of the first votes they had ever cast – have felt that, as compared with earlier times, their county and their country had become a little freer, a bit more democratic? At this remove, there can be no definitive response to any of those questions. But it is good to think that, in each case, the answer could be yes.

Acknowledgements

In 1972, while researching my PhD thesis and while scouring the Scottish Record Office, now the National Records of Scotland, for relevant information, I came across a mass of then unsorted material dating from 1847 and dealing with what were called 'disturbances in the north'. This material, I established, consisted mainly of correspondence arising from efforts to contain and suppress riot and disorder in towns and villages all around the Moray Firth. Since my thesis, afterwards published as *The Making of the Crofting Community*, was less concerned with that area than with the West Highlands and Islands, I did no more than dip into letters which, in 1972, looked to have been untouched since they were bundled away by some mid nineteenth-century clerk. But here, it occurred to me, was a topic which might someday make a book in its own right. Now, nearly 50 years later, I have at last got round to following up that thought.

In the interim, just one historian, as far as I am aware, made extensive use of that 1847 documentation. This was Eric Richards whose resulting article, 'The Last Scottish Food Riots', was published as a 1982 supplement to *Past and Present*, an academic journal. Before embarking on this book, I got in touch with Eric to tell him I was proposing to revisit those same riots. As always, Eric was encouraging. There was, he felt, much more to be uncovered about the events of early 1847 and he looked forward, he said, to seeing what I came up with. For my part, I looked forward equally to sharing my findings with Eric and getting his reaction to them. Eric's death in 2018 took away that opportunity – just as it deprived Scottish historical scholarship more generally of one of its finest practitioners.

In the course of our emailing backwards and forwards about this project, Eric Richards and I shared memories of time spent long ago in local newspaper offices – where, often in attics and basements, bound collections of closely printed weekly issues of particular papers had been left to gather dust. Always, we agreed, it was worth enduring the chill of such places in order to access the Victorian press's immensely detailed accounts of meetings, speeches, protest marches, trials and much else. Now these same accounts can be read with less effort on the ever-expanding British Newspaper Archive website – which, at the time of writing, contains more than 30 million pages culled from hundreds of British and Irish newspapers. But for that tremendous resource, this book would have been a lot harder to write.

Not everything is yet online, however. And so this project took me back to the historical search room in Register House, Edinburgh, home to the National Records of Scotland, where, over several weeks, I renewed my acquaintance with items I last glimpsed in 1972 – while also examining a great deal of other material of which I then knew nothing. Among especially valuable documents in that second category were the hundreds of pages of sworn testimony gathered in the course of inquiries into riots and into famine-related deaths. This book draws heavily on such material.

National Records of Scotland staff were, as always, unfailingly helpful – even on the occasions when I forgot that one should never lean on stitched-together and long-folded trial papers in an attempt to keep them open. Equally helpful were the many people with whom I dealt in the National Library of Scotland, in Highland Archive centres in Inverness and Wick, in the Sir Duncan Rice Library at the University of Aberdeen and in public libraries in Wick, Inverness and Elgin. Library staff at the University of the Highlands and Islands helped me access a range of electronically available sources – parliamentary reports and papers in particular. Staff at the British Library in London supplied me with photocopies of 1847 issues of the *Ross-shire Advertiser*, one of the few north of Scotland newspapers from the 1840s not to be included, so far at least, in the British Newspaper Archive. And my particular thanks are due to Patricia O'Neill of London Archive Searches who tracked down for me in the National Archives at Kew the Home Office files dealing with those 1847 rioters who, for a time anyway, faced transportation to Australia.

My repeated research trips to the National Records of Scotland were made possible by my friends David and Hilary Noble who very kindly gave me free run of their Edinburgh flat. I had very welcome assistance with research and travel costs from the Centre for History at the University of the Highlands – a centre which I helped to set up and with which I have a continuing and close affiliation.

ACKNOWLEDGEMENTS

Four friends with their own close involvements with Scottish history were good enough to read each of this book's chapters in draft. They are Marjory Harper of the University of Aberdeen, Elizabeth Ritchie of the University of the Highlands and Islands, Annie Tindley of the University of Newcastle and David Taylor, the Orkney-based author of a fine book which began as a PhD thesis I had a hand in supervising. Their many comments and suggestions have made this a better book than it would otherwise have been – though such errors and misinterpretations as it might still contain are, as always, its author's sole responsibility.

Lots of others have helped greatly to bring this project to fruition. The book's maps are owed to Jennifer Johnston and Jamie Bowie of the Geography Department at the University of Aberdeen. Its illustrations were sourced with the help of Eann Sinclair of Highlands and Islands Enterprise, Camilla Elder of Wick Harbour Authority, Fergus Mather of Wick Heritage Society, Susan Kruse of Archaeology for Communities in Highland, Jamie Gaukroger of High Life Highland's Archive Service and Scott Reid of Moray Council's Libraries and Information Services.

I am grateful to Lawrence Osborn, who edited my text, and to Roger Smith, who indexed it. As always, it has been a pleasure to work with Hugh Andrew, Andrew Simmons, Tom Johnstone, Deborah Warner, Lucy Mertekis, Jan Rutherford, Kristian Kerr and their colleagues at Birlinn. As always too, warmest thanks are due to my wife, Evelyn, who, through 47 years of marriage, has been unstintingly supportive of my efforts to make sense of northern Scotland's past.

Notes

Abbreviations

HAI	Highland Archives Inverness
HAW	Highland Archives Wick
NA	National Archives
NLS	National Library of Scotland
NRS	National Records of Scotland
NSA	*New Statistical Account of Scotland*
RA	Royal Archives

Introduction

1. NA HO18/207: Petition of Isabella Main and others, n.d.
2. *Scotsman*, 15 September 1847.
3. RA Queen Victoria's Journals, 21 August 1847.
4. *Glasgow Herald*, 3 September 1847. The imported deer came from the Duke of Richmond's properties further to the east. See *Elgin Courant*, 3 September 1847. For the background to land-use changes in the Ardverikie area, see D. Taylor, *The Wild Black Region: Badenoch, 1750–1800*, Edinburgh, 2016.
5. *Illustrated London News*, 4 September 1847; RA Queen Victoria's Journals, 8 September 1847.
6. RA Queen Victoria's Journals, 26 August 1847; *Inverness Courier*, 31 August 1847; *Scotsman*, 15 September 1847. That the three women reached Kinlochlaggan on 27 August is evident from letters mailed to the Home

Office from Ardverikie. See NA HO18/207: Correspondence and papers relating to Petition of Isabella Main and others.

7. For trial details, see Chapter 7.

8. NA HO18/207: Memorial relative to the case of Angus Davidson and others, April 1847; NA HO18/207: Waters to MacPherson, 16 August 1847. See also, family data from 1851 Census.

9. *Glasgow Herald*, 27 August 1847; *Scotsman*, 15 September 1847.

10. NA HO18/207: Waters to MacPherson, 16 August 1847; *John O'Groat Journal*, 1 October 1847; C. Dickens, *David Copperfield*, London, 1850, Chapter 37.

11. *Witness*, 8 September 1847.

12. W. Scott, *The Heart of Midlothian*, London, 1818, Chapter 37.

13. NA HO18/207: Waters to MacPherson, 16 August 1847; NA HO18/207: Note to Sir G. Grey, Home Secretary, [signature illegible], 27 August 1847.

14. *Witness*, 8 September 1847.

1 'A Winter of Starvation'

1. NRS HD7/11: Pole to Coffin, 17 January 1847; D. Monro, *Description of the Western Isles of Scotland*, [1549], Glasgow, 1884, pp. 44–45.

2. J. Wilson, *A Voyage Round the Coasts of Scotland and the Isles*, 2 vols, Edinburgh, 1842, I, p. 460; *NSA*, 15 vols, Edinburgh, 1845, XIV, p. 203.

3. N. MacLeod (ed.), *Extracts from Letters to the Rev Dr MacLeod Regarding the Famine and Destitution in the Highlands and Islands of Scotland*, Glasgow, 1847, p. 8.

4. NRS HD7/11: Pole to Coffin, 17 January 1847. *Firefly*'s specifications can be found on several websites. For example: http://www.pdavis.nl/ShowShip. php?id=1447.

5. *Edinburgh Gazette*, 22 June 1830; *Army List*, 1836 and 1843; R. H. Burgoyne, *Historical Records of the 93rd Sutherland Highlanders*, London, 1883, pp. 56–83, 406; *Correspondence Explanatory of the Measures Adopted for the Relief of Distress in Ireland* (afterwards *Correspondence Explanatory*), London, 1846, p. 81: Treasury Minute, 27 March 1846; NRS HD7/1: Statement of Pay Due for the Month of December 1846.

6. *Correspondence Explanatory*, pp. 159, 164: Pole to Trevelyan, 8 and 15 June 1846.

7. *Correspondence, July 1846 to January 1847, Relating to the Measures Adopted for the Relief of Distress in Ireland (Commissariat Series)*, London, 1847, pp. 5–6, 75: Pole to Trevelyan, 11 August, 15 September 1846.

8. *Times*, 24 December 1846.

9. *Correspondence Relating to the Measures Adopted for the Relief of Distress in Scotland* (afterwards *Correspondence Scotland*), London, 1847, pp. 259–61: Fraser-Tytler to Rutherfurd, 1 January 1847, Shaw to Fraser-Tytler, 22 December 1846, Coffin to Trevelyan, 1 January 1847.

10. *Correspondence Scotland*, p. 261: Coffin to Trevelyan, 1 January 1847; *Inverness Courier*, 16 December 1846. Fraser-Tytler was in full agreement with the *Courier*. See HAI D766/5/4/9: Fraser-Tytler to Skene, 16 February 1847.

11. *NSA*, XIV, p. 212.

12. *Report of the Royal Commission for Inquiring into the Administration of the Poor Laws in Scotland* (afterwards *Poor Law Commission*), London, 1844, Appendix, Part II, pp. 272–73.

13. NRS HD7/11: Pole to Coffin, 17 January 1847.

14. NRS HD7/11: Pole to Coffin, 17 January 1847. For Nicolson family details, see H. Scott (ed.), *Fasti Ecclesiae Scoticanae*, 7 vols, Edinburgh, 1915–28, VII, p. 196.

15. NRS HD7/11: Pole to Coffin, 17 January 1847.

16. R. Haines, *Charles Trevelyan and the Great Irish Famine*, Dublin, 2004, p. 253.

17. *Correspondence Scotland*, pp. 229–32: Pole to Coffin, 21 December 1846, Coffin to Trevelyan, 21 December 1846.

18. NRS HD7/11: Pole to Coffin, 22 January 1847; *Correspondence Scotland*, p. 306: Trevelyan to Coffin, 27 January 1847.

19. *Correspondence Scotland*, p. 259: Rutherfurd to Coffin, 5 January 1847.

20. Haines, *Trevelyan*, p. 194; NRS HD7/11: Pole to Coffin, 17 January 1847.

21. NRS AD14/47/628: Statement of Archibald MacMillan, 21 January 1847.

22. The MacMillan family details in the statements collected by Shaw are confirmed by, and can be supplemented from, information in 1841 census returns.

23. NRS AD14/47/628: Statement of John MacMillan, 21 January 1847.

24. NRS AD14/47/628: Statement of Alexander MacPhie, 21 January 1847.

25. NRS AD14/47/628: Second statement of Archibald MacMillan, 21 January 1847.

26. *Correspondence Explanatory*, p. 206: Pole to Trevelyan, 13 July 1846.

27. NRS AD14/47/628: Second statement of Archibald MacMillan, 21 January 1847.

28. NRS AD14/47/628: Statements of Neil MacNeil and Murdoch MacNeil, 21 January 1847.

29. NRS AD14/47/628: Statements of Anne MacDonald and Murdoch MacDonald, 21 January 1847.

30. NRS AD14/47/628: Statements of Mary MacDonald and Archibald MacDonald, 21 January 1847.

31. NRS AD14/47/628: Statement of Mary MacDonald, 21 January 1847.

32. NRS AD58/86: Fraser-Tytler to Rutherfurd, 15 February 1847; NRS HD19/6: Fraser-Tytler to Skene, 16 February 1847; NRS AD14/47/628: Shaw to Brodie, 8 March 1847.

33. NRS AD14/47/628: Shaw to Brodie, 23 March 1847; NRS AD14/47/628: Statement of Norman MacDonald, 17 March 1847.

34. *Report of Commissioners of Inquiry into the Condition of the Crofters and Cottars in the Highlands and Islands of Scotland* (afterwards *Crofters and Cottars*), Report and 4 vols of evidence, Edinburgh, 1884, IV, p. 2748; W. MacKenzie, *Old Skye Tales: Traditions, Reflections and Memories*, Edinburgh, 2002 [1934], p. 11. For Barra and South Uist comments about MacLeod, see *Crofters and Cottars*, I, pp. 699, 704.

35. *Crofters and Cottars*, IV, p. 2748.

36. NRS AD14/47/628: Peterkin's Memo of the Statement of the Inspector of the Poor, Barra, 17 March 1847; NRS AD14/47/628: Shaw to Brodie, 23 March 1847.

37. NRS AD14/47/628: Statement of Donald MacDonald, 17 March 1847; NRS AD14/47/628: Shaw to Brodie, 23 March 1814.

38. NRS AD14/47/628: Peterkin's Memo of the Statement of the Inspector of the Poor, Barra, 17 March 1847.

39. NRS HD7/26: Gordon to Coffin, 6 February 1847; *Inverness Courier*, 17 March 1847; NRS AD14/47/628: Statement of Archibald MacDonald, 21 January 1847.

40. Board of Supervision, *Second Annual Report*, Edinburgh, 1848, p. 67: Peterkin to Board of Supervision, 18 March 1847.

41. *NSA*, XIV, p. 216; NRS AD14/47/628: Shaw to Brodie, 23 March 1847.

42. NRS AD14/47/628: Statement of Donald Nicolson, 17 March 1847.

43. *Times*, 24 December 1846.

44. A. N. Wilson, *Victoria: A Life*, London, 2014, p. 227; RA Queen Victoria's Journals, 24–31 December 1846.

45. RA Queen Victoria's Journals, 31 December 1846.

46. RA Queen Victoria's Journals, 31 December 1846.

47. *Times*, 22 January 1847.

48. RA Queen Victoria's Journals, 5 January 1847.

49. N. Gash, *Sir Robert Peel: The Life of Sir Robert Peel after 1830*, London, 2011, p. 610. See also, D. Hurd, *Robert Peel: A Biography*, pp. 333–70.

50. M. E. Daly, *The Famine in Ireland*, Dublin, 1986, p. 69.

51. RA Queen Victoria's Journals, 12 January 1847; *Freeman's Journal*, 21 January 1847.

52. *Hansard*, 19 January 1847; RA Queen Victoria's Journals, 19 January 1847; *Times*, 20 January 1847; *Illustrated London News*, 23 January 1847.

53. *Hansard*, 19 January 1847; *Times*, 20 January 1847.

54. RA Queen Victoria's Journals, 31 December 1846; *Hansard*, 19 January 1847; *Freeman's Journal*, 21 January 1847; MacLeod, *Extracts from Letters*, p. 6; *Witness*, 19 September 1846. Much the same line as Miller's was taken by the London correspondent of the *Inverness Courier* in his column of 23 December 1846.

55. W. M. MacKenzie, *Hugh Miller: A Critical Study*, London, 1905, pp. 190–91.

56. NRS HD7/11: Pole to Coffin, 17 January 1847.

57. *Spectator*, 6 February 1847.

58. NRS AD56/308/2: Evans-Gordon to Adjutant General 24 February 1847; *Inverness Courier*, 20 April 1847; NRS AD14/47/533: Statement of Charles Evans-Gordon, 4 March 1847. The *Courier* reference relates to the paper's coverage of the trial of Wick rioters. See also, *John O'Groat Journal*, 9 April 1847.

59. NRS AD56/308/2: Evans-Gordon to Adjutant General 24 February 1847; *Inverness Courier*, 20 April 1847; NRS AD14/47/533: Statements of Cormick Dowd, John Carr, Richard Broome and Daniel Connery, 4 March 1847.

60. T. Morris, *Recollections of Military Service*, London, 1845, p. 210.

61. Morris, *Recollections*, p. 209.

62. *Times*, 4 March 1847.

63. NRS AD14/47/533: Statement of Donald Sinclair, 1 March 1847.

64. *Times*, 4 March 1847.

65. NRS AD56/308/2: Evans-Gordon to Adjutant General, 24 February 1847.

66. NRS AD14/47/533: Statement of Charles Evans-Gordon, 4 March 1847; *Inverness Courier*, 20 April 1847.

67. *Inverness Courier*, 20 April 1847.

68. *John O'Groat Journal*, 26 February, 9 April 1847.

69. *John O'Groat Journal*, 26 February 1847; HAW CC/7/10/1/1: Wick Parochial Board Minutes, 2 March 1847.

70. *Times*, 4 March 1847.

2 'Disorderly, tumultuous and turbulent assemblages'

1. S. Lewis, *Topographical Dictionary of Scotland*, 2 vols, London, 1846, I, p. 446. For a good account of fairs of this era in small Highland towns, see N. MacRae, *The Romance of a Royal Burgh: Dingwall's Story of a Thousand Years*, Dingwall, 1923, pp. 162–63.

2. NRS AD14/47/528: Statement of Charles Crichton, 14 November 1846.

3. NRS AD14/47/528: Statement of Mary Cameron, 14 November 1846.

4. Details of the Cochrane–MacColl marriage can be found in *Scots Magazine*, December 1822, p. 751. Further family details are available in 1841 Census returns. MacColl was long the commonest surname in the Appin–Duror–Ballachulish area of North Argyll. The fact that the Cochrane–MacColl wedding took place in October 1822 at Achindarroch Farm in Duror is suggestive of Susan having had a connection with that locality. Details of Mary Cameron's background are taken from statements she and others made to Sheriff Andrew Fraser.

5. NRS AD14/47/528: Statement of Mary Cameron, 14 November 1846.

6. NRS AD14/47/528: Statements of Dennis Driscoll and James Miller, 14 November 1846.

7. NRS AD14/47/528: Statements of Mary Cameron, Dennis Driscoll and James Miller, 14 November 1846.

8. NRS AD14/47/528: Statement of Mary Cameron, 14 November 1846.

9. NRS AD14/47/528: Statement of Mary Cameron, 14 November 1846.

10. NRS AD14/47/528: Statement of John Cameron, 14 November 1846.

11. NRS AD14/47/528: Statement of James Miller, 14 November 1846; NRS AD14/47/528: Fraser to Lindsay, 24 November 1846.

12. NRS AD14/47/528: Statement of Dennis Driscoll, 14 November 1846; NA WO12/8220: 76th Regiment of Foot Quarterly Pay Lists, 1846–47.

13. For the early history of the 93rd Regiment, see J. Hunter, *Set Adrift Upon the World: The Sutherland Clearances*, Edinburgh, 2015, pp. 141–54. Pole's military career can be followed in successive editions of the *Army List*.

14. J. Mitchell, *Reminiscences of My Life in the Highlands*, 2 vols, London, 1884, II, p. 55. Also, B. Farwell, *For Queen and Country: Social History of the Victorian and Edwardian Army*, London, 1981; D. Nelson, *The Victorian Soldier*, Princes Risborough, 2004.

15. Farwell, *Queen and Country*, p. 85.

16. P. Molloy, *And They Blessed Rebecca: An Account of the Welsh Toll-Gate Riots, 1839–44*, Llandysul, 1983, p. 333.

17. NRS AD56/308/2: Thomson to Lindsay, 26 February 1847; *John O'Groat Journal*, 26 February 1847.

18. *John O'Groat Journal*, 26 February 1847; NRS AD56/308/2: Thomson to Lindsay, 26 February 1847.

19. See, inter alia, J. Dunlop, *The British Fisheries Society, 1786–1893*, Edinburgh, 1978; D. Maudlin, 'Robert Mylne, Thomas Telford and the Architecture of Improvement: The Planned Villages of the British Fisheries Society, 1786–1817', *Urban History*, 34 (2007), pp. 453–80.

20. J. Thomson, *The Value and Importance of the Scottish Fisheries*, London, 1849, pp. 15, 18.

21. J. Mitchell, *The Herring: Its Natural History and National Importance*, Edinburgh, 1864, p. 25.

22. H. Miller, *Letters on the Herring Fishery in the Moray Firth*, Inverness, 1829, p. 27.

23. Wilson, *Voyage Round the Coasts*, II, pp. 156–57.

24. Thomson, *Value and Importance*, p. 16; Wilson, *Voyage Round the Coasts*, II, pp. 157–59.

25. *NSA*, XIV, p. 154; I. Sutherland, *Wick Harbour and the Herring Fishing*, Wick, n.d., p. 31.

26. J. Glover, *Man of Iron: Thomas Telford and the Building of Britain*, London, 2017, pp. 191–92; F. Engels, *The Condition of the Working Class in England*, Penguin Classics Edition, London, 2005 [1844], pp. 100–01; Maudlin, 'Telford and the Architecture of Improvement', p. 471.

27. *NSA*, XIV, pp. 121, 145, 154.

28. *John O'Groat Journal*, 11 September 1846.

29. *John O'Groat Journal*, 1 January 1847; NRS AF28/241: Report by the Commissioners of the British Fisheries, 1847, p. 2.

30. *John O'Groat Journal*, 11 September 1846.

31. *Inverness Courier*, 30 September 1846.

32. HAW CC/1/1/6: Caithness Commissioners of Supply, Minutes, 30 September 1846.

33. *John O'Groat Journal*, 25 September 1846.

34. HAW CC/7/10/1/1: Wick Parochial Board, Minutes, 4 August, 6 October, 1 December 1846; *John O'Groat Journal*, 28 August 1846.

35. *John O'Groat Journal*, 28 August 1846.

36. *John O'Groat Journal*, 26 February 1846.

37. *Correspondence Scotland*, p. 276: Elder to Lauder, 6 January 1847; *John O'Groat Journal*, 8 January 1847.

38. *John O'Groat Journal*, 29 January 1847.

39. HAW BW/1/6: Wick Town Council, Minutes, 18 January 1847; *Inverness Courier*, 13, 27 January 1847.

40. HAW CC/1/1/6: Caithness Commissioners of Supply, Minutes, 11 January 1847.

41. *John O'Groat Journal*, 22 January 1822.

42. *John O'Groat Journal*, 29 January 1847.

43. NRS AD14/47/533: Statement of James Robertson, 11 February 1847.

44. *John O'Groat Journal*, 12 February 1847; NRS AD14/47/533: Statement of James Robertson, 11 February 1847.

45. NRS AD14/47/533: Statement of Peter Taylor, 11 February 1847.

46. *John O'Groat Journal*, 12 February 1847.

47. NRS AD14/47/533: Statement of James MacKenzie, 9 February 1847.

48. NRS AD14/47/533: Statement of James MacKenzie, 9 February 1847.

49. NRS AD14/47/533: Statements of James MacKenzie and William Farquhar, 9, 11 February 1847.

50. NRS AD14/47/533: Statement of James MacKenzie, 9 February 1847; A. Alison, *Principles of the Criminal Law of Scotland*, Edinburgh, 1832, p. 531.

51. NRS AD14/47/533: Statement of James MacKenzie, 9 February 1847.

52. *Inverness Courier*, 24 March 1847.

53. NRS AD14/47/533: Statements of William Farquhar and James Miller, 11, 12 February 1847.

54. NLS Sutherland Papers 313/1174: Loch to Duke of Sutherland, 29 March 1847; A. Tindley, *The Sutherland Estate, 1850–1920*, Edinburgh, 2010, p. 13.

55. *John O'Groat Journal*, 12 February 1847.

56. NRS AD56/308/6: Thomson to Lindsay, 17 February 1847.

57. NRS AD14/47/533: Statement of Hugh MacKay, 11 February 1847; NRS AD56/308/2: Henderson to Lindsay, 20 February 1847.

58. NRS AD56/308/6: Thomson to Lindsay, 17 February 1847; NRS AD56/308/2: Henderson to Lindsay, 20 February 1847.

59. NRS AD56/308/2: Henderson to Lindsay, 20 February 1847; *John O'Groat Journal*, 19 March 1847.

60. NRS AD56/308/2: Thomson to Lindsay, 26 February 1847.

61. NRS AD56/308/2: Proclamation by the Sheriff and the Magistrates of Wick, 24 February 1847.

62. NRS AD56/308/2: Thomson to Lindsay, 26 February 1847.

63. Details drawn mostly from Thomson's eventual report to the Caithness Commissioners of Supply, printed in full in the *John O'Groat Journal* of 19

March 1847. See also, *John O'Groat Journal*, 26 February 1847; NRS AD56/308/2: Thomson to Lindsay, 26 February 1847.

64. NRS AD56/308/2: Evans-Gordon to Adjutant General, 24 February 1847; NRS AD14/47/533: Statement of Robert Thomson, 8 March 1847.

65. NRS AD56/308/2: Evans-Gordon to Adjutant General, 24 February 1847; High Court trial evidence from Evans-Gordon, *Inverness Courier*, 20 April 1846; NRS AD14/47/533: Statement of John Bain, 1 March 1847.

66. NRS AD14/47/533: Statement of Josiah Rhind, 8 March 1847.

67. NRS AD14/47/533: Statement of Robert Thomson, 8 March 1847; *Inverness Courier*, 20 April 1847; NRS AD56/308/2: Thomson to Lindsay, 26 February 1847.

68. NRS AD56/308/2: Evans-Gordon to Adjutant General, 24 February 1847; NRS AD14/47/533: Statements of Donald Sinclair and Evans-Gordon, 1, 4 March 1847; NRS AD56/308/2: Thomson to Lindsay, 26 February 1847; *John O'Groat Journal*, 26 February 1847.

69. NRS AD14/47/533: Statements of Donald Sinclair, John Shearer, James Nicol, John Bresslam and John Ricks, 24 February, 1, 4 March 1847.

70. *John O'Groat Journal*, 26 February 1847.

71. NRS AD56/308/4: John Barr and 14 others to Rhind, 25 February 1847.

72. *John O'Groat Journal*, 26 February, 5 March 1847.

73. *John O'Groat Journal*, 5 March 1847; H. Gray, *Tale of Two Streets: The Story of Wick Town Centre in the Mid-Nineteenth Century*, Wick, 2006, p. 6; H. M. Rozwadowski, *The Sea Knows No Boundaries*, Copenhagen, 2002, p. 27; J. T. Calder, *Sketch of the Civil and Traditional History of Caithness*, Wick, 1887, pp. 254–60.

74. *John O'Groat Journal*, 19 March 1847; NRS AD56/308/2: Thomson to Miller, 26 February 1847; NRS AD56/308/4: Thomson to Brodie, 27 February 27 February 1847.

75. HAW CC/7/10/1/1: Wick Parochial Board, Minutes, 2 March 1847.

76. *Caledonian Mercury*, 4 March 1847; NRS AD56/308/2: Brodie to Rutherfurd, 27 February 1847.

77. *Times*, 4 March 1847; NRS AD56/308/2: Weir to Rutherfurd, 4 March 1847; *Hansard*, 4 March 1847.

78. *Inverness Courier*, 10 March 1847; *John O'Groat Journal*, 5 March 1847; HAW CC/1/1/6: Caithness Commissioners of Supply, Minutes, 12 March 1847.

79. HAW CC/1/1/6: Caithness Commissioners of Supply, Minutes, 12 March 1847;

80. *NSA*, XV, p. 170; *Caledonian Mercury*, 4 March 1847.

3 'The year potatoes went away'

1. *NSA*, VII, p. 187.
2. N. MacLeod, *Reminiscences of a Highland Parish*, London, 1867, pp. 25–26.
3. *NSA*, VII, pp. 185–86; *Poor Law Commission*, Appendix, Pt II, p. 181; *First Report from the Select Committee on the Condition of the Population of the Highlands and Islands of Scotland and the Practicability of Affording Relief by Emigration*, 1841, pp. 100–01.
4. MacLeod, *Reminiscences*, pp. 397–400; P. Gaskell, *Morvern Transformed: A Highland Parish in the Nineteenth Century*, Cambridge, 1968, pp. 83–84; I. Thornber (ed.), *Morvern: A Highland Parish*, Edinburgh, 2002, pp. 229–30; J. Hunter, *Scottish Highlanders: A People and Their Place*, Edinburgh, 1992, pp. 53–55.
5. *NSA*, VII, pp. 185–87; *Poor Law Commission*, Appendix, Pt II, p. 181.
6. S. Johnson, *A Journey to the Western Islands of Scotland*, London, 1775, section entitled 'Ostig in Skye'.
7. Johnson, *Journey to the Western Islands*, section entitled 'Raasay'; *Poor Law Commission*, Appendix, Pt II, p. 181. This paragraph, and the two that follow, summarise findings which the author has set out in much greater detail in publications listed in this book's bibliography.
8. *Poor Law Commission*, Appendix, Pt II, p. 181.
9. *NSA*, XIV, pp. 200, 226.
10. *Morning Chronicle*, 29 September, 13 October 1846.
11. H. Miller, *Essays: Historical and Biographical, Political, Social, Literary and Scientific*, New York, 1882, p. 220; *Witness*, 19 September 1846. Accounts of the sort of families Miller had in mind can be found in Hunter, *Set Adrift Upon The World*.
12. *Poor Law Commission*, Appendix, Pt II, pp. 303, 305. See Hunter, *Set Adrift Upon The World*, for assessments of pre-clearance living conditions in the Sutherland interior. These were certainly superior to those prevailing in post-clearance coastal settlements.
13. N. M. Gunn, *The Silver Darlings*, London, 1941, Chapters 1 and 5.
14. *NSA*, XV, p. 102.
15. J. McCulloch, *The Highlands and Western Islands of Scotland*, 4 vols, London, 1824, III, p. 8; J. L. Campbell (ed.), *The Book of Barra*, Stornoway, 1998, p. 86; *NSA*, XIV, p. 213; *Inverness Courier*, 6 January 1847.
16. *Inverness Courier*, 29 July 1846; E. M. MacArthur, *Iona: The Living Memory of a Crofting Community, 1750–1914*, Edinburgh, 1990, p. 75.

17. *Inverness Courier*, 8 July 1846.

18. *Morning Chronicle*, 3 October 1846; *Inverness Courier*, 26 August 1846.

19. *Correspondence Scotland*, p. 9: Rutherfurd to Grey, 2 September 1846; H. Cockburn, *Journal of Henry Cockburn*, 2 vols, Edinburgh, 1874, II, p. 165.

20. A. W. MacColl, *Land, Faith and the Crofting Community: Christianity and Social Criticism in the Highlands of Scotland, 1843–1893*, Edinburgh, 2006, p. 27.

21. *Correspondence Scotland*, p. 24: Committee of the Provincial Synod of Argyll of the Free Church, 11 September 1846.

22. *Correspondence Scotland*, pp. 211, 260: Rutherfurd to Grey, 10 December 1846 and Shaw to Fraser-Tytler, 22 December 1846; Free Church of Scotland, *Destitution in the Highlands and Islands*, Edinburgh, 1847, pp. 14–20; *Scotsman*, 6 February 1847; MacColl, *Land, Faith and the Crofting Community*, pp. 32–33.

23. Free Church of Scotland, *Destitution*, pp. 16–20; *Inverness Courier*, 9 December 1846.

24. Free Church of Scotland, *Destitution*, pp. 17–18.

25. *Correspondence Scotland*, p. 211: Rutherfurd to Grey, 10 December 1846; *Inverness Courier*, 16 December 1846, 6 January 1847; *Observer*, 14 December 1846.

26. *Correspondence Scotland*, pp. 9, 254: Rutherfurd to Grey, 2 September 1846 and Pole to Trevelyan, 28 December 1846.

27. C. E. Trevelyan, *The Irish Crisis*, London, 1848, p. 9.

28. *Correspondence Scotland*, p. 14: Grey to Baillie, 5 September 1846; B. Ó Cathaoir, *Famine Diary*, Dublin, 1999, p. 65.

29. Cockburn, *Journal*, II, p. 78; *NSA*, VII, p. 532.

30. *Correspondence Scotland*, p. 14: Treasury Minute, 8 September 1846.

31. *Correspondence Scotland*, pp. 58, 107: Pole to Coffin, 3 October 1846 and Coffin to Trevelyan, 17 October 1846.

32. J. Sperber, *The European Revolutions, 1848–1851*, Cambridge, 2005, pp. 110–11; *Correspondence Scotland*, pp. 30, 42: Trevelyan to Horne, 20 September 1846 and Grey to McNeill, 25 September 1846; Haines, *Trevelyan*, p. 139.

33. Trevelyan, *Irish Crisis*, pp. 183–85; *Correspondence Scotland*, p. 14: Grey to Baillie, 4 September 1846.

34. *Correspondence Scotland*, pp. 78, 107–09: Coffin to Trevelyan, 9, 17 October 1846.

35. *Correspondence Scotland*, p. 255: Pole to Trevelyan, 28 December 1846.

36. Free Church of Scotland, *Destitution*, p. 14. For the origins of the Sutherland and Matheson fortunes, see E. Richards, *The Leviathan of Wealth: The Sutherland Estate Fortune in the Industrial Revolution*, London, 1973; R. J.

Crace, *Opium and Empire: The Lives and Careers of William Jardine and James Matheson*, Montreal, 2014.

37. NLS 313/1173: Loch to Duke of Sutherland, 15 November, 2, 5 December 1846. For an analysis of the extent to which the legacy of clearance loomed over later land management policy in Sutherland, see Tindley, *The Sutherland Estate*. Eventually even Loch, as Tindley shows, began to have second thoughts about the efficacy of clearance.

38. NRS HD7/26: Campbell to Coffin, 28 October 1846; Wilson, *Voyage Round the Coasts*, I, pp. 78–79; J. Hunter, *For the People's Cause: From the Writings of John Murdoch*, Edinburgh, 1986, p. 80; Correspondence *Scotland*, pp. 81–83: Campbell to Grey, 10 October 1846; M. Storrie, *Islay: Biography of an Island*, Islay, 2011, pp. 137–73.

39. J. Hunter, *Scottish Exodus: Travels Among a Worldwide Clan*, Edinburgh, 2005, p. 189.

40. *Correspondence Scotland*, p. 62: Pole to Coffin, 13 October 1846; NRS HD7/11: Pole to Coffin, 12 October 1846; *Correspondence Scotland*, p. 123: Macdonald to Grey, 21 October 1846; NRS HD6/2: Haliday to Pole, 2 March 1847 and Haliday to Trevelyan, 17 April 1847.

41. R. Somers, *Letters from the Highlands: Or the Famine of 1847*, Inverness, 1977 [1848], p. 103.

42. C. Dickens, *A Christmas Carol*, London, 1843, Stave One; *Banffshire Journal*, 20 July 1858. See also, J. M. Bulloch, *The Gordons of Cluny*, Buckie, 1911.

43. HAI D766/5/4/9: Fraser-Tytler to Rutherfurd, 1 January 1847; NRS HD7/5: Haliday to Coffin, 24 December 1846; NRS HD7/3: MacNeill to Coffin, 6 January 1847.

44. *Hansard*, 20 January, 22 February 1847.

45. *Correspondence Scotland*, pp. 80–81: Trevelyan to MacNeill, 13 October 1846; NRS HD7/5: Haliday to Coffin, 30 December 1846.

46. *Correspondence Scotland*, p. 177: Treasury Minute, 20 November 1846; *Inverness Courier*, 20 January 1847.

47. NRS HD6/2: Coffin, Final Report, October 1847.

48. NRS HD6/2: Coffin, Final Report, October 1847; Free Church of Scotland, *Destitution*, p. 4.

49. NRS HD6/2: Coffin, Final Report, October 1847.

50. *Morning Chronicle*, 24 September 1846.

51. *Times*, 22 October 1846.

52. *Times*, 1 October 1846.

53. *Inverness Courier*, 21 October 1846; M. MacGregor, 'Gaelic Barbarity and Scottish Identity in the Later Middle Ages', in D. Broun and M. MacGregor

(eds), *Mìorun Mòr nan Gall: The Great Ill-Will of the Lowlander: Lowland Perceptions of the Highlands, Medieval and Modern*, Glasgow, 2009, p. 7. For wider treatment of anti-Highland, anti-Celtic sentiment, see both the Broun and MacGregor book just cited and K. Fenyö, *Contempt, Sympathy and Romance: Lowland Perceptions of the Highlands and the Clearances During the Famine Years, 1845–55*, East Linton, 2000.

54. *Scotsman*, 30 January 1847.

55. *Scotsman*, 30 January, 3, 6, 10, 17 February 1847.

56. *Scotsman*, 3, 24 February 1847.

57. Haines, *Trevelyan*, p. 252; *Scotsman*, 3 February 1847; Edinburgh Section of the Central Board for Relieving Destitution in the Highlands, *To the Inhabitants of Edinburgh*, December 1846.

58. *Greenock Advertiser*, 25 December 1846.

59. *NSA*, VII, p. 354; Somers, *Letters*, pp. 156–60.

60. *Correspondence Scotland*, p. 327: Coffin to Trevelyan, 4, 5 February 1847.

61. NRS HD7/26: Fraser to Skene, 26 January 1847.

62. NRS HD7/26: Fraser to Skene, 26 January 1847.

63. NRS HD7/26: Fraser to Skene, 26 January 1847; *Inverness Courier*, 17 February 1847.

64. NRS HD HD7/6: Fraser to Skene, 11 February 1847; NRS HD7/11: Pole to Coffin, 21 December 1846.

65. NRS HD7/26: Fraser to Skene, 11 February 1847.

66. NRS HD7/26: Fraser to Fraser-Tytler, 6 February 1847.

67. *Correspondence Scotland*, pp. 323–25: Pole to Coffin, 31 January 1847.

68. *Correspondence Scotland*, pp. 323–25, 342–43: Pole to Coffin, 31 January 1847 and Stewart-MacKenzie to Coffin, 7 February 1847.

69. *Correspondence Scotland*, p. 343: Coffin to Stewart-MacKenzie, 10 February 1847.

70. NRS AD14/47/628: Statements of Donald and Marion Gillies, 16 March 1847.

71. NRS AD14/47/628: Statements of Donald Gillies, Marion Gillies and Flora Johnston, 16 March 1847.

72. NRS HD6/2: Rose to Trevelyan, 21 February 1847.

73. NRS AD58/84: Sitwell to Rutherfurd, 28 October and 28 December 1884; NRS AD56/308/2: Shaw to Fraser-Tytler, 4 January 1847.

74. NRS AD56/308/2: Shaw to Fraser-Tytler, 11 January 1847; *Scotsman*, 2 December 1846; *Inverness Courier*, 30 December 1846.

75. NRS AD56/308/2: Shaw to Fraser-Tytler, 11 January 1847.

76. HAI D766/5/4/9: Fraser-Tytler to Lady Dunmore, 27 January 1847; HAI D766/5/4/9: Fraser-Tytler: Fraser-Tytler to Shaw, 22 January 1847.

77. HAI D766/5/4/9: Fraser-Tytler to Shaw, 22 January 1847; HAI D766/5/4/9: Fraser-Tytler to Macconochie, 22 January 1847.

78. HAI D766/5/4/9: Fraser-Tytler to Macconochie, 22 January 1847; NRS AD56/308/4: Fraser-Tytler to Rutherfurd, 21 January 1847.

79. NRS AD56/308/4: Statements obtained from the Harris prisoners, 21 January 1847.

80. NRS AD56/308/4: Fraser-Tytler to Rutherfurd, 21 January 1847; HAI D766/5/4/9: Fraser-Tytler to Rutherfurd, 27 January 1847.

81. HAI D766/5/4/9: Fraser-Tytler to Shaw, 30 January 1847.

82. NRS AD58/84: Shaw to Fraser-Tytler, 22 February 1847; Fraser-Tytler to Rutherfurd, 1 March 1847.

4 'A pointed pistol in each hand'

1. *NSA*, XIV, p. 439; *Inverness Courier*, 27 January 1847.

2. NRS HD7/26: MacIntyre and others to Coffin, 24 November 1846; MacLeod, *Extracts from Letters*, p. 66; NRS HD7/26: MacGregor to Coffin, 13 January 1847; *Elgin Courier*, 5 February 1847.

3. HAI D766/5/4/9: Fraser-Tytler to Rutherfurd, 31 January 1847; *Inverness Courier*, 27 January 1847.

4. *Inverness Courier*, 27 January 1847.

5. *Inverness Courier*, 27 January 1847; HAI D766/5/4/9: Fraser-Tytler to Rutherfurd, 31 January 1847.

6. *Aberdeen Herald*, 23 January 1847; *Aberdeen Journal*, 27 January 1847.

7. *Aberdeen Herald*, 23 January 1847; *Aberdeen Journal*, 27 January 1847.

8. *Aberdeen Journal*, 27 January 1847; NRS RH2/4/238: Grey to Blaikie, 26 January 1847.

9. NRS AD56/308/3: Simpson to Murray, 26 January 1827; NRS AD56/308/5: Skelton to Lindsay, 31 January 1847; AD56/308/6: Boyd to Lindsay, 30 January 1827; *Aberdeen Journal*, 27 January 1847.

10. *Aberdeen Herald*, 6 February 1847.

11. *Aberdeen Herald*, 6 February 1847. See also, *John O'Groat Journal*, 1 January 1847.

12. *NSA*, XIII, p. 231.

13. *NSA*, XIII, pp. 330.

14. *NSA*, XIII, pp. 231–32, 257–58. Also, M. Gray, *The Fishing Industries of Scotland, 1790–1914: A Study in Regional Adaption*, Aberdeen, 1978. For insights into the condition of farm workers in this area at this time, see I. Carter, *Farm Life in Northeast Scotland, 1840–1914: Poor Man's Country*, Edinburgh, 1979.

15. W. Scott, *The Antiquary*, London, 1816, Chapter 11.

16. *NSA*, XIII, pp 231, 257–58.

17. *Aberdeen Herald*, 15 August 1846; *Inverness Courier*, 11 November 1846; *John O'Groat Journal*, 29 January 1847; NRS AD56/308/4: Statement of meal exports from Fraserburgh, n.d.

18. NRS AD56/308/6: Stronach to Currie, 3 February 1847.

19. For accounts and analyses of earlier riots, see, inter alia, K. J. Cullen, *Famine in Scotland: The 'Ill Years' of the 1690s*, Edinburgh, 2010; K. J. Logue, *Popular Disturbances in Scotland, 1780–1815*, Edinburgh, 1979; D. Alston, *My Little Town of Cromarty: The History of a Northern Scottish Town*, Edinburgh, 2006; M. Ash, *This Noble Harbour: A History of the Cromarty Firth*, Edinburgh, 1991.

20. Cullen, *Famine in Scotland*, p. 82.

21. *NSA*, XIII, p. 290; *Aberdeen Herald*, 23 January 1847; *Inverness Courier*, 3 February 1847.

22. *Aberdeen Herald*, 23 January 1847; *Inverness Courier*, 3 February 1847; *Banffshire Journal*, 2 February 1847.

23. *Aberdeen Herald*, 23 January 1847; *Aberdeen Journal*, 27 January 1847; *Banffshire Journal*, 2 February 1847.

24. NRS GD44/44/23: Balmer to Richmond, 19 January, 5, 8 February 1847; Balmer to Bain, 6 February 1847.

25. *NSA*, XIII, p. 262; NRS AD58/77: Allan to Gordon, 18 January 1847.

26. NRS GD44/44/23: Balmer to Richmond, 19 January 1847; NRS CR8/322: Richmond to Balmer, 28 January 1847.

27. NRS AD58/69: Lindsay to Rutherfurd, 21 January 1847.

28. NRS AD56/308/3: Davies to Pringle, 26 January 1847; NRS AD56/308/4: Currie to Rutherfurd, 27 January 1847.

29. detailed biography of George Davies can be found on the website of DNW Auctions at https://www.dnw.co.uk/auction-archive/lot-archive/lot.php?department=Medals&lot_id=283109 This is because a collection of the captain's service and gallantry medals was put up for sale in 2016.

30. NRS AD56/303/3: Davies to Pringle, 26 January 1847; Grant to Pringle, 26 January 1847.

31. NRS AD56/303/3: Davies to Pringle, 26 January 1847; Grant to Pringle, 26 January 1847.

32. NRS AD 56/303/3: Davies to Pringle, 26 January 1847; *Banffshire Journal*, 2 February 1847.

33. NRS AD 56/303/3: Davies to Pringle, 26 January 1847; *Banffshire Journal*, 2 February 1847.

34. NRS AD 56/303/3: Davies to Pringle, 26 January 1847.

35. NRS AD 56/308/4: Lindsay to Rutherfurd, 25 January 1847.

36. NRS AD 56/308/4: Proclamation by the Sheriff of Banff, 27 January 1847; *Banffshire Journal*, 2 February 1847.

37. NRS AD 56/308/4: Currie to Rutherfurd, 27 January 1847.

38. NRS GD 248/1582: Wilson to Seafield, 30 January, 6 February 1847.

39. *Banffshire Journal*, 16 March 1847.

40. NRS AD 56/308/2: Currie to Balmer, 31 January 1847; NRS GD 248/1582: Wilson to Seafield, 6 February 1847; NRS GD 44/44/23: Balmer to Richmond, 6 February 1847.

41. *Banffshire Journal*, 2 February 1847; *Inverness Courier*, 3 February 1847; NRS GD 44/44/23: Balmer to Richmond, 29 January 1847; NRS GD 44/44/23: Balmer to Bain, 6 February 1847.

42. AD 56/308/3: Currie to Rutherfurd, 31 January 1847; AD 56/308/3: Gordon to Lindsay, 1 February 1847.

5 'The sheriff of Elginshire is overpowered'

1. NRS AD 56/308/4: Lindsay to Rutherfurd, 25 January 1847.

2. NRS AD 56/308/4: Lindsay to Rutherfurd, 25 January 1847. For background information on Elginshire's sheriff, see K. Burton, *Memoir of Cosmo Innes*, Edinburgh, 1874.

3. NRS AD 56/308/4: Lindsay to Rutherfurd, 25 January 1847. The reference to Innes's build is taken from a *Scotsman* obituary of 3 August 1874. Coach timings are based on those in *Scottish Post Office Edinburgh and Leith Directory*, Edinburgh, 1847.

4. NRS AD 56/308/4: Lindsay to Rutherfurd, 25 January 1847.

5. NRS AD 56/308/4: Lindsay to Rutherfurd, 28 January 1847.

6. For a full breakdown of military strength in Scotland, see NRS AD 56/308/4: Memo from J. Eden, Strength of troops at several stations, 28 January 1847.

7. NRS AD 56/308/4: Lindsay to Rutherfurd, 28 January 1847; NRS AD 56/308/3: Lindsay to Rutherfurd, 29 January 1847.

8. NRS AD 14/47/515: Statement of C. Innes, 8 February 1847.

9. R. Young, *Notes on Burghead Ancient and Modern*, Elgin, 1867, p. 32.

10. NRS AD14/47/515: Statement of J. Allan, 10 February 1847.

11. NRS AD14/47/515: Statements of P. Christall and D. Davidson, 13, 15 February 1847.

12. NRS AD14/47/515: Statement of P. Christall, 13 February 1847.

13. NRS AD14/47/515: Statement of A. Brown, 11 February 1847; NRS AD56/308/2: Innes to Rutherfurd, 8 February 1847.

14. NRS AD14/47/515: Statements of W. Hay and A. Main, 9, 13 February 1847.

15. NRS AD14/47/515: Statement of W. Hay, 13 February 1847.

16. NRS AD14/47/515: Statement of W. Hay, 13 February 1847.

17. NRS AD14/47/515: Statements of J. Allan and W. Hay, 10, 13 February 1847.

18. NRS AD56/308/2: Waters to Innes, 10 February 1847; AD14/47/515: Statement of D. Waters, 13 February 1847.

19. AD14/47/515: Statements of C. Innes and A. Brown, 8, 11 February 1847.

20. AD14/47/515: Statements of A. Brown and W. Hay, 9, 11 February 1847.

21. E. Hobsbawm and J. W. Scott, 'Political Shoemakers', in E. Hobsbawm, *Uncommon People: Resistance, Rebellion and Jazz*, London, 1999, p. 24.

22. NA HO18/207: Declaration of J. Falconer, 13 February 1847. For an extraordinarily comprehensive assessment of wider issues touched on here, see Hobsbawm and Scott, 'Political Shoemakers'.

23. *NSA*, XIII, p. 37; NRS AD56/308/2: Waters to Innes, 10 February 1847; NRS GD44/44/23: Balmer to Richmond, 8 February 1847.

24. For Scottish Chartism in general, see W. H. Fraser, *Chartism in Scotland*, Pontypool, 2010. For Chartism in Aberdeen, see R. E. Duncan, 'Artisans and Proletarians: Chartism and Working-Class Allegiance in Aberdeen, 1838–1842', *Northern Scotland*, 4 (1981), pp. 51–67.

25. *Northern Star*, 30 January, 6 March 1841; *John O'Groat Journal*, 21 May 1841, 25 February 1842.

26. *Inverness Courier*, 7 August 1839.

27. D. Goodway (ed.), *The Chartists Were Right: Selections from the Newcastle Weekly Chronicle*, London, 2014, p. 9; F. McLynn, *The Road Not Taken: How Britain Narrowly Missed a Revolution*, London, 2012, p. 293; *Northern Star*, 17 October 1840. For much the best biography of Harney, see A. R. Schoyen, *The Chartist Challenge: A Portrait of George Julian Harney*, London, 1958.

28. *Northern Star*, 19 December 1840.

29. *Northern Star*, 2 January 1841; Goodway, *The Chartists Were Right*, p. 74.

30. *Northern Star*, 2 January 1841; *Inverness Courier*, 23 December 1840.

31. *Northern Star*, 2 January 1841; *Inverness Courier*, 23, 30 December 1840.

32. *Northern Star*, 2, 16 January, 10 April 1841.

33. NA HO18/207: Declaration of J. Falconer, 13 February 1847.

34. NA HO18/207: Declaration of A. Davidson, 17 February 1847; NRS AD14/47/515: Statements of P. Christall, D. Davidson, J. MacPherson, D. Sutherland, 5, 13, 15 February 1847.

35. J. and W. Watson, *Morayshire Described*, Elgin, 1868, p. 133; *Elgin Courant*, 29 January, 26 February 1847; *Forres Gazette*, 6 February 1847.

36. NRS AD14/47/515: Statement of W. Grigor, 7 February 1847.

37. NRS AD14/47/515: Statement of W. Grigor, 7 February 1847.

38. NRS AD14/47/515: Statement of W. Grigor, 7 February 1847; Young, *Notes on Burghead*, p. 45. Although Young's book was not published until 1867, the Granary Street inn was still owned and managed by Lewis Grant. It seems reasonable, then, to assume that the meals on offer in 1847 were as generous as those of 20 years later.

39. NRS AD14/47/515: Statements of W. Grigor, D. Davidson and J. MacPherson, 7, 15 February 1847.

40. NRS AD14/47/515: Statement of W. Grigor, 7 February 1847.

41. NRS AD56/308/3: Innes to Lindsay, 27 January 1847.

42. NRS AD56/308/3: Innes to Rutherfurd, 8 February 1847; NRS AD14/47/515: Statement of W. Hay, 9 February 1847.

43. NRS AD14/47/515: Statements of W. Grigor and W. Hay, 7, 9 February 1847.

44. NRS AD14/47/515: Statements of W. Grigor and W. Hay, 7, 9 February 1847.

45. NRS AD14/47/515: Statement of J. Grant, 10 February 1847.

46. NRS AD14/47/515: Statement of J. Gillan, 12 February 1847.

47. NRS AD14/47/515: Statement of A. Forteith, 11 February 1847.

48. NRS AD14/47/515: Statement of C. Innes, 8 February 1847.

49. NRS AD14/47/515: Statement of J. Cumming, 9 February 1847.

50. NRS AD14/47/515: Statements of J. MacPherson, W. Hay, W. Grigor and C. Innes, 7, 8, 9, 15 February 1847.

51. NRS AD14/47/515: Statements of C. Innes and F. Munro, 8, 12 February 1847; *Elgin Courant*, 29 January 1847.

52. NRS AD56/308/3: Innes to Lindsay, 27 January 1847.

53. NRS AD56/308/3: Innes to Rutherfurd, 27 January 1847.

54. NRS AD56/308/4: Innes to Rutherfurd, 27 January 1847; NRS AD56/308/3: Innes to Lindsay, 27 January 1847; NRS AD56/308/2: Innes to Rutherfurd, 8 February 1847.

55. NRS AD56/308/3: Lindsay to Rutherfurd, 29 January 1847; NRS AD56/308/3: Lindsay to Innes and Currie, 30 January 1847.

56. NRS AD11/27: Lindsay to Eden, 29 January 1847.

57. NRS AD56/308/2: Innes to Rutherfurd, 8 February 1847.

58. For a pathbreaking and deservedly influential treatment of these and related issues, see E. P. Thompson, 'The Moral Economy of the English Crowd in the Eighteenth Century', *Past and Present*, 50 (1971), pp. 76–136.

59. *Elgin Courier*, 5 February 1847.

60. NRS AD14/47/515: Statement of W. Grigor, 7 February 1847.

61. *Elgin Courier*, 5 February 1847.

62. *Elgin Courant*, 29 January 1847.

63. *Elgin Courier*, 12 February 1847.

64. *Forres Gazette*, 6 February 1847.

65. *Elgin Courant*, 29 January 1847.

66. NRS AD56/308/1: Parks to Lindsay, 2 February 1847.

67. NRS AD56/308/4: Innes to Rutherfurd, 30 January 1847; NRS AD56/308/2: Innes to Rutherfurd, 8 February 1847; AD56/308/1: Brown to Lindsay, 1 February 1847.

68. NRS AD56/308/2: Innes to Davidson, 1 February 1847.

69. NRS AD56/308/1: Copy of resolutions at meeting in Findhorn, 29 January 1847; NRS AD56/308/1: Information against J. MacKay, 4 February 1847; NRS AD56/308/1: Brown to Lindsay, 4 February 1847; NRS AD56/308/5: Innes to Rutherfurd, 4 February 1847; *Elgin Courant*, 29 January, 5 February 1847.

70. NRS AD56/308/5: Brown to Lindsay, 4 February 1847; *Elgin Courant*, 5, 12 February 1847.

71. NRS AD56/308/1: Innes to Lindsay, 3 February 1847.

72. *Elgin Courant*, 5 February 1847.

73. NRS AD56/308/5: Innes to Rutherfurd, 3 February 1847.

74. NRS AD56/308/5: Innes to Rutherfurd, 3 February 1847; NRS AD56/308/2: Innes to Rutherfurd, 8 February 1847.

6 'Acts of the most disgraceful character'

1. NRS AD56/308/2: Extract from minutes of Inverness Town Council special meeting, 2 February 1847; NRS AD56/308/2: MacKay to Lindsay, 30 January 1847.

2. NRS AD56/308/2: MacKay to Lindsay, 30, 31 January 1847.

3. NRS AD14/46/34: Statement of J. Fraser, 7 February 1846.

4. NRS AD14/46/34: Statement of J. Fraser, 7 February 1846.

5. NRS AD14/46/34: Statement of J. Kane, 14 February 1846.

6. *Inverness Courier*, 4, 11 February 1846; NRS AD14/46/34: Statement of J. Sutherland, 25 February 1846.

7. NRS AD14/46/34: Statement of W. Fraser-Tytler, 27 February 1846.

8. NRS AD14/46/34: Statement of J. Fraser, 7 February 1846; *Inverness Courier*, 11 February 1847.

9. NRS AD14/46/34: Statement of D. Fraser, 7 February 1846.

10. *Inverness Courier*, 11 February 1846; NRS AD14/46/34: Statement of J. Sutherland, 25 February 1846.

11. NRS AD14/46/34: Statements of C. MacKenzie and J. Sutherland, 10, 25 February 1846.

12. NRS AD14/46/34: Statement of J. Cameron, 9 February 1846.

13. NRS AD14/46/34: Statement of J. Masson, 10 February 1846.

14. NRS AD14/46/34: Statements of J. Masson and D. Rose, 9, 10 February 1846.

15. NRS AD14/46/34: Statement of W. Fraser-Tytler, 27 February 1846.

16. *Inverness Courier*, 11 February 1846.

17. Engels, *Condition of the Working Class*, pp. 70–71.

18. G. and P. Anderson, *Guide to the Highlands and Islands of Scotland*, London, 1834, pp. 55, 62–63.

19. G. Anderson, *Report on the Sanitary Condition of the Labouring Classes in the Town of Inverness*, Inverness, 1841, pp. 2–3.

20. *Poor Law Commission*, Appendix, Pt II, pp. 467, 470, 492; *Morning Chronicle*, 24 September 1846; J. C Leslie and S. J. Leslie, *The Hospitals of Inverness: Their Origin and Development*, Avoch, 2017, p. vi.

21. *Poor Law Commission*, Appendix, Pt II, pp. 466; *Morning Chronicle*, 24 September 1846.

22. *NSA*, XIV, pp. 17–18; *Poor Law Commission*, Appendix, Pt II, p. 467.

23. NRS AD56/308/1: MacKay to Lindsay, 1 February 1847.

24. *Inverness Courier*, 3 February 1847; NRS AD56/308/1: MacKay to Lindsay, 1 February 1847.

25. NRS AD56/308/1: MacKay to Lindsay, 4 February 1847.

26. NRS AD56/308/2: Simpson to Rutherfurd, 2 February 1847.

27. NRS AD56/308/1: MacKay to Lindsay, 3 February 1847; *Inverness Courier*, 3 February 1847; NRS AD56/308/6: MacKay to Lindsay, 5 February 1847.

28. HAI D766/5/4/9: Fraser-Tytler to Rutherfurd, 9 February 1847.

29. *Inverness Courier*, 13 April 1847.

30. *Poor Law Commission*, Appendix, Pt II, pp. 497–98.

31. HAI CI/7/8/1: Kirkhill Parochial Board Minutes, 2 December 1846, 6 January, 10 February 1847.

32. HAI CI/7/8/1: Kirkhill Parochial Board Minutes, 10 February 1847. For additional details of Callum's background, see *Poor Law Commission*, Appendix, Pt II, p. 505.

33. NRS HD19/24: Inverness District Committee Minutes, 13 March 1847; NRS AD56/308/2: MacKay to Lindsay, 6 February 1847; *Inverness Courier*, 3, 10 February 1847.

34. NRS AD56/308/2: Simpson to Rutherfurd, 2 February 1847.

35. NRS AD56/308/4: Dewar to Lindsay, 30 January 1847; NRS AD506/308/1: Dewar to Lindsay, 1 February 1847; *Elgin Courant*, 5 February 1847.

36. Somers, *Letters*, p. 45.

37. *NSA*, XIV, p. 459; Somers, *Letters*, p. 45; NRS AF56/308/1: MacKay to Lindsay, 1 February 1847.

38. NRS AD56/308/2: MacKay to Lindsay, 12 February 1847.

39. *Inverness Courier*, 13 April 1847. This account is derived mainly from the *Courier*'s report of the trial arising from the Beauly disturbances.

40. *Inverness Courier*, 13 April 1847.

41. *Inverness Courier*, 13 April 1847.

42. AD56/308/6: Jardine to Rutherfurd, 7 February 1847.

43. *Inverness Courier*, 10 February 1847; *John O'Groat Journal*, 26 February 1847; NRS AD56/308/2: MacKenzie to Lindsay, 8 February 1847.

44. NRS AD56/308/2: MacKenzie to Jardine, 12 February 1847; Scott to Eden, 11 February 1847; Jardine to Rutherfurd, 13 February 1847.

45. *NSA*, XIV, p. 393; NRS HD19/3: Gibson to Skene, 14, 17 April 1847.

46. NRS AD56/308/2: Jardine to Rutherfurd, 21 February 1847.

47. NRS AD56/308/2: Jardine to Rutherfurd, 21 February 1847.

48. NRS AD56/308/2: Jardine to Rutherfurd, 21 February 1847.

49. NRS AD56/308/2: Jardine to Rutherfurd, 21 February 1847.

50. NRS AD56/308/5: Taylor to Jardine, 30 January 1847; NRS AD56/308/1: Grigor to Lindsay, 4 February 1847; *Inverness Courier*, 10 February 1847.

51. *Poor Law Commission*, Appendix, Pt II, pp. 22, 49, 61; *NSA*, XIV, pp. 27–28. See also, Alston, *My Little Town of Cromarty*, p. 242.

52. Miller, *Essays*, pp. 213–14.

53. *Morning Chronicle*, 3 October 1846.

54. NRS HD19/24: Gillanders to Skene, 15 April 1847.

55. NRS HD19/21: Mackintosh to Skene, 15 February 1847; NRS HD19/19: Carment to Skene, 16 March 1847. Revd Carment's letter was forwarded to the Central Board by the minister's son who lived in Edinburgh.

56. *Inverness Courier*, 6 January 1847.

57. HAI CRC/1/1/1/5: Ross and Cromarty Commissioners of Supply, Minutes, 11 February 1847.

58. NRS HD19/19: Statement by the Local Committee, Rosskeen, 21 April 1847.

59. *NSA*, XIV, p. 279.

60. I. R. M. Mowat, *Easter Ross, 1750–1850: The Double Frontier*, Edinburgh, 1981, p. 72.

61. NRS AD56/308/1: Taylor to Lindsay, 4 February 1847.

62. *Ross-shire Advertiser*, 5 February 1847.

63. NRS AD56/308/1: Dewar to Lindsay, 1 February 1847; *Ross-shire Advertiser*, 5 February 1847.

64. *Ross-shire Advertiser*, 29 January, 5 February 1847.

65. *Scotsman*, 3 March 1847.

66. NRS AD56/308/5: Jardine to Rutherfurd, 5 February 1847.

67. NRS AD56/308/2: Jardine to Rutherfurd, 13, 17, 25 February 1847.

68. NRS AD56/308/5: Lindsay to Rutherfurd, 2 February 1847; *Inverness Courier*, 10 February 1847; NRS AD56/308/6: MacKenzie to Lindsay, 21 February 1847; *Scotsman*, 3 March 1847.

69. NRS AD56/308/2: Lindsay to MacKenzie, 15 February 1847.

70. NRS AD56/308/4: Manson to Lindsay, 17 February 1847; NRS HD19/25: Sinclair to Skene, 11 February 1847; *John O'Groat Journal*, 17 February 1847.

71. NRS AD56/308/4: Manson to Lindsay, 17 February 1847.

72. *John O'Groat Journal*, 5 March 1847; NRS AD56/308/2: Thomson to Lindsay, 26 February 1847.

73. NRS AD56/308/6: Traill to Crawford, 15 February 1847.

74. *John O'Groat Journal*, 26 February 1847; NRS AD56/308/2: Manson to Lindsay, 24 February 1847.

75. NRS AD14/47/624: Indictment against Donald Holme and John Munro, March 1847.

76. *Ross-shire Advertiser*, 12 March 1847.

77. NRS AD14/47/624: Statements of L. Ross, K. Robertson, E. Munro, B. MacKenzie, B. MacLean and J. Munro, 3 March 1847.

78. NRS AD14/47/624: Indictment against Donald Holme and John Munro, March 1847.

79. NRS AD56/308/6: Goodman to Eden, 3 March 1847.

80. *Ross-shire Advertiser*, 12 March 1847; NRS AD56/308/6: Goodman to Eden, 3 March 1847.

81. NRS AD14/47/624: Petition against John Munro, 18 March 1847.

82. NRS AD56/308/6: Goodman to Eden, 3 March 1847; *Ross-shire* Advertiser, 12 March 1847; NRS AD14/47/624: Statement of Catherine Munro, 3 March 1847.

83. *Ross-shire Advertiser*, 12 March 1847. Also, NRS AD56/308/6: Goodman to Eden, 4 March 1847.

84. *Ross-shire Advertiser*, 12 March 1847; NRS AD56/308/2: Taylor to Brodie, 4 March 1847.

85. *Ross-shire Advertiser*, 5 February, 5 March 1847.

86. NRS AD56/308/2: Taylor to Brodie, 8 March 1847; *Spectator*, 6 February 1847.

87. *Inverness Journal*, 5 February 1847. Although published in early February, the article from which these sentences are extracted, was written in mid January.

88. *Inverness Journal*, 12 February 1847.

7 'Chains of degradation'

1. J. N. MacLeod, *Memorials of the Rev Norman MacLeod*, Edinburgh, 1898, pp. 231–32.

2. *Scotsman*, 16 January 1847.

3. *Scotsman*, 16 January 1847.

4. https://www.nhs.uk/conditions/kwashiorkor/ [accessed 12 December 2018].

5. NRS AF67/400: Central Board circular, February 1847; T. Mulock, *The Western Highlands and Islands of Scotland Socially Considered*, Inverness, 1850, p. 81.

6. *Papers Relative to Emigration to the North American Colonies*, 1852, pp. 8–10, 17–19: Buchanan to Fleming, 26 November 1851; Douglas to Buchanan, 15 December 1851; Buchanan to Grey, 31 December 1851.

7. NRS CR8/322: Richmond to Balmer, 3, 14 February 1847.

8. NRS GD136/993: Petition to Sinclair of Freswick, 15 March 1847.

9. NRS GD136/993: Jolly to Henderson, 12 March, 7 April 1847.

10. NRS GD136/993: Jolly to Henderson, 7 April 1847.

11. For accounts of some of these sheriff court trials, see *Elgin Courier*, 9 April 1847; *Inverness Courier*, 13 April, 22 June 1847; *John O'Groat Journal*, 4 June 1847.

12. NA HO18/207: Declaration of Angus Davidson, 17 February 1847.

13. NA HO18/207: Indictment of James Falconer and others, March 1847.

14. *Scotsman*, 24 March 1847; *Elgin Courant*, 26 March 1847; *Inverness Courier*, 31 March 1847; NA HO18/207: Judge's notes of trial of James Falconer and others, 23 March 1847.

15. *Scotsman*, 24 March 1847; *Elgin Courant*, 26 March 1847.

16. *Elgin Courant*, 26 March 1847.

17. NA HO18/207: Tennent and Fraser to Grey, 26 March 1847.

18. NA HO18/207: Waters to Grey, 14 April 1847.

19. NRS AD56/308/2: Waters to Innes, 10 February 1847; *Scotsman*, 24 March 1847.

20. Burton, *Memoir of Cosmo Innes*, pp. 47–48.

21. NA HO18/207: Memorial relative to Daniel Sutherland and others, April 1847.

22. *Witness*, 27 March 1847.

23. *Northern Star*, 27 March 1847.

24. *Northern Star*, 24 April, 12 June 1847; NA HO18/207: Petition from James Clarkson and others, June 1847.

25. G. F. Millar, 'John Hope', *Oxford Dictionary of National Biography Online* at http://www.oxforddnb.com/ [accessed 21 January 2019]. Millar's entry on Hope was published in 2004.

26. NA HO18/207: Hope to Grey, 12 April 1847.

27. NRS AD14/47/533: Statement of John Bain, 1 March 1847.

28. *John O'Groat Journal*, 9 April 1847; NA HO45/1938: Resolutions of a public meeting of merchants, traders and householders of the town of Wick, 8 April 1847; *Inverness Courier*, 20 April 1847.

29. *Inverness Courier*, 20 April 1847.

30. *Inverness Courier*, 20 April 1847.

31. NA HO18/207: Hope to Grey, 19 April 1847.

32. NA HO18/207: Hope to Grey, 19 April 1847.

33. NA HO18/207: Grey to Hope, 22 April 1847; NA HO45/1938: Somerville to Miller, 8 May 1847.

34. *John O'Groat Journal*, 4 June 1847.

35. NA HO18/207: Nicolson to his parents, 3 June 1847.

36. *Morning Advertiser*, 7 July 1847.

37. *Morning Advertiser*, 8 July 1847.

38. *Manchester Times*, 21 August 1847.

39. NA HO18/207: Cowan to Rutherfurd, 23 August 1847; Cowan to Grey, 11 September, 2 November 1847.

40. NA HO18/207: Petition relating to James Nicolson, 1847.

41. NA HO18/207: Loch to Grey, 15 July 1847.

42. NA HO18/207: Petition of Mary Jack and others, n.d.

43. NA HO18/207: Rutherfurd to Grey, 7 October 1847.

44. H. D. MacLeod, *The Results of the Operation of the Poor House System in Easter Ross*, Inverness, 1851, p. 13.

45. A. Griffiths, *Memorials of Millbank*, London, 1884, p. 329.

46. *John O'Groat Journal*, 14 April 1848.

47. *John O'Groat Journal*, 22 June 1849.

48. NRS AD56/308/5: Lindsay to Rutherfurd, 11 February 1847.

49. NRS AD56/308/4: Lindsay to Rutherfurd, 25 January 1847.

50. E. Richards, 'The Last Scottish Food Riots', *Past and Present*, Supplement 6 (1982), p. 10.

51. Richards, 'Food Riots', p. 11.

52. A. McCaskill, *Twelve Days in Skye*, London, 1852, p. 35. Lady Anne's name is given on her pamphlet's title page as it is given here. But she, her husband and their children appear to have preferred MacAskill, the more usual spelling of this surname.

53. D. Ross, *The Glengarry Evictions or Scenes at Knoydart*, Glasgow, 1853, p. 12.

54. *Report of the Highlands and Islands Royal Commission*, 2 vols, 1895, II, p. 915.

55. *Crofters and Cottars*, II, p. 779.

56. McCaskill, *Twelve Days in Skye*, p. 36.

57. *Scotsman*, 22 March, 8 May 1883 and 15, 18 October 1884.

58. *Report to the Board of Supervision by Sir John MacNeill on the Western Highlands and Islands*, 1851, p. iv.

59. J. Hunter, *The Making of the Crofting Community*, Edinburgh, 1976, p. 144.

60. *John O'Groat Journal*, 4, 18 November, 9 December 1885.

61. *John O'Groat Journal*, 23 September 1885.

62. *John O'Groat Journal*, 16 December 1885.

Bibliography

Unpublished and archived material

Highland Archive, Inverness

BI/1/1/18 Inverness Town Council, Minutes, 1844–49.

BI/1/3/1 Inverness Police Commissioners, Minutes, 1847–64.

CI/1/9/1 Inverness-shire Commissioners of Supply: Constabulary Committee, Minutes, 1840–53.

CI/7/8/1 Kirkhill Parochial Board, Minutes, 1845–59.

CRC/1/1/1/5 Ross and Cromarty Commissioners of Supply, Minutes, 1839–53.

CRC/1/3/5 Ross and Cromarty Sheriff Clerk, Letterbook, 1845–50.

CRC/6/1/1 Applecross Parochial Board, Minutes, 1845–68.

CRC/6/2/1 Avoch Parochial Board, Minutes, 1845–69.

CRC/6/9/1 Knockbain Parochial Board, Minutes, 1845–55.

CRC/6/14/1 Resolis Parochial Board, Minutes, 1845–72.

CRC/6/20/1 Tain Parochial Board, Petitions for Relief, 1844–50.

D766/5/4/9 Sheriff William Fraser-Tytler Letterbook, 1846–47.

Highland Archive, Wick

BW/1/6 Wick Town Council, Minutes, 1836–55.

CC/1//1/6 Caithness Commissioners of Supply, Minutes, 1844–73.

CC/7/3/1/1 Dunnet Parochial Board, Minutes, 1845–90.

CC/7/5/1/1 Latheron Parochial Board, Minutes, 1845–51.

CC/7/10/1/1 Wick Parochial Board, Minutes, 1840–48.

National Archives, Kew

HO13/93/364–65 Correspondence and warrants relating to release of Daniel Sutherland and others, March 1848.

HO18/207 Precognitions, trial papers, petitions for clemency and associated correspondence relating to Angus Davidson, Daniel Sutherland and others, 1847.

HO19/11A Register of Criminal Petitions, 1847–49.

HO45/1938 Disturbances, Scotland, 1847.

WO12/8220 General Muster Books and Pay Lists, 76th Regiment of Foot, 1846–47.

National Library of Scotland, Edinburgh

313/863 Sutherland Papers: Correspondence and papers on Highland destitution, 1846–47.

313/1173–74 Sutherland Papers: Correspondence, J. Loch to George, 2nd Duke, 1846–47.

National Records of Scotland, Edinburgh

AD11/3 Lord Advocate's Department, Letterbooks, 1845–49.

AD11/27 Lord Advocate's Department, Letterbooks, 1847.

AD14/46/34 Precognitions against Roderick More et al., Inverness, 1846.

AD14/47/515 Precognition against James Falconer et al., Burghead, 1847

AD14/47/524 Precognition against James Ball, Ardersier, 1847.

AD14/47/528 Precognition against Dennis Driscoll, Fort William, 1847.

AD14/47/533 Precognition against James Nicol et al., Pulteneytown, 1847.

AD14/47/624 Precognition against Donald Holme et al., Invergordon, 1847.

AD14/47/628 Precognitions as to alleged deaths from starvation, South Uist and Barra, and as to the Constitution of the Parochial Board, Barra, with associated correspondence, 1847.

AD56/258/1–2 Poor and Poor Law, various papers, 1847–81.

AD56/308/1–6 Disturbances in the north, 1847.

AD58/67 Correspondence as to riots and military intervention, 1848.

AD58/69 Correspondence as to riots and civil disorder, North-East Scotland, 1847–48

AD58/77 Correspondence as to riots, Findochty and Buckie, 1847.

AD58/81 Correspondence concerning destitution, various Highland estates, 1846–47.

AD58/82 Correspondence concerning destitution, Free Kirk Relief Fund, 1846.

AD58/84 Correspondence concerning destitution, Isle of Harris 1846–47.

AD58/86 Correspondence concerning destitution, Barra and South Uist, 1846–47.

AD56/88 Correspondence concerning destitution, Argyll, 1846.

AD58/89 Correspondence concerning destitution, miscellaneous letters, 1846–47.

AD58/90 Correspondence concerning destitution, Caithness and Ross-shire, 1837–46.

AF28/240 Report by the Commissioners for the Herring Fishery, 1846.

AF28/241 Report by the Commissioners for the Herring Fishery, 1847.

AF30/11 Lossiemouth Fishery Office: Letters and Reports, 1839–54.

AF31/41 Macduff Fishery Office: Port Gordon District, Records, 1847–49.

AF34/2/1 Peterhead Fishery Office: Letter and Report Books, 1835–48.

AF36/6/11 Wick Fishery District: Private Books, 1846–48.

AF67/400 Highland Destitution Board, notices and instructions, 1847.

CR8/322 Fochabers Estate Office Records: Correspondence, Duke of Richmond to Thomas Balmer, 1846–47.

GD44/44/23 Gordon Castle Muniments: Correspondence, William Balmer to Duke of Richmond, 1847.

GD248/1582 Seafield Papers: Grant and Seafield Estate Letterbook, 1846–48.

GD136/992 Sinclair of Freswick Papers: Petition to Sinclair of Freswick by Donald Olson, 1847.

GD136/993 Sinclair of Freswick Papers: Petition to Sinclair of Freswick by tenants being removed, 1847.

HD1/19 Correspondence concerning destitution on Lord Macdonald's estate, 1847.

HD6/2 Printed Treasury Correspondence, 1847.

HD6/5 Destitution inspectors' reports, 1847–48.

HD7/1–2 Correspondence, A. Rutherfurd et al. to Sir E. Pine-Coffin, 1846–47.

HD7/3 Correspondence, Sir J. McNeill to Sir E. Pine-Coffin, 1846–47.

HD7/5 Correspondence, Major Haliday to Sir E. Pine-Coffin, 1846–47.

HD7/6 Correspondence, C. E. Trevelyan to Sir E. Pine-Coffin et al., 1847.

HD7/7 Correspondence, Sheriff Shaw, Lochmaddy, to Sir E. Pine-Coffin, 1847.

HD7/11 Correspondence, Captain G. A. Pole to Sir E. Pine-Coffin, 1846–47.

HD7/12 Representations, memorials and petitions, Home Department, 1846–47.

HD7/21 Correspondence, Sir E. Pine-Coffin to J. S. Dobree, 1847.

HD7/26 Correspondence concerning Highland destitution, 1847.

HD7/28 Correspondence, C. E. Trevelyan to Sir E. Pine-Coffin, 1847.

HD7/32 Correspondence concerning destitution in the Eastern Highlands, 1847.

HD12/1 Correspondence to W. F. Skene, Highland Relief Board, 1847.

HD16/39 Memorandum of business, first meeting, Highland Relief Board, 1847.

HD16/110 Statement as to destitution in the Highlands and Islands, 1846.

HD16/133 Printed appeal, Famine Relief Fund, 1846.

HD19/1 Local destitution committee, Alness, 1847.

HD19/2 Local destitution committee, Ardersier, 1847.

HD19/3 Local destitution committee, Avoch, 1847–48.

HD19/5 Local destitution committee, Creich, 1846–47.

HD19/6 Local destitution committee, Dores, 1847.

HD19/7 Local destitution committee, Fearn, 1847.

HD19/10 Local destitution committee, Fortrose, 1847.

HD19/11 Local destitution committee, Kiltearn, 1847.

HD19/16 Local destitution committee, Latheron, 1847.

HD19/17 Local destitution committee, Nigg, 1847.

HD19/18 Local destitution committee, Resolis, 1847.

HD19/19 Local destitution committee, Rosskeen, 1847.

HD19/20 Local destitution committee, Tain, 1847.

HD19/21 Local destitution committee, Tarbat, 1847.

HD19/22 Local destitution committee, Thurso, 1847.

HD19/24 Local destitution committee, Urray, 1847.

HD19/25 Local destitution committee, Wick, 1847.

HD19/33 Miscellaneous papers, Caithness and Sutherland, 1847–49.

HD19/34 Miscellaneous papers, Inverness-shire, 1847.

HD20/15 Local destitution committee, Sleat, 1847–48.

HD20/183 Captain Pole's memorandum of provisions sold, South Uist and Barra, 1847.

HD21/14 Local destitution committee, Applecross, 1847.

HD21/38 Report by Captain Rose on distress at Applecross, 1847.

HD22/6 Reports on various local destitution committees, 1847.

JC26/1846/3 Trial papers relating to Donald McIntosh et al., Inverness, 1846.

JC26/1846/6 Trial papers relating to Roderick More et al., Inverness, 1846.

JC26/1847/12 Trial papers relating to Dennis Driscoll, Fort William, 1847.

JC26/1847/597 Trial papers relating to John Main et al., Burghead.

JC26/1847/615 Trial papers relating to John Shearer et al., Pulteneytown, 1847.

JC26/1847/626 Trial papers relating to Donald Holme et al., Invergordon, 1847.

RH2/4/238 Home Office Domestic Entry Books, Scotland, 1846–48.

RH2/4/271 Home Office Criminal Entry Books, Scotland, 1844–48.

Published material from the time: Newspapers and periodicals

Aberdeen Herald
Aberdeen Journal
Army List
Banffshire Journal
Caledonian Mercury
Economist
Edinburgh Gazette
Elgin Courant
Elgin Courier
Forres Gazette
Freeman's Journal
Glasgow Herald
Greenock Advertiser
Illustrated London News
Inverness Courier
Inverness Journal
John O' Groat Journal
Manchester Guardian
Manchester Times
Morning Advertiser
Morning Chronicle
Nairnshire Mirror
Northern Star
Observer
Ross-shire Advertiser
Scots Magazine
Scotsman
Spectator
Times
Witness

Published material from the time: Parliamentary reports and papers

Reports from the Select Committee on the Condition of the Population of the Highlands and Islands of Scotland and the Practicability of Affording Relief by Emigration, 1841.

Report of the Royal Commission for Inquiring into the Administration of the Poor Laws in Scotland, 7 vols, 1844.

Correspondence Explanatory of the Measures Adopted for the Relief of Distress in Ireland, 1846.

Hansard (House of Commons), 1846–47.

Board of Supervision for Relief of the Poor in Scotland, *Annual Reports*, 1846–48.

Correspondence, July 1846 to January 1847, Relating to the Measures Adopted for the Relief of Distress in Ireland (Commissariat Series), 1847.

Correspondence Relating to the Measures Adopted for the Relief of Distress in Scotland, 1847.

Report of the Commissioners Appointed to Inquire into the Management of Millbank Prison, 1847.

Return of Applications for Advances under the Drainage Act, 1847.

Report to the Board of Supervision by Sir John McNeill on the Western Highlands and Islands, 1851.

Papers Relative to Emigration to the North American Colonies, 1852.

Report of Commissioners of Inquiry into the Condition of the Crofters and Cottars in the Highlands and Islands of Scotland, 5 vols, 1884.

Report of the Highlands and Islands Royal Commission, 2 vols, 1895.

Published material from the time: Books and pamphlets

Aberdeen Anti-Slavery Society, *First Annual Report*, Aberdeen, 1826.

Alison, Archibald, *Principles of the Criminal Law of Scotland*, Edinburgh, 1832.

Alison, William. P., *Observations on the Famine of 1846–47 in the Highlands of Scotland and in Ireland*, Edinburgh, 1849.

Alison, William. P., *Observations on the Management of the Poor in Scotland*, Edinburgh, 1840.

Alister, R., *Extermination of the Scottish Peasantry*, Edinburgh, 1853.

Anderson, George, *Report on the Sanitary Condition of the Labouring Classes in the Town of Inverness*, Inverness, 1841.

Anderson, George and Peter, *Guide to the Highlands and Islands of Scotland*, London, 1834.

Bain, Donald, *Observations upon the Potato Disease of 1845 and 1846*, Edinburgh, 1848.

Brown, Thomas, *Annals of the Disruption*, Edinburgh, 1884.

Bruce, James, *Letters on the Present Condition of the Highlands and Islands of Scotland*, Edinburgh, 1847.

Burton, Katherine, *Memoir of Cosmo Innes*, Edinburgh, 1874.

Calder, James T., *Sketch of the Civil and Traditional History of Caithness*, Wick, 1887.

Central Board of Management of the Fund Raised for the Relief of the Destitute Inhabitants of the Highlands and Islands of Scotland (henceforth CBM), *Correspondence of W. F. Skene*, Edinburgh, 1847.

CBM, *Destitution in the Highlands and Islands*, Edinburgh, 1847 ABS.3.203.017(2).

CBM, *Interim Instructions*, Edinburgh, 1846.

CBM, *Letter: Sir E. Pine-Coffin to W. F. Skene*, Edinburgh, 1848.

CBM, *Plan of Operation for the Distributing Committee*, Edinburgh, 1847.

CBM, *Statements as to the Destitution in the Highlands and Islands*, Edinburgh, 1846–47.

CBM, *To the Inhabitants of Edinburgh*, Edinburgh, 1846.

Cockburn, Henry, *Journal of Henry Cockburn, 1831–1854*, Edinburgh, 2 vols, 1874.

Dickens, Charles, *A Christmas Carol*, London, 1843.

Dickens, Charles, *David Copperfield*, London, 1850.

Engels, Friedrich, *The Condition of the Working Class in England*, Penguin Classics Edition, London, 2005 [1844].

Findlater, Eric J., *Highland Clearances the Real Cause of Highland Famines*, Edinburgh, 1855.

Free Church of Scotland Acting Committee on the Destitution in the Highlands and Islands, *Statement*, Edinburgh, 1846.

Free Church of Scotland Destitution Committee, *Destitution in the Highlands and Islands of Scotland*, Edinburgh, 1847.

Free Church of Scotland Destitution Committee, *Destitution in the Highlands and Islands of Scotland: With Extract Returns of Schedule of Queries*, Edinburgh, 1847.

Free Church of Scotland Destitution Committee, *Report to the General Assembly of the Free Church*, Edinburgh, 1847.

Graham, J., *On the Potato Disease*, London, 1847.

Greig, John (ed.), *Disruption Worthies of the Highlands*, Edinburgh, 1877.

Griffiths, Arthur, *Memorials of Millbank*, London, 1884.

Imlach, James, *History of Banff*, Banff, 1868.

Johnson, Samuel, *A Journey to the Western Islands of Scotland*, London, 1775.

Lewis, Samuel, *A Topographical Dictionary of Scotland*, 2 vols, London, 1846.

McCaskill, A., *Twelve Days in Skye*, London, 1852.

McCulloch, John, *The Highlands and Western Islands of Scotland*, 4 vols, London, 1824.

McLauchlan, Thomas, *The Depopulation System in the Highlands*, Edinburgh, 1849.

MacLean, J., *Reminiscences of a Clachnacuddin Nonagenarian*, Inverness, 1886.

MacLeod, Henry D., *The Results of the Operation of the Poor House System in Easter Ross*, Inverness, 1851.

MacLeod, J. N., *Memorials of the Rev Norman MacLeod*, Edinburgh, 1898.

MacLeod, Norman (ed.), *Extracts from Letters to the Rev Dr MacLeod Regarding the Famine and Destitution in the Highlands and Islands of Scotland*, Glasgow, 1847.

MacLeod, Norman, *Reminiscences of a Highland Parish*, London, 1867.

Miller, Hugh, *The Cruise of the Betsey*, Edinburgh, 1858.

Miller, Hugh, *Essays: Historical and Biographical, Political, Social, Literary and Scientific*, New York, 1882.

Miller, Hugh, *Letters on the Herring Fishery in the Moray Firth*, Inverness, 1829.

Miller, Hugh, *Scenes and Legends of the North of Scotland*, Edinburgh, 1835.

Mitchell, John, *The Herring: Its Natural History and National Importance*, Edinburgh, 1864.

Mitchell, Joseph, *Reminiscences of My Life in the Highlands*, 2 vols, London, 1884.

Monro, Donald, *Description of the Western Isles of Scotland*, Glasgow, 1884 [1549].

Morris, Thomas, *Recollections of Military Service*, London, 1845.

Mulock, Thomas, *The Western Highlands and Islands of Scotland Socially Considered*, Inverness, 1850.

New Statistical Account of Scotland, 15 vols, Edinburgh, 1845.

Rhind, William, *Sketches of the Past and Present State of Moray*, Edinburgh, 1839.

Ross, Donald, *The Glengarry Evictions or Scenes at Knoydart*, Glasgow, 1853.

Scott, Walter, *The Antiquary*, London, 1816.

Scott, Walter, *The Heart of Midlothian*, London, 1818.

Scottish Post Office Edinburgh and Leith Directory, Edinburgh, 1847

Somers, Robert, *Letters from the Highlands: Or the Famine of 1847*, Inverness, 1977 [1848].

Thomson, James, *On the Existing State of our Herring Fishery*, Aberdeen, 1854.

Thomson, James, *The Value and Importance of the Scottish Fisheries*, London, 1849.

Trevelyan, Charles E., *The Irish Crisis*, London, 1848.

Watson, J. and W., *Morayshire Described*, Elgin, 1868.

Wilson, James, *A Voyage Round the Coasts of Scotland and the Isles*, 2 vols, Edinburgh, 1842.

Young, Robert, *Annals of the Parish and Burgh of Elgin*, Elgin, 1879.

Young, Robert, *Notes on Burghead Ancient and Modern*, Elgin, 1867.

Other publications

Alston, David, *My Little Town of Cromarty: The History of a Northern Scottish Town*, Edinburgh, 2006.

Anson, Peter F., *Fishing Boats and Fisher Folk on the East Coast of Scotland*, London, 1930.

Arnold, David, *Famine, Social Crisis and Historical Change*, Oxford, 1988.

Ash, Marinell, *This Noble Harbour: A History of the Cromarty Firth*, Edinburgh, 1991.

Baines, John, Ross, John and De Comerford, Mark, *Merkinch Revisited*, Inverness, 1992.

Barrett, John R., *The Making of a Scottish Landscape: Moray's Regular Revolution, 1760–1840*, Fonthill, 2015.

Barrie, David, *Police in the Age of Improvement: Police Development and the Civic Tradition in Scotland, 1756–1865*, Cullompton, 2008.

Black, Frank G. and Black, Renee M. (eds), *The Harney Papers*, Assen, 1969.

Bohsted, John, *The Politics of Provisions: Food Riots, Moral Economy and Market Transition in England, 1550–1850*, London, 2010.

Bohsted, John, *Riots and Community Politics in England and Wales, 1790–1810*, Cambridge, MA, 1983.

Braddick, Michael and Water, John (eds), *Negotiating Power in Early Modern Society: Order, Hierarchy and Subordination in Britain and Ireland*, Cambridge, 2001.

Branigan, Keith, *The Last of the Clan: General Roderick MacNeil of Barra*, Stroud, 2010.

Brotherstone, T. (ed.), *Covenant, Charter and Party*: Traditions of Revolt and Protest in Modern Scottish History, Aberdeen, 1989.

Broun, Dauvit and MacGregor, Martin (eds), *Mìorun Mòr nan Gall: The Great Ill-Will of the Lowlander: Lowland Perceptions of the Highlands, Medieval and Modern*, Glasgow, 2009.

Brown, S. J. and Fry, Michael (eds), *Scotland in the Age of the Disruption*, Edinburgh, 1993.

Bulloch, John. M., *The Gordons of Cluny*, Buckie, 1911.

Burgoyne, Roderick H., *Historical Records of the 93rd Sutherland Highlanders*, London, 1883.

Caldwell, David, *Islay: The Land of the Lordship*, Edinburgh, 2008.

Cameron, Ewen, 'Internal Policing and Public Order, 1797–1900', in Edward M. Spiers, Jeremy A. Craig and Matthew J. Strickland (eds), *A Military History of Scotland*, Edinburgh, 2012.

Cameron, Joy, *Prisons and Punishment in Scotland from the Middle Ages to the Present*, Edinburgh, 1983.

Campbell, John L. (ed.), *The Book of Barra*, Stornoway, 1998.

Carter, Ian, *Farm Life in Northeast Scotland, 1840–1914: Poor Man's Country*, Edinburgh, 1979.

Chase, Malcolm, *Chartism: A New History*, Manchester, 2007.

Checkland, O., *Philanthropy in Victorian Scotland: Social Welfare and the Voluntary Principle*, Edinburgh, 1980.

Cochrane, Robert G., *Findhorn: A Scottish Village*, Forres, 1985.

Coleman, Terry, *The Railway Navvies: A History of the Men Who Made the Railways*, London, 2000.

Coull, James R., *The Development of the Herring Fishery in the Peterhead District Before World War I*, Bergen, 1991.

Coull, James R., *Fishing from the Moray Coast*, Aberdeen, 2007.

Coull, James R., *Fishing in the Buckie District*, Aberdeen, 2006.

Coull, James R., *Fishing in the Macduff District*, Aberdeen, 2007.

Coull, James R., *The Sea Fisheries of Scotland: A Historical Geography*, Edinburgh, 2003.

Coull, James R., 'Seasonal Migration in the Caithness Herring Fishery', *Northern Scotland*, 22 (2002), pp. 77–97.

Cowan, R. M. W., *The Newspaper in Scotland: A Study of its First Expansion*, Glasgow, 1946.

Crace, Richard J., *Opium and Empire: The Lives and Careers of William Jardine and James Matheson*, Montreal, 2014.

Cranna, John, *Fraserburgh Past and Present*, Aberdeen, 1914.

Crowther, M. A., 'Poverty, Health and Welfare', in W. Hamish Fraser and R. J. Morris (eds), *People and Society in Scotland, 1830–1914*, Edinburgh, 1990.

Cullen, Karen J., *Famine in Scotland: The 'Ill Years' of the 1690s*, Edinburgh, 2010.

Currie, Jo, *Mull: The Island and Its People*, Edinburgh, 2000.

Daly, Mary E., *The Famine in Ireland*, Dublin, 1986.

Dando, William A., *The Geography of Famine*, London, 1980.

Darling, F. Fraser, *West Highland Survey: An Essay in Human Ecology*, Oxford, 1955.

Davidson, Neil, Jackson, Louise A. and Smale, David M., 'Police Amalgamation and Reform in Scotland: The Long Twentieth Century', *Scottish Historical Review*, 95 (2016), pp. 88–111.

Delaney, Enda, *The Great Irish Famine: A History in Four Lives*, Dublin, 2014.

Devine, T. M., *Clanship to Crofters War: The Social Transformation of the Scottish Highlands*, Manchester, 1994.

Devine, T. M. (ed.), *Conflict and Stability in Scottish Society, 1700–1850*, Edinburgh, 1990.

Devine, T. M., *The Great Highland Famine*, Edinburgh, 1988.

Devine, T. M., *The Scottish Nation, 1700–2007*, London, 2006.

Dodgshon, Robert A., 'Coping with Risk: Subsistence Crises in the Scottish Highlands and Islands, 1600–1800', *Rural History*, 15 (2004), pp. 1–25.

Dodgshon, Robert A., *No Stone Unturned: A History of Farming, Landscape and Environment in the Scottish Highlands and Islands*, Edinburgh, 2015.

Donnelly, Daniel and Scott, Kenneth (eds), *Policing Scotland*, Cullompton, 2005.

Douglas, Robert, *Sons of Moray*, Elgin, 1930.

Duncan, Robert E., 'Artisans and Proletarians: Chartism and Working Class Allegiance in Aberdeen, 1838–1842', *Northern Scotland*, 4 (1981), pp. 51–67.

Dunlop, Jean, *The British Fisheries Society, 1786–1893*, Edinburgh, 1978.

Draper, Nicholas, 'Scotland and Colonial Slave Ownership: The Evidence of the Slave Compensation Records', in T. M. Devine (ed.), *Recovering Scotland's Slavery Past: The Caribbean Connection*, Edinburgh, 2015.

Dressler, Camille, *Eigg: The Story of an Island*, Edinburgh, 1998.

Duthie, R. J., *The Art of Fishcuring*, Aberdeen, 1911.

Dyer, Michael, *Men of Property and Intelligence: The Scottish Electoral System Prior to 1884*, Aberdeen, 1996.

Farwell, Byron, *For Queen and Country: Social History of the Victorian and Edwardian Army*, London, 1981.

Fegan, Melissa, *Literature and the Irish Famine*, Oxford, 2002

Ferguson, Ronald, *George MacLeod: Founder of the Iona Community*, London, 1990.

Ferguson, William, *Scotland: 1689 to the Present*, Edinburgh, 1968.

Fenyö, Krisztina, *Contempt, Sympathy and Romance: Lowland Perceptions of the Highlands and the Clearances During the Famine Years, 1845–55*, East Linton, 2000.

Foden, Frank, *Wick of the North: The Story of a Scottish Royal Burgh*, Wick, 1996.

Fraser, W. Hamish, *Chartism in Scotland*, Pontypool, 2010.

Fraser, W. Hamish and Lee, Clive H. (eds), *Aberdeen, 1800–2000: A New History*, East Linton, 2000.

Fraser, W. Hamish and Morris, R. J. (eds), *People and Society in Scotland, 1830–1914*, Edinburgh, 1990.

Fry, Michael, *Patronage and Principle: A Political History of Modern Scotland*, Aberdeen, 1987.

Garthwaite, Kayleigh, *Hunger Pains: Life Inside Foodbank Britain*, Bristol, 2016.

Gash, Norman, *Sir Robert Peel: The Life of Sir Robert Peel after 1830*, London, 2011.

Gaskell, Philip, *Morvern Transformed: A Highland Parish in the Nineteenth Century*, Cambridge, 1968.

Glover, Julian, *Man of Iron: Thomas Telford and the Building of Britain*, London, 2017.

Goodway, David (ed.), *The Chartists Were Right: Selections from the Newcastle Weekly Chronicle, 1890–97*, London, 2014.

Grant, Donald M. A., *Old Thurso*, Thurso, 1967.

Gray, Harry, *Tale of Two Streets: The Story of Wick Town Centre in the Mid-Nineteenth Century*, Wick, 2006.

Gray, Malcolm, *The Fishing Industries of Scotland, 1790–1914: A Study in Regional Adaption*, Aberdeen, 1978.

Gray, Malcolm, 'The Fishing Industry', in Donald Omand (ed.), *The Moray Book*, Edinburgh, 1976.

Gray, Malcolm, *The Highland Economy, 1750–1850*, Edinburgh, 1957.

Griffiths, Trevor and Morton, Graeme (eds), *A History of Everyday Life in Scotland, 1800 to 1900*, Edinburgh, 2010.

Gunn, Neil M., *The Silver Darlings*, London, 1941.

Haines, Robin, *Charles Trevelyan and the Great Irish Famine*, Dublin, 2004.

Handley, James, *The Navvy in Scotland*, Cork, 1970.

Harries-Jenkins, Gwyn, *The Army in Victorian Society*, Hull, 1993.

Hay, Robert, *How an Island Lost its People: Improvement, Clearance and Resettlement on Lismore, 1830–1914*, Kershader, 2013.

Hobsbawm, Eric, *The Age of Capital, 1848–1875*, London, 1997.

Hobsbawm, Eric, *The Age of Revolution, 1789–1848*, London, 1977.

Hobsbawm, Eric and Rudé, George, *Captain Swing*, London, 1969.

Hobsbawm, Eric and Scott, J. W., 'Political Shoemakers', in Eric Hobsbawm, *Uncommon People: Resistance, Rebellion and Jazz*, London, 1998.

Holmes, Richard, *Redcoat: The British Soldier in the Age of Horse and Musket*, London, 2001.

Horne, John, *The County of Caithness*, Wick, 1907.

Hughes, Robert, *The Fatal Shore: A History of the Transportation of Convicts to Australia*, London, 1987.

Hunt, Tristram, *The Frock-Coated Communist: The Revolutionary Life of Friedrich Engels*, London, 2009.

Hunter, James, *A Dance Called America: The Scottish Highlands, the United States and Canada*, Edinburgh, 1994.

Hunter, James, *For the People's Cause: From the Writings of John Murdoch*, Edinburgh, 1986.

Hunter, James, *The Making of the Crofting Community*, Edinburgh, 1976.

Hunter, James, *Scottish Exodus: Travels among a Worldwide Clan*, Edinburgh, 2005.

Hunter, James, *Scottish Highlanders: A People and Their Place*, Edinburgh, 1992.

Hunter, James, *Set Adrift Upon the World: The Sutherland Clearances*, Edinburgh, 2015.

Hurd, Douglas, *Robert Peel: A Biography*, London, 2008.

Hustwick, Iain, *Moray Firth Ships and Trade During the Nineteenth Century*, Aberdeen, 1994.

Hutchison, I. G., *A Political History of Scotland, 1832–1924: Parties, Elections and Issues*, Edinburgh, 1986.

Jeffrey, Alex, *Sketches from the Traditional History of Burghead*, Aberdeen, 1928.

Johnson, W. Branch, *The English Prison Hulks*, Chichester, 1970.

Kelly, John, *The Graves are Walking: The History of the Great Irish Famine*, London, 2012.

Kidd, Sheila M., '*Caraid nan Gaidheal* and "Friend of Emigration": Gaelic Emigration Literature of the 1840s', *Scottish Historical Review*, 81 (2002), pp. 52–69.

Kinealy, Christine, *Charity and the Great Hunger in Ireland: The Kindness of Strangers*, London, 2013.

Kinealy, Christine, *The Great Irish Famine: Impact, Ideology and Rebellion*, Basingstoke, 2002.

Kinealy, Christine, *This Great Calamity: The Irish Famine, 1845–52*, Dublin, 2006.

Knox, W. W. J. and McKinlay, A., 'Crime, Protest and Policing in Nineteenth-Century Scotland', in Trevor Griffiths and Graeme Morton (eds), *A History of Everyday Life in Scotland, 1800 to 1900*, Edinburgh, 2010.

Lawson, Bill, *Harris in History and Legend*, Edinburgh, 2002.

Lengel, Edward G., *The Irish Through British Eyes: Perceptions of Ireland in the Famine Era*, Westport, 2002.

Leslie, J. C. and Leslie, S. J., *The Hospitals of Inverness: Their Origin and Development*, Avoch, 2017

Levitt, Ian (ed.) *Government and Social Conditions in Scotland, 1845–1919*, Edinburgh, 1988.

Levitt, Ian and Smout, T. C., *The State of the Scottish Working Class in 1843*, Edinburgh, 1979.

Logue, Kenneth J., *Popular Disturbances in Scotland, 1780–1815*, Edinburgh, 1979.

MacArthur, E. Mairi, *Iona: The Living Memory of a Crofting Community, 1750–1914*, Edinburgh, 1990.

MacAskill, John (ed.), *The Highland Destitution of 1837: Government Aid and Public Subscription*, Edinburgh, 2013.

MacColl, Allan W., *Land, Faith and the Crofting Community: Christianity and Social Criticism in the Highlands of Scotland, 1843–1893*, Edinburgh, 2006.

Macdonald, Norman and Maclean, Cailean (eds), *The Great Book of Skye: From the Island to the World: People and Place on a Scottish Island*, Portree, 2014.

McGarvey, Darren, *Poverty Safari*, Edinburgh, 2018.

McGeachy, Robert A. A., *Argyll, 1730–1850*, Edinburgh, 2005.

MacGregor, Martin, 'Gaelic Barbarity and Scottish Identity in the Later Middle Ages', in D. Broun and M. MacGregor (eds), *Mìorun Mòr nan Gall: The Great Ill-Will of the Lowlander: Lowland Perceptions of the Highlands, Medieval and Modern*, Glasgow, 2009.

MacKechnie, Aonghus, *Inverness Castle: A Preliminary Historical Account*, Inverness, 2015.

MacKenzie, W. C., *History of the Outer Hebrides*, Paisley, 1903.

MacKenzie, W. M., *Hugh Miller: A Critical Study*, London, 1905.

MacKenzie, William, *Old Skye Tales: Traditions, Reflections, Memories*, Edinburgh, 2002 [1934].

MacKinnon, Iain, 'Colonialism and the Highland Clearances', *Northern Scotland*, 8 (2017), pp. 22–48.

Mackintosh, Herbert B., *Elgin Past and Present: A Historical Guide*, Elgin, 1914.

MacLaren, A. Allan, *Religion and Social Class: The Disruption Years in Aberdeen*, London, 1974.

MacLeod, John, *None Dare Oppose: The Laird, the Beast and the People of Lewis*, Edinburgh, 2010.

McLynn, Frank, *The Road Not Taken: How Britain Narrowly Missed a Revolution*, London, 2012.

MacRae, Norman, *The Romance of a Royal Burgh: Dingwall's Story of a Thousand Years*, Dingwall, 1923.

Marsden, Richard A., *Cosmo Innes and the Defence of Scotland's Past*, Farnham, 2014.

Maudlin, Daniel, 'Robert Mylne, Thomas Telford and the Architecture of Improvement: The Planned Villages of the British Fisheries Society, 1786–1817', *Urban History*, 34 (2007), pp. 453–80.

Miller, James, *The Gathering Stream: The Story of the Moray Firth*, Edinburgh, 2012.

Miller, James, *Inverness*, Edinburgh, 2004.

Miller, James, *Salt in the Blood: Scotland's Fishing Communities Past and Present*, Edinburgh, 1999.

Mitchison, Rosalind, 'The Making of the Old Scots Poor Law', *Past and Present*, 63 (1974), pp. 58–93.

Mitchison, Rosalind, *The Old Poor Law in Scotland: The Experience of Poverty, 1574–1845*, Edinburgh, 2000.

Mitchison, Rosalind, 'Poor Relief and Health Care in 19th Century Scotland', in O. P. Grell, A. Cunningham and R. Jutte (eds), *Health Care and Poor Relief in Eighteenth and Nineteenth Century Northern Europe*, Aldershot, 2002.

Mokyr, Joel, *The Enlightened Economy: Britain and the Industrial Revolution, 1700–1850*, Yale, 2009.

Molloy, Pat, *And They Blessed Rebecca: An Account of the Welsh Toll-Gate Riots, 1839–44*, Llandysul, 1983.

Mowat, Ian R. M., *Easter Ross, 1750–1850: The Double Frontier*, Edinburgh, 1981.

Mowat, W. G. *The Story of Lybster*, Lybster, 1959.

Murray, Donald S., *Herring Tales: How the Silver Darlings Shaped Taste and History*, London, 2016.

Nally, David P., *Human Encumbrances: Political Violence and the Great Irish Famine*, Notre Dame, 2011.

Nelson, David, *The Victorian Soldier*, Princes Risborough, 2004.

Newby, Andrew, 'Emigration and Clearance from the Island of Barra, c.1770–1858', *Transactions of the Gaelic Society of Inverness*, 61 (2003), pp. 116–48.

Ó Cathaoir, Brendan, *Famine Diary*, Dublin, 1999.

Ó Gráda, Cormac, *Black '47 and Beyond: The Great Irish Famine in History, Economy and Memory*, Princeton, 1999.

Ó Murchadha, Ciarán, *The Great Famine: Ireland's Agony, 1845–1852*, London, 2011.

Omand, Donald (ed.), *The Caithness Book*, Inverness, 1973.

O'Rourke, John, *The History of the Great Irish Famine of 1847*, Dublin, 1902.

Ó Súilleabháin, Séamus, *County Limerick in Crisis: The Progress of Destitution, Hunger and Despair in a Rich Land*, Broadford, 2015,

Omand, Donald (ed.), *The Moray Book*, Edinburgh, 1976.

Omand, Donald (ed.), *The New Caithness Book*, Wick, 1989.

Omond, G. W. T., *The Lord Advocates of Scotland, 1834–1880*, London, 1914.

Paterson, Audrey, 'The Poor Law in Nineteenth-Century Scotland', in Derek Fraser (ed.), *The New Poor Law in the Nineteenth Century*, London, 1976.

Pickering, Paul A. and Tyrell, Alex, *The People's Bread: A History of the Anti-Corn Law League*, London, 2000.

Piketty, Thomas, *Capital in the Twenty-First Century*, London, 2014.

Polson, Alexander, *Easter Ross*, Tain, 1914.

Prebble, John, *The Highland Clearances*, London, 1963.

Randall, Adrian and Charlesworth, Andrew (eds), *Markets, Market Culture and Popular Protest in Eighteenth-Century Great Britain*, Liverpool, 1996.

Randall, Adrian and Charlesworth, Andrew (eds), *Moral Economy and Popular Protest: Crowds, Conflict and Authority*, Basingstoke, 2000.

Reay, Barry, *The Last Rising of the Agricultural Labourers: Rural Life and Protest in Nineteenth-Century England*, Oxford, 1990.

Reed, Mick and Wells, Roger (eds), *Class, Conflict and Protest in the English Countryside, 1700–1880*, London, 1990.

Reid, Peter H., *Port Gordon: The Life and Times of a Village*, Portgordon, 1997.

Renwick, Chris, *Bread for All: The Origins of the Welfare State*, London, 2017.

Rice, Duncan C., 'Abolitionists and abolitionism in Aberdeen: A test-case for the nineteenth-century anti-slavery movement', *Northern Scotland*, 1 (1972–73), pp. 65–87.

Rice, Duncan C., *The Scots Abolitionists, 1833–1861*, London, 1981.

Richards, Eric, *The Highland Clearances: People, Landlords and Rural Turmoil*, Edinburgh, 2008.

Richards, Eric, *The Highland Estate Factor in the Age of the Clearances*, Laxay, 2016.

Richards, Eric, 'The Last Scottish Food Riots', *Past and Present* Supplement 6 (1982).

Richards, Eric, *The Leviathan of Wealth: The Sutherland Estate Fortune in the Industrial Revolution*, London, 1973.

Richards, Eric, *Patrick Sellar and the Highland Clearances*, Edinburgh, 1999.

Richards, Eric and Clough, Monica, *Cromartie: Highland Life, 1650–1914*, Aberdeen, 1989.

Richards, Eric and Tindley, Annie, 'After the Clearances: Evander MacIver and the Highland Question, 1835–73', *Rural History*, 23 (2012), pp. 41–57.

Riding, Jacqueline, *Peterloo: The Story of the Manchester Massacre*, London, 2018.

Rixon, Denis, *Knoydart: A History*, Edinburgh, 2011.

Robertson, A. G. R., *The Lowland Highlanders*, Tain, 1972.

Robertson, Iain J. M., *Landscapes of Protest in the Scottish Highlands after 1914: The Later Highland Land Wars*, Farnham, 2013.

Robins, Nick S. and Meek, Donald E., *The Kingdom of MacBrayne: From Steamship to Car Ferries in the West Highlands and Hebrides*, Edinburgh, 2006.

Rosie, George, *Hugh Miller: Outrage and Order: A Biography and Selected Writings*, Edinburgh, 1981.

Rozwadowski, Helen M., *The Sea Knows No Boundaries*, Copenhagen, 2002.

Rudé, George, *Ideology and Popular Protest*, London, 1980.

Rule, John and Wells, Roger (eds), *Crime, Protest and Popular Politics in Southern England, 1740–1850*, London, 1997.

Salaman, R. N., *The History and Social Influence of the Potato*, Cambridge, 1949.

Schoyen, Albert R., *The Chartist Challenge: A Portrait of George Julian Harney*, London, 1958.

Scott, Hew (ed.), *Fasti Ecclesiae Scoticanae*, 7 vols, Edinburgh, 1915–28.

Seabrook, Jeremy, *Pauperland: Poverty and the Poor in Britain*, London, 2013.

Sen, Amartya, *Poverty and Famines: An Essay on Entitlement and Deprivation*, Oxford, 1981.

Sellar, W. D. H., *Moray: Province and People*, Edinburgh, 1993.

Smith, J. S. and Stevenson, D., *Fermfolk and Fisherfolk: Rural Life in Northern Scotland in Eighteenth and Nineteenth Centuries*, Aberdeen, 1989.

Smout, T. C., *A Century of the Scottish People, 1830–1950*, London, 1986.

Smout, T. C., 'Famine and Famine Relief in Scotland', in L. M. Cullen and T. C. Smout (eds), *Comparative Aspects of Scottish and Irish Economic and Social History, 1660–1900*, Edinburgh, 1977.

Smylie, Mike, *Herring: A History of the Silver Darlings*, Stroud, 2004.

Sperber, Jonathan, *The European Revolutions, 1848–1851*, Cambridge, 2005.

Storrie, Margaret, *Islay: Biography of an Island*, Islay, 2011.

Sutherland, David K., *Fisher Lore of Avoch*, Inverness, n.d.

Sutherland, Iain, *Caithness:1770 to 1832*, Wick, 1995.

Sutherland, Iain, *The Fishing Industry of Caithness*, Wick, n.d.

Sutherland, Iain, *From Herring Fishing to Seine Net Fishing on the East Coast of Scotland*, Wick, n.d.

Sutherland, Iain, *Wick Harbour and the Herring Fishing*, Wick, n.d.

Sutton, John, *Food Worth Fighting For: From Food Riots to Food Banks*, London, 2016.

Taylor, David, *The Wild Black Region: Badenoch, 1750–1800*, Edinburgh, 2016.

Taylor, Michael A., *Hugh Miller: Stonemason, Geologist, Writer*, Edinburgh, 2007.

Thompson, Edward P., *The Making of the English Working Class*, London, 1980.

Thompson, Edward P., 'The Moral Economy of the English Crowd in the Eighteenth Century', *Past and Present*, 50 (1971), pp. 76–136.

Thomson, Paul, *Living the Fishing*, London, 1983.

Thornber, Iain (ed.), *Morvern: A Highland Parish*, Edinburgh, 2002.

Tindley, Annie, *The Sutherland Estate, 1850–1920*, Edinburgh, 2010.

Tindley, Annie, '"They Sow the Wind, They Reap the Whirlwind": Estate Management in the Post-Clearance Highlands', *Northern Scotland*, 3 (2012), pp. 66–85.

Tivy, Joy, 'Easter Ross: A Residual Crofting Area', *Scottish Studies*, 9 (1965), pp. 64–84.

Trevelyan, Laura, *A Very British Family: The Trevelyans and Their World*, London, 2012.

Turnock, David, *The Making of the Scottish Rural Landscape*, Aldershot, 1995.

Watson, James, *Our Church Fathers*, Elgin, 1899.

Wells, Roger, 'The Irish Famine of 1799–1801: Market Culture, Moral Economies and Social Protest', in Adrian Randall and Andrew Charlesworth (eds), *Markets, Market Culture and Popular Protest in Eighteenth-Century Great Britain*, Liverpool, 1996.

Whatley, Christopher A., *Scottish Society, 1707–1850*, Manchester, 2000.

Wightman, Andy, *The Poor Had No Lawyers: Who Owns Scotland and How They Got It*, Edinburgh, 2010.

Williams, David, *The Rebecca Riots: A Study in Agrarian Discontent*, Cardiff, 1986.

Wilson, A. N., *Victoria: A Life*, London, 2014.

Wilson, A. N, *The Victorians*, London, 2003.

Wilson, Alexander, *The Chartist Movement in Scotland*, Manchester, 1970.

Wood, Sydney H., *The Shaping of Nineteenth-Century Aberdeenshire*, Stevenage, 1985.

Woodham-Smith, Cecil., *The Great Hunger*, London, 1962.

Worthington, David, 'The Settlements of the Beauly-Wick Coast and the Historiography of the Moray Firth', *Scottish Historical Review*, 95 (2016), pp. 139–63.

Unpublished thesis

Duncan, Robert E., *Popular Radicalism and Working Class Movements in Aberdeen, 1790–1850*, (M.Litt. Thesis), University of Aberdeen, 1976.

Selected websites

Royal Archives: Queen Victoria's Journals: http://www.queenvictoriasjournals.org/home.do

Oxford Dictionary of National Biography: http://www.oxforddnb.com/

The History of Parliament Online: http://www.historyofparliamentonline.org/

ScotlandsPeople: https://www.scotlandspeople.gov.uk/

Index